Men and Women of the Corporation

Rosabeth Moss Kanter

Basic Books, Inc., Publishers

NEW YORK

Library of Congress Cataloging in Publication Data

Kanter, Rosabeth Moss.
  Men and women of the corporation.

  Bibliography: p. 326
  Includes index.
    1. Organizational behavior. 2. Industrial
organization. 3. White collar workers. 4. Women
in business. I. Title.
HD58.7.K36   301.18'32   76-43464
ISBN: 0-465-04452-2

Copyright © 1977 by Rosabeth Moss Kanter
Printed in the United States of America
DESIGNED BY VINCENT TORRE
10 9 8 7 6 5 4 3 2 1

For B.A.S.

CONTENTS

Part III

Structures and Processes

Success as vertical mobility in the large corporation, in the absence of alternatives; how opportunity to get ahead defines the
ways people involve themselves in work; the seductiveness of
opportunity in contrast with the characteristic responses of
those who find themselves stuck; how relative opportunity
creates self-fulfilling prophecies and also accounts for what
might otherwise seem to be "sex differences" in work behavior.

The meanings of power and its importance for leadership in
large organizations; how power accumulates through activities
and alliances; the sources of bureaucratic powerlessness and
the responses it engenders, trapping the powerless in downward spirals of ineffectiveness. The problems of women and
leadership in organizations reveal themselves as matters of
power, not sex.

Relative numbers of socially different people—being among
the many or among the few—are seen to have a powerful impact on individuals' fates; "tokens" (the numerically rare) and
how they manage their special situations; certain popular findings about "women's behavior" in the professions or management dissolve into more universal human responses to the
dilemmas of token status.

Part IV
Understanding and Action

Appendices

PREFACE

This book has a circuitous history. I had first set out to write a rather theoretical account of how consciousness and behavior are formed by positions in organizations, in order to show how both men and women are the products of their circumstances—if not mechanically "manufactured" by their jobs, then at least limited by them. Having been heavily involved in projects to create dramatically new organizational forms, I wanted to show that structural change is a necessity if the human problems of modern bureaucracies are to be solved. Problems and solutions do not lie in the hands of individuals alone. This perspective, I thought, would also give organizational decision makers and policy planners a handle for understanding the human dilemmas of particular ways of organizing work so that they would have some guidance for making improvements in the quality of work life and organizational effectiveness.

At the same time, I was also motivated by my involvement in the women's movement to seek understanding of the fate of women as well as men in organizations. I was disappointed by a reductionist thrust in one intellectual wing of the movement which often fell back on "women are different" arguments. In one version, it was deemed important that women reach more organizational and political leadership posts because society would thereby be humanized. This concerned me, because my evolving theory held that as long as organizations remained the same, merely replacing men with women would not alone make a difference. I needed to offer alternatives.

Meanwhile, I had begun my acquaintance with the company I have called Industrial Supply Corporation (Indsco) a few years earlier, in the course of several research and action projects for which I was an outside consultant. The projects all involved issues where I felt the data and conclusions would benefit Indsco's workers. But these inside glances at life in the large corporation were also interesting enough to register in me the notion that "someday" I might like to write an ethnography of a corporation. I continued to collect data on Indsco, and to work on projects for other large organizations, without making the connection between my far-off future idea and my current activities, and I built a network of contacts at Indsco and elsewhere without any idea that I would be using the information given me as the subject of a book (even though Indsco staff encouraged me to publish the results of specific pieces of research).

Then the two streams came together. My observations at Indsco made the theory come alive. I saw there people behaving in just the ways the evolving theory would predict. New extensions and concepts were emerging out of the experiences of Indsco's men and women, as they relayed them in formal interviews and informal conversations. That future ethnography of a corporation could be written now. It would combine theory with rich descriptive material interesting to anyone who wanted to see life in the large corporate bureaucracy from the inside. It would use my data to build concepts that could guide practical change strategies for the benefit of Indsco and its people. When this decision was made, my use of available opportunities became more systematic. Consequently, I want to thank all the men and women of Indsco with whom I had contact through the years for sharing their experiences. I hope the final product justifies the use I made of our meetings.

INTELLECTUAL DEBTS

There are several important thinkers whose writings can be considered the intellectual ancestors of this book. First, C. Wright Mills wrote, just after World War II, what is still the best American account of the history and content of white-collar work, and his investigations and criticisms of managerial elites served as a reminder that politics was being conducted behind the doors of supposedly "rational," impersonal, and universalistic corporations. While other sociologists of his time were constructing ever more abstract conceptions of social systems, he continually returned attention to concrete individuals and the content of particular roles. And, as a radical, he refused to take the current system as a "given" or as the most naturally efficient. Everett C. Hughes considered the relations of "men and their work," especially the informal features connected with pursuit of an occupation, such as the nature of a colleague group or the meaning of being "different" from others in one's line of work, issues I take up in Chapter 8. Robert K. Merton's incisive comments about the effects of social structure (bureaucratic roles, mobility prospects) on "personality" variables (occupational outlook, group identification) showed that functional analyses of social systems could include, and in some cases even subsume, individual psychology as an explanation for behavior. Georg Simmel, though of another continent and generation, represented for me a reminder that forms and numbers give rise to distinctive modes of interaction. Chris Argyris' notions of the interplay between personality and organization structure have been an important source of insights. And two recent books have been especially influential: Michel Crozier's *The Bureaucratic*

Phenomenon and James Thompson's *Organizations in Action*. Both consider the interlinking between formal, technical aspects of organizations and informal, personal aspects; I note my debts to them often in the text.

Although this book lies within such intellectual traditions in social science, it also owes a debt to debates within feminism. Most discussions of women's work behavior have been either highly macroscopic (considering global variables such as general rates of work force participation by time period and social class) or very microscopic (focusing on issues such as the psychology of women and the dispositions implanted by nature or by socialization). Participation in many feminist conferences helped lead me to a third, intermediate level analysis, one that I think has a great deal more potential for building theory, explaining observed behavior, and making change. Undeniably, macroscopic societal patterns and individual psychologies interact in influencing behavior, but the nature of the institutions that serve as intervening links still needs to be made clear. My examination of how forms of work organization, and the conceptions of roles and distributions of people within them, shape behavioral outcomes leaves very few verifiable "sex differences" in behavior that are not better explained by roles and situations—and thus able to account for men's behavior, too. There is a system of relations in place in modern organizations in which many features are interlocked and mutually reinforcing. The only effective long-term changes will be those that address the nature of such systems, that break into a number of vicious cycles, which I describe in detail particularly in Chapters 3, 4, 6, 7, and 8.

PERSONAL DEBTS

There were a number of agencies and individuals who helped me in the translation from ideas to book. The John Simon Guggenheim Memorial Foundation provided a fellowship year, spent at Harvard Law School, which enabled me to complete the manuscript; I am especially grateful for the Guggenheim Fellowship. A contract with the Division of Public Administration and Finance of the United Nations (research project on improving personnel systems in the public sector) enabled me to work on the first version of the ideas in Chapter 10. The Center for Research on Women in Higher Education and the Professions at Wellesley College, under the direction of Carolyn Elliott, provided some support for the completion of a paper that became Chapter 8, as well as a seminar of very helpful colleagues.

Many anonymous Indsco people gave generously of their time and insight. Zick Rubin provided detailed comments on some of the chapters and continual good cheer and encouragement, as well as the benefit of his own considerable background and knowledge of the literature. Arlene Daniels rescued me, in her own inimitable way, during a low period between drafts. Allan Cohen offered many incisive observations on an entire early draft. Diane Fassel contributed field work on all-women's organizations, reported in Appendix II. Margaret Torrey kindly supplied data from a survey of headmasters' wives, referred to in the notes for Chapter 5.

I also want to thank the following colleagues and friends for reactions to bits and pieces of the book as it emerged in various forms, and as I presented it at meetings in various stages, although I did not always take their advice: Chris Argyris, Louis B. Barnes, Wendy Barnes, David Bradford, Lee Bolman, Nancy Chodorow, Rose Coser, Margaret Cussler, Susan Eckstein, Roslyn Feldberg, Gordon Fellman, William Form, Linda Frank, William Gamson, Oscar Grusky, Jeanne Guillemin, Robert Guillemin, Marcia Guttentag, Joanna Hiss, Joan Huber, Judith Long Laws, Sara Lightfoot, Judith Lorber, Phyllis Marx, Marcia Millman, Marcy Murninghan, Jerome Neu, Albert J. Reiss, Jr., Kristine Rosenthal, Carol Rubin, Janice Sanfacon, Alice Sargent, Carol Schreiber, Otis Stephens, Carol Tavris, Shelley Taylor, Barrie Thorne, and William Torbert.

Portions of this book appeared in embryonic form in a number of my articles: "Women and the Structure of Organizations: Explorations in Theory and Behavior," *Sociological Inquiry*, 45 (1975): pp. 34–74 and *Another Voice*, M. Millman and R. M. Kanter, eds. (New York: Doubleday Anchor, 1975); "The Impact of Hierarchical Arrangements on the Work Behavior of Women and Men," presented at the 1975 Meetings of the American Sociological Association and published in *Social Problems*, 23 (1976): pp. 415–30; "Policy Comment VI," presented at the Conference on Occupational Segregation of the American Economic Association, 1975, *Signs*, 1 (1976): pp. 282–91, and *Women in the Workplace*, M. Blaxall and B. Reagan, eds. (Chicago: University of Chicago Press, 1976); "Women and Organizations: Sex Roles and Group Dynamics," *Beyond Sex Roles*, A. Sargent, ed. (St. Paul, Minn.: West, 1976); "Interpreting the Results of a Social Experiment," *Science*, 192 (14 May 1976): pp. 662–63; "Organizational Structure and Occupational Role Definition," presented at a plenary session of the section on organizations and occupations, American Sociological Association, 1976; and "Some Effects of Proportions on Group Life: Skewed Sex Ratios and Responses to Token Women," *American Journal of Sociology*, 82 (1977).

This book would never have been finished on time if it were not for the typing help of Wanda Koetz, Gwen Whately, Lorraine Gorfinkle, and Carolyn Wadhams' excellent staff at Report Production Associates, especially Susan Memno. I am also extremely grateful to Erwin Glikes of Basic Books and Harper & Row—a "water walker" if I ever saw one—who took time out from his own executive tasks to work with me, very helpfully, on the book. I appreciate Carol Vance's and Julie DeWitt's help too. And my husband, Barry Stein, was, as usual, the best of colleagues along with everything else: a fountain of creative suggestions, new insights, and esoteric references buried in second-hand books.

ROSABETH MOSS KANTER

Cambridge, Mass., June 1976

Men and Women

of the Corporation

Introduction

It is not the consciousness of men that determines their existence, but, on the contrary, their social existence determines their consciousness.
  —Karl Marx, *A Contribution to the Critique of Political Economy*

But the understandings of the greater part of men are necessarily formed by their ordinary employments.
  —Adam Smith, *The Wealth of Nations*

The shift in the structure and character of work has created a demand that work produce more than purely economic benefits. To make a living is no longer enough. Work also has to make a life.
  —Peter Drucker, *Management*

The most distinguished advocate and the most distinguished critic of modern capitalism were in agreement on one essential point: the job makes the person. Adam Smith and Karl Marx both recognized the extent to which people's attitudes and behaviors take shape out of the experiences they have in their work.

If jobs "create" people, then the corporation is the quintessential contemporary people-producer. It employs a large proportion of the labor force, and its practices often serve as models for the organization of other systems. How people-production happens in all large bureaucracies, but especially in one manufacturing firm, is the subject of this book. The case of the organization I have named Industrial Supply Corporation (Indsco) provides the context for illuminating the ways in which organization structure forms people's sense of themselves and of their possibilities.

Indsco is a good place to visit, not only because it is among the biggest and most powerful of the multinationals that dominate American industry but also because it is socially conscious. In the past decade, Indsco has taken an active look at its employment practices in an attempt to benefit workers and live up to the self-chosen designation of "people-conscious organization." Thus, the human problems that remain in a place like Indsco illustrate irresolvable dilemmas of the large hierarchical organization as a social form—and not the difficulties of a backward corporation. Indsco is anything but backward, and it is anything but unaware that social responsibility may be the business issue of the future.

There is a need for studies that take a close look inside one organization. Large corporations are often formidable and mysterious to people outside them, like giants that populate the earth but can only be seen through their shadows. Yet informed participation in civic culture requires knowing more about how corporations operate or what people in them do than is contained in stereotypes of ambitious organization men or insensitive bureaucrats. Corporations are often equally mysterious to the people inside, whose views can be limited and parochial because they rarely get a sense of the whole. With the interest of villagers who have never seen the rest of the world, insiders often ask an outsider who has just traveled to another part of the organization, "Is it all like it is in my little corner? Is it the same other places?" Insiders, too, need the larger view in order to manage their situations, to understand the forces acting on them, to see options, and to consider alternatives.

My focus is on the people who work in offices, who run the administrative apparatus of the large organization. They consist of two major groups. First are the managers, professionals, and technical personnel who make up what Norman Birnbaum called the "new middle class," those who are "workers in all but name and consciousness" and whose "very careers entail not only acceptance of hierarchy but factual complicity in its maintenance, in the actual exercise of power." [1] At the very top of this group are the corporate executives Birnbaum termed the "new elite," who have effective control of the collective property represented in the corporation, along with privileged access to stock ownership. Far below in status and class position but contiguous in office space are the corps of paper-handlers, record-keepers, and data-manipulators—the clerical and service personnel who make up "an army of those skilled in one or another organizational technique, or in more specific techniques placed at the service of organizations. They are subordinate, even if the possibility of ascent is open." [2] In both of these organizational classes, my concern is with individuals and their work experiences rather than with the conflict between classes or the operation of interest groups. With the possible exception of those at the very top, who receive only passing mention in this study, groups in the white-collar ranks tend not to act as organized, official power blocs.

The stage is set in Chapters 1 and 2. I first consider the development of the white-collar administrative classes with the growth of large corporations and present statistics on the distribution of men and women among managerial and clerical jobs. The ideologies and theories that legitimated the position and defined the characteristics of managers and clericals are described. Chapter 2 is a tour through Indsco: its offices and people, ranks and grades, history and culture, activities and rewards. Here the people of the corporation begin to speak for themselves, as they do through the rest of the book.

The next chapters consider the dilemmas and choices inherent in three roles, and how images develop that further constrain the people in them. Each role shapes the person in it by confronting him or her with characteristic dilemmas and constricting the range of options for response. For managers, the critical issue is why social conformity is such an important part of being a manager, and the forces that lead management to become a closed, exclusionary circle. These forces are located in the uncertainties of legitimacy, evaluation, communication, and loyalty inherent in a manager's place in the organization. For secretaries, the critical problems stem from a patrimonial relationship with bosses that represents one of the final outposts of the personal inside the bureaucratic. The role pressures on secretaries encourage them to become timid, emotional, parochial, praise-addicted, and wedded to a single boss. Around wives the question that must be asked is whether or not they should even be considered part of the system. But then, this very question creates the first dilemma corporate wives-of-managers face in their "careers": inclusion/exclusion. Other dilemmas are created for wives as their husbands' careers unfold.

Managers, secretaries, and wives all must choose a stance that solves the problems created by their position in the network of organizational relationships, but the roles come to serve organizational functions that make change difficult. We also see that "masculine" or "feminine" images embedded in the roles are inherent neither in the nature of the tasks themselves nor in the characteristics of men and women; instead, they are developed in response to the problems incumbents face in trying to live their organizational lives so as to maximize legitimacy or recognition or freedom.

The third part of the book looks at how people respond to their position in a structure of opportunity (Chapter 6), power (Chapter 7), or relative numbers (Chapter 8). In these chapters I develop the elements of an integrated theory of behavior in organizations. Regardless of specific role, people have more or less opportunity for advancement, growth, and challenge, as we see in Chapter 7. Indeed, the hierarchy at a place like Indsco makes most people feel that "success" must be equated with vertical mobility, so people who become stuck or hit early dead ends are especially disadvantaged. Engagement with work (how much ambition, how much commitment), ways of seeking social recognition, and amount of risk-taking are all bound up with opportunity. Those low in opportunity are unlikely to develop the motivation to improve their situation and, therefore, a downward cycle of deprivation is set in motion. Thus, questions about great discrepancies in opportunity must be raised, since there appear to be costs both to the success-striving of those high in opportunity and the disengagement of the disadvantaged.

The problems of power and powerlessness are taken up in Chapter 7. If power is defined as efficacy (the ability to mobilize resources) rather than domination, then the importance of power to the lives of people in organizations makes sense. In the large bureaucracy, power is a virtual requisite for effective performance in jobs with accountability for others, and subordinates have good reasons to prefer to work for the more powerful leaders. The specifically organizational ways in which power accumulates are examined: through activities (often made possible by job attributes) and through alliances with sponsors, peers, and even subordinates. But the several sources of bureaucratic powerlessness (accountability without power) are also made clear; the struggles of people to operate in a powerless situation leads them to tend toward rigid, rules-minded, controlling, and possessive styles. So a major cause of ineffective, stereotypically "bureaucratic" behavior is seen to lie in the extent to which too few people are empowered in large organizations; the solution becomes a wider sharing of power. Indeed, the problems of women in managerial roles (a preference for male bosses, an image of women's controlling style) spring into focus as problems of powerlessness, not sex.

Chapter 8 considers how relative numbers—social composition of groups—affect relationships between men and women (or any two kinds of people). Wherever occupational sex segregation has been in effect, as it has in the managerial and professional ranks of corporations like Indsco, those women who do break into men's territories find themselves in the position of the very few among the very many. This position as "tokens" (representatives of their category rather than independent individuals) accounts for many of the difficulties such numerically scarce people face in fitting in, gaining peer acceptance, and behaving "naturally." The existence of tokens encourages social segregation and stereotyping and may lead the person in that position to overcompensate through either overachievement or hiding successes, or to turn against people of his or her own kind. Thus, numbers—proportional representation—are important not only because they *symbolize* the presence or absense of discrimination but also because they have real consequences for performance.

The implications of my analysis are considered in Chapters 9 and 10. Chapter 9 presents the outlines of the theory, considering the advantages of a social structural model over more traditional social psychological and individual models of the sources of work behavior. Chapter 10 suggests a large number of specific kinds of interventions and changes, policies and programs, that would enhance opportunity, distribute power more broadly, and help balance numbers. Although optimistically encouraging reform, the discussion also points to problems inherent in the large hierarchical organization that no amount of reform can solve: barriers to change and limits to change. There is an extent to which only larger-scale system change can fully improve the conditions of work for the majority of the population.

Some of the context behind my analysis is unique to the administrative ranks of profit-making, shareholder-owned, manufacturing corporations: the high salaries and luxurious fringe benefits for top people; the emphasis on upward mobility and increasing status as a measure of achievement; the frequency of executive transfer among geographic areas and the stringency of constraints on executive wives; the preeminence of sales and marketing functions; a strong technical orientation and a non-intellectual (or even anti-intellectual) culture; and an official political ideology that is pro-capitalist, anti-regulation, barely tolerant of unions, and generally conservative.[3] In short, many details of life and behavior inside Indsco reflect the culture, language, and style of mainstream American industry three-quarters of the way through the century.

But in other ways, the specific details of the case are incidental to the roles and images, structures and processes, described. What happens to the white collarites in Indsco is only one instance of more general phenomena that occur especially inside government bureaucracies, public commissions, communications establishments such as television networks and large publishing firms, banks and insurance companies, and, to a lesser extent, in the administration of big universities, school systems, and hospitals—wherever there is a large administrative apparatus that is hierarchically organized. The consequences of high or low opportunity, high or low power, and high or low numerical representation are also likely to affect professionals as well as administrators, production workers as well as clericals.

Furthermore, regardless of the formal ownership and control of economic and other job-providing institutions, a number of important issues must be addressed by every system: power and authority, equity and fairness; who governs organizations and who has access to the governing structure; and social responsibility for the individual consequences of organization membership. Even if a social revolution were to try to transform private ownership (already largely collective—the essential meaning of the corporation) to some kind of socialized public ownership, and managerial control to worker control, we would still face vexing organizational questions: how to divide labor, make available power and opportunity, and distribute people across tasks. Indeed, some might say that such considerations are important *especially if* a socialist transformation were coming, for contemporary American socialist theory tends to lack a coherent vision of the concrete form organizations might take that will make them more responsive to the people in them as well as productive—in short, how they will solve universal bureaucratic dilemmas. Institutions for supplying work and products must exist in the post-industrial age, and they must be run. *How,* and with what consequences for members, is as important for socialists as for capitalists to know.

On the other hand, should the future unfold differently, and corporations, along with other large hierarchical organizations, continue as essentially the only game in town, then they must be made aware of how to handle their social responsibilities. Those people inside concerned with organizational policy, and those outside concerned with public policy, must join in considering the modification of hierarchy, the opening of opportunity, the broadening of participation in decisions, and the increase of worker discretion, if they are to alleviate some of the stresses, tensions, and inequities of current organization structures. The extension of legal-democratic principles from the polity to the economy [4] is a worthwhile goal; what this means in terms of concrete practice and specific structural arrangements is a matter that merits considerable attention.

One major modification with which growing numbers of people from both sides of the political spectrum are likely to agree is a decrease in the size of economic units, as the popularity of E. F. Schumacher's *Small Is Beautiful* attests.[5] Recent evidence suggests that economic efficiency is possible in much smaller units than had been conventionally believed.[6] At the same time, it should become clear from the analysis of behavior inside organizations in this book that the problem of large size is a common thread connecting many of the dilemmas people face at work. Size is often accompanied by hierarchy and centralization of power, which renders many individuals, even those with high status, relatively dependent and powerless. The consequences are either ineffective behavior or attempts to bypass the formal structure through informal (and exclusionary) political arrangements. Size makes face-to-face working relationships an impossibility for the people whose activities intersect with others across departments and areas, creating a reliance instead on superficial cultural and social similarity—on social conformity—in the managerial ranks. And even as large size opens more job options, it also tends to add more layers and levels, increasing the gap between categories of workers.

The women's issue also appears as an important sub-theme in this book. Why is the women's issue joined with examination of the effects of organization structure? There are several important reasons. First, no study of human behavior can any longer be considered complete that ignores the special roles, positions, and constraints affecting women in the public arena, as well as the men who have traditionally peopled organizational research. At the same time, the fate of women is inextricably bound up with organizational structure and processes in the same way that men's life-at-work is shaped by them. Differences based on sex retreat into the background as the people-creating, behavior-shaping properties of organizational locations become clear. Findings about the "typical" behavior of women in organizations that have been assumed to reflect either biologically based psychological attributes or characteristics developed through a long socialization to a "female sex role" turn out to reflect very reasonable—and very universal—responses to current organizational situations. Even discrimination itself emerges as a consequence of organizational pressures as much as individual prejudice. Thus, specific attention to women as well as men is one way to demonstrate the utility of the perspective that "the job makes the person." And, in turn, to help women.

Even more critically, the women's issue (along with general considerations of equal employment opportunity) is a good place to try to arouse the interest of organizational policy-makers in socially beneficial change. Affirmative action is as immediate and costly an issue as it is controversial.[7] Any analysis that can provide officials with concrete understanding as well as action possibilities would have more than just academic interest.

As important as opportunity for women might be in itself, however, it is only one instance of an increasing tendency for external (governmental) intervention in the internal practices of organizations. The very emphasis on EEO programs makes it clear that public policy does not consider corporations to be merely money machines that turn out shareholder profits. The public interest requires a scrutiny of employment practices because of the centrality of organizations as producers of jobs as well as products—jobs that have important individual and social consequences. As Philip Selznick wrote: "In recent years we have seen a transition from preoccupation with freedom *of* association to a concern for freedom *in* associations. This renewed awareness stems from a realization that the private organizations can be more oppressive than the state. The loss of a job, or the right to pursue a profession, or the opportunity to continue one's education, may be far more hurtful than a term in jail. When these deprivations are inflicted arbitrarily, and there is no recourse, a gap in the legal order exists. We become more sensitive to that gap when the decisions are made by organizations that seem large, powerful, and impersonal, and by men who have the look of officialdom."[8]

In this perspective, then, the women's issue is one example of the pressure for development of appropriate concepts of individual rights to a good quality of life inside organizations, as well as structures that maximize the exercise of these rights. Selznick argued that "industrial justice" requires extension of the concept of "citizenship," with its traditional democratic privileges and safeguards, to all members of those organizations that are, in effect, "private governments." [9] "It is in no sense a figure of speech to refer to a business company as a private government," Beardsley Ruml commented in an essay series on the social meaning of legal concepts. "A business is a *government* because within the law it is authorized and/or organized to make rules for the conduct of its affairs. It is a *private* government because the rules it makes within the law are final and are not reviewable by any public body." [10] Thus, public policy has a legitimate interest in the inner order of the organization, especially in the operation of power and authority and the access to opportunity. Employment practices that enhance individual welfare and the quality of work life should not be private decisions based on the voluntary goodwill or *noblesse oblige* of employers but rather a question of vital social concern to those outside the enterprise. Such issues move far beyond the existing body of labor law (which tends to treat individual "corporate citizens" only in their capacity as group members) to a radically different view of the purposes and practices of organizations and the role of legal intervention in internal affairs.

This book, then, locates a large measure of the responsibility for the behaviors people engage in at work and their fate inside organizations in the structure of work systems themselves. Life does not consist of infinite possibility because situations do not make all responses equally plausible or equally available. But the limits are not as much internal, rooted in the person, as they are structural and situational. In the view advanced here, people are capable of more than their organizational positions ever give them the tools or the time or the opportunity to demonstrate.

There is both tragedy and hope embodied in this perspective.

Tragedy lies in the self-defeating traps into which individuals fall when they try to make the most of a disadvantaged situation, only to sink further into "failure" and to generate a cycle that makes rescue increasingly unlikely. Some of the ways people choose to gain recognition and value and to fight for a piece of autonomy, when their situations greatly constrain their bargaining tools, only bind them further to the constraining situation. Or, the dilemmas people confront can provide them with a set of choices that are equally restricting, from which there is no escape.

Behavior in organizations can only be fully understood when there is adequate appreciation of the self-perpetuating cycles and inescapable dilemmas posed by the contingencies of social life: Managers who solve the "trust" problem inherent in delegating decision-making discretion by insisting on outward, social conformity, only to put themselves in a conformist box, and one where outward appearance becomes manipulated so that it is even less a sign of trustworthiness, and conformity must be even more tightly controlled.

Secretaries who do work that is so lowskill and replaceable that their only way to get recognition and perhaps advancement is to develop a relationship of personal service with a boss, only to find themselves tied further to that boss and rewarded for things that are not generalizable or useful anywhere else in the organization. Wives who must choose how to handle a formal exclusion from the company and an informal set of restrictive social demands. People at dead ends who lower their aspirations, stop trying, disengage, and make it less likely that they will ever get unstuck. "Token" women who are always different from their peers, no matter what they do, so that they can never be just normal members of the organization but always symbols of their kind. The people with advantage, for whom the cycles are always upward (opportunity creating more opportunity, power generating power), are equally responding to their situations, but they are fortunate in being provided with more of the tools that make success possible.

However, the tragedy in this highly dilemma-laden view of life in organizations is balanced by a hopeful vision of the transforming power of outside intervention. Situations can be modified. The net of rewards and constraints can be rewoven. New tools can be provided. The people who are stuck can be offered challenges. The powerless can be given more discretion, more influence over decisions. Tokens can be provided with allies. And more. If it is organization structure rather than intrinsic character that determines organizational behavior, then self-defeating, self-perpetuating cycles can be interrupted. The fabric of job relationships can be changed.

Part I

The Players and the Stage

1

Men and Women of
the Corporation: The Population

For just experience tells, in every soil
That those that think must govern those that toil.
—Oliver Goldsmith, "The Traveller"

"Women are temperamentally unfit for management."
—Respondent to a *Harvard Business Review* survey

"Woman's place [has been] at the typewriter."
—Margery Davies, *Radical America*

Every day a large proportion of all Americans don their figurative white collars and go to work in offices, where they take their stations in the administrative machines that run large organizations.

Large organizations not only dominate economic and political life (one common prediction holds that 200 multinational corporations will run the world's economy by the year 2000); they also control most of the jobs. The possibilities people experience in work, then, are often limited by the job structure made available by the design of large organizations. Nearly 20 percent of the total nonagricultural employed labor force works for local, state, or federal government.[1] Another 30 percent are employed by business enterprises with more than 500 people on the payroll.[2] And that half of the labor force does not include a variety of other large organizations that cannot be called "businesses" but are often run like them: private universities, private hospitals. Over 12 million Americans work in firms that employ over 10,000 people. In manufacturing, the dominance of large organizations in providing jobs is even more striking. As Table 1–1 shows, 60 percent of all persons employed in manufacturing in 1967 were in firms with at least 1,000 people, 42 percent in companies with over 10,000 employees. At the same time, the labor force is con-

TABLE 1–1

*Number of Employees in Business Enterprises by Employment-Class
Size of Enterprise (1967)*

	Number of Employed Persons	
Employment-Size Class	All Enterprises	Manufacturing
All companies	41,921,345	21,376,976
Less than 500 employees		
per company	22,285,503	6,504,130
500–999 employees	1,773,665	1,120,253
1,000–2,499 employees	2,202,239	1,490,980
2,500–4,999 employees	1,849,658	1,306,255
5,000–9,999 employees	2,222,868	1,677,240
10,000–24,999 employees	3,556,178	2,750,566
25,000–49,999 employees	2,955,729	2,556,543
50,000–99,999 employees	1,793,947	1,273,488
100,000 or more employees	3,281,558	2,697,521

Source: *U.S. Bureau of the Census, 1967,* Enterprise Statistics, *Part I, General Report on Industrial Organization (January, 1972), pp. 164–5, 124.*

centrated in white-collar jobs, like the professional and technical workers, salaried administrators and managers, sales workers and clerical workers that together made up 45 percent of the employed persons in 1974.[3] Both men and women work in large organizations, then, but their experiences are shaped by very different distributions across administrative positions.

Sex polarization and sex segregation of occupations is a fact of the American work world. From 1900 to 1970, in every census year, most female workers were concentrated in occupations that were predominantly female; in 1970 half of all women workers were employed in 17 occupations, as contrasted with the 63 occupations in which half of the men were located. Between 1960 and 1969 there was a disproportionately small growth in the numbers of women in the professional and technical group, in skilled trades, and among salaried managers and officials, but a disproportionately large increase in women clerical workers compared with the growth rate of women workers generally.[4] Women's rising labor force participation, then, has not resulted in women getting a chance at the higher-paying and more powerful jobs. Such statistics led economist Hilda Kahne to write that "women's work setting does not reflect the man's work world."[5]

Women populate organizations, but they practically never run them, especially the large businesses and public establishments that are the model when commentators speak of "modern organizations" or refer to America as an "organizational society." The title of William H. Whyte's 1952 best seller, *The Organization Man,* did not reflect an unwitting failure to use a better generic term for all of humanity; there were then and still are so few women in management that "the organization *man*" meant exactly what it said. By now, figures like these on management are familiar: as of the last census, men constituted over 96 percent of all managers and administrators earning more than $15,000 yearly and nearly 98 percent of those earning over $30,000 yearly.[6] A recent national personnel survey of 163 U.S. companies (98 of them with over 1,000 employees) discovered that the further up the management ladder, the even scarcer are women. In over half of the companies, women held only 2 percent or fewer of the first-level supervisory jobs (including such positions as manager of secretaries). In three-fourths of the companies, women held 2 percent or fewer of the middle management jobs; and in over three-fourths of the companies, they held *none* of the top management jobs.[7]

The exact proportion of men and women in management positions varies from industry to industry. There has been virtually no room for women, as a reading of the statistics and the opinions of executives themselves tell us, in the management of construction, mining, and oil companies, basic industrial goods manufacturing, and production—or in top management in general.[8] These, of course, are areas in which engineering backgrounds may count a great deal. Women have had more opportunities in certain other fields: education, the arts, social service, retail trade, office management, personnel work, advertising, public relations, and staff support positions.

Even in areas decreed by tradition to encompass "female concerns," such as the service fields, and in areas where the workers are largely women, managers are still overwhelmingly likely to be men. The number of male and female bank tellers in the U.S. in 1969 was nearly equal, for example (255,549 men and 220,255 women), but bank officers and financial managers were largely men (82.48 percent). Officers, of course, rarely come up from the ranks or from such jobs as teller; yet even such a low-status administrative position as office *manager* (generally supervising women clericals) is still more likely to be occupied by a man—60 percent of the time—than by a woman.[9]

At the same time, women are to clerical labor what men are to management—in almost the same proportions. According to Census Bureau data, there were over 10 million female "clerical and kindred workers" in the U.S. in 1969—73.78 percent of the total employed workers in this category. The small group of men in the clerical labor force tends to be concentrated in a few occupations where men far outnumber women, several because the jobs require technical knowledge or physical movement (computer operators, messengers, mail carriers, shipping and receiving clerks, and stock clerks). The rest of the occupations, the core of office work, are heavily female. Women comprised 82.14 percent of the bookkeepers, 81.84 percent of the billing clerks, 68.96 percent of the payroll and timekeeping clerks, and 82.08 percent of the file

clerks in a recent census. In secretarial and related functions, men are as un-
derrepresented as women are in management. In 1969, women were 93.46
percent of the stenographers, 94.18 percent of the typists, 94.65 percent of the
receptionists, and 97.71 percent of the secretaries. In fact, these four positions
account for nearly 40 percent of the 1969 female "clerical and kindred workers"; secretaries alone account for 25 percent of the 1969 female clerical labor
force. Labor Bureau statistics for 1970, calculated on a slightly different basis,
show even fewer men in such positions; of the category "stenographers, typists, and secretaries," 98.6 percent are female and only 1.4 percent are male.[10]
Work in America, a task force report to HEW, concluded that the job of secretary is symbolic of the status of female employment, both qualitatively and
quantitatively. Office jobs for women have low status, little autonomy or opportunity for growth, and generally low pay.

Managerial and clerical jobs, then, are the major sex-segregated, white-
collar occupations, brought into being by the development of the large corporation and its administrative apparatus. A sex-linked ethos became identified with each of these occupational groupings. Ideologies surrounding the
pursuit of these occupations and justifying their position in the organization
came to define both the labor pool from which these occupations drew and
ideal images of the attributes of the people in that pool.

CORPORATE CAPITALISM AND THE GROWTH
OF MANAGERIAL IDEOLOGIES

The large corporation began to emerge as a dominant organizational form
in the decades between 1890 and 1910. The Industrial Revolution had already
taken place, but the "Administrative Revolution" did not occur until the turn
of the century. The nature of factory jobs had been determined decades earlier; white-collar work was just beginning to take shape. The proportion of the
total labor force engaged in manufacturing was growing (from 18 percent in
1880 to 26 percent in 1920), but the big spurt in employment was in white-
collar jobs.[11] The number of white-collar workers in the labor force doubled
between 1900 and 1920, whereas manual-service workers increased by a factor
of only 1½.

Women were still employed as seamstresses and in a variety of domestic
occupations. They were beginning to enter offices to handle growing piles of
paperwork, but they had not yet fully taken over clerical work. Management
as a profession was just appearing on the horizon as "family capitalism" and
small business gave way to bank control and finance capitalism in the age of

mergers. A few conglomerates like Standard Oil had existed before 1890, but it was during the following decades that mergers brought together formerly small and far-flung enterprises. *Historical Statistics of the United States* recorded 1,208 mergers in 1899, a number exceeded only by those in 1929. In 1901 the formation of the U.S. Steel Corporation brought together around 158 companies.[12] These new giants needed to be administered, and professional managers came into being. Whether or not capital owners actually faded into the background and lost control of their enterprises—a fact of some dispute [13]—the new breed of professional managers developed to take charge of the ongoing functioning of corporations. Modern administrative practices were invented, first in banks and later spreading to other organizations. Issues such as labor recruitment, disciplined work schedules, cost reckoning, and the seeking of customers were addressed and the solutions built into systems.[14]

Interorganizational consolidation was matched by functional consolidation; an increasing number of functions were brought together and merged in a single corporate administration. More and more formerly independent occupations became located inside large organizations under the "guidance" of professional managers. Earlier, businesses had contracted for the performance of certain tasks such as sales and distribution; during this period, they were taken over by the company. It was a way to gain control over activities that would otherwise have a high quotient of uncertainty, and coping with uncertainty was a principal aim of the new forms of organization. For example, Pittsburgh Plate Glass Company, dissatisfied with the practices of jobbers, established a chain of its own warehouses throughout the country.[15] Inventors and lawyers went to work for the company. Public relations departments were established a few decades later. The practice of "inside contracting," in which foremen were treated as independent contractors with the power to hire, fire, and manage, gave way to central personnel functions and centralized administration.[16] The need to coordinate different operations at scattered sites made management a specialized occupation, and managerial skills began to be more rewarded in business than technical manufacturing work, especially the tasks that came to be the province of managers, internal professionals, and clerks.[17]

The tools, techniques, and functions of management had to be invented, and an occupational culture had to be put in place. The development of titles and labels, such as "vice-president of marketing," and names for specialized officers emerged with the railroads in the mid-nineteenth century, but they did not catch on with other large companies until the twentieth.[18] The first school of business at an American university was the Wharton School of Finance and Commerce at the University of Pennsylvania, founded in 1884; the name provides a clue to the training the school was intended to provide. Management as a separate field was not introduced until several decades later at the Harvard Business School, which itself produced the *crème de la crème* of the managerial elite. Titles and schools supported the development of a new occupation.

The new career managers lacked a class position buttressed by tradition that would provide grounds for legitimation of their authority. After all, they were neither owners nor a traditional "ruling class." (Reinhard Bendix discussed the concerns about authority this evokes in *Work and Authority in Industry*.[19]) Managers had to seek legitimation instead in the increasing professionalization of management, in the development of a "spirit of managerialism" that gave ideological coherence to the control of a relatively small and exclusive group of men over a large group of workers, and that also differentiated the viewpoint of managers from that of owner-entrepreneurs.[20] The managerial viewpoint stressed rationality and efficiency as the *raison d'être* for managerial control. Without the power of property to back them, the new managers created and relied, instead, on a claim of "efficiency," in order to "justify the unilateral exercise of power by management."[21] Control by managers was held to provide the most "rational" way to run an enterprise, and, as Michel Crozier pointed out, rationality represents one of the best grounds for challenging entrenched power groups.[22] On their claims to hold the keys to efficiency, then, and to know the "one best way" to organize work, managers provided a basis for their ever-extending role. A review of the origins of modern management theory shows just how "masculinized" and paternalistic the definition of this role was. To paraphrase Max Weber's classic title, the evolving "spirit of managerialism" was infused with a "masculine ethic."

Although the history of management theory, from scientific management through the human relations school, has been recounted many times, it is worth examining again in the light of its implications for the stratification of organizations by sex.

Scientific Management and the Image of Managers

Management found its first prophet in Frederick Winslow Taylor, the steel company engineer turned management consultant, and its theory in Taylor's "scientific management." Taylor gave a name and rationale to the concept of the rational manager who made decisions based on logical, passionless analysis.

The "rational manager" created by scientific management and its successors was presented as very different from the intuitive entrepreneur of the nineteenth century, in image if not in practice. The tools, techniques, and strategies of modern management had not yet been born. This picture of Cornelius Vanderbilt, the railroad builder who left $104 million when he died in 1877, described qualities in him that were to become objects of scorn for theorists of the new profession of management.

> In his big transactions he seemed to act almost on *impulse* and *intuition.* He could never explain the mental processes by which he arrived at important decisions, though these decisions themselves were invariably sound. He seems to have had, as he himself frequently said, almost a *seer-like faculty.* He saw visions, and he believed in *dreams* and *signs.* The greatest practical genius of his time was a frequent attendant at spiritualistic seances; he cultivated personally the society of mediums, and in sickness he usually resorted to mental healers, mesmerists, and clairvoyants. Before making investments or embarking on his great railroad ventures, Vanderbilt visited spiritualists; we have one circumstantial picture of his summoning the wraith of Jim Fiske to advise him in stock operations.[23] [Italics mine.]

In contrast, Taylor wrote that "no great man can (with the old system of personal management) hope to compete with a number of ordinary men who have been properly organized so as efficiently to cooperate." Taylor's scientific management was labeled and introduced to the public by Louis D. Brandeis in 1910 in direct response to men like Vanderbilt, for Brandeis opposed the trusts and powerful corporations spawned in the preceding decades and wanted to substitute the "efficiency" and "rationality" of management for the greed of the capitalists.[24] In the process, intuition and reliance on non-rational factors in decisions were also firmly rejected.

Taylor's premise was the application of the systematic analysis of science to management methods, emphasizing routines, order, logic, production planning, and cost analysis.[25] His ideas influenced task specialization, time and motion studies, and assembly line philosophies. Taylor's work also supported professional management at a time when unions were gaining in strength and employers were waging militant anti-union campaigns. Taylor separated technical ability to perform a limited task from cognitive ability to abstract, plan, and logically understand the whole process; the latter was the special ability of management. He wrote, "The workman who is best suited to actually doing the work is incapable of fully understanding" the science underlying it "without the guidance and help of those who are working with him or over him." [26]

Although the specifics of Taylor's thought were not necessarily adopted, his general ideas influenced managerial thinking and helped create what has become known as "classical" administrative theory, a set of theories of organization that "operate on the principle of establishing in advance of performance the methods of work and areas of responsibility for each position in the structure. . . . The manifest intention of this rationalization is to direct energy in quantity, time, and place according to an overall plan of organization function at all status levels. The latent effect, of course, is the centralization of management control in a hierarchy of line and staff positions." [27]

Chester Barnard, president of New Jersey Bell and the next great father of modern management, modified the idea of rationality but preserved its flavor. His conception of the rational organization was based on information and decisions rather than on routines and the orderly structuring of positions. He stressed communication (including informal channels) rather than hierarchy, but the mandate of a class of decision-makers was clear. Goals were the special responsibility of the manager, whose functions included abstract generalizing and long-range planning. Authority was a necessary by-product of these decision-making functions. [28]

Early management theory thus developed rationality as the central ideal of the organization and the special province of managers. Organizations were considered tools for generating rational decisions and plans. Workers were motivated to participate on utilitarian grounds and could contribute specific skills, but the real effectiveness of the organization was seen to lie in the efforts of management to design the best way for individuals to fit together in an overall scheme. The rationality of the formal organization was thought to arise not so much from the nature of its participants as from the superiority of the plan created by management. This design could minimize the non-rational, efficiency-undermining feature of human beings to the extent that the participants consented to the authority up the line. The very design of organizations thus was oriented toward and assumed to be capable of suppressing irrationality, personality, and emotionality.

For Max Weber, who saw rationalization of social life as the thrust of Western history, this gave bureaucratic organizations their advantage of efficiency over other types of organized groups. Bureaucracy was the truly "passionless" organization; it was singularly unromantic—even singularly inhuman. As Weber wrote, "Its specific nature . . . is developed the more perfectly bureaucracy is 'de-humanized,' the more completely it succeeds in elimination from official business love, hatred, and all purely personal, irrational, and emotional elements which escape calculation. This is the specific nature of bureaucracy, and it is appraised as its special virtue." [29]

A "masculine ethic" can be identified as part of the early image of managers. This "masculine ethic" elevates the traits assumed to belong to some men to necessities for effective management: a tough-minded approach to problems; analytic abilities to abstract and plan; a capacity to set aside personal, emotional considerations in the interests of task accomplishment; and a cognitive superiority in problem-solving and decision-making. These characteristics supposedly belonged to men; but then, practically all managers were men from the beginning. However, when women tried to enter management jobs, the "masculine ethic" was invoked as an exclusionary principle.

The first thrust in management theory—planning and decision-making to order the tasks and functions of an impersonal bureaucracy—put the "rational man" into management. The second thrust concerned motivation and morale, acknowledging the human order behind the machine. Yet it did not significantly change this aspect of the manager image.

Human Relations in Industry

The 1930s and 1940s gave rise to another theory of management: the human relations model. A group of researchers working with Elton Mayo at Harvard Business School, beginning in the mid-1920s, discovered the importance for productivity of primary, informal relations among workers in the well-known experiments at the Hawthorne plant of Western Electric.[30] They developed the concept of "informal organization" to include the emotional, non-rational, and sentimental aspects of human behavior in organizations, the ties and loyalties that affected workers, the social relations that could not be encompassed by the organization chart but shaped behavior anyway. Other theorists influential in the development of this perspective included Mary Parker Follett, whose interest in management grew out of her experiences with the administration of social welfare organization, a setting in which many women exercise their managerial talents.[31] In short, the human relations model assumed that people were motivated by social as well as economic rewards and that their behavior and attitudes were a function of group memberships. The model emphasized the roles of participation, communication patterns, and leadership style in affecting organizational outcomes.

This theory introduced social and emotional considerations, focusing on the human side of organization. The extent to which it affected managerial practice is not known, but as ideology, it did not challenge the image of the rational manager. Early human relations analysts supported the concept of managerial authority and managerial rationality. In Mayo's view workers were controlled by sentiment, emotion, and social instincts, and this phenomenon needed to be understood and taken into account in organizational functioning. On the other hand, managers were rational, logical, and able to control their emotions in the interests of organizational design.

For managers in Mayo's model, the workers' emotionality offered another set of important factors to take into account in rational planning, and this should be added to the technical training of managers. However, managerial elites were urged to develop their own logic to the fullest and to control their own emotional reactions. In 1933 Mayo wrote that "the administrator of the future must be able to understand the human-social facts for what they actually are, unfettered by his own emotion or prejudice. He cannot achieve this ability except by careful training—training that must include knowledge of relevant technical skills, or the systematic ordering of operations, and of the organization of cooperation." [32] Reinhard Bendix argued that a consequence of this perspective was a simplified version that viewed the successful manager as the man who could control his emotions, whereas workers could not. According to a 1947 management manual, "He [the leader] knows that the master of men has physical energies and skills and intellectual abilities, vision and integrity, and he knows that, above all, the leader must have emotional balance and control. The great leader is even-tempered when others rage, brave when others fear, calm when others are excited, self-controlled when others indulge." [33] (The truth of this image in practice is, of course, another matter.)

Although the emphasis on informal, social factors could not be further from the factors considered important by scientific management, the view of the role of management in an organization was strikingly similar, as Bendix pointed out. "Mayo certainly shared Taylor's belief in science as the foundation upon which an enlightened management should base its approach. Taylor had advanced the idea of a managerial elite, which by means of a 'mental revolution' could increase wages as well as profits. . . . Though Mayo did not accept Taylor's techniques, his conception of a managerial or administrative elite which would bring about industrial harmony and increased production had much in common with Taylor's idea of a managerial elite." [34] If the human relations school's metaphor was the "family" rather than the "machine" of classical models, the organization was still thought to require a rational controller at its head. Writers on management practice and organization theory distinguished between the managers' logic of efficiency and the workers' logic of sentiment. [35] "Informal organization"—the play of emotion, sentiment, and politics—continued to be studied primarily among lower-ranking personnel, leaving the impression that only workers, and not managers, base their actions on "irrational" factors. [36]

The "rational" thread in management theory has continued, even though a long line of critics, especially Chris Argyris, has also challenged the rationalist assumption on both scientific and moral grounds (that it is an inaccurate or an undesirable model of how organizations are and ought to be). [37] When human relations theory filtered into the management level of corporations in the form of sensitivity training groups in the late 1950s and 1960s, it coexisted alongside theories and techniques for rational decision-making. Sensitivity groups were considered a vehicle for learning about relationships so as to master, not unleash, emotional factors counter-productive to the organization.

Human relations theories have made inroads, adding what some have called a "feminized" element to the old "masculine ethic," and new forms of organization, such as team-oriented matrix and project management systems, are in use in many organizations. Yet for most of the twentieth century a "masculine ethic" of rationality dominated the spirit of managerialism and gave the manager role its defining image.[38] It told men how to be successful as men in the new organizational worlds of the twentieth century.

Such an image also provided a rationale for where women belonged in management. If they belonged at all, it was in people-handling staff functions such as personnel, where their emotional fine-tuning, according to the stereotype in operation, was more appropriate than in decision-making functions. Personnel staff are like the social workers of management. One management writer commented that "it's taken for granted that women will be found in personnel jobs. . . . There is a feeling that women can do these jobs, that they understand people better. . . . Part of this misconception that women can only do personnel work stems from the old idea that personnel is a do-good operation." [39]

If women have been directed into the "emotional" end of management, they have also been excluded from the centers of power in management for the same reason. Perhaps the most pervasive stereotype of women in organizations is that they are "too emotional," whereas men hold the monopoly on rational thought. Women represent the antithesis of the rational manager. They were considered by some people in a *Harvard Business Review* survey to be "temperamentally unfit for management." Among the "top ten gripes" of women executives in a *Business Week* survey was the complaint that a display of emotion was not tolerated in a woman, although it was accepted and common in men.[40] Male managers in the corporation I studied expressed the fear that a woman would cry in their office or fly off the handle if they criticized her, so they avoided giving negative reactions to women, whether secretaries or colleagues. The women who could get in were the ones who could demonstrate the ability to "think like a man."

While management was being defined as a "masculine" pursuit, more routine office chores were being "feminized."

THE EVOLUTION OF OFFICE WORK FOR WOMEN

Women did not always dominate the clerical labor force; office work in the nineteenth century was first a male preserve. The same turn-of-the-century period (1890–1910) that brought large organizations and the growth of the

professional manager also witnessed the emergence of the modern office with
its invention of new roles for women. "Rational" planning and record-keeping
required clerks. The three-person office of mid-nineteenth century Dickens
novels was socially reorganized into departments and functional areas headed
by office managers, and this change—itself a product of bureaucratization
and machine technology—permitted the massive introduction of office machines. Although invented in the 1870s, the typewriter was not widely used
until the twentieth century; but from 1900 to 1920 office employment rose
dramatically, and typing soon became women's work.[41]

The rise in the employment of women in the office around the turn of the
century was dramatic, and it corresponded to a large decrease in "household
occupations" (servants, dressmakers and seamstresses outside of factories, and
laundresses). In 1870 the "clerical group" (clerks, stenographers, typists,
bookkeepers, cashiers, and accountants) accounted for less than 1 percent of
the women employed outside of agriculture; by 1920 it accounted for over 25
percent of female non-agricultural employment. In 1880 the proportion of
women in the clerical labor force as a whole was 4 percent; in 1890 it was 21
percent. By 1910 women were already 83.2 percent of the stenographers and
typists; by 1920 they were 91.8 percent of the stenographers/typists and 48.8
percent of the bookkeepers, cashiers, and accountants. Between 1910 and
1920 the number of female clerks (excluding store clerks) quadrupled; female
stenographers and typists more than doubled. Slightly more women were still
employed in factory than in clerical jobs in 1920 (about 1.8 compared with 1.5
million women), but less than 1 percent of those in industry could be classified
as managers, superintendents, or officials.[42] The growth of modern administration brought women into domination in the office but left them absent in
management. Whereas factory jobs were divided between men and women,
clerical jobs rapidly became the work almost exclusively of women. As an
economist observed in 1929, "The influx of women into the clerical occupations
within the last few decades has become one of the most phenomenal, if also
one of the least conspicuous, of the economic changes which have been transforming the lives of women during this period. The seven women stenographers and typists recorded by the census takers in 1870 would hardly have
conceived it possible that they were precursors of a host which had become
half a million by the census of 1920."[43]

Popular images changed along with the labor force shifts, promoting the
"feminization" of the clerical labor force that was occurring. In 1900 the *Ladies
Home Journal* was urging women to stay out of offices, but by 1916 the same
magazine was glorifying the feminine traits of stenographers: their ability to ra-
diate sympathetic interest, agreeableness, courtesy. Magazine fiction began to
build romantic stories around the young girl working in an office who would

find her true love, leaving at that point, of course, to get married. Office work was acceptable to the extent that women emphasized their femininity rather than their skills and saw it as clearly subordinate to the ultimate goal of marriage. A 1905 *Ladies Home Journal* column advised, "Do not suppose that the prize and success it, the business world, holds out to you will at last outweigh the nearer, dearer blessings of home and home life." [44]

The typing pool acquired its Harvard Business School in 1911.[45] The first U.S. typing school was opened by the New York YWCA in 1881, but it was the Katharine Gibbs School that prepared young women for the elite secretarial jobs. Gibbs, a widow, founded her first school in Providence, Rhode Island, with one student. In 1917 the Boston school started, and in 1918 came one in New York. Remaining a family company until bought out by Macmillan in 1968, the schools have turned out about 55,000 secretaries tutored in the basics: typing, shorthand, and personal grooming.

Both men and women held clerical jobs when the Gibbs schools were founded, but women's work was typically more menial. As the first institution of its kind to teach women accounting and grammar as well as the "basics," the Gibbs schools helped get women more responsibility, but this was in keeping with its elite tradition rather than feminist leanings. "Gibbs girls" came from well-to-do backgrounds and got the best of the jobs. Tuition was high and the atmosphere that of a finishing school, with daughters of Gibbs girls coming for *their* preparation. (In the early 1930s some early spring classes were held in Bermuda for those who could afford it.) Though open to both sexes, only one man has ever enrolled full time. A look at the curriculum makes this easy to explain. The concern with appearance and grooming reflected in lectures on posture and hand care extended to a strict regimen, along with dress and conduct rules.

While the secretarial image was taking shape, the organization of office work was also developing. The increased use of office machines as well as the expansion of the office affected the arrangement of tasks; this was the theme of C. Wright Mills' excursion into "the enormous file" in *White Collar*. Specialists in the running of one machine or the processing of one kind of paperwork developed, working factory-style at row after row of desks supervised by office managers. Secretarial work was divided into two kinds: marriage-like and factory-like. The elite corps of private secretaries were directly attached to one or more bosses for whom they did a variety of tasks and from whom they derived status. Other secretarial work was done in steno and typing pools whose occupants were little more than extensions of their machines—and highly replaceable at that. The contrast in the privileges, rewards, and status of these two types of work enhanced the desirability of the private secretarial position, making it seem the culmination of a clerical worker's aspirations.

Although the reporting arrangements and personnel policies around secretaries were formalized in large organizations, the actual content of a secretary's role, beyond the basics like typing, was defined by a relationship to a specific boss. Here the fact that most secretaries were female helped shape or reinforce the definition of the secretarial role. Men type and run machines too, and they often act in a service-like capacity for bosses. However, the nature of the secretarial role, as found in practically all large organizations, is heavily bound up with the feminization of the occupation.

Wives

One additional group of women may find their lives bound to the corporation, even though they are not recorded in official labor force statistics: the wives of management, particularly those women not otherwise employed in paid work. This is a sizable group. In 1969, 93.19 percent of the male managers earning $15,000 or more (nearly all of the managers to begin with) were married, 72.25 percent to women not in the paid labor force. As income and status goes up, even fewer of the wives hold paid jobs, and even more of the men are married. An earlier American Management Association survey of 335 company presidents turned up only five bachelors. Less than a fourth of 210 wives of headmasters of private schools felt, in another survey, that their school would hire a headmaster without a wife; among the 210 wives, only 16 percent held outside paid employment, and almost all of those worked in a neighboring school. Men have reported the pressure they feel to acquire a wife at a certain stage in their careers due to the prejudice of some companies against single men. As much as men themselves may want to get married because of what wives can give them, it is almost as though organizations give them that little extra push by insisting they bring a wife along as a backup person for their jobs.[46]

Men and women of the corporation, then, relate to each other and to their work through jobs that are often sex-segregated and laden with idealized images of the capacities of the people in them. These views define the principal players. The stage setting is an industrial giant like Industrial Supply Corporation.

2

Industrial Supply Corporation:

The Setting

"We're a nice quiet organization. Know your place."
— Longtime Industrial Supply manager

"At times I feel more like part of an army than a team."
— Young sales worker

"I'm a very integral part of the team. However, at times other members of the team are not in the same game."
— Junior manager

"Industrial Supply is a 'Puritan Ethic' company. If you don't make it, you don't deserve it."
— Executive from a minority group

Industrial Supply Corporation (Indsco) is not a real name, but it is a very real place. Some of the details of its existence are disguised, too, to protect confidentiality, but the overall picture is true to the life of this organization, as it revealed itself through surveys, interviews, meetings, and documents in the 1970s.[1]

Indsco was one of those hybrid firms that grew during the first great wave of corporate mergers at the beginning of the century, a conglomerate that developed out of a number of smaller companies employing new technology and later diversified. Consolidation of the loose divisions comprising the corporation took place after World War II, especially in the 1960s. Indsco is one of the world's largest producers of industrial goods, a multinational on the *Fortune* magazine list of 500 leading industrial firms; its stock is actively traded. It dominates two or three of its markets (including areas in which it supplies its major competitors) but competes with a range of firms, including smaller ones, in other markets. Until recently, it has had a low public profile because its primary sales were to other firms and its consumer products were known by a variety of different and unrelated brand names. For employees, Indsco also had had limited corporate identity; employees were most likely to feel a part of their own division rather than the corporation. A recent set of institutional ads, coupled with a series of corporate reorganizations over the past decade, is moving Indsco in the direction of a single-umbrella identity. The ads show the range of goods coming out of Industrial Supply, some as finished products and some as material supplied to other manufacturers.

Industrial Supply Corporation was not implicated in any of the corporate scandals of the 1960s and 1970s. It has never been accused of bribery, and it has never been the target of protests about the manufacture of war products. It is known as straitlaced and honest, if a bit stodgy. Said one executive, "Indsco is a moral company—high ethics. Things like cheating on wives don't go over big. High puritan ethics. Bribe stuff wouldn't happen here—partly because the company is too cheap and partly because there has always been a demand for its products. And, of course, we now see the situation." (But one officer confessed privately that he had reservations about the public proclamations of the Board of Directors that Indsco was free of corruption: "It makes me nervous to hear them say that. The organization is so large, so many people—I can't know if it's true. It worries me a lot.")

Industrial Supply had more than 50,000 employees in the 1970s, 16 percent of them women and 9 percent minorities. Over 3,000 people worked in the headquarters office, about half of them clerical personnel. In 1974 in one division, women constituted 87 percent of the clerical and office workers, 21 percent of the professionals, and only 2 percent of the officials and managers. Indsco's size and divisional structure make an organization chart very complicated. People liked to laugh about it, saying that the organization chart was two inches wide and three feet long, printed on adding machine tape. A series of reorganizations, beginning in 1964, developed the present matrix structure. Each division is more closely connected to the central corporation. It in turn is divided into both functional areas and profit centers for each product. One division had 40 profit centers and over 230 products. Each division had its own structure of officers, and managers reported to two bosses: one for their function and one for the profit center.

There have been a number of other experiments along the way to the present structure. In the early 1970s, for example, titles were taken away from people like division presidents and vice-presidents because business was bad and the corporation was "punishing" them. They were given the titles of division manager and assistant division manager, but they got around it by having two sets of stationery, one for internal correspondence that said "division manager," and one for external correspondence that said "president, _____ division." (The titles were given back two years later when business improved.) During this same period, the director of one function experimented with flattening the hierarchy. He tried to collapse three levels of managers into one, giving them all the same titles and having them report directly to him. He hoped thereby to improve communication. However, he was soon moved to South America; and after his departure, the new director reinstituted the titles. In any case, responsibilities had not changed, and everyone knew that levels 1, 2, and 3 within the new management positions corresponded to the old hierarchical grades.

The next major organizational innovation was to develop a comprehensive management system, complete with its own language and procedures, based on a system of "management by objectives" that would standardize procedures throughout the corporation. It was also hoped that the new system would encourage people to focus on targets and results and would involve more people in planning. Along with the matrix, this represented the corporation's attempt to move from a fairly standard pyramidal bureaucracy to a more dynamic system. It was also established along with a series of what the company calls "people-conscious" programs: a career planning process for exempt employees that was beginning to filter down to nonexempts by the middle 1970s, a standardized performance appraisal system, and a more comprehensive set of continuing education programs offered by the corporation itself. All of these things were seen as important selling points in attracting good young people to the company. It worked. The company got about 50 percent of the sales workers to whom it made offers—slightly higher than the industry average, which was about 44 percent. It was thought that this was because the company was competitive on salaries, had a good reputation, produced high-quality products, provided opportunities for career growth (alternative plans, a career development program), and because new hires were recruited by "real professionals" inside the company who were enthusiastic.

Until the reorganizations of the 1960s, the company had a small-town, small-company atmosphere. Divisions were independent enough and sometimes small enough that people inside them often felt that they were working for a very small rather than a very large company. Gossip and rumors flowed freely, and people tended to feel as though they knew one another; they could rely much more on personal contact and much less on formal procedures. With the reorganization, all that started to change. In terms of rumor circles, it remained a small company—in terms of the size of the world that mattered to a particular employee and who passed what along to whom. However, the circles increasingly seemed to be small and parochial networks. Only in the smaller functions or profit centers could people's paths still crisscross enough that they could feel a part of a larger whole.

Attitudes were changing in response. One new trainee described the feeling of insignificance he had as he first encountered the organization in its orientation program. Along with thirty other new hires in sales, he faced confusing organization charts, "six hundred handshakes," and lunch with the chairman of the board. He felt like "a small cog in a big wheel." A staff official responsible for many of the new employee programs commented, "The company is so large now that when someone wants to develop an innovation, he runs up against the inability of doing it because it has ripples beyond the small group. So you have to be content to make small changes. In a company this big, that's all you can do. You do a few small things, but you make sure they are sustained. Lower your sights." A high-ranking executive in a subsidiary said that his small company had been bought by Indsco in order to learn its secrets of success in its field, but as soon as the company became part of the corporation, the virtues of its small size and flexibility disappeared, and "I became the highest paid bookkeeper in the corporation." A manager in his thirties, destined to go places in the company, described this reaction to a new job he was about to take: "I have a stack of papers eighteen inches high that people have been sending me in anticipation of my starting the job next month. I had it sitting on top of the credenza at home, and I finally stuffed it away inside the credenza, deciding that it was too much to be thinking about—to do all that planning in advance. I had a fantasy: what does it all matter anyway? What would happen if I did nothing? Everything is on a fail-safe basis anyway, and it will be done automatically if no one stops it. Then I could just drift along, and things would take care of themselves. It probably wouldn't make any difference."

Legends told by old-timers who had been around the company a long time tended to reflect nostalgia for the good old days when the company was smaller and when people had a closer relationship across hierarchical levels. One story was told about a past president. "There was a time when every salesman wore a hat, even on an elevator—bowlers. Some men couldn't afford it on their salaries. One got on an elevator in the old headquarters building when the president was standing in the back. The president said, 'Mr. Stevens, don't we pay you enough so that you can afford to purchase a hat?' Stevens replied, 'No.' " Shortly thereafter, legend has it, he got a raise. There are also many stories about an early president who retained his interest in scientific research, despite his lofty position, and continued to go down to the lab and play around with the scientists.

A new series of legends has grown up about a recent divisional president who had died unexpectedly a few years earlier, a great loss to the organization; but this was partly because he was so unique. He managed to inspire people to their best efforts so that even down at the plant, the story was told, production workers would say, "I'm doing this for Tom." A manager reminisced, "He resembled a military leader like Patton. Things for him took on similarities to a war or battle. We'll put on our best effort and either win and share in the glories or lose and go down together. For example, he took over a plant that was failing and put himself on the line. He told the guys under him that if they lost the battle and he was out, they'd be fired ten minutes before. People were willing to accept the risk because they wanted leadership like that. They felt part of the team doing something important. Or he went down into a plant on Black October, when we had to cut back. We had to let many people go. He said, 'I make the decisions. I'll take the heat.' So he went down and dropped the bomb himself. He got much flak, but he took it, and those who were left had higher allegiance to him afterwards. Too bad we don't have more guys like that, but the company really doesn't support them."

Like most large corporations, Indsco moved managers from place to place very frequently, but it was size issues that in part accounted for the ambivalence people expressed about moving to the headquarters office in a large city. On the one hand, they would have exposure and make connections that would further their careers. No one ever advanced who had not spent some time in headquarters. Even an ambitious secretary working in a field office just outside of the headquarters city turned down a promotion in her own office because she was holding out for a job in headquarters. On the other hand, many people were concerned about the costs involved in getting swallowed up by a large and anonymous environment. There was enough resistance about moving to the home office that the corporation was considering a move to a smaller city, where at least the surroundings would provide a greater sense of smallness.

Still, most people at the upper levels of Indsco seemed to think they were pretty well situated. When they made comparisons with other companies in the industry, Indsco looked good by contrast. It was seen as more casual and less tradition-bound than one, which required salespeople to begin in inside technical jobs first. It was considered looser and more relaxed than another: "At _____, people always seemed to be looking over my shoulder. They were concerned if I came in five minutes late. 'Performance appraisal' was whatever the boss said; I had no inputs, no rewards. It's much better here at Indsco." There was also curiosity about the culture of major rivals and how their system and policies might contribute to profitability and job satisfaction. But, for the most part, complaints about size and bureaucratic annoyances at Indsco were balanced by the obvious pride many people took in working for a large and powerful organization, one whose headquarters towered many stories in a major city—a monument to the company's importance.

Corporate headquarters occupied many floors in a glass and steel office building in a large city. The surroundings were luxurious. At ground level was a changing art exhibit in glass cases with displays of awards to Indsco executives for meritorious public service or newspaper clippings about the corporation. There might be piles of company newspapers on a nearby table or special publications like the report by foreign students who spent the summer with Indsco families. Such public displays almost always stressed Indsco's contributions to the welfare of the larger community. Across from gleaming chrome elevators and a watchman's post were doors leading into the employees' dining room. In the morning a long table with coffee, sweet rolls, and bagels for sale was set up outside the dining room; during the day coffee carts were available on each floor. Inside, the dining room was divided into two parts: a large cafeteria for everyone and a small area with already set tables, hostess seating, menus, and waitress service. Those tables were usually occupied by groups of men; the largely female clerical work force tended to eat in the cafeteria. Special luncheon meetings arranged by managers were held in the individual executive dining rooms and conference areas on the top floor; to use these rooms, reservations had to be made well in advance by someone with executive status.

Indsco executives were also likely to go out for lunch, especially if they were entertaining an outside visitor, to any of the numerous posh restaurants in the neighborhood. At these lunches a drink was a must; at one time it was two extra-dry martinis, but more recently it became a few glasses of wine. However, despite the fact that moderate social drinking was common, heavy drinking was frowned upon. A person's career could be ruined by the casual comment that he or she had alcoholic tendencies. Stories told about men who cavorted and caroused in bars, staying up all night, were told with the attitude that "that was really crazy."

The office floors were quietly elegant, dominated by modern design, white walls, and beige tones. At one end, just off the elevators, sat a receptionist who calls on a company telephone line to announce visitors. A secretary would then appear to escort a visitor to his or her appointment. Offices with windows were for higher-status managers, and their secretaries were often proud of having drapes. Corner offices were reserved for the top. They were likely to be larger in size, with room for coffee tables and couches, and reached through a reception area where a private secretary sat. Inside offices went to assistants and other lower-status-salary personnel; conference rooms were also found along the inside rim. Secretaries and other hourly workers occupied rows of desks with banks of cabinets and files in the public spaces between. There were few signs of personal occupancy of space, except around the secretaries' desks. Managers might put up a painting or poster on the wall, and they usually had a small set of photographs of their families somewhere on or near their desk. Rarely would more than a few books or reports be visible, and the overall impression was one of tidiness, order, and uniformity from office to office. In fact, it was often true that the higher the status of an executive, the less cluttered was his desk. Office furnishings themselves reflected status rather than personality. There was a clear system of stratification. As status increased, desks went from a wood top with steel frame through solid wood to the culmination in a marble-top desk. Type of ashtray was also determined by the status system; and a former executive secretary, promoted into a management position herself, reported that her former peers were upset that she took her stainless steel file trays with her because a secretary working for her would not be entitled to such luxurious equipment. The rational distribution of furniture and supplies was thought to make the system more equitable and to avoid competition for symbols of status.

Discreet bulletin boards near every cluster of secretaries served as office information centers, passing on news of people's travels and making apparent a wide range of company activities such as the women's bowling league standings as of the last week, the camera club contest winners, a notice regarding medical plan benefits, when to sign up for beginning tennis, when the men's softball team would be playing—announced by a Peanuts cartoon—"Your Benefits Plan Corner" in question-and-answer format with this month's question ("Why it takes so long to get money from the sale of Indsco stock"), a cartoon of a man asking why he doesn't get a promotion and spilling water all over his boss, the week's menu for the employees' cafeteria, a similar menu for the restaurant, a notice to salaried employees about a change in the pension plan, a notice about a plant location that was no longer on direct dial, a letter from the corporate executive vice-president to the Indsco executive list on the appointment of a president to a newly formed division, a letter from a divisional president on the appointment of a new vice-president, and a copy of one of the company's new institutional ads containing an especially touching picture. The bulletin board reflected the essence of the image the company wanted to convey—the caring, welfare-oriented organization that could meet all of its employees' needs and provide a total home. Indeed, the company employed a large staff of its own chefs and food-service personnel. Though its primary business was manufacturing, it found itself in many secondary social and service operations. It was becoming increasingly true that the corporation employed people in practically every occupational category.

Physical height corresponded to social height at Indsco, like other major corporations. Corporate officers resided at the very top on the forty-fifth floor, which was characterized by many people in Indsco as "a hospital ward." The silence was deafening. The offices were huge. According to one young executive who had served as an assistant to an officer, "One or two guys are sitting there; there's not much going on. It's the brain center, but there is no activity. It's like an old folks' home. You can see the cobwebs growing. A secretary every quarter mile. It's very sterile." An executive secretary told the story of her officer boss's first reaction to moving onto the forty-fifth floor. "He was the one human being," she said, "who was uncomfortable with the trappings of status. When he moved up, he had to pick an office." She wouldn't let him take anything but a corner—it was the secretary who had to tell him that. Finally he agreed for the sake of the corporate image, but he was rarely there, and he set up the office so that everything was in one corner and the rest was useless space.

Some people felt that the physical insulation of top executives also had its counterpart in social insulation. Said a former officer's assistant, "There are courtiers around the top guys, telling them what they want to hear, flattering them. For example, there was a luncheon with some board members. The vice-chairman mentioned that he was looking for a car for his daughter. A courtier thought, 'We'll take care of it.' He went down the line, and someone in purchasing had to spend half a day doing this. The guy who had to do it resented it, so he became antagonistic to the top. The vice-chairman had no idea this was going on, and if he had known, he would probably have stopped it; but you can't say anything at the top without having it be seen as an order. Even ambiguous remarks may get translated into action. At the top you have to figure out the impact of all of your words in advance because an innocent expression can have a major effect. A division president says, 'It might be a good idea to _____.' He's just ruminating, but that gets sent down to the organization as an ultimatum, and everyone scrambles around to make sure it gets done. He looks down and says, 'What the hell is happening?' " At the same time, officers could also be frustrated by their distance from any real action. One remarked, "You get into a position like mine, and you think you can get anything done, but I shout down an order, and I have to wait years for any action. The guy in the plant turns a valve and sees the reaction, or the salesman offers a price, but I may never live to see the impact of my decisions." For this reason, it was known that once in a while officers could be expected to leave their protected environment and try to get involved in routine company activities. Some would go down and try to do something on the shop floor. Once in a while one would make a sales call at a very high level or make an appearance at a customer golf outing. It was also a legend that an early president had his own private laboratory outside of his office—his own tinkering room. As a manager put it, "He would close the door and go play. It was almost as though he was babied. He was given a playroom."

Mornings and evenings elevators at headquarters crowded with the two major types of corporate administrative personnel: carefully dressed men in dark, tailored business suits and more colorfully, casually dressed women who were almost exclusively nonsalaried workers and largely secretaries. The great divide in company personnel terms was the exempt/nonexempt distinction. "Nonexempts" were the workers paid weekly and covered by wage-and-hour laws; for example, they must be paid overtime rates for extra hours. In the office and administration side of the company, nonexempts were almost all women, although there were a few nonexempt men at both low and high status, such as mail messengers on the low end or accounting clerks on ladders leading to exempt jobs. "Exempts" were on annual salary; they were the managers, the professionals, and the sales and technical workers, who were still practically all men. Exempt jobs all had a rating for salary purposes that was universal throughout all levels of the company. However, exempt jobs were also graded on a scale of one to twenty-four, corresponding to a title hierarchy: supervisor, manager, director, officer. Officers, including both divisional and corporate presidents and vice-presidents as well as board officials, began at grade 20. Beginning at grade 18, people were in jobs where they reported directly to officers. Jobs with management responsibility began at about grade 9. The number of people at each level got thinner and thinner, of course, as grades increased; the corporation resembled not so much a pyramid as the Eiffel Tower. The number of women above grade 10 anywhere in the corporation could be counted in single digits.

Dress differences between exempt and nonexempt employees coincided largely, but not only, with male/female differentiation. Exempt and nonexempt categories also carried their own styles. Managers of whatever sex were likely to present a tailored, conservative appearance. They were also frequently, though not invariably, physically attractive. Staff of a training facility commented, for example, that people who were physically impressive and athletic seemed to get instant respect. Nonexempts, on the other hand, were likely to be dressed much less "professionally." "You can easily tell the professional women from the secretaries by their shoes," one person reported. "The professionals wear pumps; the secretaries wear four-inch wedgies." Indeed, the range, casualness, and hip-fashion air of younger secretaries' dress made some men uncomfortable, although others seemed to enjoy having young women around. (There were also many matronly looking older secretaries.) Heavy eye makeup, teased hair, see-through blouses, and flamboyant dress were the subject of some discussion at a task force meeting on the management of nonexempts, and consideration was given to a dress manual for nonexempt employees.

The contrasting styles and relationships to the company of exempt and nonexempt employees were visible from their very first day on the job. New exempts participated in a one-week orientation program. Upon entering the auditorium at headquarters, they were given an attractive binder and a note pad, printed name tags, a copy of local entertainment magazines, and invitations to cocktail and theater parties. Top-ranking officials appeared to present the history of the corporation and a demonstration of its social concerns. The exempts heard discussions of Indsco's activities in environmental protection and occupational safety, of its community service activities, of its support for minority enterprises. Films were shown of a variety of plants and activities, and opportunities for continuing education and for learning the management system were discussed. By contrast, the nonexempt orientation took half a day. A personnel staff member presented the Indsco benefits plan (for example, pensions, educational refund plans), described available company social events (tennis club, bowling tournament), showed a film on office safety, and showed a general company propaganda film. Not only was the exempt welcome more elaborate, but also it was clear that the company thought that they were the only ones who needed to be concerned about larger social issues and further opportunities for growth.

Once on the job, differences in treatment continued. There were elaborate personnel systems for the handling of exempt employees; only toward the middle 1970s were such programs contemplated for nonexempts, and then primarily as a response to affirmative action pressures. People in the exempt ranks could anticipate an ever-increasing flow of luxuries as they moved up in grade. (They could also anticipate working longer hours. Some sales managers who found themselves putting in 80-hour weeks felt they had "two full time jobs for the price of one.") In sales and management, company cars were taken for granted as "bennies" (fringe benefits). The entire sales force was treated to a week at a fancy resort hotel, and only half of the time was officially scheduled for meetings; the rest was devoted to a series of sports events that were set up by committees of sales workers and managers themselves. The company spent a great deal of money moving its exempt people from place to place. One manager's move from a field office to headquarters cost the company $33,000. Indsco paid moving expenses, real estate agent fees, loss from the sale of the original house, plane trips back and forth, and hotel bills while getting settled in the new city. Of the $33,000, the moving cost of household goods represented only $9,000.

Nothing seemed to be too good for valued exempt employees, and they came to believe that this was a very special organization that cared deeply about its people. These were the kinds of stories they told. A man was on the West Coast on a trip with his wife in the company car. He was in back, and she was driving. They were in an accident, and he was killed immediately. Corporation vice-presidents got involved. The widow was entitled to insurance only if her husband was on business, so they put pressure on the insurance company. The president made a statement that the whole services of the corporation would be put behind the wife. He even flew out to the funeral. In another instance, the father of a salesworker's wife died. She was pregnant at the time, and the doctor said she should not fly commercially. The salesworker's boss called a director, who arranged a corporate jet to be ready at a local airport with full services, and they could even take the doctor with them. This was set up within five to six hours. A manager in the territory where the wife's father had lived put himself at the widow's disposal, and he met the husband at the airport when he came for the funeral. In still another case, in which a manager was having personal problems with a divorce, the company relocated him so that he could be closer to his former wife and children, even in this period of separation. "This company really cares about its people," would be the message conveyed by the people who told such stories. Yet when I would ask if such treatment ever extended down to nonexempts, there would often be surprise at my question, and respondents would have to confess that they simply had not thought about it. Nonexempts were not given the same luxurious treatment as exempts, and they also did not have the same kinds of stories to tell, except in the case of secretaries who had a special relationship with a particular boss.

One of the corporation's major suburban office facilities differed in particulars from urban headquarters but created some of the same atmosphere. It sprawled horizontally instead of vertically, looking out at woods and rolling hills, and the carpet colors were often brighter—blues and reds. The building reflected the latest in "office landscaping": mobile beige partitions instead of walls, large potted jungle trees, an indoor bridge running from the office part to the cafeteria, where carpet samples might occasionally be tested. The atmosphere was somewhat less formal. The men sometimes came to work in sports jackets, blazers, or even open shirts. Secretaries, clerks, and exempts all ate together in one cafeteria. There was also a company store where employees could buy products that contained Indsco materials at special prices.

Here also the company had built an up-to-date training facility for sales and marketing, complete with video cameras, film projectors, and other recording equipment, large meeting rooms, and small model offices for role plays of sales calls. This attention given to sales and sales management training reflected the importance of this function for the company, especially because the company sold primarily to other firms in rather large quantities. At one time, all Indsco executives had had technical and then financial backgrounds, but now sales was one of the prime routes into management.[2] It was well known that in sales people could move higher younger. For example, at the 1973 salary range of $21,500 to $25,500, the average age of people in production was thirty-four, in research and development thirty-six-and-a-half, in engineering thirty-two, and in sales thirty-one. At a salary range of $28,500 to $33,500 (managerial grade), the average age was forty-two in marketing, forty-three in research and development, forty-three in production, forty-five in engineering, but only thirty-seven in sales. People who entered through sales generally had technical backgrounds in science and engineering, but there were also liberal arts graduates. Sales workers entered at grade 6, already well on their way up the ladder. "It's the best function," a rising young manager commented. "There's the best training, the most money spent on boondoggles, the most recognition, and the loosest climate—we have the most fun." The sales function was divided by product type and by region. Area sales offices occupied suites generally in suburban office parks, which included people in all divisions. One floor of corporate headquarters was also given over to the local sales office. Increasing size affected field sales offices as well as corporate headquarters, and people from one sales force often did not know their counterparts in others.

There was both a formal and an informal company culture, reflected in language, rituals, and styles of communication.[3] Officially, the corporation was trying to promote a terse language system called a "comvoc," for "common vocabulary." To the formal Indsco terminology was added a long list of specialized terms used by people in different functions. A group of wives, whom I asked to list all of the words they heard their husbands use that required definitions, generated a list of 103 words—and said there were more, if they hadn't been told to stop. And then there was the folk language of the corporation. People used a colorful, graphic, highly pictorial language, in which abstract concepts were captured in concrete images: "looking for a person to hang his hat on" meant a manager was looking for a promising subordinate he could promote and improve his own prospects in the process; "bennies" meant fringe benefits, but the term also was intended to convey an element of addiction, as to a drug. The development of multiple terms for a single phenomenon also reflected the major concerns of the corporate culture, just as all cultures elaborate the language around those phenomena that represent central issues.[4] There were six words in common use to describe people who were "comers" and on the move in the organization: fast trackers, high fliers, superstars, one performers, boy (or girl) wonders, and (with provocative imagery) water walkers. (Upward mobility was clearly a central issue.)

Concrete picture language reflected an avoidance of abstraction that was also reflected in the lack of introspection encouraged in interpersonal relations. For people in the exempt ranks of Indsco, at least, life was comparatively safe and secure as long as they committed no major blunders. This was reflected in an atmosphere that was rather bland and easygoing—even emotionless. It was one of apparent comfort (vice-presidents sitting around and singing with the junior people at sales meetings, everyone on a first name basis—"very little mistering," one person said—friendly greetings on elevators) but emotional distance. Emphasis was placed on getting along, "keeping your nose clean," and on having a smooth interpersonal style. Introspection was out. Intellectuals were suspect. Difficult or controversial subjects were avoided. Staff of training programs invariably commented that differences and anger were very difficult to express; instead, the atmosphere was expected to exemplify collaboration, agreement, and consensus. There were few, if any, rewards in fighting for something too hard or too openly. The manager of one new function became this sort of advocate of his work, and it nearly cost him his mobility within the company. Even years later people got back at him in stories that questioned whether he was fully living up to the commitment he had expressed in developing the function in the first place. A tremendous value was placed on team membership and getting along with peers: "Peer acceptance" was considered a factor in promotions. "Individual performers" were generally not promoted. What emotional expression there was generally occurred through joking relationships. Jokes were a very important part of company culture, and having a good sense of humor also seemed to be a requisite for mobility. It was a ritual, for example, to have a party in someone's honor when they left a job or moved to a new location. On these occasions, the person being honored would have to sit still while he or she was made the brunt of everyone else's jokes. Such "roasting" was perhaps a way of expressing affection, but there were people even within Industrial Supply who were concerned that it could not be expressed more directly.

It was as though people did not want to have to think too closely about themselves or their situation.[5] There were small hints of this from time to time. Occasionally, fears emerged from behind the apparent ease that people projected. For example, there was a great deal of paranoia about the use that would be made of information gathered on surveys, even though people were promised confidentiality and anonymity. There was also an issue of confidentiality in training programs. It took a great deal of experience to convince some people that the things they revealed about themselves in the course of learning new behavioral skills would not somehow be fed back to their managers and used against them. Once in a while, too, a person exhibited signs of a controlled rebellion, of testing the system to see how far he could go. In one case, a young man who was clearly seen as a comer made a point of being open about his criticisms of the company. He took pleasure in defying the system whenever he could. He was fairly open about disdain for many of the people who had made it in the corporation, and he planned to bring marijuana to a company meeting, even though organization morality was strictly against it. Testing behavior also occurred in the jokes and dirty talk made in or near the presence of women, who were now starting to enter the exempt ranks.

Many men at Industrial Supply Corporation seemed more confused than hostile about the trickling in of women into management, professional, and sales positions; but there were those who were also openly angry. A few of the young men admitted to feeling competitive and having concerns that affirmative action would make women their age go whizzing by them on their way to the top. The older men did not have that worry; and after all, the trickle was still a trickle. However, the whole issue was raising organizational and personal self-consciousness, something that people at Industrial Supply preferred to avoid. It pointed out that the system was not working as well as people wished to believe, and it aroused whatever fears people had about their own involvement in their work. Some managers were ready to relax at any sign of progress and say, "The problem is solved. Women are here to stay. So what's all the fuss? Stop giving them preferential treatment." However, "great signs of progress" at Indsco meant a change in the number of exempt women in one division from 4 percent to 8 percent—and most of those were in traditional women's jobs such as personnel and advertising. Others did not know how to respond to this change in their world. Some of them—the ones who went to all-male technical schools, for example—had literally never interacted with a woman who was anything but a secretary or a wife. Sometimes they did not know how to behave. (The wife demanded one thing, the women at work another.) So they avoided the new woman or acted in an old-fashioned, chivalrous manner. Other men were more sophisticated. A few were even eager to support enlarged opportunities for women in the company because they believed in Indsco's commitment to be "progressive" and because they had daughters they would like to see have a chance.

The women's issue had the potential to make the system transparent to itself in a way it had never been before. The absence of women from management would have to be explored. The clustering of women in secretarial and clerical functions could not be ignored, and neither could the people in those functions. The relationship of wives to the company might also be considered.

In any case, there was one thing that could be said for sure about the relationship between men and women as it appeared at Indsco: raising the issue was causing talk.

Industrial Supply Corporation is neither a good nor a bad example. It is, rather, a case that is used to exemplify a type. Though concrete particulars reflect a unique organization, the principles underlying patterns of behavior in a place like Indsco are more widespread and more universal. The issues, the processes, the structural dilemmas, and the concerns of the people illuminate aspects of behavior in organizations that are shared by all large corporations and, in many ways, by modern organizations in general, whether economic, educational, political, or service systems. Indsco's "woman problem" is no worse than that of other large organizations, and it is much closer to resolution than in some. Many of the people at Indsco are doing the best they can to handle their situations and even to conceive of value-oriented change. But it is in the workings of the total system—the structure of decision-making, opportunity, and power, the problems of hierarchy and the problems of size—that the options for behavior are given to the people of Indsco. If there are no villains at Indsco, there are few heroes either. There are just ordinary people, reflecting the dilemmas created for them by the way they make their living.

Part II

Roles and Images

3

Managers

The corporation seems to seek an arrangement which is surely an anomaly in human society, that of homosexual reproduction.
—Wilbert Moore, *The Conduct of the Corporation*

Managers at Indsco had to look the part. They were not exactly cut out of the same mold like paper dolls, but the similarities in appearance were striking. Even this relatively trivial matter revealed the extent of conformity pressures on managers. Not that there were formal dress rules in this enlightened company, like the legendary IBM uniforms, but there was an informal understanding all the same. The norms were unmistakable, after a visitor saw enough managers, invariably white and male, with a certain shiny, clean-cut look. The only beards, even after beards became merely daring rather than radical, were the results of vacation-time experiments on camping trips, except (it was said), for a few in R & D—"but we know that scientists do strange things," a sales manager commented. An inappropriate appearance could be grounds for complaint to higher management. A new field supervisor was visited by his boss for a "chat about setting a good example for the guys" after his longish hair, curling the slightest way down the nape of his neck, caused comment. "Appearance makes a big difference in the response you get around this company," the boss insisted. Another executive was upset because a staff expert he frequently called upon for help seemed to change his appearance or hairstyle with each fashion wind. "What are you trying to do now?" he once asked the staffer exasperatedly. "We get used to you one way, then you have to change. Why must you always be changing?"

If differences in appearance were not easily tolerated in the ranks of those called managers, neither were a wide range of other sorts of differences. It is not news that social conformity is important in managerial careers. There is ample evidence from organizational studies that leaders in a variety of situations are likely to show preference for socially similar subordinates and help them get ahead. As Clark Kerr and his colleagues wrote, "Incumbents in the managerial hierarchy seek as new recruits those they can rely upon and trust. They demand that the newcomers be loyal, that they accept authority, and that they conform to a prescribed pattern of behavior." [1]

Unlike a more communal environment, where eccentrics can be lovingly tolerated because trust is based on mutual commitments and deep personal knowledge, those who run the bureaucratic corporation often rely on outward manifestations to determine who is the "right sort of person." Managers tend to carefully guard power and privilege for those who fit in, for those they see as "their kind." Wilbert Moore was commenting on this phenomenon when he used the metaphor of a "bureaucratic kinship system" to describe the corporation—but a kinship system based on "homosexual reproduction," [2] in which men reproduce themselves in their own image. The metaphor is apt. Because of the *situation* in which managers function, because of the position of managers in the corporate structure, social similarity tends to become extremely important to them. The structure sets in motion forces leading to the replication of managers as the same kind of social individuals. And the men who manage reproduce themselves in kind.

Conformity pressures and the development of exclusive management circles closed to "outsiders" stem from the degree of uncertainty surrounding managerial positions. Bureaucracies are social inventions that supposedly reduce the uncertain to the predictable and routine. Yet much uncertainty remains—many situations in which individual people rather than impersonal procedures must be trusted. "Uncertainty," James Thompson wrote in a recent major statement on organizations, "appears as the fundamental problem for complex organizations, and coping with uncertainty as the essence of the administrative process." Thompson identified three sources of uncertainty in even the most perfect of machine-like bureaucracies: a lack of cause-effect understanding in the culture at large (limiting the possibility for advance planning); contingencies caused by the fact that the bureaucracy is not alone, so that outcomes of organizational action are in part determined by action of other elements in the environment; and the interdependence of parts, the human interconnections inside the organization itself, which can never fully be reduced to predictable action. [3] The requirements for a perfectly technically "rational" bureaucracy that never has to rely on the personal discretion of a single individual can never be met: complete knowledge of all cause-effect relationships plus control over all of the relevant variables. [4] Thus, sources of uncertainty that are inherent in human institutions mean that some degree of reliance on individual persons must always be present.

It is ironic that in those most impersonal of institutions the essential communal problem of trust remains. For wherever there is uncertainty, *someone* (or some group) must decide, and thus, there must be personal discretion. And discretion raises not technical but human, social, and even communal questions: trust, and its origins in loyalty, commitment, and mutual understanding based on the sharing of values. It is the uncertainty quotient in managerial work, as it has come to be defined in the large modern corporation, that causes management to become so socially restricting: to develop tight inner circles excluding social strangers; to keep control in the hands of socially homogeneous peers; to stress conformity and insist upon a diffuse, unbounded loyalty; and to prefer ease of communication and thus social certainty over the strains of dealing with people who are "different."

If conditions of uncertainty mean that people have to be relied on, then people fall back on social bases for trust. The greater the uncertainty, the greater the pressures for those who have to trust each other to form a homogeneous group. At different times in an organization's history, and at different places in its structure, a higher degree of uncertainty brings with it more drive for social similarity. If this issue can be understood theoretically and in its historical manifestations, then the present-day behavior of Indsco's managers makes more sense.

UNCERTAINTY, DISCRETION, AND THE NEED FOR TRUST

Uncertainty is a feature of the early stages of organizations. The beginnings of all organizations, even those for which there are preexisting models, involve a set of choices requiring discretion on the part of decision-makers, so new organizations almost invariably begin by choosing a homogeneous rather than a diversified group to make initial decisions.[5] Similarity of outlook guarantees at least some basis for trust and mutual understanding. If beginnings always tend to create pressures for similarity among those who begin, then the organizations that start without maps, guides, or the accumulated experience of those who have been there before—the organizations that must invent the models—are even more likely to face the trust issue.

The first large corporations had the uncertainty of how to proceed to organize, as well as the uncertainty of any beginning. How to organize was a task equaling, if not surpassing, in importance the task of coordinating whatever was organized. The early corporations also had to bring under control the potential for violations of trust inherent in instances of manager disloyalty or misbehavior—the possibility that the first managers would become so caught up in their own power they would forget their larger purposes.[6]

Closed inner circles in which trust is assumed can be achieved by two kinds of homogeneity: similarity of social background and characteristics, or similarity of organizational experience. The latter is possible, of course, only when the organization or its models are no longer new—when organizational routines have been established and people have remained in their positions long enough to make shared socialization and shared experience a meaningful basis for trust. However, when organizations are new or changing rapidly, elites have to fall back on social homogeneity—on being part of the same social circle. In the military, for example, Oscar Grusky found that slower turnover of managerial personnel, when there was time for shared understanding to develop, was associated with homogeneity of organizational experience; but rapid turnover, signifying rapid change, was associated with greater homogeneity of their social characteristics.[7] For the first corporations, then, we would expect social similarity to be a factor in the selection of trusted managers, and management to evolve as a socially closed circle.

The Trust Issue and Delegation from Entrepreneur to Manager

At the end of the nineteenth century, when the large-scale enterprise began to dominate American commerce, uncertainty about the tasks and purposes of the new management, described in Chapter 1, must have been more than matched by concerns about abuse of the power delegated to professional managers. The social-psychological climate of the emergent corporations must have put pressures on capital owners and their lieutenants to make loyalty and trustworthiness prime criteria for the selection of managers. In the early days of industrial capitalism in the eighteenth and nineteenth centuries, a dominant view preached avoidance of a system of large-scale management because "managers who had to be given any measure of power or responsibility were not to be trusted." Adam Smith himself argued for the virtues of small owner-managed businesses and the defects of delegation to "disinterested" managers or directors: "The directors of [joint stock] companies, being the managers rather of other people's money than of their own, it cannot well be expected that they should watch over it with the same anxious vigilance with which the partners in a private copartnery frequently watch over their own. . . . Negligence and profusion . . . must always prevail, more or less, in the management of the affairs of such a company. . . ."[8]

The trust issue was a real one. In Britain many disasters were recorded among early experiments with larger organizations and professional managers: bribery, money channeled into the pockets of promoters instead of toward productive purposes, indulgent spending on overhead and status symbols, and instances of managers defrauding proprietors and then disappearing. In America there were similar problems. Agent-stealing was a frequent practice in the life insurance business around the turn of the century; loyalty to a company seemed to be the exception rather than the rule.[9] In the highly competitive and politically charged atmosphere in which the new conglomerates waged their battles for control of the economy, tales of greed, corruption, and theft among appointed managers were common.

No wonder capitalist-owners so reluctantly gave up their control or substituted a formal, decentralized management structure with delegated authority. Peter Drucker criticized the nineteenth-century entrepreneurs for their refusal to accept managers and management. He cited the case of Henry Ford, who built Ford Motor Company into the world's largest and most profitable manufacturing establishment by 1920. By 1927, however, this "seemingly impregnable business empire," said Drucker, "was in shambles." Why? Because Ford believed that all a business needed was the owner maintaining his monopoly on decision-making, with a set of "helpers" to carry out orders.[10] Yet such a position should not be viewed only as an "irrational" holdover from an earlier era of smaller, owner-run enterprises. Concerns about trust and loyalty must have been major issues for the first decades of organizations too large to be controlled by one person or a small group. Why should an owner give discretion over his or her property to strangers?

The large capital owners of the late nineteenth century ensured monopolistic control of the market by means of financial trusts. To stretch a metaphor, they maintained control of the organizations they spawned by means of "social trusts"; that is, by confining management to a closed circle of homogeneous peers. (In 1912, for example, J. P. Morgan testified before the House Committee on Banking and Currency and insisted that what ruled the financial world was not money, but character. When the committee counsel asked him, "Is not commercial credit based primarily upon money or property?" Morgan replied, "No, sir. The first thing is character . . . because a man I do not trust could not get money from me on all the bonds in Christendom.")[11] At the same time that managerial theories were creating a "scientific" underpinning for the tasks of management, social pressures within the growing organizations were confining those new tasks to a small and socially similar group, sometimes to members of the immediate family. As the major life insurance companies grew in the 1890s, "clusters of brothers, nephews, cousins, and sons-in-law of top executives appeared everywhere."[12] If there were too few relatives available for the management of complex and far-flung enterprises (a likely occurrence), there was still a network of trustworthy peers and sons-of-peers. Excellence by the standards of the new management was not always the selection criterion, as a reading of business history suggests. Predictability and trustworthiness, by virtue of membership in the right groups—which themselves could serve control functions—were more likely to be factors in the choice of key managers, since owners and directors appointed those they felt they could "count on," those whose loyalty and obligation to the system could be demonstrated. Keeping privilege in the family was perhaps one impetus for the development of closed management circles; keeping control over managers was probably as important. Marrying the boss's daughter was a way for an upwardly mobile young manager to get ahead, but it was just as advantageous for the boss, because it enabled him to keep control in the family, where sanctions were more easily exercised.

Discretion and Hierarchy Today

There is still a great deal of personal discretion required in positions with a high uncertainty quotient. Uncertainty can stem from either the time-span of decisions and the amount of information that must be collected, or from the frequency with which non-routine events occur and must be handled. The impossibility of specifying contingencies in advance, operating procedures for all possible events, leaves an organization to rely on personal discretion. (It is also this pressure that partly accounts for the desire to centralize responsibility in a few people who can be held accountable for discretionary decisions.) Commented a sales manager at Indsco, "The need for flexibility is primary in my job. The situation changes from minute to minute. One minute it's a tank truck that collapsed. Another it's a guy whose wife just had a hysterectomy and is going to die. . . . I'm dealing with such different problems all the time."

The importance of discretion increases with closeness to the top of a hierarchical organization. Despite the institutionalization and routinization of much of the work of large organizations and despite the proliferation of management experts, uncertainty remains a generic condition, increasing with rank. Jobs are relatively unstructured, tasks are non-routine, and decisions must be made about a variety of unknown elements. Issues such as "direction" and "purpose" cannot be reduced to rational formulae. Organizational improvement, or even maintenance, is not a simple matter that can be summarized in statements about "the ten functions of managers" or techniques of operation. If the "big picture" can be viewed from the top, it also looks bigger and fuzzier. Computers have not necessarily reduced the uncertainty of decisions at the top; in some cases, they have merely increased the amount of information that decision-makers must take into account. A major executive of Indsco confessed in a meeting that "we don't know how to manage these giant structures; and I suspect no one does. They are like dinosaurs, lumbering on of their own accord, even if they are no longer functional."

Criteria for "good decisions" or good management performance also get less certain closer to the top. The connection between an upper management decision and a factor such as production efficiency several layers below or gross sales is indirect, if it is even apparent. (An Indsco division president said,

"In the 1960s we thought we were really terrific. We patted ourselves on the back a lot because every decision was so successful. Business kept on expanding. Then came the recession, and we couldn't do anything to stop it. We had been lucky before. Everything turned to gold in the 1960s. But it became clear that we don't know the first thing about how to make this enterprise work.")

Financial measures of performance are sometimes even artifactual because of the juggling of figures; for example, when and how a loss is recorded. There are also a variety of dilemmas in trying to evaluate the success of managers: qualitative versus quantitative measures, short-run versus long-run outcomes. Decisions that look good in the short term might be long-term disasters, but by that time the failure can be blamed on other factors, and those responsible for the decisions might be so entrenched in power that they now call the shots anyway. A former public relations manager at DuPont formulated what he called the Law of Inverse Certainty: "The more important the management decision, the less precise the tools to deal with it . . . and the longer it will take before anyone knows it was right." One example was a rigid cost cutter who helped increase profits by eliminating certain functions; by the time the company began to feel the loss of those functions, he had been promoted and was part of the inner power group. Someone else picked up the pieces.[13]

The uncertainty up the ranks, like the uncertainty of beginnings, also puts trust and homogeneity at a premium. The personal loyalty normally demanded of subordinates by officials is most intense at the highest levels of organizations, as others have also noted. The lack of structure in top jobs makes it very important for decision-makers to work together closely in at least the harmony of shared understanding and a degree of mutual trust. Since for an organization to function at all requires that, to some extent, people will pull together around decisions, the solidarity that can be mustered through common membership in social networks, and the social control this provides, is a helpful supplement for decision-makers. Indeed, homogeneity of class and ethnic background and prior social experiences is one important "commitment mechanism" found to build a feeling of communion among members of viable utopian communities.[14] Situational pressures, then, place a great emphasis on personal relations and social homogeneity as functional elements in the carrying out of managerial tasks. And privilege is also kept within a small circle.

The social homogeneity of big business leaders from the early-to-middle twentieth century has been noted frequently by critics such as C. Wright Mills as well as business historians. Their class background and social characteristics tended to be similar: largely white, Protestant men from elite schools. Much attention has also been paid to the homogeneity of type within any particular company. In one industrial organization, managers who moved ahead needed to be members of the Masonic Order and the local yacht club; not Roman Catholic; Anglo-Saxon or Germanic in origin; and Republican.[15]

At Indsco, until ten years ago, top executives in the corporation were traceable to the founders of the company or its subsidiaries—people who held stock or were married to people who did. There was a difference between who did well in the divisions, where performance tended to account for more, and who got into top positions in the corporation itself. To get ahead in the corporation, social connections were known to be very important. Indeed, corporate staff positions became a place to put people who were nonmovers, whose performance was not outstanding, but were part of the "family." The social homogeneity of corporate executives was duly noted by other managers. One asked a consultant, "Do all companies have an ethnic flavor? Our top men all seem to be Scotch-Irish." (But as management has become more rationalized, and the corporation has involved itself more heavily in divisional operations, there has also been a trend, over the past five years, toward more "objective" criteria for high-level corporate positions.)

We expect a direct correlation, then, between the degree of uncertainty in a position—the extent to which organizations must rely on personal discretion—and a reliance on "trust" through "homosocial reproduction"—selection of incumbents on the basis of social similarity.

Reduced Uncertainty: More Heterogeneity

The uncertainty quotient in organizational roles varies with the historical time, with the organization's stage of development, and with the routinization of functions. Today, a variety of forces vastly reduce the amount of uncertainty in many jobs. Computers take over many complicated forecasting and analysis functions. There are commonly known techniques for doing managerial tasks and a vast quantity of supplies—from guide books to desk calculators to management consultants—to help do them. There are clearly established patterns and rituals for working in an organization, holding meetings, solving problems, getting information, dividing up tasks, and so on. Anyone who wanted to start a traditional organization from scratch today can do so easily; the patterns and equipment are all there. Furthermore, a group of people have been well socialized as to what it means to run something for an interest other than theirs and to handle other people's money with as much care as they would their own, without making it their own.

The reduction of uncertainty reduces the need for homogeneity and makes it possible to accept more kinds of people in management positions. Clark Kerr and others have argued that the stress on trust and loyalty becomes less important when society has developed a high degree of consensus about the functions and tasks of management. When managerial jobs are routinized and output can be measured, the personal characteristics of the people doing them become less important. When personal trust is rendered irrelevant because social consensus ensures reliability and organizational control mechanisms are strong enough to induce loyalty and conformity by themselves, it is possible to open the closed circle. As corporate executives themselves have become subject to more control inside the organization or from outside agencies and as their tasks and decisions have become more routine, they also have less privilege to protect and pass on to just their own kind—and less opportunity or reason to do so. Finally, as training both in the skills and culture of management has been made available, such training could begin to substitute for membership in a social group as an assurance of reliability, predictability, and the proper outlook.

People who do not "fit in" by *social* characteristics to the homogeneous management group tend to be clustered in those parts of management with least uncertainty. They are in places where what to do and how to judge its doing tend to be more routine. They are found in increasing numbers away from the top, and they are found in staff positions where they serve as technical specialists. Some women have succeeded in management because of their membership in the ruling family; they were already part of the inner circle. However, most women in business have found their management opportunities in low uncertainty, non-discretionary positions that bear the least pressure to close the circle: closer to the bottom, in more routinized functions, and in "expert" rather than decision-making roles. They are also found in those areas where least social contact and organizational communication are required: in staff roles that are administrative rather than line management and in functions such as public relations, where they are removed from the interdependent social networks of the corporation's principal operations.

If the desire for social homogeneity is fostered by organizational uncertainty, the need for smooth communication sets up another set of exclusionary pressures.

COMMUNICATION AND THE PREFERENCE FOR

SOCIAL CERTAINTY

The tasks of managers constitute a "social event," as William Henry put it, "not an individual event." One psychologist explained it this way: "The individual manager does not have a clearly bounded job with neatly defined authorities and responsibilities. Rather, he is placed in the middle of a system of relationships, out of which he must fashion an organization which will accomplish his objectives." Research on executive time use support these propositions. In one study, four executives in England were found to spend 80 percent of their time talking. A Harvard Business School study estimated that 50 to 60 percent of a department head's time was spent talking to men other than his immediate subordinates. Robert Dubin found that in several samples as little as 28 percent down to 6.3 percent of an executive's time was actually spent making decisions as opposed to other kinds of more social activities.[16]

That what managers did was communicate with people was certainly true at Indsco. A sample of twenty managers told me how they spent their time, and I generated this composite list: Paper work and mail; sales calls and negotiating contracts; reviewing telegrams at the office and at home; receiving and making phone calls (including unsuccessful repeat calls); talking to subordinates; interviewing recruits; reviewing with secretaries; teaching trainees; contracts, monthly summaries, weekly summaries, forecasts, sales plans, and quarterly reviews; reviewing subordinates' expense accounts, career reviews (preparation and feedback); performance appraisals; meetings with others in the function, including technological, professional and associated functions; entertainment such as golf and skiing, travel; training programs; handling specific crises; entertaining out of town dignitaries; active recruiting on campus; discussions with others about competitors' activities; organizing meetings; reviewing business plans continuously; watching video tape cassettes sent from headquarters; travel, and time waiting for planes or appointments; solving problems of interface with people in other functions; and special task force meetings.

They estimated that from 30 percent to 55 percent of their time was spent actually in meetings with other people. This did not include time with secretaries, on the telephone, or in routine communication around the office. Time not spent talking could still involve communication. Many of them found, in fact, that the demands made by superiors for communication—even if those superiors were at a considerable distance, such as in the home office—could be quite irritating and represented distraction from a task they considered more important. Telegrams were one source of annoyance; they would even be sent to the manager's home. One manager estimated that after being away from his office for two days, he could expect to find a stack of mail four inches deep when he returned, and "half of it not worth reading." Another commented, "The mail is important and we've got to pay attention to it, but there is too much of it. It is time-consuming and nonproductive to go through it. It gets worse and worse day by day because of the matrix. It is self-generating. If I write a note on a piece of mail and send it back, then my boss says, 'You're not communicating.' " And, "We tend to over-communicate. I get more than one copy of the same thing. Neither one seems to know that he's sending the same thing." Still another manager estimated that he spent 20 percent of his time on the phone trying to make calls or actually talking.

Then there were the numerous special events that were deliberately social: Business luncheons. Dinners for trainees. Entertaining superiors who decided to drop in. "You have to be there when these cats, the heavies, the dignitaries, fly through and say, 'I want to spend a day with your people at Blump-te-de-blump.' And they come through and sit down in your office, from the corporate vice-president on down." Some people called them "snow birds"; others called them "the Monday evening supper club." Total time spent entertaining depended on the season, the customers, and demand on the managers. But one man estimated that he spent nine days during the first quarter of the year on entertainment, not including business lunches.

One typical day, a Monday in March in the Midwest, began at 7:30 when the manager arrived at the office. From 7:30 to 9:00 he finished reading his mail, wrote letters, and called headquarters. From 9:00 to 10:30 he met informally with sales people and customer service people to discuss current problems and offer help. From 10:30 to 11:30 he interviewed a job candidate. From 11:30 to 12:00 he returned phone messages, and from 12:00 to 1:00 he had lunch with a sales person in order to conduct an informal performance appraisal before the formal meeting. From 1:00 to 2:00 he read more mail, and from 2:00 to 2:30 he answered phone messages, again from the headquarters office. At 2:30 he received a wire on the state of the business, which he was expected to communicate to the field and solicit a response to. He began on this and continued until 3:30. From 3:30 to 4:30 he worked on his quarterly review and at 4:30 left for home. Tuesday and Wednesday were spent out of town visiting another office. Thursday and Friday he returned to his own office, and Friday evening he attended a senior executive dinner from 7:00 to 11:00 P.M.

There were several striking features of the communication dominating managerial tasks, because of the sheer size, complexity, and geographic spread of the organization: Communication had to be rapid, since each episode was squeezed in among many more. It had to be accurate, since it was part of a network of interdependencies and contingencies. And it had to travel long distances, sometimes by impersonal means and through channels where people were not directly known to one another. Common language and common understanding were thus very important. People had neither the time nor the backlog of joint experience to make appropriate calibrations for differences in meaning systems or messages that seemed incomprehensible.

The structure of communication involved in managerial jobs generated a desire for smooth social relationships and a preference for selection of those people with whom communication would be easiest. Indsco managers identified social and interpersonal skills as important characteristics of the "effective manager." After a group generated their list of twenty-four such attributes in a meeting, someone pointed out that missing from the list was "knowing the business you're in." But then another manager replied that he knew of many effective executives who knew nothing about their product or field. "Winning acceptance" and being able to communicate seemed much more important. And the group agreed that no one without peer acceptance could get ahead.

One way to ensure acceptance and ease of communication was to limit managerial jobs to those who were socially homogeneous. Social certainty, at least, could compensate for some of the other sources of uncertainty in the tasks of management. It was easier to talk to those of one's kind who had shared experiences—more certain, more accurate, more predictable. Less time could be spent concentrating on subtle meanings, and more time (such an overloaded resource for managers) on the task. The corporation's official language system and cryptic jargon (A/C scribbled at the bottom of a note signified "agreement and comprehension" of its message) could be supplemented by the certainty that socially similar communicators would have more basis for understanding one another. Hence, another force pushed for the confinement of managerial work to a closed circle of homogeneous peers, people who had been through the same things together and could readily understand one another.

There was a decided wish to avoid those people with whom communication was felt to be uncomfortable, those who took time to figure out or seemed unpredictable in their conduct. Deviants and nonconformists were certainly suspect for this reason. Even people who looked different raised questions, because the difference in appearance might signify a different realm and range of meanings in communication. It was all right to be somewhat controversial, as long as a person fit within the same value system and was consistent. ("All of our top executives have been 'radicals,' " a young manager who had worked for a time with officers remarked. "They sometimes did things differently and pushed the rest of us a little further, but they were always consistent. You knew where you stood.")

Women were decidedly placed in the category of the incomprehensible and unpredictable. There were many reports that managers felt uncomfortable having to communicate with women. "It took more time," they said. "You never knew where you stood." "They changed their minds all the time; I never knew what they'd do from one minute to the next." "With women's lib around, I never know what to call them, how to treat them." "They're hard to understand." "It takes a lot of toe testing to be able to communicate." "I'm always making assumptions that turn out to be wrong." Some managers were willing to admit that this was "90 percent my problem, mostly in my head." But this was another example of the preference for dealing with people who were similar. The structure of the managerial role made it more comfortable to try to exclude those people seen as "different." A homogeneous network reinforced the inability of its members to incorporate heterogeneous elements.

UNCERTAINTY OF EVALUATION AND
PRESSURES FOR SOCIAL CONFORMITY

It has been said that managerial occupations call for skills and knowledge that are stated only in general terms and measured imprecisely, if at all.[17] Uncertainty of prediction, measurement or evaluation may leave managers uncertain about the basis of their power or the effectiveness of their functioning. As Wilbert Moore commented, "Managers . . . and particularly the top managers or executives of the large corporations, find themselves without a sure basis for their autonomous power, for their own selection to wield power, or for their financial compensation for doing so." This is shown, Moore said, in the doubts, anxieties, and tension-produced disorders of executives themselves, and the outside pressures and criticisms of managerial power.[18] Indeed, there is a large critical literature questioning the necessity for large numbers of managers and wondering whether managerial functions should be distributed among those with operating responsibility. The necessity (in economic and social terms) for hierarchical structures laden with managers has yet to be demonstrated definitively, as the conflicting results of several studies of the association between the size of an administrative apparatus and organizational effectiveness indicate.[19] Barry Stein has marshaled evidence to indicate that the presumed efficiencies of scale in large organizations are instead often inefficiencies, and administrative costs are one important cause.[20] A recent study of 167 large corporations over a twenty-year period concluded that much of the variance in sales, earnings, and profit margins could be be explained by factors other than the impact of management.[21] Neo-Marxist theorists, such as Harvard economist Stephen Marglin, have answered the question of "what do bosses do?" by arguing that hierarchical arrangements and rule by managers constitute a device for (a) fragmenting the work process so that control from the top is maintained, since workers are rendered incapable of integrating their outputs by themselves; and (b) thereby ensuring the accumulation of capital. They question whether managerialism makes the contribution to organizational efficiency that has always provided the ideological basis for corporate hierarchies.[22]

Secrecy around salaries may be one reflection of this general uncertainty about the fairness of the distribution of rewards in large corporations. Un-

certainty of merit criteria or patent unfairness of income differentials may
result in deliberate concealment or obfuscation of the factors in the judgment
of individual cases.[23] There is also, of course, the problem of direct comparison of performance across functions. Indsco kept salary information secret,
revealing the range for a grade only if a person requested it, and never revealing individual salaries. No one was supposed to have access to the overall salary picture, except those who administered it and decision-makers at the top.
Lower-level managers often received clues by accident: "I asked for something for one of my people and was told, 'You can't get that.' That's how I
found out what the range was. There are so many things we're not supposed to
know. . . ." To the question of the basis for income differentials within the
managerial ranks could be added, of course, the more serious question of the
basis for the wide gaps in reward between managers and operating workers.

Uncertainty of criteria for management evaluation was a major issue at
Indsco. There were definite variations in the extent to which functions could
measure and reward for performance in general, let alone the work of managers, variations corresponding to the extent to which the function remained
non-routinized and discretionary. The highest-ranking salary administrator
concluded after a long review that engineering and R & D did the best job of
rewarding for performance. In these areas, of course, performance in general
was easiest to measure, since workers did roughly the same thing in centralized locations, and the exercise of managerial discretion was minimal compared to functions like sales or marketing. But when the administrator looked
at the extent to which previous performance ratings had predicted who did
well as officers during a five-year period (something for which he felt there
should be about 75 percent accuracy), he found little correlation between ratings of "potential," "performance," and "growth," and actual behavior.

Managers themselves experienced uncertainties about evaluation. Said a
sales manager, "It's hard as a manager to know when you're doing well. You
can't *really* take credit for improvements in sales." The further away from first-
line involvement with operating tasks, the more managers seemed to be aware
of the increasingly vague performance criteria. When the new Indsco management system was introduced, everyone above grade 5 generated a position
charter and wrote, in conjunction with his or her boss, a statement of objectives and performance standards. It was hard to prevent generalities from
creeping in. A manager in one field office heard that the corporation president
wrote as one of his performance standards: "The Chairman of the Board thinks
I'm doing a good job." So the manager tried to put in his: "My boss thinks I'm
doing a good job." That was the best and most precise measure he felt he could
develop. (His boss did not accept this, but the problem was made clear to everyone concerned.)

There were other examples of the difficulty in pinning down what made a good manager. An executive personnel committee generated a list of characteristics that would make a person "officer material" (although they also denied that such a list existed). The traits were so vague as to be almost meaningless, and they included a large number of elements subject to social intrepretation: "empathy; integrity; acceptance of accountability; ambition; makes decisions; intelligent; takes appropriate risks; smart; uses the organization through trust and delegation; a good communicator; a good track record." A group of junior managers also made a list, as part of a training activity, and it did not succeed in being any more specific. If anything, the young managers' list increased the judgmental, interpretive social components: "good communicator; well organized; good interpersonal skills; a successful performer; high peer acceptance; a risk taker; highly visible to other managers; able to recognize opportunities; results oriented; and possessing the requisite amount of prior experience in the company and in the function."

Although the characteristics of a good manager were far from easily or directly measureable, there was agreement that being a good team player who fit into the organization and had strong "peer acceptance" was essential for moving into the managerial ranks in the first place. "Individual performers" who did a job unusually well but were not organization men could be rewarded by raises but not by promotions. Respondents to my sales force survey were asked to rank order twelve possible factors in both managerial promotions and salary increases. As Table 3–1 shows, the factors contributing to both promotions and raises were given approximately the same rank—except in the case of the item reflecting exceptional performance of the job content. This was seen as very important for a raise (ranked second) but much less important for promotion (ranked sixth). For promotion, such factors as reliability and dependability, skill with people, and seniority were considered more important. Fitting in socially was a requisite for the transition to managerial status.

Furthermore, in the absence of clear and objective measures, organizations can fall back on a routinized system, in which advancement proceeds automatically when it is scheduled to happen—something the Indsco sample felt was very *unimportant* in managerial promotions—or social, "non-ability" factors[24] can enter into career decisions. "Social credentials" are common substitutes for ability measures in management positions. A University of Michigan team identified a number of forms of "non-ability" traits and social credentials that were important in executive selection in industrial firms in the Midwest: having the right social background; living in a good section of town; belonging to the right club or lodge; being white; graduating from a high-prestige college; being native born; having "solid respectability"; getting along with coworkers; and having superficial presentability.[25] Indeed, the vagueness of the

TABLE 3–1

*Rank Order of Perceived Factors in Managerial Promotion Versus Salary Increase,
According to Sales Force Respondents of Indsco*

Order of Factors in Promotion * (N = 162)	Order of Factors in Salary Increase * (N = 155)
item (mean rank)	item (mean rank)
1. overall performance record (2.41)	1. overall performance record (2.06)
2. organizational, managerial ability (4.07)	2. occasional spectacular sales performance (3.91)
3. reliability, dependability (4.09)	3. reliability, dependability (4.49)
4. skill with people (4.58)	4. organizational, managerial ability (5.03)
5. seniority (5.14)	5. seniority (5.26)
6. occasional spectacular sales performance (5.48)	6. skill with people (5.64)
7. amount of education, special training (6.84)	7. routine action—time scheduled to happen (6.36)
8. an "in" with management (6.89)	8. amount of education, special training (7.28)
9. reports from customers (8.10)	9. an "in" with management (7.42)
10. routine action—time scheduled to happen (8.11)	10. reports from customers (8.18)
11. luck, good fortune (8.12)	11. personal need (8.78)
12. personal need (9.53)	12. luck, good fortune (8.97)

* The rank orders were computed from the mean score given each item (taking a rank of 1 as a score of 1, a rank of 12 as a score of 12, etc.). There were no ties. Degree of agreement over all respondents ranged from .47 to .88, with a mean degree of agreement of .69. The greatest agreement and smallest standard deviation occurred for the item ranked #1 on both lists; the largest spread was around the items on an "in" with management, routine action, and education.

line between job-relevant and private conduct gave organizations the right to generate norms for the appropriate out-of-work behavior of higher ranking members, and it gave management incumbents a rationale for distinguishing between candidates on the grounds of social acceptability. Indsco clearly prided itself on not going as far in this respect as other companies. (Managers liked to contrast Indsco with a competitor, headquartered in a company town, that told recruits what residential sections of town were appropriate for their status, what clubs they should join, and where to send their children to school.) But the similarity in manner and style among management people and the Anglo-Saxon flavor of the place led one young man with a very Italian name to legally change his name in order to take his wife's decidedly British name. And "peer acceptance," as we have seen, was considered essential to managerial success.

Thus, two sources of conformity pressures are generated. Social criteria (both intra- and extra-organizational) can serve as measurement surrogates; and they can also ensure that managers reproduce themselves. Keeping man-

agement positions in the hands of people of one's kind provides reinforcement
for the belief that people like oneself actually deserve to have such authority.
"Homosocial" and "homosexual" reproduction provide an important form of reassurance in the face of uncertainty about performance measurement in high-
reward, high-prestige positions. So management positions again become easily closed to people who are "different." Finally, since uncertainty about evaluation also raises questions about the criteria for determining who "wins" in a
competitive situation, the pressures for on-site and off-work lifestyle conformity also constitute, as William Henry put it, a "self-protective system assur-
ing in some degree that competitive peers are held to some common standards." [26]

Evaluation uncertainty generates another conformity pressure in the
demand for total loyalty and devotion to the organization.

THE DEMAND FOR LOYALTY:

MANAGEMENT AS TOTAL DEVOTION

There has traditionally been no such thing as a part-time manager. Wom-
en's advocacy agencies trying to find more part-time opportunities for women
have discovered the concept very difficult to sell for managerial jobs. In addition, full time for a manager is not confined to normal working hours; in some
cases, it literally means every waking hour. Managers have a great deal of
discretion over how they use their time and when they leave their desk and
sometimes even where they work; but the organizational situation surrounding business management has made it among the most absorptive and time-
consuming careers. In the midst of organizations supposedly designed around
the specific and limited contractual relationships of a bureaucracy, managers
may face, instead, the demand for personal attachment and a generalized, diffuse, unlimited commitment.

The importance of loyalty in corporate careers was made clear in several
different places on my sales force survey. Nearly half of those responding (42
percent) indicated that they had considered leaving Indsco within the last six
months; only 5 percent said that they had never considered leaving. But in
response to an open-ended question about why they had stayed, 17 percent of
the potential leavers wrote that they had stayed out of *loyalty* to the company,
even in the absence of concrete rewards such as a better job at Indsco.
Another set of items asked people to rate themselves in terms of their strength
on twenty-seven personal characteristics, on a five-point scale, running from
"very strong" to "weak, need improvement." "Loyal" netted the highest mean
rating (1.9), beating out "ambitious" (in second place with a mean rating of

2.1), and only closely followed by "helpful" and "friendly" (tied at 2.2). ("Knows business trends" received the lowest mean rating, at 3.1). Loyalty was thus an important part of the self-perception of Indsco's upper-level workers, and it showed in their acceptance of demands for unbounded commitment.

Indsco managers tended to put in many more hours than workers, and they spent more of their so-called leisure time in work-related activities. One manager even dreamed about the company. At 4:30, when the working day ended, people stuffed the elevators in the rush to get out. Some of the men stayed behind for an occasional dinner or training program or important meeting. Into the briefcase went those inevitable papers or a trade publication or even a book on work-related issues that certainly could not be read in the office. "No one would believe that an executive was working if he were found at his desk reading a book," one commented. (On the other hand, another manager said that *visibly* working very long hours could also be slightly suspect. People would begin to wonder about the competence of someone who seemed to have to work much longer than others at the same job.)

Managers routinely felt that too many people were making too many demands on their time: "There's *no way* this is a forty-hour week." "When I walk through the office five people will say, 'Slow down.'" "It's a juggling act. There are twenty balls up in the air at any one time." "There's no such thing as relaxing or thinking time." "Part of *my* time I have to spend placating my wife for all the rest of the time I'm not spending with her." "Going up the line, it doesn't get better." Sixty-hour work weeks were typical. Sales managers agreed that even though some functions do not spend as much time traveling as do people in sales, they spend more time in team meetings. Furthermore, the tendency of Indsco to do more and more work through committees and task forces put an additional pressure on managers. They were on committees to work on transportation, packaging, training, corporate relocation, minority relations, or to solve particular organizational problems. The immediate response to any problem in the corporation was to form a committee, and managers were likely to get an announcement in the mail that they were appointed to one. In the sales force survey, 83 percent of 205 respondents reported that they now did what they considered "extra work," beyond the bounds of a reasonable working day.

Some managers and professionals work so hard because the organization piles on tasks; others do it to get ahead; still others because they love the work. When asked why they did extra work, the sales force respondents indicated it was because of the work load (46 percent), commitment to the company (24 percent), or interest in the work itself (21 percent). (It is striking that interest in job content was mentioned with least frequency.) In any case, many companies resemble Indsco in actively encouraging work-absorption. A first-line manager told this story, which sent sympathetic chords through a group at Indsco to whom I showed it: "I used to work for another firm, and they really pushed for production, which was okay with me. I can work as hard as the next guy. My line produced as much as any of the others and more than most. You won't believe this, but upper management expected you to come in on Sundays too—not to work, but just to be seen on the premises—supposed to show how much you loved the damn place. . . . Well, I have a family. What are you supposed to do, live at the plant? Lots of the foremen came down to the lounge on Sunday and drank coffee for a couple of hours. I did a few times, and then said to hell with it—it's not worth it. . . . I started to get passed over on promotions, and I finally asked why. My boss said they weren't sure about my attitude and for me to think about it. Attitude! How does that grab you? So I quit and came here." [27]

The organization's demands for a diffuse commitment from managers is another way to find concrete measures of trust, loyalty, and performance in the face of uncertainties. It is the answer to a series of questions about control over the performance of people given responsibility for the organization's fate. *Question:* How do managers show they are trustworthy? *Answer:* By showing they care about the company more than anything else. *Question:* How does the organization know managers are doing their jobs and that they are making the best possible decisions? *Answer:* Because they are spending every moment at it and thus working to the limits of human possibility. *Question:* When has a manager finished the job? *Answer:* Never. Or at least, hardly ever. There is always something more that could be done.

There is an expectation, furthermore, that people in management form their careers largely around one organization. This expectation not only built loyalty but it also ensured that managerial personnel have a common core of organizational experience that would establish trustworthiness and translate into smooth and accurate communication. Thus, managers became members of Industrial Supply Corporation rather than of a community or even a nation. Those on management ladders at Indsco planned their career, sought jobs within the company, as though all of life could be encapsulated within the corporation. They resigned themselves to the necessity of geographic relocations, and even built this expectation into the rhythm of their family. Houses were selected for their resale value, and they were often identical versions of the same suburban split-level all over the country. When the company announced a decision to move headquarters to X-ville, some managers answered my question about how they spent their time by a joking reference to having to move: "I spend my time looking for property in X-ville." One manager had considered himself very lucky. In twenty years with the company, he had been able to remain at or near headquarters and to establish solid roots in a suburban community. He "loved the city," he said, and both he and his wife dreaded moving, yet if the corporation moved, he would go with it. He never even considered looking for another job so that he could stay in his community.

A number of analysts have commented on the multiple functions served by frequent personnel transfers on the managerial level, beyond the official reason of "broadening a manager's experience, providing wide exposure": to break up cliques, to reduce directly personal competition by shuffling people through locations.[28] But it is also clear that transfers serve to reduce the efficacy of commitments other than to the corporation. Just as long-lived utopian communities built commitment in part by establishing strong boundaries between themselves and the outside world, making it difficult for people to maintain any ties outside the community,[29] so do corporations like Indsco create organizational loyalty by ensuring that for its most highly paid members the corporation represents the only enduring set of social bonds other than the immediate family. And the family, too—at least the wife—can be drawn in. The demands of executive work have often had two effects: time demands reduce the participation of men in their families, and demands on wives (as Chapter 5 indicates) have sometimes absorbed them into the realm of corporate loyalty and corporate control.

The concern with organizational commitment showed in a number of other ways. People who seemed to have competing loyalties were considered slightly suspect. It was a bad sign when someone in the sales force turned into a "customers' man"—identifying with the customers and looking out for their interests—even if this resulted in higher sales. Similar reasoning might be behind the traditionally lower status of people in staff positions in corporations. Certainly staff are immune from the direct responsibilities for production that characterize line managers, and therefore their contribution to the organization's functioning is even more uncertain. But also, their professional affiliations make their loyalties flow outward but not necessarily upward, so to questions of the worth of the staff function are added concerns about the loyalty of staff people themselves.[30] Indeed, at Indsco one highly promising manager with a shot at a vice presidency fell from grace after he took a temporary personnel staff assignment and began to devote himself to the professional aspects of the work, joining outside associations, attending meetings, and seeming to become more the professional and less the company man.

If pressures for total dedication sometimes serve to *include* wives in peripheral and auxiliary roles, they also serve to *exclude* many other women from employment as managers. Women have been assumed not to have the dedication of men to their work, or they have been seen to have conflicting loyalties, competing pulls from their other relationships. Successful women executives, as Margaret Hennig showed in her interviews with a hundred of them, have often put off marriage until rather late so that they could devote their time during the important ladder-climbing years to a single-minded pursuit of their careers.[31]

Concerns expressed by men in management about the suitability of women for managerial roles reflect these themes. Questions about turnover, absenteeism, and ambition are frequently raised in meetings at Indsco, when affirmative action officers try to enlist the support of other managers. Sets of statistics and information countering prevalent myths have been prepared to hand out in response to such likely questions. The issue behind them often has to do with marriage.

The question of marriage is experienced by some women in professional, managerial, or sales ladders at Indsco as full of contradictory injunctions. Sometimes they got the message that being single was an advantage, five women reported, sometimes that it was just the opposite. Two single women, one of them forty, in quite different functions, were told by their managers that they could not be given important jobs because they were likely to get married and leave. One male manager said to a female subordinate that he would wait about five years before promoting a competent woman to see if she "falls into marriage." On the other hand, they were also told in other circumstances that married women cannot be given important jobs because of their family responsibilities: their children, if they are working mothers; their unborn children and the danger they will leave with pregnancy, if currently childless. One woman asked her manager for a promotion, to which he replied, "You're probably going to get pregnant." So she pointed out to him that he told her that eight years ago, and she hadn't. A divorced woman similarly discussed promotion with her manager and was asked "How long do you want the job? Do you think you'll get married again?" One working mother who had heard that "married women are absent more," had to prove that she had taken only one day off in eleven years at Indsco.

A male manager in the distribution function who supervised many women confirmed the women's reports. He said that he never even considered asking a married woman to do anything that involved travel, even if this was in the interests of her career development, and therefore he could not see how he could recommend a woman for promotion into management.

IMPLICATIONS

Management becomes a closed circle in the absence of better, less exclusionary responses to uncertainty and communication pressures. Forces stemming from organizational situations help foster social homogeneity as a selection criterion for managers and promote social conformity as a standard for conduct. Concerned about giving up control and broadening discretion in the organization, managers choose others that can be "trusted." And thus they reproduce themselves in kind. Women are occasionally included in the inner circle when they are part of an organization's ruling family, but more usually this system leaves women out, along with a range of other people with discrepant social characteristics. Forces insisting that trust means total dedication and non-diffuse loyalty also serve to exclude those, like women, who are seen as incapable of such a single-minded attachment.

There is a self-fulfilling prophecy buried in all of this. The more closed the circle, the more difficult it is for "outsiders" to break in. Their very difficulty in entering may be taken as a sign of incompetence, a sign that the insiders were right to close their ranks. The more closed the circle, the more difficult it is to share power when the time comes, as it inevitably must, that others challenge the control by just one kind. And the greater the tendency for a group of people to try to reproduce themselves, the more constraining becomes the emphasis on conformity. It would seem a shame, indeed, if the only way out of such binds lay in increasing bureaucratization—that is, in a growth in routinization and rationalization of areas of uncertainty and a concomitant decline in personal discretion. But somehow corporations must grapple with the problem of how to reduce pressures for social conformity in their top jobs.

4

Secretaries

Skewered through and through with office-pens, and bound hand
and foot with red tape.
> —Charles Dickens, *David Copperfield*

If a man has an office with a desk on which there is a buzzer, and if he
can press that buzzer and have somebody come dashing in response—then he's an executive.
> —Elmer Frank Andrews, Address to the Trade Association
> Executives' Forum of Chicago, 1938

Secretaries added a personal touch to Industrial Supply Corporation workplaces. Professional and managerial offices tended to be austere: generally uniform in size and coloring, and unadorned except for a few family snapshots or
discrete artworks. ("Welcome to my beige box," a rising young executive was
fond of saying to visitors.) But secretaries' desks were surrounded by splashes
of color, displays of special events, signs of the individuality and taste of the
residents: postcards from friends' or bosses' travels pasted on walls, newspaper
cartoons, large posters with funny captions, huge computer printouts that
formed the names of the secretaries in gothic letters. It was secretaries who
remembered birthdays and whose birthdays were celebrated, lending a legitimate air of occasional festivity to otherwise task-oriented days. Secretaries
could engage in conversations about the latest movies, and managers often
stopped by their desks to join momentarily in a discussion that was a break
from the more serious business at hand. It was secretaries who were expected
to look out for the personal things, to see to the comfort and welfare of guests,
to show them around and make sure that they had what they needed. And it
was around secretaries that people at higher levels in the corporation could
stop to remember the personal things about themselves and each other (appearance, dress, daily mood), could trade the small compliments and acknowl-
edgments that differentiated them from the mass of others and from their for-

mal role. In many ways—visually, socially, and organizationally—the presence
of secretaries represented a reserve of the human inside the bureaucratic.

Nowhere were the contradictions and unresolved dilemmas of modern
bureaucratic life more apparent than in the secretarial function. The job, made
necessary by the growth of modern organizations, lay at the very core of bureaucratic administration; yet, it often was the least bureaucratized segment of
corporate life. The product of the rationalization of work and the vast amount
of paperwork that entailed, it still remained resistant to its own rationalization.
At Indsco, secretarial positions were unique in a number of ways; for one
thing, they were the only jobs in the company ranked merely by the status of
the manager, and attempts to change this arrangement were resisted. The secretarial job involved the most routine of tasks in the white-collar world, yet the
most personal of relationships. The greatest time was spent on the routine, but
the greatest reward was garnered for the personal.

Understanding the nature of this bureaucratic anomaly sheds light on
several features of life in the corporation: the functions served by pockets of
the personal inside the bureaucratic, but the tradeoffs for people who become
trapped as an underclass in those pockets; the sources of both the intensity and
the awkwardness that can emerge in relationships between bosses and secretaries; and the origin, in job conditions, of those work orientations that tend to
be adopted by secretaries. Secretaries' characteristic ways of managing their
organizational situation—their strategies for attaining recognition and control—as well as the behaviors and attitudes they develop, can all be seen as a
response to the role relations surrounding the secretarial function. Here also
are found the sources of resistance to change in the secretarial function: by the
organization at large, by managers, and by secretaries themselves. From
awareness of the resistances can come better designs for change.

THE SECRETARIAL LADDER AT INDSCO

The first fact about the several thousand secretaries at Indsco was that
they were all women, except for two men at headquarters who were classified
as typists. If they entered at the bottom, Indsco secretaries were generally
hired out of high school or a secretarial finishing school like Katharine Gibbs.
There was a tendency in corporate headquarters to recruit from parochial
schools, which meant that a very high proportion of secretaries were white and
accustomed to hierarchical discipline. The bulk of hiring took place in June,
after high school graduation. New hires, who had to have typing and shorthand skills, were put in the entry level position of "stenographer." After a

several-day orientation, covering the cafeteria, library, medical department, policies and benefits, and classes in Industrial Supply style for letters and telephone calls, new stenographers entered a "pool."

Pool arrangements at Indsco were dispersed throughout its offices rather than centrally located, but secretaries were considered part of a pool as long as they had no permanent assignment (filling in as vacation relief, for example) and were supervised by secretarial assignment coordinators rather than by those whose work they were doing. For about six months, all correspondence they handled was sent to a training staff member, who evaluated it for proficiency. After six months, they were promoted to Secretary I and given a permanent assignment, typically working for more than one boss. From this point, there was little training or retraining, although secretaries were sometimes encouraged to go back to school on their own, and the management of secretaries was decentralized, either in the hands of their bosses, most frequently, or under secretarial coordinators, in one department that retained the pool longer.

"Bosses" were not only managers but anyone in the exempt ranks whose work required secretarial services: professionals, sales workers, and staff officials as well as people formally labeled managers, directors, or officers. One of the striking things about secretaries, then, was that their presence made nearly everyone in the exempt ranks a "boss," generating a shared managerial orientation among exempt personnel and further drawing the caste lines between exempt and nonexempt groups.

The secretarial ladder was short, and rank was determined by bosses' statuses. A secretary with three to four years' experience was eligible for promotion to Secretary II, working for a PRO (person-reporting-to-officer). Secretary IIIs had seven to twelve years' experience and worked for divisional vice-presidents. Secretary IVs worked for division presidents and executive vice-presidents. At the top were executive secretaries of corporate officers. Sometimes these women took on some supervisory responsibility for the secretaries of lower-level managers, distributing extra work or discussing personnel problems. A survey [1] of eighty-eight nonexempt women at one location in 1974 indicated just how limited the secretarial-clerical opportunity structure was. Though 25 percent of the women had worked for the company over fifteen years, only 12 percent had held more than three jobs in the corporation. An old hand recalled: "A person used to be forty-five before becoming an executive secretary and stayed there for fifteen to twenty years. Now they move much faster. They get there at twenty-nine and have no place else to go." Salaries were also not high. Over half of the nonexempt women earned less than $11,000 a year, despite so many with long service.

The executive secretarial position was the peak for nonexempt women at

Indsco. Only in very special situations did they move into exempt jobs—sometimes secretaries in a field sales office rose into a customer service job, and a few executive secretaries moved into secretarial personnel administration. But these cases were extremely rare. They stood in dramatic contrast to the situation for nonexempt men, who, as accounting clerks, could easily move by a standard route into the exempt ranks. The ceiling for secretaries was set by how high a boss they could snare.

For a secretary, to be handled by and bound to particular bosses was by far the preferred arrangement. In those offices where secretaries remained in a pool and had to report to assignment coordinators, turnover was much higher than in situations where they were responsible only to bosses. (A divisional comparison showed 22 percent turnover in a year, as against 6 percent where secretaries reported only to a boss. One area with assignment coordinators lost thirty-two out of eighty-five secretaries one year.) The greater satisfaction with direct supervision by bosses rather than coordinators could be explained in several ways. First, the coordinators were perceived by many secretaries as "busybodies" who encroached on their freedom, and there were complaints about closeness of supervision. Indeed, the coordinator position was developed in offices where bosses were likely to be away much of the time, as in the sales force, as an attempt to fill the gap and provide daily direction for secretaries even when their bosses traveled. Second, coordinators were relatively powerless women, and bosses were overwhelmingly likely to be more powerful men. Bosses could do more for secretaries in the long and short term than coordinators could. And because they had to compete with more powerful pulls from bosses, coordinators often became coercive and bossy in their supervisory styles (a phenomenon addressed in Chapter 7).

Under pool arrangements, furthermore, secretaries functioned in machine-like fashion. In one field office, men avoided interaction with the pool secretaries, going instead to their managers or coordinators to talk about problems or needs. One male manager with supervisory responsibility for secretaries and clerks in this office reported: "I was kind of a labor contractor. The men using the secretaries' services abdicated everything but a utilitarian viewpoint: What could this secretary do for me? If there was a problem, there was no attempt to find out why. They assumed the problem was hers, not theirs, and they would come to either me or the supervisor and say, 'Hey, you've got to do something about her.' But men, if they can avoid it, will try not to deal with women on that critical level, so they get someone else to do it. It was detrimental to morale."

There was thus not much incentive for secretaries to aspire to "managerial" posts in their own hierarchy, since occupants of such positions met with resentment, resistance, and even ostracism in the office social network. There was little chance of leaving the secretarial ranks for another job at Indsco. And there were decided benefits to escaping from the pool, where one was an interchangeable machine, to an assignment to a particular boss or two, where one was at least a noticeable person. So secretaries learned to count on a relationship with a boss for their rewards. The secretary-boss relationship, in turn, was a relic of patrimony within the bureaucracy. In the early 1970s Indsco added a new, centralized personnel administration to place secretaries, monitor budgets, rationalize demands, and provide upward mobility. But this new system, as we shall see later, was often circumvented by those who were benefiting from the old ways: some bosses and some higher grade secretaries. Patrimony proved resistant to change.

PATRIMONY IN BUREAUCRACY

Max Weber, in his classic rendering of the character of modern organizational life, considered the universalism, legalistic standards, specialization, and routinization of tasks in the bureaucracy the antithesis of traditional feudal systems ruled by patrimonial lords. As Weber saw it, bureaucracy vested authority in offices rather than in persons and rendered power impersonal, thereby undercutting personal privilege that stood in the way of efficient decisions. But despite Weber's claims, not all relationships in modern organizations have been rationalized, depersonalized, and subjected to universal standards to the same degree. The secretary-boss relationship is the most striking instance of the retention of patrimony within the bureaucracy. Fewer bureaucratic "safeguards" apply here than in any other part of the system. When bosses make demands at their own discretion and arbitrarily; choose secretaries on grounds that enhance their own personal status rather than meeting organizational efficiency tests; expect personal service with limits negotiated privately; exact loyalty; and make the secretary a part of their private retinue, moving when they move—then the relationship has elements of patrimony.

Reinhard Bendix summarized Weber's view of patrimonial rule by saying: "(A) patrimonial ruler resists the delimitation of his authority by the stipulation of rules. He may observe traditional or customary limitations, but these are unwritten; indeed, tradition endorses the principled arbitrariness of the ruler. . . . His entirely personal recruitment of 'officials' makes the supervision of their work a matter of personal preference and loyalty. . . . All 'offices' under patrimonial rule are part of the ruler's personal household and private property. His 'officials' are personal servants. . . . Official business is transacted in personal encounter and by oral communication, not on the basis of impersonal documents." [2] Many of these features characterized the power of bosses over secretaries in Industrial Supply Corporation. Secretaries were bound to bosses in ways that were largely unregulated by rules of the larger system and that made the relationship a highly personalized one.

There were three important aspects of the social organization of the relationship: *status contingency* (the fact that secretaries, primarily, and bosses, secondarily, derived status in relation to the other); *principled arbitrariness* (the absence of limits on managerial discretion); and *fealty* (the demand of personal loyalty, generating a non-utilitarian aura around communication and rewards).

STATUS CONTINGENCY

Reflected status was part of the primary definition of the secretarial position. *Secretaries derived their formal rank* and level of reward not from the skills they utilized and the tasks they performed but *from the formal rank of their bosses.* A promotion for secretaries meant that they had acquired a higher-status boss, not that their own work was more skilled or valuable. Most often, above the early grades, secretaries were not actually promoted at all on their own; they just remained with a boss who himself received a promotion. It was common practice at Indsco for secretaries to move with their bosses within the same geographic area, as though they were part of the private retinue of a patrimonial dignitary.

Before Indsco created a centralized personnel administration for nonexempt positions, there was no way to determine secretarial salaries other than status contingency. Personnel records had been minimal, and there were no written job descriptions or standardized means for evaluating and rating actual job content. This led to a widespread feeling throughout Indsco that secretaries were not being rewarded for their own work but rather only for their bosses' prestige and power. Some people thought that secretarial promotions meant secretaries had *less* work to do and made less use of their skills. Secretaries felt that the hardest work, with the most demands and variety in technical requirements, was performed on the lowest levels. Women at the higher levels consequently talked about their work with a degree of discomfort, indicating the trouble they had justifying their greater pay and lighter work, except by insisting, as many did, "I worked hard to get here."

There were small ways in which greater responsibility revolved around secretaries in the upper grades: a few administrative duties, the fact that mistakes might have larger ramifications. But for the most part, life got easier as the bosses' status rose. Secretaries could stop worrying about improving their own skills and work on their relationship with the boss. They could orient their work life around their connection with this one person. Some executive secretaries acquired their own corps of typists to do routine work, devoting their time to the social and interpersonal aspects of their jobs. They acquired more privileges and perquisites through their bosses: freedom to come and go, to set their own hours; office status symbols such as drapes, outside offices with windows, special ashtrays, and steel file trays. They got gifts that no one else did. If there was a cocktail party for people who worked on a project, for example, the top secretary was invited, not the lower-level nonexempts who actually worked directly on the task.

Even more important was the fact that the *boss's status determined the power of the secretary.* Even on the lowest levels, secretaries had some influence through their bosses, mostly in terms of people: the secretaries' assessment of other people in the office or their evaluation of new candidates for clerical jobs. Higher up, secretaries' power derived from control of bosses' calendars. They could make it easy or difficult to see a top executive. They could affect what managers read first, setting priorities for them without their knowing it. They could help or hurt someone's career by the ease with which they allowed that person access.

If the secretary reflected the status of the boss, she also contributed in minor ways to his status. Some people have argued that *secretaries function as "status symbols"* for executives, holding that the traditional secretarial role is developed and preserved because of its impact on managerial egos, not its contribution to organizational efficiency. Robert Townsend, iconoclastic former president of Avis, claimed in *Up the Organization* that the existence of private secretaries was organizationally inefficient, as proven by his experience in gaining half a day's time by giving up what he called "standard executive equipment." One writer was quite explicit about the meaning of a secretary: "In many companies a secretary outside your door is the most visible sign that you have become an executive; a secretary is automatically assigned to each executive, whether or not his work load requires one. . . . When you reach the vice-presidential level, your secretary may have an office of her own, with her name on the door. At the top, the president may have two secretaries. . . ." [3] A woman professional at Indsco agreed with the idea that secretaries were doled out as rewards rather than in response to job needs, as she talked about her own problems in getting enough secretarial help.

At Indsco, the secretary's function as a status symbol increased up the ranks as she became more and more bound to a specific boss. "It's his image, his status, sitting out in front," a personnel administrator said. "She's the first thing people see about him." For this reason, personal appearance—attractiveness and social skills—was a factor in the career prospects of secretaries, with task-related skills again playing a smaller role as secretaries moved up the ranks. "We have two good secretaries with first-rate skills who can't move up because they dress like grandmothers or housewives," another official complained. "Even those executive secretaries who are hitting sixty don't look like mothers. Maybe one or two dowdy types slipped in at that level, but if the guy they work for moves, they couldn't be sold elsewhere at the same grade." Appearance was so important that secretaries would be sent to Katharine Gibbs as much as for the personal side as for the skills training. Gibbs taught posture, hand care, the use of deodorants, and the importance of clean underwear in addition to filing methods and telephone responses; only recently has Gibbs stopped insisting on the wearing of hats and gloves. This was all designed to make the secretary into a "pretty package." [4] Herbert Marcuse, in *One-Dimensional Man,* even considered the secretary to represent a touch of "managed sex" in the office, a part of the "large-scale sexual manipulation" of the modern employee: "Without ceasing to be an instrument of labor, the body is allowed to exhibit its sexual features in the everyday work world and in work relations. . . . The sexy office and sales girls, the handsome, virile junior executive . . . are highly marketable commodities. . . . Sex is introduced into work and public relations and is thus made more susceptible to (controlled) satisfaction." [5]

Indsco personnel administrators also found that bosses tended to want highly skilled, highly educated secretaries, whether or not the work load demanded it, as a way of inflating their own importance and deriving status from a secretary. One manager, looking for a new secretary for his department, described the job in glowing terms, stressing the amount of intelligence and independent decision-making it required. The actual job content turned out to be largely typing, filing, and recording material on standardized forms according to a highly routinized procedure. "Managers don't level about what a job really is," reported an executive secretary. There was a story circulated among top-level secretaries about a co-worker who did nothing but type from written material, with no opportunity to use initiative, let alone technical skills like shorthand. She soon left the job, and the manager put out a request for a replacement, asking for a "very experienced secretary," to the amusement of those reporting the incident.

The bosses' image of what their secretaries did and the secretaries' views were often discrepant. Bosses tended to report routine tasks in overblown ways that made their own work load sound impressive; secretaries consistently saw the same tasks as less important. At one point, some secretaries asked for more administrative responsibility, so personnel staff talked to top managers.

The managers invariably replied, "She is already doing administrative tasks." They included under this label such matters as keeping the calendar, collating reports, and reading the newspaper to mark items of interest—all of which the secretaries considered routine. Indsco had a problem with the boredom and dissatisfaction of educated, intelligent women assigned to men who requested someone with education and skills but made no use of them.

Derived status between secretaries and bosses spilled over in informal as well as formal ways. *The parties became fused in the awareness of other organization members.* Secretaries became identified with bosses in a number of personal and informal ways. Secretaries could get respect from their peers because of feelings about their bosses, but they could also be disliked and avoided if their bosses were disliked. "There are problems for secretaries if they become trapped in their managers' fights," a secretary said. "They are usually the ones who are caught, and they have few resources with which to defend themselves." There were also "shadow hierarchies" at Indsco, in which secretaries to higher-level executives received deference at informal social events from the secretaries of lower-level staff and were more likely to assume leadership of employee events. At the same time, a socially skillful secretary could help smooth over some relationships for difficult bosses.

Despite the fact that bosses could derive some informal status from characteristics of their secretaries, *status contingency operated in largely nonreciprocal ways.* It was the boss's *formal* position that gave the secretary formal rank; he, in turn, wanted to choose someone whose *personal* attributes made her suitable for the status he would be conferring. As in the patrimonial official's private ownership of his servants, the secretary was seen by the boss as "my girl." This attitude was made clear to a personnel administrator who was finding secretaries for two vice-presidents under the new, centralized system. She located two candidates and sent them both to see both men, who called her in anger when they discovered this: "You mean *the women* are making the choice?" One of the executives made an offer to a candidate, only to find that she still wanted to see the other manager. He told the administrator, "If she looks at the other job, I don't want her." (The secretary made her own angry retort, and took the second job.)

The secretaries' position in the organization, then—their reward level, privileges, prospects for advancement, and even treatment by others—was contingent upon relationships to particular bosses, much more than on the formal tasks associated with the job itself.

PRINCIPLED ARBITRARINESS

The second patrimonial feature of secretarial role relations was the *absence of limits on managerial discretion,* except those limits dictated by custom or by abstract principles of fair treatment. Within the general constraints of Indsco tradition and the practice of other managers, bosses had enormous personal latitude around secretaries. The absence of job descriptions, before the new personnel administration began to generate them, meant that there was no way to insure some uniformity of demands across jobs with the same general outlines. There was no way for personnel staff to help match secretaries' skills to the job, or to compare positions so as to determine whether and how a secretary could be moved. Thus, it was left to bosses to determine what secretaries did, how they spent their time, and whether they were to be given opportunities for movement. There was no such thing as career reviews for secretaries, or for nonexempt personnel in general. A secretary's fortunes, especially in finding other work in the corporation, were in the hands of the boss. Bosses received notices of job openings for nonexempts in envelopes marked "private and confidential," and it was their choice whether or not to share this information with their secretaries. Only a rare and lucky secretary, like one who was finally promoted into an exempt job, had a boss who would help her find another job because he had reached his level and she would go no further if she stayed with him.

Furthermore, until the advent of the centralized nonexempt administration, bosses prepared their own salary budgets for the nonexempts reporting to them. This made the reward system seem to secretaries even more arbitrary than it actually was, increasing their sense of dependence on the whim of the manager. Central guides were invisible, and secretaries tended to feel that their salary was based on whether or not they were liked or what department they happened to be in. There were also no written company policies around personal days and vacation days, so bosses had the power to make decisions about the category into which time off fell, being thus able to punish or reward a secretary.

Managerial discretion in job demands combined with another feature of secretarial work to contribute to the sense of personal dependence on arbitrary authority. It was a job with low routinization in terms of time planning, characterized instead by a *constant flow of orders.* Unlike other parts of the bureaucracy, where the direct exercise of authority and the making of demands could be minimized through understood routines and schedules of expectations, secretarial work might involve only the general skeleton of a routine, onto which was grafted a continual set of specific requests and specific instructions. The boss did not merely set things in motion; he might make demands on the half hour. Even if boss and secretary developed a set of routines that reduced the number of direct face-to-face demands (e.g., he put work to be typed in an in-box; she knew to bring coffee in at 10:15), continual demands and new orders could not be eliminated entirely. Indeed, the secretarial position was often there in the first place to provide a person capable of responding to momentary demands and immediate requests generated on the spot. There was variation, of course, in the extent to which secretaries had to wait for their bosses to tell them what to do; in some cases, they were given or carved out an autonomous territory that they controlled independent of instructions. But by and large, the job was characterized by a degree of availability for unpredictable orders. Power could not be rendered impersonal by the use of routinized schedules.

Arbitrariness was embedded in the *personal services* expected of secretaries. The list of items included in the secretaries' own description of their duties on the first wave of performance appraisal forms for a hundred Indsco secretaries made clear how much variation there was in a secretary's understanding of her official responsibilities from boss to boss, even in the same nominal job at the same level. Some secretaries included personal services in the core definition of their job, giving them equal importance with the communication functions (like typing and telephones) for which Indsco had hired them. One secretary included among her major responsibilities: "office household duties: watering plants, cleaning cups, sharpening pencils, straightening desks, etc." (A personnel administrator commented about such items, "Does she think that's what the company is paying her for?") And despite media publicity for the controversy over whether or not secretaries should make and serve coffee, Indsco secretaries still performed this service, especially for visitors to their bosses' offices.

Journalists have found good material for their criticisms in the range of personal services secretaries perform: cutting the boss's hair, dog-sitting while he and his wife are on vacation, returning his wife's mail order shoes, and providing homemade (by the secretary) coffee cake at board meetings. One secretary told a writer: "His wife does everything for him at home; I do everything for him here. The only thing he does for himself is well, you know." [6] Many Indsco secretaries seemed to feel the same way. Resentment over personal work was the biggest single issue raised by secretaries when Industrial Supply brought an experimental group of them together with their bosses for "expectation exchanges." The secretaries felt that the official definition of their jobs was fuzzy enough that they were concerned about refusing to do personal things for their bosses even when they would have preferred not to. Demands were limited only by customary practice, the boss's conscience, or the secretary's negotiating skills or ability to embarrass her boss enough that he would stop asking for personal favors. But there was disagreement among secretarial administrators and supervisors themselves about how much the manager's right to expect personal service was built into the job. At a meeting in which the secretarial function was discussed, a woman supervisor of several dozen secretaries, who herself had been promoted to this exempt job from an executive secretary's slot, insisted that, in her words, "The 'girl' is there to serve the man." A reform-minded personnel administrator countered, "No. The secretary is there to *assist* a manager."

There was another kind of personal service that was even more difficult for secretaries to talk about, since it tread the fine line between official and unofficial, legitimate and illegitimate. This was the secretaries' involvement as critical ingredients in their bosses' presentation of a "front." They participated in the behind-the-scenes transformation of chaos into order, or rough ideas into polished, business-like letters and documents. They had access to confidential files that told the real story behind the front. They knew how bosses really spent their time. They set the stage for an atmosphere that was designed to awe or impress visitors. They served as a buffer between the boss and the rest of the world, controlling access and protecting him from callers. And on occasion, they were asked to collude in lies on behalf of this front, from such routine lies as "Mr. Jones is not in just now" when Mr. Jones wanted to sit at his desk undisturbed, to more major lies such as Rose Mary Wood's alleged erasure of a portion of the Nixon tapes. At the managers' discretion, then, secretaries could be implicated in major and minor moral dilemmas.

The first kind of lie was a source of discomfort for some secretaries at Indsco who generated this case for discussion at a secretaries' seminar: "P.Q. is a marketing secretary in the division. One of her marketing officers is a specialist in his field. The demand for his time from field office managers, salespeople, and clients is great, and because of this P. is faced with the constant frustration and pressure of explaining to persistent and demanding callers that her boss is not available. . . . [For example], Mr. S. has given strict orders not to be disturbed. Suddenly a caller appears in person and wishes to see her boss. Because he is now at her desk and can see that Mr. S. is in his office, the secretary cannot excuse her boss and is faced with a further uncomfortable situation as the caller continues to stand at her desk until Mr. S. is free." Having no official recourse to higher authority, secretaries could deal with such binds by deciding to suspend their own judgment and make the automatic assumption that, however arbitrary or suspect the demand, bosses knew best. This attitude, in turn, supported managerial authority and allowed bosses to expect whatever they wished.

The secretarial job thus rested on a *personal set of procedures and under-*

standings carved out by secretary and boss. As we have seen, the corporation provided only the merest skeleton for the relationship; its substance depended on the unique qualities and agreements of the two people involved. Unlike other bureaucratic relations, which certainly included *some* component of special understandings generated by the unique personalities of those who interact, the secretary/boss relation was defined *largely* by the special relationship developed by two particular individuals. Secretaries and bosses created unique relationships that did not remain, that were not necessarily institutionalized as part of the built-in structure of that secretarial job. When either of the parties left, the job reverted to its skeletal outline, again to be remade. Several examples illustrated this aspect of secretarial role relations.

One enterprising secretary with a newly promoted boss (who had never had a private secretary before) was able to make herself into an assistant. When he gave her performance appraisals to type, she added her own comments. She began writing as well as typing the monthly memo-newsletter. Asked to come to a committee meeting to take notes, she wrote the reports and eventually asked to be made an official member of the team. Then she was promoted as part of an affirmative-action effort. The next woman to take the job was more conventional, and the position slid back into the standard typing job. How the first secretary shaped the role did not remain a permanent feature of the system. Had *she* stayed while her boss moved on, it would also have been possible for a new manager to take away all of the creative, independent, and exciting privileges she had developed. In other words, it was the manager's largesse and the secretary's ability to convince him to use it that gave her special privileges.

Another secretary had a similar experience, although this time she was the one who remained while bosses changed. "In this office, all the men are on a rotating assignment; I've been here a long time and have been given a lot of responsibility. But each time they come in new, I go back to being a new-hire again. I have to take a role off to the side until they get ready to delegate back to me the things I was doing before they came. I get ignored until the boss gets used to what his job is. I have to be patient and wait for them to notice me and make me part of the gang again. I've got time, more than they do, but I wish I could ram it down their throats. I have to earn their respect to get my job back. Even if the previous guys say something nice about me and what I can do, the new ones have to learn it for themselves. I had to realize what change like this does to me: it turns me upside down, inside out."

The fifth aspect of principled arbitrariness in the relationship of bosses to secretaries was the use of *particularistic criteria for evaluation.* Because of the absence of job descriptions, performance standards, or rationalized mechanisms for determining rewards, bosses were relatively free to determine their own standards for judging the performance of their secretaries. The first batch of forms from the pilot project to develop performance appraisals for nonexempts indicated that managers used a variety of standards for determining a clerical subordinate's worth, and such standards often depended on the unique values and preferences of the bosses themselves. As we shall see, managers often rated secretaries in terms of the quality of their relationship rather than in terms of skills that could benefit the corporation at large.

FORCES TOWARD FEALTY

The third patrimonial feature of secretarial role relations had to do with the social psychological tone of the relationship: an expectation of personal loyalty, that secretaries should derive their primary rewards from the relationship with their particular bosses. This arose, in part, as a consequence of the first two features of social organization of the job. Because of characteristics of the organization of the work itself, bosses developed a stake in seeing that secretaries: (1) identify their interests with that of their bosses, subordinating any desires for their own career advancement; (2) suppress resentments of the differential material privileges of bosses and clerical workers by valuing instead the symbolic and emotional rewards of the secretarial job; and (3) develop attitudes that made it easy for bosses to exercise their authority. An expectation of fealty helped bosses manage their own situation vis-à-vis secretaries.

First, the secretary's collusion in the boss's front and her access to the real story behind the presentation and to the boss's secrets made it important that she not be in direct competition for the boss's job, for she would have a potent set of weapons to use in the struggle for the position. The possibilities for blackmail inherent in her access, the threat that she might "blow his cover," made it important that she identify her interest as running with, rather than against, his. Thus, forces were generated for the maintenance of a system in which the secretary occupied a separate career ladder, was not considered eligible for positions such as that of the boss, and was to find her status and reward level dependent on the status and, hence, success of her boss.

Beyond reducing direct competition with the boss, the demand that she identify his interests with her own helped insure that she would not seek advantage in the system by forming coalitions with competitors of her boss or by using her access to his secrets against him. It was not unheard of that secretaries act as spies or agents for someone else outside or inside of the organization; the organization could guard against this only by structuring a reward system that induces loyalty. Many other patrimonial features of the secretarial position became understandable in this light: particularistic rather than universalistic performance standards, which made secretaries dependent on a specific boss's criteria for approval and reward; status only by reflection of the boss's status rather than as a result of the secretary's skills; and the tendency for a higher-status secretary's mobility to be tied to that of her boss, so that she moved—or didn't move—when he did.

The second pressure for fealty emerged from the great discrepancies in material rewards and power between bosses and secretaries. The close daily interaction of secretaries with bosses was itself an anomaly in a bureaucratic system, since most bureaucratic positions generally have close contact only with those immediately above or below them in the hierarchy. Hence, the lines of privilege separating organizational castes were highly visible. The stability of secretaries, for example, contrasted with the mobility of managers in every sense: daily work and career progression. Managers might do much of their work out of the office; secretaries needed permission to leave their desks. Managers moved ahead every three to five years; secretaries could stay where they were for twenty years or more. It was thus important to the maintenance and legitimacy of the system that secretaries not develop resentments about their caste position. One way to ensure this, of course, was to recruit the secretarial population primarily from among those least likely to see themselves as bosses and most likely to accept differential status—young women from parochial high schools—as Indsco did.[7] It was not clear which came first, the availability of a particular labor force or the social organization of the job, but each functioned to reinforce the other. A second way was to develop relationships of fealty and to offer secretaries symbolic rewards.

Finally, the authority relationship itself, the existence of principled arbitrariness and continual order-giving, led bosses to value the complex of traits contained in the notions of fealty and low mobility for secretaries. The authority relationship was non-reciprocal. Only the boss commanded, restricting and controlling the secretary's freedom above and beyond the generalities of company policy, but she lacked similar rights to restrict his. He evaluated her, but only in rare circumstances did she evaluate him; her opinion of him did not control his fate in the company the way his did of her. Whenever there are relationships of such unequal and non-reciprocal authority, both systemic and social psychological pressures arise that attempt to prevent the parties at the receiving end from ever gaining authority on their own. For the system, the threat of retaliation is what must be guarded against. The danger is that one-sided authority relations generate resentments that would be turned against former superiors if subordinates ever got authority on their own. There was thus a systemic interest in keeping secretaries in a separate hierarchy remote from the possibility of organizational authority, even though individual secretaries with proven loyalty might occasionally trickle up.

For the bosses themselves there was the threat of embarrassment that could occur when meeting a former servant as a peer, an embarrassment typical of other situations where those once highly subordinated suddenly turn up as colleagues. The embarrassment partly stemmed from the possibility that the truth about the relationship, a truth buried in the authority relation, would now be told. Managers generally did not want their secretaries evaluating them or even giving them unofficial feedback, Indsco's personnel administrators found when they tried to include reciprocal evaluations in performance appraisals. It was very difficult for some people to shift from a relationship of superordination to one of equality, so they might fumble awkwardly in trying to accommodate to the former secretary's new status or try to avoid altogether the person causing them discomfort. A former secretary promoted into a professional job at Indsco reported that her months of transition were "pure hell" because of the problems managers and professionals had in relating to her and accepting her.[8] The existence of such a person—one of the servant class now turning up as a master—put bosses on notice that "servants" were eligible for mobility, that underlings might someday be peers. This notice could interfere with their comfort in commanding the current generation of servants, causing bosses to redouble their wish that secretaries never enter the managerial ranks and instead remain loyal serfs. Finally, the need to give continual orders generated the possibility for resistance on the part of secretaries, even though they must eventually give in or lose their jobs. Secretaries could make order-giving more or less comfortable for the order-givers; they could reduce or increase the embarrassment many Americans feel about commanding. For this reason, good order-taking tended to be a prime characteristic demanded in the fealty relation between secretaries and bosses, and there was a further stake in keeping secretaries content to be order-takers.

FEALTY

Hence, fealty became the third feature of the ideal boss-secretary relationship, from the boss's perspective, making the relation a highly personal rather than a purely instrumental one. *Secretaries were rewarded for loyalty and devotion to their bosses.* They were expected to value non-utilitarian, symbolic rewards—which did not include individual career advancement—and to take on the emotional tasks of the relationship. Secretaries were rewarded for their attitudes rather than for their skills, for their loyalty rather than their talent. Given the low skill required by the actual tasks they were given to do, and the replaceability of personnel with basic secretarial skills, secretaries found it to their advantage to accept fealty as their route to recognition and reward.

Expectations of loyalty were bound up with the sense on the part of bosses that they were making secretaries part of their personal estate. This was behind the outrage experienced by some executives at the thought that secretaries might shop around for a job rather than wait to be chosen by a particular manager. It was also involved in the wishful statement made by some managers to a central personnel administrator that "my secretary wouldn't *want* another job." (The staff official indicated that she knew that many of their secretaries were indeed actively looking for other opportunities.) Members of an Indsco task force on upward mobility for clerical workers considered a major barrier to change the fact that "some men felt the secretaries worked for them personally, not for the corporation." They found managers reluctant to suggest competent secretaries for other positions; instead, bosses wanted to claim ownership and, in turn, demand loyalty. One case was presented to a new nonexempt personnel manager in which a male boss was trying to increase a secretary's salary above the pay ceiling that had just been established for that grade, limiting the discretion of bosses to pay whatever they chose. The manager pointed out the difficulties: "He wants more for her, he wants her paid for potential—she has an M.A. But she can't get paid just because one person thinks she's deserving. She has to do more or move on. But the man and the secretary say they don't want to be separated." In these instances, fealty served to create a close bond, but one that worked for bosses and secretaries in different ways, in that a "loyalty oath" to a particular boss could hold back only the secretary's career, not the boss's.

The ideals bosses held for the relationship were captured in the pilot program to develop standardized performance appraisals for nonexempt employees. When the procedure was first proposed and discussed with managers, the bosses contacted generally preferred, they said, a section dealing with "attitude" rather than one concerning "job objectives." This was at a time when Indsco was converting fully to a system of management-by-objectives, which made results-as-weighed-against-goals the most important single standard in exempt performance appraisals. Yet, managers wanted to continue to evaluate secretaries on the basis of their "attitudes."

When the first wave of performance appraisals were completed, managers' concerns with the personal rather than the skills side of the relationship were demonstrated throughout the form. After collecting data on a hundred forms, I found that there were two "central traits" that recurred and tended to determine a secretary's overall rating. (That certain central traits influence perceptions and judgments is a classic finding in social psychological research; whether a person was presented as "warm" or "cold," for example, could influence responses to a wide variety of identical characteristics.[9]) According to my data, the two central traits for secretaries were "initiative and enthusiasm" and "personal service orientation" (as one manager put it, "ability to anticipate and take care of personal needs"). Content analysis showed that where variants of these traits were found, the secretary was generally rated high on most other abilities, including basic skills like typing. Where they were not present, or where managers commented on their absence, secretaries tended to be rated low on basic skills, too. In other words, secretaries were rewarded for the quality of their relationship with bosses: appearing to like their jobs and being willing to take care of bosses' personal needs. They were also rewarded for minimizing the bosses' need to give orders. Such attitudes created a halo for the secretary who had them. But they were not necessarily rewarded for professional skills. One secretary was rated high for setting up a room for a meeting and serving coffee—not for organizing the meeting and writing the agenda, which she also did.

If secretaries were evaluated on non-utilitarian grounds, they were also *expected to accept non-utilitarian rewards.* In many cases, secretaries willingly did so. Theorists have pointed out that the interstitial position occupied by some white-collar workers makes them manipulable by esteem and prestige symbols, by normative rather than material rewards.[10] Clerical workers traditionally viewed themselves as "privileged" in comparison with blue-collar workers, and this sense of privilege was often considered sufficient reward in itself, so, as a political scientist noted as early as 1929, "It has been customary both among clerical workers themselves and among others to regard clerical workers as outside the range of attention to working conditions. Clerical workers had 'positions,' not jobs; they were paid 'salaries,' not wages; and they had attained a status where investigators did not penetrate and legislation did not corrupt the free play of economic opportunity." [11]

"Love" was one non-material reward secretaries were supposed to appreciate. Some Indsco secretaries reported that their bosses managed to turn their complaints about salary or working conditions into expressions of concern about whether or not they were "loved," assuming that women at work were motivated by such noneconomic, emotional factors. One member of the non-exempt task force thought that managers did not suggest opportunities to women secretaries because they assumed the women would feel "rejected" if a suggestion was made that they move on. A woman manager, promoted out of an executive secretarial position, thought that these views of what secretaries really wanted spilled over into the treatment she was getting. She had an offer from another department, which she was considering because of the extra pay and challenge, and in trying to keep her, her own department said, as she reported, " 'We love you. We want you to stay.' They didn't say, 'We'll pay you more.' I couldn't get that from them. Just, 'We love you.' I wanted to say to them, 'I get the love from my husband. I work for other reasons.' "

The idea that women wanted "love" above all was translated into constant praise for secretaries. Women were supposed to be managed through flattery. Especially at the upper levels, it was common for the constant flow of orders for particular tasks to be accompanied by a constant flow of "thank you's" and compliments for jobs well done. The rapid cycle of beginnings and completion meant that there were many tasks for which secretaries could be thanked, and bosses assumed that being a good boss was to generate these courtesies. Elaborate praise for what were, after all, relatively minor tasks requiring few advanced skills, coupled with flowery requests for services, also helped bosses reduce any embarrassment involved in order-giving, any concern they had about their position of differential authority. When secretaries' rights organizations began to agitate for "raises, not roses," they were challenging this notion of what motivated women.

Yet many Indsco secretaries *were* content to settle for symbolic rewards, for prestige and daily flattery rather than higher pay, job control, and independent recognition. There was a shared feeling on the part of some secretaries that women did better in the higher-level executive secretarial positions than they did in the lower exempt jobs, even taking into account the pay differential. "I'd have to give up my drapes and my outside office and settle for a tiny inside cubicle," one executive secretary said. Despite the large numbers of routine and boring tasks secretaries carried out, the little corners of reflected power in the job gave some of them a sense of reward. The upper-grade secretary had access to inside information. She knew who the "fast track" people were; who the boss would see no matter how busy he was; who goes to lunch, who goes to meetings, who got invited to personal dinners at home. The gifts of knowledge, the invitations to special events, the bits of power secretaries picked up from their bosses' status—all this made it hard for some secretaries to see any other options for themselves.

Through their bosses, secretaries acquired contact with the power and knowledge elite of the organization. One of the attractions clerical work held for women from the early twentieth century was the opportunity for contact with those in powerful positions.[12] The sentiments of a private secretary to a corporation president were echoed by women in Indsco in explaining why they were content to be secretaries: "I enjoy one thing more than anything else on this job. That's the association I have with the other executives, not only my boss. . . . . I feel like I'm sharing something of the business life of the

men. So I think I'm much happier as the secretary to an executive than I
would be in some woman's field, where I could perhaps make more money.
But it wouldn't be an extension of a successful executive. I'm perfectly happy
in my status." [13] A former Indsco secretary echoed this sense of the secretary's
reward-through-relationship: "If a girl [sic] has built her whole life career
around a particular manager, and he doesn't take her with him when he
moves, it is completely shattering."

The symbolic rewards of identification were related to another aspect of
the secretary-boss relationship. A *tone of emotional intensity* may come to per-
vade it. A "division of emotional labor" may be developed, in which the secretary comes to "feel for" the boss in both senses: to care deeply about what happens to him and to do his feeling for him. Secretaries represented a reserve of
permissible emotional expression in the office. Executives unwound to their
secretaries, according to an Indsco informant. "They say things they would not
say anywhere else. If something goes wrong at a meeting, they will tell their
secretary more than their wife." A journalist romanticized this aspect of the
relationship in an advice book to managers: "During the many hours you
spend working closely with your secretary, she'll inevitably share your moments of triumph and distress, of accomplishment and frustration. Her position at your side stimulates a common bond of understanding." A revealing
picture of the division of emotional labor appeared in this sketch of Rose Mary
Woods, secretary to Richard Nixon, a man described by observers as wooden
and unfeeling: "A woman with red hair and an Irish temperament beneath a
cool exterior, in pre-White House days she occasionally scolded politicians and
reporters she felt had been unfair to Nixon. *She cried* when Nixon was chosen
as General Eisenhower's running mate in 1952 because she thought the job
was a dead end for him. *She hid her tears* behind dark glasses in Caracas,
Venezuela, in 1958 when his car was stoned. But ten years later, in the Wal-
dorf-Astoria ballroom, *her tears flowed unashamedly* while he made his victory
statement." [14] [Italics mine]

In return for the secretary's devotion and emotional support, the boss
may take on the traditional patrimonial ruler's attitude of caretaking toward his
underlings. An Indsco manager told a group of managers, who were discussing
the position of women in the company, how his feelings of responsibility
changed when he acquired a secretary of his own, after years of sharing secretarial services with other bosses: "In the old job I shared a secretary with up to
six people, and I didn't feel very personally responsible. Now I have this personal feeling that I am responsible for the care and feeding of that person—my
secretary—the nurturing of her emotions, giving her a shoulder to cry on. I'm
the one who remembers her anniversary. I'm the one constantly checking on
her sensitivities, treating her emotions, stopping to notice that, hey, she's not

having a good day. I have to make sure she's feeling all right." Note the certainty of this man that what his secretary wanted existed primarily in the emotional realm.

In a relationship of fealty, then, secretaries were expected to be bound by ties of personal loyalty, to value non-utilitarian rewards, and to be available as an emotional partner. The image of what secretaries wanted—and, by extension, working women—was shaped by these expectations.

THE MARRIAGE METAPHOR:
SECRETARY AS "OFFICE WIFE"

The three patrimonial elements in secretarial role relations (status contingency, principled arbitrariness, and fealty) have led to the frequent use of the marriage metaphor to describe the relationship between secretaries and bosses.[15] The metaphor aptly fits many elements of the position: reflected and derived status; greater privileges and lesser work for women attached to higher-status men; choice of a secretary on the basis of personal qualities like appearance; fusion of "the couple" in the eyes of others; a non-rationalized relationship with terms set by personal negotiation; expectations of personal service, including office "housework"; special understandings that do not survive the particular relationship; expectations of personal loyalty and symbolic or emotional rewards; and an emotional division of labor in which the woman plays the emotional role and the man the providing role. Indeed, the progression from the secretarial pool and multiple bosses to a position working for just one manager resembles the progression from dating to marriage, echoed in managers' own comments about special feelings of responsibility toward a private secretary. A working woman was better off when she could be attached to a single man. Some writers, such as Mary Kathleen Benet in *The Secretarial Ghetto,* have also suggested that the more elevated the executive, the more closely their duties approximate that of a wife rather than of a stenographer-typist, including bill-paying, sending Christmas cards, preparing refreshments, providing protection from subordinates/children, or making travel arrangements.[16]

But the marriage metaphor is not just a catchy description used by critics. It was also implicit in the way many people at Indsco talked about the relationships between secretaries and bosses. Over time, a serious emotional bond could develop. One executive secretary promoted into management described leaving her old boss as a "divorce." "I worked with a really fine man before this slot opened, which is one of the hazards of a secretarial job. You work for truly fine people, and you get so identified with them that you really don't have a career that's your own. I'm sure I really felt a marriage was ending when we both talked about my moving. It was almost as sad as getting a divorce. I was as emotionally involved in it. While in my explanations to myself I said it was fear of going to a new job, I think it was also fear of ending a relationship with a man I really enjoyed." For the first few months after her promotion, she stopped in to see him every morning, hanging her coat in her old office instead of the new one, and finding herself concerned if he had a cold or looked unhappy.

Some secretaries made the inevitable comparison between how *they* treated a boss and how the wives did. As a secretary said: "I think if I've been at all successful with men, it's because I'm a good listener and interested in their world. . . . Most of the ones I'm referring to are divorced. In looking through the years they were married, I can see . . . what probably happened. I know if I were the wife, I would be interested in their work. I feel the wife of an executive would be a better wife had she been a secretary first. As a secretary, you learn to adjust to the boss's moods. Many marriages would be happier if the wife would do that." [17] On the other hand, there were also executive wives to whom I spoke who compared what *they* did for their husbands to the tasks of a good secretary. And, one manager suggested a *ménage à trois* in his remark to the real husband of a woman assisting him, "You have her body; I have her head."

If the marriage image had applicability, it also needed to be differentiated. There were *types* of office marriages at Indsco. Some were very traditional, perhaps among the remaining bastions of female submissiveness and deference. The traditional secretary, usually an older woman, knew her place, served with a smile, was willing to be scapegoated and take the blame for the boss's mistakes, and did not presume. For example, compare this description of Eugene McCarthy's secretary, Jean Stack, his "protective alter ego," with the Victorian wife: "She knew his reactions so well that his staff went to her for guidance. She paid family bills, scheduled his speaking dates and negotiated fees for him, protected him, anticipated his orders—and even took his clothes to the cleaner's. She was always careful to note, however, that she was not an adviser, and her favorite line was, 'When Mr. McCarthy hired me, he told me he wasn't hiring me to think.' She worked for him for 18 years, and she never called him by his first name." [18]

At the other end of the continuum were the new "liberated" office marriages, generally involving younger women. Some secretaries refused to do "housework" and insisted on participating in a process of contracting that defined the relationship as they wanted it defined, indicating their needs and limits. The secretary to the manager of a field office, who proved herself intelligent and capable, made her job an administrative one. She demanded (and won) the title of assistant to the manager and the right not to type unless absolutely necessary. (A special typist was hired part time.) The manager, a casual, easygoing, and very liberal man, gave her highly desirable office space, taking less for himself, and tried to accommodate all of her wishes. But he wistfully mentioned that he longed sometimes that she would take more responsibility for seeing that the office stayed clean. And even this liberated secretary was still merely "the wife," without a clear career territory of her own, but in a new kind of "marriage" in which she could demand privileges.

THE SECRETARY'S RESPONSE: WORK ORIENTATIONS
UNDER PATRIMONIAL CONDITIONS

Perhaps no other job category in the large corporation displays so vividly the constraints that give rise to characteristic behaviors, attitudes, and styles on the part of workers. In the case of secretaries, they were assumed to display the properties of "women as a group." But what they really displayed were the orientations of people whose strategies for achieving recognition and control were constrained by the social organization of their job. There were four work orientations that derived from the secretarial function at Indsco: parochialism, timidity and self-effacement, praise-addiction, and emotionality.

Parochialism

There was a tendency for secretaries to narrow their interests and involvements over time, to fail to see beyond the bounds of their own small locale in the organization or to understand their job in terms larger than their personal relationship with a boss. There was little incentive for secretaries to look beyond their own organizational unit. Instead, their work demands and reward structure almost demanded parochial attitudes. This orientation was a major problem for personnel managers looking for secretaries promotable into exempt jobs, for they could find few women who had not become narrowly specialized in the operations of one department and the outlook of one boss.

The sources of parochialism lay in the nature of the job itself. The relatively low-level and easily learned skills required in the most universal technical aspects of a secretary's job (e.g., typing, telephone-answering) posed a problem for the secretary who wanted to achieve recognition for herself in order to keep, let alone improve, her job. The simplicity of the formal job requirements made secretaries highly replaceable and interchangeable, on the formal level, with a vast number of other people who could type. There were two possible solutions to this problem: to demonstrate initiative and enterprise or to personalize the relationship.

The initiative/efficiency route, for example, was taken by a secretary who made herself virtually an assistant to her boss by actually writing the reports and newsletters she was formally expected only to type. (She felt she could "get away" with this because he had never had a private secretary before and did not know the "rules of the game" at Indsco.) Such a strategy was risky, however, especially in light of expectations for the secretarial function and reward allocation criteria of the organization. It would be difficult for both boss and organization to admit that major portions of the boss's work were being done by a low-paid employee in a job with low-level entrance requirements. For one thing, wage and hour laws served as limits, in the eyes of Indsco's legal department, on the extent to which secretaries could be officially turned into administrators. To take initiative without taking over the job, then, marked a fine line the more ambitious secretaries walked. They ran the risk that the more they did or the better they did, the more threatening they became to bosses and Indsco; doing better in this case might be self-defeating. There was also the possibility that each task secretaries did more efficiently than bosses would become downgraded in bosses' minds, secretaries' efficiency exposing bosses' deficiency. One writer argued that the things secretaries do well become redefined to their detriment: "A man who is sloppy will not only expect his secretary to compensate for his sloppiness but will inevitably suggest that her neatness and capacity for organization are proof of a tidy, and therefore limited, mind, while his sloppiness is the sign of unfettered creativity, making her feel guilt for possessing exactly those abilities he lacks, so that the more successful she is at straightening the mess, the more she proves her inability to *really* succeed." [19]

The second strategy for winning recognition was far safer and likelier to succeed, given the patrimonial features of the secretarial job. Secretaries could make themselves unique by becoming absorbed in the routines and procedures associated with their jobs, by specializing in the particulars of that boss's needs, wants, and interests. They could learn the *boss* rather than the organization. They could induce a relationship of dependency with bosses, in which bosses would come to count on their ability to anticipate needs, to respond to requests without explicit orders, to know exactly what the boss would do at any one time. This response was congruent with demands of personal service and fealty. And it tied the parties in the relationship closer together. A boss came to depend on the secretary not for interchangeable technical skills (the universalistic parts of the job that could be taught in schools, written in books, or conveyed in training programs) but for the unique knowledge of him and for the unspoken understandings that developed about how the work was to get done.

Parochialism was found, then, in those secretaries who became over-identified with a particular boss and who saw themselves as working for that boss's function rather than for the organization. They substituted depth of knowledge about one person for breadth of knowledge about the corporation. They were interested in little that occurred at Indsco except for those things that directly impacted on their department, and they were surprisingly ignorant of basic facts about the company. Their conversations concerned people and local gossip.

Timidity and Self-Effacement

Another cluster of attitudes and behaviors that could come to characterize secretaries over time derived from lack of independence and autonomy in the job, from status contingency and the principled arbitrariness of bosses. Older women and those with longer service were reinforced for timid, self-effacing, non-assertive responses to the organization. (Such attitudes were not found as often in younger women.) Older secretaries, especially, seemed concerned with security and unwilling to take risks; they also failed to see that they had independent talents. One secretary who had "trained" several new managers in the routines and procedures of their job, still failed to see that she had "managerial" skills. Another one was reluctant to make decisions on her own, even when the boss delegated this responsibility. In another case, a member of the personnel development staff was interviewing members of an organizational unit to start a career development system, when he realized that the secretary was not being included. The consultant called the secretary to ask to interview her. She turned him down, not realizing she had anything to say. According to the boss, she was a powerful force in the unit and had further influence on his set of priorities, choosing callers, deciding what she could handle and what needed his decision. But the secretary did not see her importance, only, as the personnel man put it, that "she was working through him, he's the powerful one."

In this self-effacement, secretaries shared a tendency with nonexempt women in general, who learn through their low-level, nonautonomous clerical jobs that they have few assets to offer the organization; and their jobs do not give them the chance to develop their talents. On the nonexempt personnel survey, a large percentage of the eighty-eight women secretaries and clerks reported that they had *no* skills whatsoever in these areas: developing programs (74 percent of the women reported *no* skills); motivating and persuading (49 percent); interviewing and selecting (84 percent); administering discipline

(64 percent); setting goals and objectives (37 percent); conducting meetings (76 percent); and leading others (47 percent). Most felt themselves skilless.

Some secretaries adopted a passive stance toward fulfillment of their own needs and self-interest. In keeping with the fealty inherent in the job and the bosses' positions as provider/caretakers, some women waited for their bosses to recognize that they needed something rather than asking directly. Some had enormous patience. One secretary complained to a personnel manager that she had had no salary increase in seven years. The manager asked "What did your manager say when you asked him about it?" The secretary replied, "Oh, I wouldn't speak to my boss about *that*." Also typical and revealing was the following set of events. A staff member sent out requests for an assistant, to be chosen among executive secretaries. Like other job information in Indsco, this was circulated only to managers on a "personal and confidential" basis. Three weeks later there had been only two responses from managers suggesting candidates. But the staffer heard from the gossip network that at least five or six people were interested, out of thirty executive secretaries. They knew about the job, because they could read "confidential" memos, but they were waiting for their bosses to mention it to them. They did not even call the staff member, although they knew her well. So there were twenty-eight bosses who had not mentioned the job to their secretaries, and perhaps as many secretaries who were too timid to ask. (The staff member thought one of the two candidates suggested by managers did take the initiative.) The staff member eventually called one of those who she had heard was interested to ask why she had not brought up the opening with her boss. The secretary replied, "I was waiting until he returns from his vacation. I'm on pins and needles wanting to know what to do, whether to call you or to wait for him. I decided to wait."

Praise-Addiction

The emotional-symbolic nature of rewards in the secretarial job; the concern of some bosses to keep secretaries content through "love" and flattery; and the continual flow of praise and thanks exchanged for compliance with a continual flow of orders—all of these elements of the position tended to make some secretaries addicted to praise. Praise-addiction was reinforced by the insulation of most secretaries from responsibility or criticism: their power was only reflected, the skills they most exercised were minimal, and authority and discretion were retained by bosses. Thus, many years in a secretarial job, especially as private secretary to an executive, tended to make secretaries incapable of functioning without their dose of praise. And it tended to make some wish to avoid situations where they would have to take steps that would result in criticism rather than appreciation. Their principal work orientation involved trying to please and being praised in return.

One older executive secretary with long tenure at Indsco was a victim of praise-addiction. Though happy as a secretary, and well-respected for competence, she accepted a promotion to an exempt staff job because she thought she should try it. After a year and a half, it was clear to her and to those around her that she could not take the pressures of the new job. Her nervousness resulted in an ulcer, and she asked to return to the secretarial function. In the exempt job she had supervisory responsibilities and had to make decisions for people—sometimes unpleasant ones, such as terminations. Her manager thought she spent much too long making such decisions, "moaning" afterwards even if she knew she had made the right decision. But she felt herself to be in an intolerable position. She had a feeling she was not appreciated. No one said "thank you" for her work in the new job. As the manager put it, "She was used to lots of goodies from her boss—'Hey, that's a good job.' Here we have to be of service to managers as well as subordinates. The managers feel we're one of them, so they don't go out of their way to thank us. And subordinates don't thank managers. So she was missing something she had been used to."

The kinds of orientations that secretaries can develop out of the social organization of their work, the arousal and reinforcement of needs for social appreciation and emotional expression, were demonstrated in a survey of attitudes toward thirty promotional outcomes among a sample of Indsco's nonexempt men and women. The twenty-three men surveyed were largely accounting clerks on a promotional ladder into exempt jobs; the eighty-eight women were pricing clerks and secretaries. Respondents rated the thirty outcomes on nine-point scales for both desirability and likelihood. The men, in keeping with their greater opportunity, rated the bulk of the positive outcomes much more likely than the women did, since they could more appropriately expect promotion. The women found it more desirable than likely that they would be in positions involving independence, decision-making responsibility, or business risks. But among those items rated as much *less desirable* by the women than the men though their likelihood was greater than their desirability, the effects of praise-addiction were manifest. (Statistical significance was at the .05 level.) Undesirable job characteristics included: "having a job where my work will be subject to both praise and criticism"; "being in a position where it is necessary to be outspoken"; "being in a position where it is necessary to be unemotional"; "being in a position where I must show confidence." The secretaries had become accustomed to praise for taking orders; they did not want to stick their necks out and risk criticism.

Emotionality and Gossip

Secretaries had few weapons at their disposal to use in negotiating and bargaining when there was something they wanted from bosses. Their easy replaceability, contingent status, expected fealty, and the non-reciprocal nature of the authority relationship left secretaries with only limited power strategies. Some secretaries felt that they could count on the "goodwill" of their bosses. Through appeals to conscience or principles of fairness, they felt they could win favors, raises, opportunities, or adjustment of working conditions. But this was, of course, the essence of "principled arbitrariness": bosses had the power, limited only by appeal to larger principles. Additional power tactics were necessary. In this situation, many secretaries turned to classical ways members of the subordinate or the victim class manage to get what they want from the more powerful: through assumed helplessness and emotional manipulation. And they earned status with others through gossip.

This was a game some secretaries played extremely well. Whether or not they, as women, were intrinsically any more "emotional" than men, they learned to display their emotions as a very useful way to get what they wanted. As a former executive secretary said, "Women, like men, learned what the rules of the game are. A secretary goes in to see her boss and quivers and cries. Not because she's so emotional, but because she knows the rules. She gets the raise because he can't stand to see her cry. . . . We have to use the rules we have available to us. Women in business use what they can."

Exaggerating emotionality was one of the safest strategies secretaries could use to manage their situation. The discomfort of bosses in the presence of an emotional woman often led them to give in quickly, just to stop the interaction from going any further. It was easier to give the secretary the day off than to listen to her pleas or to have her mope around the office depressed. Giving in to a person in need also spoke to bosses' images of themselves as "good people." And conceding something to a helpless, suffering person did not threaten the definition of the overt power distribution in the relationship. Bosses were still the strong ones, secretaries the weak and helpless.

But at the same time that secretaries using these tactics gained an immediate advantage, they also became more and more accustomed to emotional display. Other women clerical workers were in a similar situation with respect to their learned strategies for exercising influence in their authority relations. The items rated by nonexempt women and men on the survey of attitudes toward promotion included one specifically geared to this issue of emotionality: "being in a position where it is necessary to be unemotional." The women secretaries and clerks rated this much lower for desirability than did the men junior accountants, even though the women found it more likely than desirable. On a nine-point scale, with a score of one representing the maximum of undesirability and nine representing the maximum of desirability, the mean score for eighty-eight women on this item was 4.82, compared to a mean of 6.21 for twenty-three men. (The difference was statistically significant.) It seemed that women did not want to give up those few weapons, and those few freedoms, available to them in the clerical hierarchy.

The other way to gain some control and power in the secretarial job was to make use of the secretary's privileged access to information. So gossip became a commodity in which secretaries traded. The secretaries' gossip network was also useful for the organization; low-status people can spread things unofficially that official spokespersons would have to deny. Secretaries were free to engage in informal relationships and to spend time talking to others because their jobs were not often overly demanding, and gossip was a way to make the day more interesting. Their assumed freedom from political ambitions of their own enabled secretaries to form alliances with each other across units of the organization that otherwise had no formal linkage or were connected only at very high and abstract levels. Communication through secretaries could open otherwise closed channels. Those who wanted to bypass the formal system could use secretaries to get an inside reading of a situation. And secretaries could feel more important in the process.

Others have also pointed to the centrality of the secretary in information exchange in large corporations and the reasons for it: "Although informal communication is a game that any one and indeed any number can play, the finger of suspicion points strongly to official communicators as being the chief unofficial ones as well. I mean secretaries. They have knowledge without official power, and they constitute a kind of 'shadow' organization by their extensive dispersion in physical and social space. The fact that secretaries are also commonly female has, in my opinion, very little relevance. I doubt if a fair case can be made for the special proclivity of women to gossip, except, as with secretaries, when gossip is one of the few available ways of exercising some power. Gossip, whether benevolent or malicious, accurate or distorted, is simultaneously a way of bypassing formal agencies of communication and of enhancing the power of the individual over a system he does not control." [20]

In using available power and control tactics, then, some secretaries also reinforced stereotypes of women as gossip-prone and emotional.

WHY SECRETARIES STAY PUT:

FORCES PERPETUATING LOW MOBILITY

Secretarial role relations and the work orientations developed by secretaries both served to perpetuate the differentiation of the clerical and man-
agerial/professional hierarchies—to reinforce the low job ceiling for secretaries
and to block their movement into the exempt ranks. A critical paradox in the
secretarial career was responsible. Secretaries, if they wanted to keep and
improve their job, had to keep "doing better" at it. But "doing better," under
a patrimonial system, could also mean: (1) getting progressively less able, in
behavior and attitudes, to hold down a management position; and (2) becoming progressively more indispensable to the organization as a secretary—thus
remaining stuck.

The first factor was what Thorstein Veblen called *trained incapacity*. As
Robert Merton wrote, "Trained incapacity refers to that state of affairs in
which one's abilities function as inadequacies or blind spots. Actions based
upon training and skills which have been successfully applied in the past may
result in inappropriate responses *under changed conditions*. . . . [John]
Dewey's concept of occupational psychosis rests upon much the same observations. As a result of their day to day routines, people develop preferences, an-
tipathies, discriminations, and emphases." [21] In other words, training that
makes people fit for one position may make them progressively less fit for any
other.

This happened to many Indsco secretaries. Rewarded more and more for
personal and particularistic transactions, they were reinforced for the least
transferable portions of their knowledge and abilities, forced to narrow rather
than broaden their focuses as their work life continued, and rewarded for the
development of work orientations diametrically opposed to those required in
high-status, independent, decision-making positions in the exempt ranks.
Contrast secretarial parochialism with the increasing generality and wide exposure throughout the organization required in managerial positions, where
people were rewarded for ability to deal with uncertainties, not for superb
handling of the routine. Contrast timidity and praise-addiction with the necessity to take risks, make unpleasant decisions, and await long-term consequences in management and professional positions. Contrast emotional vul-
nerability as a control tactic with the appearance of managerial "rationality."
Thus, success as a secretary made some secretaries unfit for mobility out of the
secretarial ranks. Paradoxically, though people who succeeded in accommo-
dating to the secretarial job and adopting appropriate attitudes were promoted

within the clerical hierarchy, the ceiling for their careers could be simultaneously reinforced. *The pool of secretaries who reached the top, and hence became eligible for what little mobility existed, might also be the group least fit, by learned response to their own job conditions, to handle it.*

The second factor limiting mobility was the *dilemma of indispensability.* The secretary who succeeded might become progressively more indispensable—to the boss and to the organization—as a secretary. Indsco, like many large corporations headquartered in urban areas in the 1970s, was finding it hard to attract competent secretaries. Thus, there was a widespread fear of losing those people who *were* good secretaries by giving them exempt opportunities. Bosses often stood in the way of recognition that might generate mobility for a good secretary: by failing to tell them of job opportunities, by downgrading their performance evaluations, by keeping them from wider exposure in the organization. If the indispensability trap was defeating for the secretary, it was also self-defeating for the organization, because one of the reasons Indsco was having such a hard time finding competent people to be secretaries was the low mobility in the job.

In both cases, the process was circular. The existence of a low-skill, low-mobility job, with highly replaceable personnel subject to contingent status and a high degree of managerial discretion, encourages the development of a personal service relationship as a recognition and tenure mechanism. But this in turn reinforced the low mobility of the job and its confinement to a separate, low-status career ladder.

ATTEMPTS AT STRUCTURAL CHANGE—

AND RESISTANCE TO CHANGE

Under affirmative action pressures in the early 1970s, in the wake of growing complaints from younger women or those stuck in lower-level slots in the clerical hierarchy, and in the desire to extend modern management systems to all parts of the white-collar organization, Industrial Supply Corporation established a centralized administrative apparatus for nonexempt personnel. Managers were appointed to handle this function, and these managers, in turn, created a task force composed of exempt personnel who managed different groups of nonexempts. They took the first steps to generate job descriptions, monitor budgets for secretaries, announce job openings and keep a file of candidates, begin a centralized performance appraisal system for secretaries, find opportunities for secretaries to move into exempt jobs, ensure universal standards in secretarial jobs, approve promotions, and insist that secretaries not automatically move with their bosses. Steps were also being taken to devise ways to uncouple a secretary's status from that of her boss.

The processes that concerned clerical workers as a whole, especially male accounting clerks, were accepted readily, but those changes specifically designed for secretaries garnered no widespread support, even on the task force itself. Other committee members joked that their chairperson, a supporter of change, was "on her secretarial kick again" when she brought up the subject. There was disagreement among secretaries themselves. Those who thought change should be made were generally the ones trapped by the old system. The ones who benefited from the old ways, like executive secretaries, resisted change and even refused to participate in data-gathering that was part of the change effort. The more open, equitable centralized search procedures for job candidates were consistently voided by the actions of some managers. One manager called the nonexempt administrator on a Thursday night about a job opening and left a message. By the time the administrator returned the call Friday morning, the manager said he already had a preferred candidate. When the personnel staff told an executive moving to officer level that he could not automatically take his secretary with him, but that she could compete for the new job along with other people, he complained about adjusting to someone new and insisted on taking her anyway, despite the new system. Lower-level managers, not so powerful, merely flooded the office with complaints that they did not have the final say about who worked for them. And, in a year, no one had been promoted off a list of nonexempts eligible for promotion that was circulated by the personnel function.

Initial experiences with the performance appraisal process for secretaries were also revealing. For some, it worked. Many secretaries were grateful for the opportunity to seek feedback and clarify their job objectives for the first time, and they found the process potentially educational. Those for whom the appraisal worked well felt that they had career direction for the first time and could take themselves more seriously. One woman attached a long list of extra-company community leadership positions and newspaper clippings about herself to the form; it was the first personnel people knew of the existence of a secretary with such demonstrated leadership skills, and they put her on the promotion eligibility list.

But some bosses refused to go through the performance appraisal process in any but a perfunctory way. Some forms had check marks where required but no comments in the major spaces left for remarks. Most responses did not seem highly differentiated. Bosses tended to give secretaries about the same ratings on all items. And, in some cases, personnel staff could recognize outright distortions and lies on the forms. One pool secretary-receptionist had been the subject of many long complaining phone calls from the manager in charge to the personnel office, in which the manager blasted the woman's incompetence and insisted that something be done about her. But her appraisal form contained a large number of items checked "outstanding."

Problems with the performance appraisal process merely underscored the dilemmas identified in secretarial role relations: the problematic nature of male-female communication, especially around criticism; the fact that bosses were not speaking with peers or people seen as potentially promotable into the ranks of peers; the subjective nature of job standards; managers' concerns about being evaluated in return for their actual secretarial needs and their skills at managing; the fact that interpersonal or emotional issues could be important parts of the job, an area where communication is always more difficult; the reluctance of managers to lose good secretaries and therefore the wish to avoid discussing their career possibilities or indicating promotion readiness; and the tendency of some bosses to see secretaries as working for them rather than for the corporation. All of these concerns showed up in the resistance to the new evaluation process.

But there were also larger issues involved in resistance to change in the organization of the secretarial job, issues that made clear what human and organizational functions were being served by the traditional system.

THE PERMISSIBLE PERSONAL

Because the secretarial function in Indsco represented a repository of the personal inside the bureaucratic, the last relic of *Gemeinschaft* emotion-laden relations of individual loyalty within a *Gesellschaft* system of contractual, limited, interchangeable, instrumental involvements, many people were reluctant to tamper with it. If it was the last place where people could be personal beings, they were reluctant to risk losing this reserve of personal territory.

In the first place, since secretaries were largely defined out of the mobility game, they could afford to carry the human side of the office. The reward system and authority structures in their jobs, as we have seen, encouraged secretaries to be leading actors in many forms of personal and emotional communication.

For bosses, the traditional secretarial system offered something many of them found nowhere else in their work. It was a pocket of personal privilege in a setting where few areas of completely individual discretion and control were allowed. Secretaries offered an arena of power and control—and sometimes adoration—for bosses who were otherwise rendered powerless and not very important by the routinization of their own job or the numerous constraints upon bureaucratic action. In the person of the secretary was someone over whom bosses could claim at least partial "ownership" and to whom they could give orders that rarely had to be justified to anyone else. Here was someone to whom they were critically important and in whose eyes they could *be* important. Here also was someone who provided them a chance to exercise the sentimental and emotional sides of themselves discouraged elsewhere in the organization, someone who needed and depended upon them, someone to whom they could make gestures indicating what good persons they were underneath. (The story was told of a top-ranking Indsco officer who called his former secretary from his field office days to apologize personally for the closing of that office, which put her out of a job. "See what a wonderful human guy he is," the storyteller said.)

For the secretaries themselves, there were tradeoffs involved in their position. Although they were subject to the personal whim of their bosses rather than to impersonal rules and orders scrutinized for fairness, they also retained a direct and special relationship to a person they could influence and manipulate. They had only one or two people to please, rather than being enmeshed in the larger bureaucratic tangle, where they would have to manage multiple relationships to get ahead. Although they were rewarded for someone else's achievements and status rather than directly for their own talents and skills, they also could derive much closer contact with power and privilege than they could ever attain on their own. So for many secretaries, too, the personal, non-rationalized residue in their position made life in the corporate bureaucracy easier to live.

Private secretarial setups, or even the small pool attached to a small group of bosses, thus provided more advantageous work conditions than those most clerical workers faced. The present personalized arrangements looked good especially in contrast to an alternative: mechanized systems in which secretaries, like other clerks, became wedded to their machines and to their routine tasks. It was such mechanization of the office that struck C. Wright Mills when he wrote *White Collar* just after World War II. And it is the continuation of trends toward rationalization through mechanization that has led other analysts to write of the "proletarianization" of the clerical labor force and to encourage unionization as the solution to the problems of women clericals.[22] Indeed, nonexempt personnel staff at Indsco were investigating the use of "Word Processing" systems in other companies. Word Processing is a system that, in effect, replaces the private secretary with the assembly line. All communication is sent to a single department that takes dictation over the phone, transcribes tapes, types documents, sends out mail, and performs other "secretarial" tasks, using the latest computerized equipment. In some cases, an "administrative assistant" remains with a unit to handle organizational tasks, but the great bulk of employees are, by and large removed from access to the traditional secretarial privileges. But if Word Processing is the only alternative, rather than a genuine upgrading of the secretarial or clerical job so that it has autonomy, pay, status, and mobility opportunity associated with it, then many secretaries prefer the old system.

Resistance to change in this function can be seen as resistance to further bureaucratic encroachment. Inequities in the situation of secretaries seem to demand change, but any change must also acknowledge the reluctance of people to give up preserves of the personal. There needs to be some such relationship in the organization, but it should not be a "hereditary" or "patrimonial" one. Indsco secretaries were locked into self-perpetuating, self-defeating cycles in which job and opportunity structure encouraged personal orientations that reinforced low pay and low mobility and perpetuated the original job structure. The fact that such jobs were held almost entirely by women also reinforced limited and stereotypical views of the "nature" of women at work.

How to restructure the job to enhance opportunity and eliminate patrimonial inequities, but how to simultaneously provide outlets for the needs of human beings for personalized relationships and personal territory—this is the dilemma of the corporate bureaucracy.

5

Wives

Perpetual devotion to what a man calls his business, is only to be sustained by perpetual neglect of many other things.
—Robert Louis Stevenson, *Virginibus Puerisque*

Women are still expected to do things because of love or duty.
—Jessie Bernard, *Women and the Public Interest*

Some of the most important role-players at Industrial Supply Corporation were never seen on company premises. They were clearly outside the official boundaries of corporate administration, listed nowhere, paid nothing, and discouraged from visiting their husbands' offices (even on weekends, because of security considerations). They are the managers' wives. There was no employment relation between Indsco and management wives, and no legitimate claims of one party on the other. As in the bureaucratic theory that helped give rationale and form to the modern corporate organization, men were presumed to leave their private relationships at the door to the company when they entered every morning. Wives stood on the other side of the door. At an off-site research meeting of junior executives and wives, paid for by their department, it was announced that only "Mr." should show on the hotel register; if "Mr. and Mrs." appeared, the manager footing the bill would need a letter from a vice-president.

Yet there were signs that the supposedly neat boundary between inside and outside the system marked by the legal employment relation was not so crystal clear. In Indsco offices were some obvious manifestations of the wives' involvement with the organization. Photographs of wives and children adorned men's offices so commonly that they seemed almost mandatory. Wives were automatically mentioned by name in articles in company newsletters about husbands' accomplishments: "Joseph Jones lives with his wife, Margaret, and their three children in Anytown Heights." Being a "family man" was a clear sign of stability and maturity and was taken into account in promotion decisions; sexual promiscuity on the part of Indsco's management men was frowned upon, despite a culture that joked about sexual pursuit. Wives were clearly seen by some of their husbands as a motivational factor in their careers, in answers to questions about why they worked at Indsco: "Providing for a family is a large reason why I work here. It gives me great gratification to know that I can give to my wife and kids at such a luxurious level." On my sales force survey, a high proportion of the men indicated that family was a major life interest for them. When given an open-ended chance to respond to the question, "What are the important things to you?" following a scaled commitment item asking whether "my work is among the most important things in my life," 62 percent of 205 respondents wrote in "family," while only 17 percent wrote in "career."

Personnel staff and executives were aware of the wives around certain critical issues where their reactions could influence the husbands or where they could unleash a storm of protest. Pre-retirement career planning sessions and orientations to international transfers included wives, and a proposal for spouse workshops around any transfer was under discussion. To soothe wounded feelings about being left behind, an expensive gift (an engraved crystal candy dish) was distributed to all the wives whose husbands were being sent, alone, to a glamorous setting for a meeting and recreation. And, of course, wives were essential elements at social gatherings, sometimes acting as hostesses for people with whom the company wanted a good relationship. Such events occurred outside the business day but hardly outside the business boundaries. In all these ways, wives were part of the organization.

From the wives' perspective, the company was a critical part of their lives, defining how they spent their time and influencing what was possible in their relationships with their husbands. One wife in her mid-thirties, married to a rising manager, put it this way: "Until two years ago, when I thought about going back to school, I was an Indsco wife, married to the company as much as to Fred. No one ever demanded anything of me *per se* except going out to dinner with so-and-so. But in my own being, I was very dependent on Fred's experiences in Indsco. It chose the area we lived in. Our friends, except for a few neighbors, were Indsco friends, made *because* of the company. I always felt that our goal was to settle down, to set down roots when the kids were in junior high school. Now they are, and the company tells us to move, so we move, pushing that goal further ahead. . . . If Fred was doing well, I felt *I* was doing well. I'm the woman behind the man, I could take some pride in his achievements."

Young wives anticipated increasing sacrifices for the company as their husbands' careers progressed, pointing to effects on their marriages of the men's daily fatigue, travel, and evenings away, and demands that they play a growing role in official entertaining. "Husband-absence" also gave them exclusive child care responsibilities. Some wives considered themselves unpaid workers for the corporation, in the sense both of direct services and of opportunity costs for options in their own lives they had forgone. As wives saw it, then, they were very much inside the corporate system.

The existence of wives also had implications for women officially employed by the company. Just as the image of the secretary spilled over and infused expectations about other women workers, the image of the wife affected responses to career women at Indsco. Because corporate wives were generally seen to be content to operate behind the scenes and to be ambitious for their husbands rather than themselves and because they made use of social rather than intellectual skills in their hostess role, the image of women that emerged for some management men from knowing their own and other wives reinforced the view that career women were an anomaly, that they were unusual or could not really be ambitious, or that their talents must be primarily social and emotional rather than cognitive and managerial. Some men, especially those who had attended engineering schools and were accustomed to an all-male colleague environment, explicitly said they took their sense of how to treat professional and management women from their wives' preferences—often leading to awkward and uncomfortable situations. Such men were then also likely to resent the career women who made them feel uncomfortable, wishing they were more like their wives. (This process of translation could also work *for* employed women, as in the case of a senior executive married to a prominent professional woman, a man who was a strong and public supporter of affirmative action for women.) Professional women sometimes said they felt pressure from male managers to live up to the expectations clearly stemming from what the wives were expected to do. On one occasion, the automatic assumption was made that a woman would not be attending a two-day off-site meeting because one of her children had a bad cold. The child, a boy, actually preferred to have his father take care of him when he was sick, but regardless, the woman thought it should be her own decision, not her manager's. Another example was a dialogue in which a woman said she would go on a business trip out of the country, and her manager kept telling her to "think about it overnight." She finally understood that he was expecting her to ask her husband before agreeing to go.

Some of the expectations stemming from the existence of wives had another, more general, effect. Men could bring two people with them to the organization, and indeed, preferential hiring of married men and occasional attention to the wives' own characteristics frequently ensured that this was so. But career women, especially in the managerial ranks, did not have this advantage. There was no "corporate husband" role equivalent to that of corporate wife. Husbands of higher-ranking women who were not themselves part of Indsco sometimes resisted having anything at all to do with the company. One husband refused to attend official dinners or social events with his wife, a marketing executive. At the same time, married women employed by the company were also reminded by their managers of their responsibilities as wives and mothers—or managers expressed concerns that these responsibilities would deflect energy or lower commitment. Thus, while men symbolically brought two people to their jobs, women were seen as perhaps bringing less than one full worker.[1]

Finally, concerns of the women outside the office were transferred directly to those inside. Wives' concerns about the sexual potential of office relationships occasionally pitted the two sets of women against each other as rivals. Even if overt sexuality did not occur, the competitive threat was still there, as noted by a psychiatrist: "As people who have interesting careers have always known, work is very sexy, and the people with whom one is working are the people who excite. A day spent launching a project or writing a paper or running a seminar is more likely to stimulate—intellectually and sexually—than an evening spent sharing TV or discussing the lawn problems or going over the kids' report cards."[2]

The competitive potential of office relationships was always there. Several saleswomen at Indsco felt, rightly or wrongly, that they were the targets of the sexual fantasies of male peers. Some said that men used them to taunt their wives, e.g., by making innuendos about going out on a sales call with one of the women. For this reason, many saleswomen felt it important that they establish good relations with the wives, giving women an additional task men did not have. Wives, in turn, not themselves directly participating in the work world, could fear what would happen when their husbands worked with women as peers, such as the Newton, Massachusetts, policemen's wives who protested the hiring of policewomen, giving as one reason the sexual potential of long shifts shared by men and women in patrol cars.[3] A few men played on these concerns and then used their wives' jealousies as reasons why women should not be hired for certain jobs, like those that involved travel with men.

For all of these reasons, wives cannot be ignored when looking at men and women in the administration of corporate bureaucracies. But at the same time, it is hard to know exactly where they do fit in the system or how to conceptualize their nature as both insiders and outsiders. They are sometimes directly involved with the organization, sometimes involved only with and through their husbands, and sometimes completely uninvolved.

INDUSTRIAL SUPPLY'S POLICY DILEMMAS:

WHAT TO DO ABOUT WIVES

How to understand and take into account the position of wives is an intellectual task with relevance for both organization theory and organization policy. At Indsco, there was considerable debate over whether the organization should get involved in the family lives of managers at all, even in relatively innocuous ways like offering programs with serious educational content for wives dragged along to business conferences or running workshops on couple issues as an adjunct to career planning and development.

The "libertarian" position held that anything wives did was strictly voluntary, their own choice. Employees' private lives were—officially—their own business, and the company had no right to interfere. To think otherwise smacked of the worst kind of paternalism not in keeping with modern management, as in practices like wife-screening (never an explicit policy at Indsco) or company housing in company towns or the packaged social life complete with corporate country club provided by IBM. As one rising young executive said, he came to Indsco in the first place, rather than a rival company with a strong paternalistic heritage and a tradition of involving managers in a complete, ritualized (and somewhat stodgy) lifestyle, because he was "looking for a job, not a closed community." A few women with important careers in their own right, married to Indsco executives, resented the notion that the company could even take an interest in their lives, which they wanted to see as totally independent.

Yet, this "libertarian" position was also used to avoid the issue of how much Indsco was already constraining salesmen's and managers' families; it helped evade any organizational responsibility. To throw a party at an expensive restaurant for husbands and wives, for example, was considered within a manager's prerogative, but to spend the same amount of money to bring spouses on-site to teach them about company policies or what their husbands did all day long was inappropriate. The most recurrent complaint from Indsco wives had to do with the limits of the role they were given to play: on the one hand, faced with strong demands to be gracious, charming hostesses and social creatures, supporting their husbands' careers and motivating their achievements, with the boundaries of their own life choices set by the company; but on the other hand, kept away from opportunities to see, understand, and even participate in their husbands' jobs. They simultaneously wanted to be left alone to live their own lives *and* to be more involved in their husbands'.

Corporate policy and practices, then, were viewed by a second school of thought in the company as a source of marital tension and severe strain for wives which, in turn, had bearing on men's work performance. These people supported the idea that more attention be paid to work-family issues and that wives be seen as "inside" the company's boundaries. As Sam Culbert and Jean Renshaw, a consultant-research team, pointed out, the relationship of many organizations to the family has been one-sided: "The boundary between the organization and the family has remained too long inaccessible. A double standard of participation has left the families open to exploitation. On the one hand, their strengths are drawn upon to help make and implement critical organizational decisions which the employee cannot manage by himself. On the other hand, they are denied formal channels of participation, and, therefore, can neither initiate discussions nor react to proposals that affect them." [4] The "social welfare" advocates of this second view at Indsco felt the company had a responsibility to wives.

Clearly, then, understanding the corporate wife role and its appropriate connection to the organization is not a simple matter. It requires taking into account a number of circumstantial variations and developing a theoretical framework for identifying the constraints within which organization wives must operate.

TOWARD A PERSPECTIVE ON THE CORPORATE WIFE

Other writings on organization wives do not provide much help in advancing intellectual understanding. Most of them belong in the "wife-as-victim" category.

The corporate wife as a social role captured public attention in the early 1950s when William H. Whyte, Jr., wrote a series of articles in *Fortune* and elsewhere revealing the extent to which corporations looked over and made rules for wives of men they were considering for executive positions.[5] The corporate wife's acceptance of her fate was taken by Whyte as another sign of the rise of "groupmindedness," which he later documented in *The Organization Man*. Whyte's picture, as well as that presented by later journalists and psychiatrists, tended to show the corporate wife as a helpless casualty, even when a willing one. Moving from place to place frequently, subject to rules and constraints, excluded from the office world, stuck with almost exclusive household responsibilities, and lacking their husbands' opportunities for learning and adventure, corporate wives were portrayed as victims of a too-demanding system. And with reason. Alcoholism, unwanted pregnancies, divorce, and bouts of depression in women have all been attributed to features of the managerial lifestyle.[6] More recently, the suffering of wives of politicians was described in popular articles and books: Margaret Trudeau's emotional collapse, Joan Kennedy's mental distress, Abigail McCarthy's divorce, Angelina Alioto's runaway revolt.[7] Feminist writings also pointed out the costs of reflected identity or vicarious achievement for wives, and through them, for children. Lack of an independent sense of self was considered a cause of depression. One wife told Robert Seidenberg, "I bask in my husband's reflected glory. I don't have to be anything myself. His status is my status. Sometimes I feel he's living his life to the fullest, and I'm living his life to the fullest." [8]

The actual casualty rate among corporate wives has never been fully known, and at every wave of criticism and protest there was also a chorus of apparently contented wives waiting in the wings to insist that the advantages outweighed the disadvantages. However, no one disagreed that marriage to successful men was constraining, shaped role demands for wives, and often put the family last in the men's priorities. William Henry had this to say after a study of the personalities of successful executives: "They are . . . corporate men, not family men. Wives must actively subordinate themselves to the husbands' work aims or, at the very least, not interfere with them. The key to an effective partnership, and we use this neutral word intentionally, would in fact be the degree to which the wife actively adopted the corporate goals and skillfully aided the husband in that direction. This makes of the wife a kind of high-class assistant, bound by marriage rather than salary but otherwise facilitating the work goals with the same sense of efficiency the husband would expect of his secretary and other office personnel. The all-embracing demands of corporate life do not permit distractions." [9]

The second theme in the victim critique focused on economic exploitation: wives as unpaid workers. Some writers pointed to the direct and indirect services wives performed for their husbands' careers and organizations. Four kinds of task contributions were among those noted. *Direct substitution* involved the wife in work that could also be done by a paid employee; she substituted permanently, temporarily, or on an ad hoc basis, either at the office or at home. The wife might stuff envelopes, do some typing, answer phones, deliver packages, or keep accounts and records, like the wife of a consulting engineer mentioned in one report who kept his files and scrapbooks up to date and helped him make business contacts at conferences. The winners of one company's award for exceptional salesmanship (American Cyanamid Company's Golden Oval) all had wives without outside jobs, most of whom reported to an interviewer in 1973 that they spent a considerable amount of time helping their husbands with sales work. (In one case of a man who had won this award twice, his wife filled in when his secretary was on vacation, traveled with him on business, helped him entertain customers, and talked to him about his work even when *she* was bored.) *Indirect support* included those entertainment functions that were assumed to be part of the wife's "hostess" role, using her assumed skill as a relationship builder. Such services might be purchased if unavailable from a wife. *Consulting* involved discussion and advice on business matters, like those discussions that might be held with a management consultant. The wife acted as a business adviser, a psychotherapist, a listener, or even an "expert" on some part of her husband's work, helping him make decisions or choose between options. *Emotional aid,* a part of the conventional housewife role, involved such services as "sending him off in a good frame of mind" and keeping him satisfied with his work. As Whyte summarized these latter functions, the wife was a "wailing wall, a sounding board, and a refuelling station." [10] She was an important adjunct to the company's motivational apparatus but was never rewarded directly by it for her services.

Though economic benefit supposedly came to the wife through the boost to the husband's career, a chord of protest was sounded by some critics and some wives, who found this situation unfair. As one wife complained, "I am paid neither in job satisfaction nor in cash for my work. I did not choose the job of executive wife, and I am heartily sick of it." [11] The argument was made that wives at least should be compensated for out-of-pocket expenses in their work for their husbands. The economic exploitation theme is also highlighted in recent feminist writings urging pay for housework, since work at home is involved in the "reproduction of labor power" and thus should be compensated by the work systems it benefits.

Corporate wives, in short, have been seen as outsiders, swallowed up by a greedy organization [12] that tries to absorb totally the lives of its managerial employees. But the closest to a theory of why this arose or what wives actually did was offered by Hanna Papanek in her discussion of the "two-person single career," the combination of formal and informal institutional demands placed on both members of a married couple, although only the man is officially employed. She wrote: "Large, complex institutions employing highly educated men . . . develop their own version of the two-person career pattern among their employees . . . [communicating] certain expectations to the wives. These expectations serve the dual function of reinforcing the husband's commitment to the institution and of demanding certain types of role performance from the wife which will benefit the institution in a number of ways. A pattern of pressures is generated for both members of the couple which is closely related to social mobility, mobility within the employing institution, loyalty, and interpersonal rivalry." [13]

The idea of a "career" for corporate wives points to a way to identify the particular dilemmas they face, the characteristic forces shaping their behavior.

What the wife does, what she must contend with, is a function of the husband's career stage and the nature of managerial work in the large corporate bureaucracy. Thus, her role and the reasons for her implication in the organization at all are bound up with human issues in management itself: issues such as uncertainty, trust, and loyalty; internal company politics and external needs for legitimacy.

THE CORPORATE WIFE'S CAREER PROGRESSION

Three phases can be identified in the career of a corporate wife in Industrial Supply Corporation and other industrial bureaucracies, each distinguished by a set of dilemmas and choices particular to it. The three phases partly overlap, and all three sets of functions may be performed simultaneously, but the distinction between them reflect differences in the critical issues in the husband's career. The first is the *technical* phase, roughly corresponding to husbands' pre-management jobs and early rungs on management ladders, when the constraints on a wife flow directly from the husband's immediate job conditions, and any involvement on her part in his work is in the form of technical assistance or personal support directly to him. The most critical factor in husbands' careers is whether they can carry out the technical requirements of their jobs. At this point, wives form an anonymous mass, with little if any direct connection with the organization.

Then, as a husband enters middle and upper management, a second phase, the *managerial* phase, begins. Here the wife's role is shaped by the growing importance of the husband's involvement in company social networks. As he takes on "people-handling" tasks and becomes enmeshed in the informal political structure of the company, the wife adds social tasks that involve her more directly in a social network of other husbands and wives. The uncertainties in evaluation of managerial performance and the concomitant importance of such non-ability factors as trust, loyalty, and fitting in well in corporate society give shape to this phase. As the uncertainty factor increases in the husband's career, the visibility factor increases in the wife's. Entertaining and sociability, more or less private matters during the technical phase, may now receive official notice and scrutiny, taking on political meaning.

Finally, the *institutional* phase centers around the husband's location at the top of the organization or in a position where he must represent it to the outside. Diplomatic functions become important, for the organization seeks legitimacy and support from its environment (major suppliers, the immediate community, governmental agencies, the public-at-large) not only in formal ways but also through the persons of its leaders. At the very top, the wife-of-the-chief has an official role to play in the organization's diplomatic system: official hostess, link to the community, caretaker and mobilizer of other wives, and public relations professional. Wives-at-the-top are no longer hidden and officially excluded, and they may even have a budget for the conduct of their position. Names like "First Lady" or "Wife of the Ambassador" or "Chief Executive's Wife" can describe an organizational title as well as a marital bond. The wife may, at this point, form a visible team with her husband. However, just as the corporate wife's role becomes more rewarded and rewarding closer to the top, it also becomes more controlled. In the institutional phase, the wife may be less free to arrange for her own private life and more constrained by the needs of the organization.

We can see in the "career progression" of a corporate wife, then, an increase in visibility with each shift in phase and a change in the principal orientation of the activities she might choose to perform. In the first phase, her activities take place primarily with respect to her husband; in the second, around a social network internal to the company; and in the third, around the organization itself. Each of these phases presents the wife with a set of decisions and dilemmas.

THE TECHNICAL PHASE:

HANDLING EXCLUSION/INCLUSION

The first dilemma faced by Industrial Supply Corporation wives revolved around *exclusion/inclusion*. Wives of men in sales and low-level management positions faced a system that shut them out officially of their husbands' job worlds, at the same time that job conditions limited their husbands' availability. Wives complained that there was too little left over after work: "His high at work made me angry. He was so involved there but under-involved at home. He'd be withdrawn and too democratic at home, completely abdicating any responsibility for what we shared, telling me that whatever I wanted was fine. He just didn't have any energy left."

Furthermore, the jargon-laden company culture created a communication problem—sometimes overtly denied by wives who would pretend to be interested while understanding little of what was said. At a research meeting, twelve wives whose husbands worked in the same unit generated a list of words and phrases they had heard their husbands use but that they could not define; it ran to 103 entries, before the group stopped for lack of time. Knowledge of their husbands as workers was minimal, and the wish was frequently expressed by both women and men that a wife have a chance to "see who he is when he is doing his job, to learn what it does to him." In keeping with the knowledge gap, the wife's-eye view of the corporation was a highly distorted one, with only bits and pieces of information filtering through. One wife wanted to see the organization chart, which she claimed must be twelve feet wide and two inches high, from what she had heard, printed on adding machine tape and requiring two people to hold it up. Another said she got the impression from her husband's conversation that everyone at Indsco was a manager; there seemed to be no one underneath.[14]

There were several ways in which this situation was handled. One option was to settle for total exclusion, with the wife choosing a path of her own that took her farther away from any direct involvement with her husband's job or with Indsco. Sometimes this occurred because she had a career of her own; if it were in a similar field, as for the psychologist wife of a counsellor in the personnel department, colleagueship could at least be maintained. But more often, in the early 1970s at Indsco, it took the form of diverging roles of husbands and wives, with the wife erecting an exclusionary barrier over her own technical domain of home and children and getting angry if the husband threatened her power there. She might want the husband to do some of the work of the household, but she also made clear that she was the boss, a pattern in several marriages of relatively young managers whom I observed at home. Such a choice set a vicious cycle in motion: The more the husband was away from the family system (through fatigue, travel, work absorption, or excitement the wife did not share), the more the family operated without him, closing him out or punishing him on reentry for his absence, thereby intensifying any desire he had to get away. Wives who began to move in this direction were those who felt helpless to do anything meaningful with respect to his career because there was no direct way to make a contribution; they then tended to confirm the fact that they could not make a contribution by, in some cases, becoming drains on their husbands and detriments to their success.

Attempts at inclusion were limited by the wife's position on the other side of official organization boundaries. Some who wished to render the kinds of job assistance mentioned earlier in the chapter found that they could do so in only limited and fairly menial ways (such as typing, running errands) that utilized relatively few of their talents and kept them distinctly subordinate. (The routinized tasks available to wives paralleled those menial jobs performed by official women's auxiliaries that spring up around public service organizations like hospitals.) As one husband indicated, "It's hard to use wives' skills even if they are highly educated because they can't learn enough details of the job." This narrowed the wife's choice of roles enough that many women gave up the assistant's role for that of hostess, in which they could have an independent territory, at least, that they could manage and be praised for.

But there were also those ambitious wives who refused to believe they could be left behind, who thought they could remain included in their husbands' jobs by dint of their own effort. One young wife said determinedly: "I don't feel that travel is a threat to our marriage. Indsco is no threat. What he doesn't tell me, I find out about myself. I go to his desk and read everything on it. *This chicken is going to learn.* I'm going to learn and know every aspect from A to Z. There's no such thing as an F in this school. When he comes home, it's bringing Indsco to me. I'm entitled to two hours of his time myself for me to learn." In reply, a more experienced Indsco wife said: "You can read, but you won't learn everything that your husband will. It's a unique experience." Retorted the first: "That's the way you interpret it; I might not." The second answered flatly: "You can't do it."

Tensions around inclusion/exclusion were translated into anger at the company for keeping the wives so separate and uninformed and for so constraining the wives' options for involvement. Those lavish social events to which wives were invited were seen as meaningless "bribes": "They're getting the little wife out of the kitchen for an evening so she won't feel left out," one wife said sarcastically. On the other hand, an experimental attempt to run an educational program for wives and husbands in one unit, part of a research effort, revealed how little wives felt it took to make them feel included. Four wives wrote: "Watching our husbands exercising the skills they have learned bridged the gap of corporate man and family man. Participating in some of the tasks that our husbands are involved in daily was very valuable. The entire experience enabled us to help them to cope with the intellectual, emotional, and physical demands made on them. It succeeded in bringing the company and its functions closer to us and helped to make us feel that we, too, are a part of Industrial Supply Corporation. When a wife is included, the corporation may not seem so large. All of this can result in nothing less than a wonderful sense of sharing between husband and wife in relation to what our men are doing all day, five days a week." Despite the wives' enthusiasm and increased commitment to Indsco, however, this event was not repeated, and their exclusion returned.

THE MANAGERIAL PHASE:

HANDLING INSTRUMENTALITY/SENTIMENTALITY

As a husband moved up the managerial ladder and became enmeshed in company politics, the wife's role with respect to the social network formed by the organization loomed larger, and she faced the issue of charting a course between instrumentality and sentimentality in her dealings with other people around Indsco. Choices revolved around the degree to which authenticity and feeling in relationships were subordinated to deliberate image manufacture and manipulation for political advantage.

In this phase, wives also became a large consideration in company policy, and the issue of whether wives would be judged as part of their husbands' evaluations began to be raised. Though Indsco had no formal wife-screening process, informally information about wives formed part of the scuttlebutt surrounding managers. Such a process seemed almost unavoidable, even though, as Wilbert Moore pointed out in *The Conduct of the Corporation,* "moral shades grow darker when wives have to meet tests" because judging the wife muddles competence criteria for the man. Harry Levinson, an organizational psychiatrist, justified wife-scrutiny this way: "When a man comes to an organization, he is likely to be a family man. The organization takes little official notice of that fact. . . . Yet if the man is in managerial ranks, before he advances very far in some companies or governmental units, his wife will be judged just as he is being judged. . . . Some will object that it is unfair to evaluate a man's wife. He, not she, is being employed. As a matter of fact, when a man has a responsible leadership post, *for all practical purposes both he and his wife are employed.*" [15] [Italics mine]

Indsco wives of middle managers and top divisional managers were aware of the decisions highlighted by William Whyte's "organizational man" studies; at a certain point in their husbands' climb to the top, wives realized that friendships were no longer a personal matter but had business implications.[16] Social professionalism set in. The political implications of what had formerly been personal or sentimental choices became clear. Old friendships might have to be put aside because the organizational situation makes them inappropriate, as in the case of one officer husband who let his wife know it would no longer be seemly to maintain a social relationship with a couple to whom they had previously been very close because the first husband now far outranked the second. The public consequences of relationships made it difficult for some wives to have anything but a superficial friendship with anyone in the corporate social network. Yet, since so much of their time was consumed by company-related entertainment, they had little chance for other friendships, and reported considerable loneliness. A few wives complained about other costs to instrumentalism in relationships: having to entertain in their homes people they did not like and would not otherwise have invited, the need to be consistently cheerful and ready to be on display. Duplicity in relationships was one result.

The tightly controlled social network of wives that can evolve around a corporation was well documented by Whyte and other critics in the 1950s. Whyte, for example, identified a number of "rules" guiding the behavior of wives of "organization men": do not invite superiors in rank before they invite you; do not talk shop gossip with the other wives; do not turn up at the office; never get drunk at a company party; do not be too outstanding, too good; blend with the group; do not get too chummy with wives of associates your husband might pass on the way up. One woman complained in *McCall's* in 1958 about the oppression of company-oriented social life: friendships that had to be based on status rather than attraction; the lack of privacy in the company community, in which "every purchase, every remark, every action was dissected over the telephone or the bridge table." Several management consultants reported instances in which wives of top executives antagonistic to another man's wife were able to hurt the man's career through their husbands. The picture men hold of the kinds of wives who could hurt a husband's company or career was also made clear. A study of the attitudes of 300 top executives toward management wives identified the following kinds of wives as troublemakers: the "shrew" who made a man unhappy at home, the "show-off" in front of other wives, or those who pushed their husbands to advance too fast, discussed company business inappropriately, were too outspoken or critical, or who implied that they ran the company. The benefits that could accrue to a husband's career because of the connections made by a wife were also made apparent.[17]

There were a number of reports of unfavorable comments about wives who failed to conform or fit in at Indsco, although no one admitted outright that wives' behavior affected husbands' careers. The wife seemed more important in field locations in smaller towns, where the corporate network might in fact become a closed social community. But all wives, even those living in the large and rather anonymous suburbs surrounding corporate headquarters, had to face the issue of how far to trade sentimentality for instrumentality. Some wives made instrumentality into a way of life—at least as seen by others, for part of the talent of such people was to retain the pretense of sentiment even in the most instrumental of dealings. Having operated politically in the rise of their husbands, they then claimed the right to "rule" the wives' network, standing, like the wives of ambassadors in the foreign service,[18] at the peak of a system of protocol that awarded them deference and gave them the right to scrutinize and comment on the lifestyle and manners of other wives. In exchange for helping their husbands, they demanded political influence. Instrumentality gave them an arena in which to wield power, even at the cost of superficiality, loneliness, and duplicity. Yet it was to gain public importance, something not possible in the technical phase or without a career of their own.

To choose sentiment, on the other hand, might mean opting out, a choice ill-afforded by those wives whose support and satisfaction were tied to their husbands' successes. Even for those desiring authenticity and feeling in their relationships, however, pure sentiment was no longer possible. Awareness of the operation of the social network meant that a degree of calculated choice had to enter into even fully sentimental ties. Wives and husbands alike could protest the unfairness of social network influences in career mobility, as many did; here wives were adamant in wishing they could live their own lives apart from social scrutiny. A few commented that the insidiousness of the gossip network in this respect lay in its insulation: gossip and gossip-carriers could not be confronted directly, since, in the official system, they were presumed not to exist.

THE INSTITUTIONAL PHASE:
HANDLING PUBLICNESS/PRIVATENESS

It is one of the prevailing ironies of modern corporate life that the closer to the top of the organization, the more traditional and non-"modern" does the system look. As Max Weber noted, at this point more charismatic, symbolic, and "non-rational" elements come into play.[19] At the top—and especially in interaction with its environment—the organization is most likely to show strong elements of a personal, familistic system imbued with ritual, drawing on traditional behavior modes, and overlaid with symbolism. The irony stems from the fact that it is the top level that prescribes routine and impersonality— the absence of particularism and familism—for the rest of the organization. The modern organization formally excludes the family from participation in organizational life and excludes family ties as a basis for organizational position, even to the extent of anti-nepotism rules. Yet, at the top the wife may come into the picture as a visible member of the husband's "team"; she may be given a position and functions (and, in some cases, may even jump over qualified employees in taking on an official, paid, executive position).[20] The wife who is excluded below may be included at the top, as part of the diplomatic apparatus of the corporation. And she has little freedom to refuse partici-pation.

The dilemma that can confront people at this level is the issue of public-ness/privateness. Both husband and wife can be made into public figures, with no area of life remaining untinged with responsibilities for the company. Here, as Wilbert Moore said, "The man, and his wife, simply cannot divest themselves of corporate identification. Their every activity with persons out-side the immediate family is likely to be tinged with a recognition of the man's position. He represents the company willy-nilly. His area of privacy, and that of his wife, is very narrowly restricted." [21] One rising young Indsco executive felt that the following had to be considered the "modern risks" of corporate vice presidential and presidential jobs: traveling 80 percent of the time, get-ting shot at or kidnapped by radicals, prostituting yourself to customers, and opening your private life to scrutiny.

The higher executive's work spills over far beyond the limits of a working day, as we saw in Chapter 3. [22] There may be no distinction between work and leisure. Activities well out of the purview of the organization's goals and de-fined as pleasure for other people (golf club memberships, symphony atten-dance, party-giving) are allowable as business expenses on income tax returns because the definition of what is "business" becomes so broad and non-specific. People entertain one another on yachts or over long, lavish lunches—all in an attempt to mutually obligate, to create personal relations that will give someone an inside track when it comes to more formal negotiations. When-ever "selling" is a part of the organization's relations with its environment and sufficient sums of money rest on each deal, those who sell tend to offer gifts (tickets to a sports event, dinners at fancy restaurants, expensive pen and pen-cil sets) to those who buy, trying to bind the others beyond the limits of a ratio-nal contractual relationship. Entertaining in the home with the wife as hostess is especially binding, since it appears to be a more personal offering not given to all, sets up a social obligation, implicates others, and also calls on ancient and traditional feelings about the need to reward hospitality.

Fusion of business and private life also occurs around longer-term rela-tionships. At the top, all friendships may have business meaning. Business relations can be made because of social connections. (One unlikely merger be-tween two companies in very different fields was officially said to result from one company's need for a stock exchange listing held by the other, but off the record it was known to have been brought about by the friendship of the two presidents and their wives.) Charitable and community service activities, where the wife's role is especially pivotal, may generate useful business and political connections. Wives may meet each other through volunteer work and bring their husbands into contact, with useful business results. Stratification of the volunteer world paralleling class and ethnic differentiation in the society ensures that husbands and wives can pinpoint the population with which they desire connections by an appropriate choice of activity. As one chief executive wife wrote, "Any public relations man worth his salt will recognize the corporate wife as an instrument of communication with the community far more sincere and believable than all the booze poured down the press to gain their favor." [23]

The importance of the wife stems not only from her own skills and activities (which could be, and are, performed by paid employees) but also from the testimony her behavior provides, its clue to the character and personal side of her husband. The usefulness of this testimony, in turn, is derived from unique aspects of top leadership. Image, appearance, background, and likability are all commodities traded at the top of the system, where actors are visible and where they put pressure on one another to demonstrate trustworthiness, as Chapter 3 argued. Farther down a hierarchy, jobs can be broken down into component skills and decisions about people and jobs made on the basis of ability to demonstrate those skills. At the top, decisions about people are not so easy or mechanical; they rest on personal factors to a degree perhaps much greater than systems themselves officially admit. The situations that a corporation president or a president of a country face are not routine and predictable; indeed, constituents are less interested in their handling of routine matters than in their capacities for the unexpected. So there is no test except a vague one: Is this person trustworthy? Even questions about philosophy and intelligence are proxies for trust.

Furthermore, the capacities of an organization itself are unknown and cannot be reduced precisely either to history or to a set of facts and figures. Thus, the character of its leaders can become a critical guide to making a decision about a future relationship with it: whether to invest, to donate funds, to allow it into the community, to provide some leeway in the regulation of its activities. Indsco was always concerned about character in its managers. Company newspapers from field locations routinely stressed church leadership in articles about individual managers, and "integrity" and "acceptance of accountability" appeared on the list of eleven traits that must be possessed by candidates for officer level jobs. Disclosures of corrupt practices by other companies in the mid-1970s enhanced Indsco's concerns about public respectability. Whereas, at lower levels of the organization, there was a tendency to formalize demands, to create routinized job descriptions, to ensure continuity of functioning by seeing to it that the occupant did not make over the job in his own image, and to exclude as much as possible of the personal and emotional life of the worker, close to the top, opposite pressure prevailed. Those with whom leaders entered into relationships looked for the private person behind the role and for the qualities and capacities that could not be encompassed by a job description but on which they must bet when deciding to trust the leader or the organization. Here's where the wives are important.

One way leaders can offer glimpses of their private beings is by bringing along their wives, by inviting others into their homes, and by making sure that their wives confirm the impression of themselves they are trying to give. By meeting in social circumstances, by throwing open pieces of private life for inspection, leaders try to convey their taste and their humanity. Wives, especially, are the carriers of this humanity and the shapers of the image of the private person. Of course, to the extent that social events and "informal" occasions are known to communicate an image for the purposes of making appropriate relationships, they may come to be as carefully managed and rationally calculated as any production task within the organization. The public relations department might even stage-manage the performance of the leader and his wife; when Dollie Ann Cole, wife of a General Motors president, wrote that p.r. departments no longer tell the wife what to wear and what to say, she made it explicit that they once did: ". . . a new day has dawned. Corporate wives no longer ask the public relations office what charity they should work with or whether they can debate for a cause on a local or national radio or television show—or even who is coming for dinner." [24]

The wife is thus faced with an added task at the boundary of the public and the private: to make an event seem personal that is instead highly ritualized and contrived. She must recognize also the meanings conveyed by small acts (who sits next to whom, how much time she and her husband spend with each person, the taste implied by objects in the home, how much she drinks, who seem to be the family friends) and manage even small gestures with extreme self-consciousness, as one high-level wife at Indsco recalled she did at managers' meetings: "I had to be very careful to be invariably cordial, friendly, to remember everyone's names—and then to stay away. If I was too involved with someone, it would look like I was playing favorites; that would set up waves in highly inappropriate ways. Some of the young wives were terrified, but there was only so much I could do because I had other things to worry about."

Private life thus becomes penetrable and not very private at the top. Wives face the demand to suppress private beliefs and self-knowledge in the interest of public appearance. As an instrument of diplomacy and a critical part of her husband's image, the corporate wife must often hide her own opinions in order to preserve a united front, play down her own abilities to keep him looking like the winner and the star. The women's intelligence and superior education—assets when the men looked for wives—give way to other, more social traits, such as gregariousness, adaptability, attractiveness, discretion, listening ability, and social graces.

Thus, unless serving as a surrogate for the husband, voicing opinions was not easily allowed of corporate wives at Indsco, like those political wives who must beware of outshining their husbands. An aide to Eleanor McGovern spoke of the contradictory pressures on a candidate's wife: to be able to give the speech when he can't make it but to shut her mouth and listen adoringly when he is there. Indeed, Eleanor was told to stop looking so good when she started getting better press notices than George. Abigail McCarthy recalled the anxiety she felt about how words would affect her husband's prospects: "After every interview, I lay awake in a black nightmare of anxiety, fearful that I had said something which would do Gene irreparable harm." [25] Betty Ford became an object of controversy (and of admiration) precisely because she violated these rules of the game and refused to distort her private life. Yet, wives of upper management at Indsco felt they did not have that luxury, even though they characterized the pressure to suppress independent opinions as "nonsense" and "frustrating." Not everyone complained. One wife reported that she was proud of never having unburdened herself, even to a confidante, and never having forgotten her public role throughout her husband's career.

Stresses, choices, and dilemmas in the institutional phase, then, center around the tension between the public and the private. If wives at the top gained public recognition, they also lost private freedoms. The emotional pressure this entailed was too much for some wives, as literature in the corporate-wives-as-victims tradition made clear; but it should be pointed out, too, that emotional breakdowns and secret deviances could also reflect defiant independence, unobtainable in any other way under constraining role definitions. The wishes expressed by wives in this position were of two kinds. Some women said that if they were going to be used by the company anyway, they would like the opportunity to do a real job, exercise real skills—by which they meant take on official areas of responsibility. Others wanted merely to be able to carve out more areas of privacy and independence in an otherwise public existence.

IMPLICATIONS: THE ORGANIZATION AND THE WIFE

There is much disagreement, among social scientists as well as Indsco
employees and families, about the importance of wives to the organization or
to their husbands' careers. Some writers have commented that a denial system
operates to minimize attention to the contribution made by wives to their successful husbands. David Riesman noted that it was a male trait to claim individual credit for achievements and to forget the infrastructure that helped
make them possible. Hanna Papanek argued that wifely collaboration in a husband's career was not openly acknowledged because of what she called the
"fragility of male self-esteem." [26] But aside from any such masculinist biases,
there were also organizational pressures to minimize the actual or reported
role of wives in Indsco. Above all, the organization prided itself on "fairness,"
and its legitimacy among employees rested on belief in the attempt to create a
just system that rewarded merit, even though it was known that internal politicking could not be completely eliminated. To admit to what one wife called
"influence through the pillow" on decisions, or to acknowledge that someone
other than an official employee was engaged in the company's work, would be
to pose a challenge to legitimating ideologies. Thus, wives are relegated to the
background and often accept this place. One wife of a high-ranking Indsco executive reported that both she and other executive wives of her acquaintance
tended to deny that they played a part in their husbands' work—even when
they knew they had been influential.

With respect to the corporation itself, the issue of the wife's importance is
inextricably bound up with the notion that anything she does is voluntary, a
matter of personal choice. Indeed, there *is* a degree of choice built into the
roles wives play. There may be a wide range of options about when and how
the wife participates, many of them negotiated privately between husband and
wife. Many of the things a wife does would simply go undone if she were not
there to perform them; organizations would be unlikely to replace most of a
wife's services with that of a paid employee. The seeming voluntariness of the
decisions of a wife to participate in her husband's career, along with the facts
that some men do manage without a wife and that some wives have independent careers of their own, all help organizations to view the informal "women's
auxiliary" as nothing more than a luxury. It is seen as a peripheral part of the
system somewhere on the other side of its boundaries, sometimes helpful,
sometimes a nuisance, but there not because the organization wants it to be
but because employees have lives and relationships beyond the organization.
The voluntary nature of the wife's involvement is also supported by a system
in which, as Jessie Bernard put it, women are expected to do things out of

love, duty, or personal loyalty; [27] in short, they are seen as perpetual volunteers.

But examination of what the organization does in fact demand of wives—either indirectly, through husbands' job conditions, or directly—makes clear that there are degrees of voluntariness. Organizations themselves may vary in the extent of the demands and constraints they place on wives. It is possible to identify a number of conditions that tend to activate an organization's use of wives, especially as diplomats and committed advocates. There are five circumstances most likely to implicate wives in their husbands' careers and their husbands' organizations: (1) *In small cities and towns.* If the organization plays a major role in the community in which it is located, if it is a major employer, it needs good community relations. There is also a tendency for organization leaders to be public figures in the town and wives to become known. (2) *In political situations.* When the organization (or leaders) needs to win continual approval from constituents, to win votes or to raise funds from donors or to secure favorable legislation, its diplomatic apparatus becomes important. Wives of top politicians have major roles to play. (3) *In "total institutions."* If the organization is highly absorptive of the lives of members and is more than a nine-to-five involvement, as in the military or for staffs of boarding schools or small-town colleges, wives become involved for two reasons. The boundary between work and non-work life becomes fuzzy, with the organization encompassing much of members' lives; and the greater legitimacy needs of such demanding organizations make it more important to secure the support of families. A survey of wives of headmasters of private schools, for example, showed how much more constraining the wife's role was, how much more she had to do, in boarding schools (the total institution situation) compared with day schools. [28] (4) *In controversy.* Where the organization is controversial or makes controversial decisions, diplomacy, especially as performed by unpaid volunteers like wives, is important. (5) *In entrepreneurial climates and times of change.* When the organization is growing, transforming itself, or facing a rapidly changing environment, it can make use of new connections made socially with other systems; it needs to count on the total dedication and achievement drives of managers (and therefore on the motivation, understanding, assistance, and support of their families); and it can benefit from people with ties to the community who can provide useful information. Wives of entrepreneurs often play critical roles in their husbands' businesses.

Whether or not the wife is important in the conduct of the corporation, however, the corporation is central in the conduct of her life. The behavior of wives, and the marital issues that arise, must be seen in the way we are viewing the behavior of all corporate workers: as a function of their location in the system, as a response to the role constraints within which they operated in the Industrial Supply Corporation of the 1970s.

There are also some larger issues raised by the situation of corporate wives. Through them it is possible to see a side of corporate life usually kept hidden and unexamined: the operation of corporate diplomacy, the personalism and familism remaining at the top of corporate bureaucracies, processes of image creation and image management in career politics, and the existence of a "shadow organization" outside the official boundary marked by paid employment but making random and occasional contributions. Here we see some of the human and social factors that limit the full operation of bureaucratic rationality. Clearly wives are not nearly as involved or central or critical in an organization's functioning as are paid workers, but the fact that they are peripheral does not make them irrelevant.

The very ambivalence of corporations toward the "wife problem" (William Whyte's label) indicates a fundamental tension in social life between the demands of organizational work and the pulls of family, at least in individualistic societies. Is the wife a helper to be embraced, or a danger to be minimized? Is she an unpaid worker, or a separate reality irrelevant to the organization—an independent person on whom the organization has no claims? From the corporation's perspective, is the family, the intimate tie, to be included in the organization to make more committed members, or is it to be discouraged, kept away, so that participants will feel no competing pulls? [29] Whose interests do the "women's auxiliaries" serve—their own, their husbands', the corporation's? What responsibilities do organizations have when their policies and practices impact on the family outside? These questions cannot be answered by default, by pretenses that wives are not part of the system. Issues remain: the nature of corporate responsibility; the limits on corporate greed—in this case, the organization's tendency to swallow up its members and consume them and their families.

From the perspective of individuals and *their* welfare, there are other problems organizations can address. [30] Some require delicate balancing: How to minimize wives' feelings of exclusion while permitting them independence. How to reduce the stresses of publicness and reduce image pressures. How to give families a voice in policies affecting them. Whether job pressures drive wedges between husbands and wives, and how these can be modified. How to help involve wives in husbands' work (and vice versa) without making them subordinated assistants. How to redefine success so as to minimize political manipulation and instrumentality. How to create positive relations between the women inside and the women outside the organization. Whether to compensate professional and managerial women for their lack of a "wife." As pressure mounts for more explicit national family policy, questions of the impact of forms of employment on family life cannot be avoided.

Perhaps the atomization of contemporary family relations—the desire of each member for an independent domain—will solve these problems for the corporation by reducing the population of those willing to fit the corporate wife mold. Already, there were signs that women married to Indsco men no longer deserved to be known only as "wives" in the conventional sense; their primary identities lay elsewhere. But it would be a mixed blessing indeed if the resolution to the dilemma of fusion or separateness in the work-family relationship always had to be resolved in favor of separateness.

Part III

Structures and Processes

6

Opportunity

General question to an Indsco meeting:
  "How do you spend your time?"
Answer from a manager:
  "We worry about our careers a lot. Don't we, guys?"
            —Exchange at Industrial Supply Corporation

Success is counted sweetest
By those who ne'er succeed.
            —Emily Dickinson, "Success Is Counted Sweetest"

In order that people may be happy in their work, these three things
are needed: They must be for it. They must not do too much of it.
And they must have a sense of success in it.
            —John Ruskin, *Pre-Raphaelitism*

It was hard for success to mean anything else but movement in a large hierarchical organization like Indsco. The incentives were all for mobility. Long service or good continuing performance in one job took a distinct back seat. It was hard to raise the issue of alternative definitions of success.

Good work got a person a salary and the standard 15 percent in benefits. But there were upper limits on pay within a job classification, and after a time, good performance could be rewarded only through promotions. Once in a while, the idea of incentive payments came up, something strongly favored by exempt personnel (184 out of 205 respondents on the sales survey said they would like such a system because it would reward people more appropriately and improve motivation), but a satisfactory system was never designed, and the idea was dropped. A salary administrator said, "Money is not a motivator, anyway. It's just a way for the company to cut its losses by ensuring that people do their job at all. The reward we really control is the ability to promote." This was one of the reasons Indsco began a career planning process in the late 1960s: to openly encourage aspirations for "career" growth among exempt employees.

Long service also meant very little, if it was not coupled with rising status and authority. The twenty-five-year watch and luncheon on retiring hardly matched the recognition that came automatically with higher-grade jobs. A change in title, a promotion, was a significant event in company culture, one that would be duly noted in newsletters and internal communications; continuing to do the same thing well over time seemed hardly to deserve anyone's notice. Many employees believed that more time in their job and more knowledge of company operations should earn them a greater voice, more autonomy, or more control over their own function. But given the labyrinthine complexities of the corporate bureaucracy, there was no way to make that autonomy or participation real as long as people remained in the same job classification; they would have to be upgraded. It took a move from Statistical Clerk I to Statistical Clerk II to win the right to send out correspondence without the approval of a supervisor. And given the centralization of power and absence of vehicles for employee participation in decisions, a greater voice really required moving up through the management ranks. There was no way to value increasing wisdom if it did not come with increasing official authority.

Some jobs, furthermore, lost their meaning and became, instead, stepping-stones on the path to upper management. Sales was the prime example of a management supply function, much to the annoyance of those who wanted to create a "professional sales force" and pride in the sales job. "Everyone gets plugged into the same pipe as though they were management candidates," a first-line sales manager said. "All people hired off a campus are evaluated in terms of what kind of manager they will make. Ninety-five percent of them say, 'In five years, I want to be a manager.' That's where the gravy is. And if they don't say it, we'd probably not hire them." Another one complained: "People think they have to move, to progress to gain respect, so even if they love selling, they think they're going to have to move on." If they do not move into management, many salespeople think they have failed. Attempts to upgrade such jobs by giving salespeople their own mobility tracks, like the creation of a "professional sales ladder," were a poor substitute; the ladder was inevitably shorter and the rewards slimmer.

In other functions, too, movement was intimately associated with career progress. The appropriate pathway to the most desirable managerial jobs was to hold a variety of positions across functions for two or three years each, including a stint of service in central headquarters. Depending on the times, the kinds of experience seen as prerequisites for prestigious positions would vary. According to a manager who himself had traveled through several offices and functions: "Some people get pushed into jobs whether they want to or not or whether they have the qualifications, because something is identified as 'that's the job to get in.' Some people fit, some don't, but they've got the job of the week, which changes from year to year. 'I want to be a production manager,' a guy says; then he asks, 'What does a production manager do?' Well, the answer is, he gets experience in operations so he can go on to something else. People want to jump into jobs only so they can jump out as a manager."

Moving around often became an end in itself. There were many organizational benefits to having lots of jobs, as long as the overall direction was upward: more exposure and visibility, the kind of broad view of the organization said to be desired in top executives, the opportunity to build political alliances in many parts of the company through the exchange of favors. Indeed, until the establishment of universal and comprehensive career review and performance appraisal systems in the 1970s, which could feed information about people across functions and units and into central personnel decisions, frequent movement through jobs and locations was one of the best ways (and sometimes the only way) to guarantee being noticed in such a large organization. The chance to move became equivalent to a sign of recognition.

It was not as though alternatives to success-as-climbing-the-corporate-ladder could easily be sustained, when all parts of the system conspired to make even other human values attainable only through mobility. Autonomy and independence, growth and a sense of challenge, the chance to learn—all were earned through increasing hierarchical position. Changing the system, improving the conditions of work, encouraging social action—individual status was a prerequisite to having either the credibility or the clout to work on such goals, at least within the formal system as it was then constituted. And then, organizational rewards aside, career movement also hooked whatever human desire there is for a sense of progress.

Indsco's people got the message: Be promoted or perish. You are not really successful, or you do not mean much to the company, unless you get the chance to move on. Thus, jobs and job categories were evaluated in terms of their advancement prospects, quite apart from job content or actual grade level and salary. Many clerical positions had low status because they led nowhere; sales could attract good people because it promised a route into management. Line management jobs were generally more desirable than staff jobs (except where these were designed as flow-through slots) because they included longer and more varied chains of career opportunity. The manager of a staff function, an organizationally savvy man, turned down a corporate directorship in personnel, despite high pay and elevated title, because it was a dead end. A promising executive, a former accountant whose real interests lay in the human relations, social action, and community service parts of the company, took a technical management position as a division controller (after running a training function and a company-sponsored community improvement project) because it would increase his opportunity to move back into the areas he valued at a higher level. A junior management woman, currently at grade 6, turned down a promotion to grade 9 because, "They were remaking another 6 job into a 9 just for me—but that meant it was still really a 6 in terms of leading anywhere or giving me a chance to grow."

But it is not as though career ladders and paths and tracks had all been clearly identified. One of the problems of such a large corporation was a general lack of clarity for many positions about what should lead where. There was much speculation but little real information. Management had a general sense of what kinds of experience should be necessary for people to move into certain kinds of jobs, and this helped people conceive of their career development in terms of seeking job changes that would put them in a place to win further mobility. Some jobs became generally known as dead ends because no one was ever seen to move from them, not because the job itself did not have possibilities. Corporate staff jobs, for example, were thought to be for nonmovers who had family ties with Indsco. Similarly, high promotion rates from certain positions often came about not because career paths automatically flowed from that position but because the job provided a person with exposure, visibility, and connections. Central headquarters jobs often could have that potential, so people lined up to move to headquarters almost regardless of the nature of the specific opening. People in the same position disagreed among themselves about its place on the organizational career map. Twenty distribution managers identified seven routes to their job, two that seemed to be the path taken by most people, and two that they considered lateral moves. And they imagined that there were three likely and seven rare moves from their job, including one lateral move ("a guy's got poor judgment if he does it"), one demotion, and one lucky double jump (called a "double dipper").

Only a few years earlier had Indsco routinized time-in-grade considerations for promotions, and that was mostly at lower levels and not written anywhere. The career review and planning process was similarly just a few years old, and it did not yet extend below the exempt ranks. Personnel planners, in fact, had never even thought of pathways through and out of nonexempt jobs until affirmative action pressures. The entire system was further complicated by five-year evaluations of the grade and salary level of jobs, which could result in shifts downward or upward and change the picture of what jobs constituted a path. Overlaid on top was the increasing tendency most informants perceived for the corporation to formalize tracks, making some moves (particularly speedy or advantageous ones) even rarer.

The differentiated hierarchical form of Indsco, then, created a structure of opportunity, which in turn defined the ways people perceived themselves and their jobs. The fact and possibility of movement affected attitudes toward work and personal feelings of achievement. Arnold Tannenbaum and colleagues noted this general psychological consequence of hierarchical organizations: "Hierarchy, in American plants at least, represents to many organization members the path of achievement; movement along the hierarchy implies personal success or failure. Thus, hierarchy, which is a basic *organizational* characteristic, has profound *psychological* implications for members." [1] [Italics mine] But mobility also defined more than self-evaluation. Relative opportunity could account for the ways people involved themselves in work.

THE SEDUCTIVENESS OF OPPORTUNITY

Especially advantaged were those people placed on "fast tracks." They were identified as "officer material" or outstanding performers and moved up the ladder faster than the norm. People being fast-tracked were known in company culture as "water walkers," boy or girl "wonders," "high fliers," "one performers," or "superstars." They were given career reviews much more often than usual (every year to eighteen months, as opposed to every three years) and placed in positions that would maximize their exposure. Perhaps five or six out of every fifty people in the exempt category were singled out for such close attention and special observation. It was often denied by vice-presidents that officer material was judged so low down the ranks, but if people asked their managers, they were generally told whether they were on fast tracks. One manager estimated that 90 percent asked. There was a tendency for peers not to talk about it with each other, however, because if they were fast-tracked, they might not want competition, and if they were not, they would not want to admit it. Beyond career reviews and moves, the signs included exposure to top people (e.g., lunch invitations), project assignments to task groups with more senior people, and placements where they really "wore two hats" in the matrix, building more connections because they related to two different functions.

Fast-tracking happened in "strange and devious ways," said one young "water walker." "The first indication was that certain people liked me. They were friendly, knew my name, had personal details. I found myself going to meetings where people I didn't know would say they had heard of me. Then powerful people started offering me jobs and through the back door—pulling me aside, not through channels. Pirating: 'I'd really love to have you on my team; how would you like that?' Then I'd hear through third parties that others think well of me. I'd indicate a desire to do something, and I'd see by the amount of activity how people felt about me. And by how peers respond. Respect? They almost seem to warm up to you regardless. You could see the brown-nosing; others would seem to want to be your friend. Then I looked back over my career and saw that I was the youngest person in my job in the history of the function."

Opportunity bred more of it for the selected few. ("Superstars don't get as many fouls called against them in basketball. People who get all A's sometimes get one when they don't deserve it," said another manager, explaining the greater latitude on fast tracks.) But it also made people in high opportunity positions very sensitive to the organizational politics that would actualize their opportunity. They anticipated their move upward by attuning themselves to what was going on further up the hierarchy. "For a high performer to sustain and grow in this organization is tricky," one said. "There are many pitfalls. It takes timing. Making strong allegiances—the right ones. Being noncommittal sometimes. It's situational. Laying back for a few years and being persistently patient, patiently persistent. You can become a pawn in other people's power struggles if you're not careful. You need humility. You can be rising as a water walker one day and be a bum the next. And what if they put you on the water and you don't walk?"

For those that had it, opportunity was seductive, and it tied self-image close to career progress. Those on the move invested themselves heavily in work and concerned themselves with learning those things that would be useful to them on their journey upward. One young, high-performing sales-man was first interviewed in 1970, when he was 26 and had been with the company three years, and then interviewed again in 1973 and 1975. He saw himself in 1970 as spending two more years in sales, then two getting experi-ence in production, four years as a marketing manager, and then rising to a directorship a few years later. By 1975 the first set of his predictions had come true, even though the pathway had been different, for that year he took on a prestigious job as an assistant manager in a major function at headquar-ters. In 1970 his learning goals all had to do with organizational politics, unlike less mobile peers who were still interested in doing their sales job more effec-tively. He wanted to learn "internal selling" within Indsco, a more compre-hensive understanding of company management, the ability to convey ideas within the company, and the ability to express dissent diplomatically within Indsco. He wanted more participation and involvement, to be asked his opin-ions, to be valued for his ideas. In 1975 he openly admitted that he knew how to be political, how to watch what he said and to whom.

As he moved, he was willing to take on nearly any extra task that would advance his career. He jumped on the bandwagon for new ideas and was known as an innovator. Though critical of the corporate lifestyle and con-cerned about the decreasing time he had to spend with his family (especially because of the longer commute to headquarters), still he woke up many mornings to realize that he had just been dreaming about Indsco. The company was always on his mind. A warm and sociable person who obviously cared about people, he had many relationships inside and outside of the company—some inside who were not as mobile as he—and he made a point of trying to warm up the atmosphere in his headquarters office. Yet, he saw other people as a way to help advance his career, because they could help each other learn and do each other favors. "I can't say I have many friendships here. Just mutual strong business relationships. I talk only business at lunch." Over the years, he seemed to become more work-consumed, more upward-oriented. He was on his way to being a "success."

Aspirations, work commitment, and a sense of organizational responsibility could also be aroused by a dramatic increase in opportunity. (This is the Gerald Ford syndrome; not aspiring to the Presidency until becoming President.) A twenty-year Indsco secretary was upgraded from executive secretary to assistant manager to manager of her function, with a chance, for the first time, to reach higher management positions. Before the promotion, she had never wanted to be anything but a secretary: "I made up my mind very early—I was in junior high school—and I never changed it. I really never thought about another career." She married in her thirties, and when her children were born, work suddenly was less important. It seemed to be the classic "female" pattern. Her explanation was that "being a secretary didn't seem to be a good enough reason for leaving the children. You could pick up being a secretary and put it down and pick it up again, and I had a lot of guilt feelings about leaving them because my contribution to work really didn't mean that much." She might have left the company then if her boss at the time had not planted the first seeds of ambition by deciding she was a good candidate for promotion to assistant manager. At first she was reluctant to accept the job because it meant leaving a solid group of friends, but the excitement of opportunity soon took hold. She pushed her husband to share child care, she reorganized household chores, and her aspirations soared. Her enthusiasm in taking on ever-increasing responsibility, initiating corporate programs in her area, acting as an advocate for opportunities for women and blacks, and seeking education, brought her another promotion after nine months. "Now I'm ambitious, probably overly so. I will probably work twenty more years, and I expect to move at least six grade levels, maybe to vice-president. Isn't that something from me? It's the climate for women now, plus the doing. You know, as you do, you learn you can, so you want to do more." She had been turned around and turned on by her jump in opportunity.

The stuck told a different story. These were the people with low ceilings in their jobs, the people at dead ends. Blocked from movement, lacking opportunity in a system where mobility above all meant success, they made a variety of adjustments to their situation. They related to work, involved themselves in the organization and with its people, very differently from high-opportunity movers.

WHO HITS DEAD ENDS: SOURCES OF LOW OPPORTUNITY

"Stuck" is a relative concept. In hierarchical systems, it has to do with how far one can go in relation to the total system, how much of the system's rewards will increasingly be possible over time, how many more perquisites and privileges of a qualitatively different sort will be added, and how many changes in position and jumps in status are defined as objectively possible. It also has a temporal dimension. Since people are not constantly changing jobs, one only becomes stuck after movement has stopped for a long enough time and the probability of movement has also declined. Age evaluation can help define for people whether or not they are moving quickly, slowly, or not at all, relative to peers in a similar situation. Occasionally, people at Indsco were told rather directly that they had "reached their level" and were in a terminal job. But more often, awareness of being stuck came more indirectly: through seeing the low promotion rate from one's job category, or knowing that there would be no place to go beyond the next job, or by seeing that one was getting "old" in one's position—beyond the average age in that job, or beyond the average number of years of service.

Mobility could be blocked in several ways. The largest category of people among the stuck were those who never had much opportunity to begin with. Low promotion rates, or short ladders and low ceilings in their job category, meant that few expectations were ever created for such jobs to involve movement. Most women clericals, supervisors of office workers, and some exempt staff, especially in personnel functions, were in this situation. The biggest group was certainly the clerical workers. At most, people could hope for a few steps toward more independence and slightly higher pay during a working lifetime, as in a move from Secretary I to Executive Secretary. Until recent attempts to extend career planning to nonexempts, they were not expected to have career goals—or at least no one bothered to ask them. And in many cases, as we saw in Chapter 4, long-term loyalty and single-job stability were encouraged in secretaries.

Among people in such low or blocked mobility jobs, peer and occupational culture was likely to develop around and support the generally lower level of aspirations, concern with security and low-risk activities, and recognition through sociability that reflected adjustments to the stuck situation. But

they were also not necessarily disaffected in terms of organizational participation, since their expectations were low to begin with, and they had an alternative vehicle for involvement provided by the peer culture. (It is interesting
that personnel and organizational development staff, at least, also had a peer
network devaluing mobility: their "professional" organizations.)

The next set of the stuck were the ones who had lost out in the competition. Though they began in positions with mobility prospects, they were
passed over for promotions or moved aside to jobs known to be dead ends.
This happened because of their own lackluster performance (which was rarely
the case, since true incompetents were usually weeded out earlier), or because of political factors like an alliance that turned out to be wrong, or simply
because of the pyramidal squeeze: fewer than the eligible number could keep
moving up. These people had to operate in the midst of an occupational culture of mobility; any network they formed with people in a similar situation
was always a subgroup surrounded by people in the contrasting situation. The
social recognition they substituted for organizational recognition consequently
came not as often from peers inside the company as from people junior to
them (from whom they could elicit respect for superior knowledge or experience) or outside the company (to whom they could represent the organization
or who would not be aware of their comparative status). The reactions of this
group of the stuck often reflected frustrated expectations and were more likely
to be tinged with hostility than those of the first group.

Such people could constitute a considerable problem for the organization,
for they could occupy key positions and be relatively highly paid. They were
often people with seniority who had been valued performers in the past; their
disaffection represented a real cost. There were those within the company
who felt that Indsco had brought this problem on itself by promising too
much, by valuing mobility more than job substance, by ignoring alternatives
to career competitiveness as a value, and by not making real the rewards and
recognition that should come with technical competence itself. "The organization can promise too much. People think they can move to very high levels
when they can't. Indsco needs to tell people earlier that they won't be a vice-
president in fifteen years. Too many people think they can be. But not everyone is a candidate for stardom. People are stacked up on top of each other in
central office jobs because there has been an exodus from the field to get
headquarters experience in order to rise. But they are stagnating there. The
worse problem is, if you don't tell people early enough, you create frustrations
among people in key positions—ten-, twelve-, fifteen-year people at the peak
of their careers. They are *running* the company. And they can be totally
disgruntled by the reality of opportunities."

The last, and smallest, group was stuck even though people had moved into jobs that usually carried opportunity—but they had come through the wrong path. Though they could get into and handle their present job, they lacked the experience, background, attitudes and knowledge, or connections that could lead them any further, and they were now too old or too senior to go back and fill in some of the missing pieces. This was the dilemma, for example, of anyone promoted through the ranks to a managerial job in that function; they were able to manage that function but were ineligible for any other (or higher) management position. This could happen to production workers who made it up to plant manager, to plant workers who became sales trainees, to secretaries who became personnel administrators, or to clerical workers in the sales and marketing division who became customer service representatives. What was more typically a first or early job was for such people likely to be their last or nearly last job. For old plant workers, for example, sales—usually a high opportunity position—was likely to be a dead end. Salespeople were usually college graduates, so it took a great deal of company experience for a production worker to become eligible. But then they were "trainees" at a much older age than the norm and likely to get stuck at a junior level. Many women and minorities in exempt jobs also found themselves in this situation: stuck because they had not come through the usual route or had been placed even though they skipped some of the experience usually required to get into their present position. Their past positions and present skills made them suitable for the job currently held, but did not constitute "preparation" for the future jobs that could unfold from it. A black man, for example, who had been a stockbroker and was hired into a personnel function, with which he had experience, was promoted into a managerial position where he supervised people with a technical background that he lacked, and it was clear to him and those around him that he would not be able to go any further in a line management position. A woman went through the secretarial ranks into a good exempt job managing administration for a group of clerical workers, and she wanted to go further in the employee relations function. But she had no plant experience—then considered a prerequisite for higher level jobs—and all of the plant jobs were several grades below her present level.

People in this last type of situation were frustrated because their expectations of opportunity were simultaneously aroused and capped. Many thought that the company felt it had done enough by just getting them into a good professional or managerial job, since people like them usually did not have this chance. But they had been hoping to go even further. Thus, they could share some of the disaffection of the competition losers. At the same time, some of them exhibited the self-doubts about competence that often characterized people who had always been in low-mobility job categories; after all, they lacked some official "credential" that would get them further than their present job. A few people in this situation found their social recognition by identifying with nonexempts or minorities, turning to them for social support or championing their cause. Others did not take this value position, yet still retained an attitudinal framework characteristic of low-opportunity personnel, such as low-risk, security orientations.

Though the group of people blocked because they had come through a wrong route was small in relative numbers, it was critical for the organization in other respects. These were generally the people who reflected whatever commitment the company had to improving opportunities for the disadvantaged—for women and minorities, for clerical and factory workers. The difficulties encountered by the few people promoted from low-opportunity jobs as clericals or factory workers in going any further pointed to a major difficulty of the large corporate organization: that the blue-collar and clerical ranks came to constitute castes with rigid barriers from which mobility was really not possible under the present system. There was just enough openness and an occasional example to keep the illusion that even people in low-status jobs or without all of the right credentials could eventually work their way up, but the professional or management post that represented the way out of the low-mobility job cluster was likely to come with its own very low ceiling.

The three ways in which opportunity could be blocked confronted people with slightly different organizational situations, particularly in terms of how many of their peers faced the same set of circumstances. (Fig. 6–1 summarizes the contrast.) But many of the alternatives for responding to low opportunity were similar regardless of organizational level or job category. People who were stuck could respond with a number of forms of disengagement, substitute social recognition, and conservative resistance.

FIGURE 6–1

Types of Dead Ends and Their Consequences

Source of Opportunity Blockage	Amount of Disaffection	Common Alternative for Recognition
low ceiling occupation	low	peers
individual "failure" in high ceiling occupation	high	outsiders
wrong route to high ceiling occupation (lack background for further progress)	moderate	subordinates or less advantaged

DISENGAGEMENT

One way that people coped with a lack of opportunity was to disengage. They wrote off the organization or their career as something to be involved with or care about for anything short of strictly instrumental (monetary) reasons. This could take the form of depressed aspirations, low commitment, or non-responsibility.

Depressed Aspirations

There is much evidence that people have low aspirations when they think their chances for mobility are low. Research on auto workers, for example, has documented their very limited interest in or hope for promotion in response to notoriously poor mobility opportunities. In one company there was one foreman's job opening a year for 120 workers; in the plant observed by Ely Chinoy for *Automobile Workers and the American Dream,* there were ten to twelve a year for 6,000 workers. In assembly line plants, furthermore, there were relatively few skilled jobs to which the unskilled could aspire, and there were no natural ladders of promotion. Men were hired for a job and expected to stay with it. In such a situation, when workers hoped for "better" jobs, they tended to mean those that were easier or cleaner rather than those that advanced them in the hierarchy. Similarly, Henry Purcell's study of workers in three meat-packing plants showed them to be negative about their chances for advancement, and many of them denied that they would even *want* a promotion. Surveys, too, have found a correlation between negative mobility perceptions and low aspirations.[2]

Aspirations are not necessarily low to begin with, but they may be lowered as people encounter the realities of their job situation. Things may become evaluated as less desirable as they become less likely. This was clear among clerical workers at Industrial Supply, and especially among the women, whose objective opportunities were much more limited than those of the men. One source of evidence was an attitude survey of nonexempts in one Indsco unit, for which G. Homall collected the data.[3] It demonstrated the connection between realistic expectations and desires. Men's mean score on an overall measure of motivation to be promoted was significantly higher than women's[4]—but so were the men's objective prospects for advancement. There were more than twice as many women as men in the clerical ranks of this unit of Indsco (reflected also in the numbers in the sample: eighty-eight women and twenty-three men), and the men were clustered in jobs like accounting clerk that opened up into the exempt ranks and eventually into management. The women were in lower-level clerical jobs or junior secretarial positions, where ladders were short, ceilings low, and the chance for a move into exempt status extremely low. The men were also more likely than the women to be young, to have been with the company less than five years, and to have even held a supervisory position—all indications that there was opportunity ahead of them. The men reported a greater amount of encouragement from superiors to improve and to advance, and a greater company awareness of their contributions. (See Table 6–1.) And they generally saw themselves as acquiring more skills from their jobs than the women, especially in areas critical for promotion such as report writing, budget preparation, leading others, calculating and estimating, setting goals and objectives, and motivating and persuading.

But the depressing of aspirations in the face of realistically lower opportunity was even clearer in ratings of both the desirability and the likelihood of thirty possible outcomes of a promotion. The men's scores on both desirability and likelihood tended to be higher, especially on those items having to do with increased responsibility and managerial tasks. (There were no significant differences between the sexes on those items having to do with certain social aspects of a job.) But when I looked at the comparison of women's scores on desirability and likelihood on those same items, I saw that, first, women rated *all* of them above the median on desirability and tended to see *all* of them as *more desirable than likely.* It was as though women's perceptions of the lower likelihood that any of them would come true made them rate those outcomes as less desirable than did the men, for whom they were more realistically likely to happen. The greatest gap between sense of likelihood and desirability

TABLE 6–1

Situations Reflecting Opportunity Differences for Men and Women Nonexempt Personnel at Indsco

	Men (N = 23)	Women (N = 88)	
Proportion under 25 years old	44%	30%	
Proportion with the company less than five years	65%	40%	
Proportion who have *ever* held a supervisory position	57%	20%	
Mean rating on scale of 1–9 of:			
Amount of encouragement received from superiors to improve	7.62	6.20	$p < .05$
Amount of encouragement received from superiors to advance	7.18	6.32	$p < .05$
Amount of company awareness of one's contributions	7.15	6.10	$p < .05$

(*Figures reported with the permission of G. Homall*)

was in those items most clearly reflecting promotions into management (the opportunity to lead others; making decisions on promotions, raises, and terminations; and independent thought and action). It was highly unrealistic for women clericals during the time of the survey to aspire to such positions. On the other hand, the smallest gap between likelihood and desirability occurred for those items having to do with personal characteristics, which were much more under the control of the worker herself (being objective; being outspoken; being aggressive and competitive; getting additional training). There was also a key to the job opportunities the women faced in their response to the promotional outcomes that had something to do with the degree of occupational segregation and limited opportunities for women at Indsco. They saw it as *much* more desirable than likely, and close to a nonexistent possibility, that they have opposite sex co-workers—meaning, in essence, that they moved out of a "female"-labeled, sex-segregated, and thus low-status job. At the same time, they saw as more *likely* than desirable (indicating their fears about what would really happen) that they would have an opposite sex boss, have difficulty being accepted by others at a new level, and have co-workers of the same sex. (See Table 6–2.)

TABLE 6–2

Comparison between Ratings of Desirability versus Likelihood of Possible Outcomes of a Promotion by Nonexempt Women

(Rated on 9-point scales, with 1 the least and 9 the most desirable or likely)

Items reflecting managerial tasks	Desirability (Mean score)	Likelihood (Mean score)
Responsibility	7.18	6.41
Decision-making	7.23	6.45
Job not predictable, routine	6.93	6.26
Opportunity to lead others	6.92	5.17
Independent thought, action	7.54	6.52
Being outspoken	5.71	5.26
Being aggressive, competitive	5.95	5.36
Getting additional training	6.23	5.77
Being objective	6.64	6.44
Making decisions on promotions, raises, terminations	5.53	4.10
Items reflecting occupational segregation		
Having opposite sex co-workers	5.64	2.25
Having an opposite sex boss	6.65	7.63
Having difficulty being accepted as an equal by others at the new level	4.12	4.53
Having same sex co-workers	4.44	4.92

(Figures reported with the permission of G. Homall)

Low Commitment

Those with low opportunity may also be less committed to the organization or to their work in general. A common research finding is that people at the upper levels of organizations tend routinely to be more motivated, involved, and interested in their jobs than those at lower levels. But even within similar ranks, upward mobility has tended to be associated with identification with the organization. Managers who experienced maximum career mobility in one study were generally more strongly committed to the organization than the less mobile.[5]

And, of course, a number of classic studies of blue-collar men have found that work commitment is low under conditions of low opportunity. Robert Dubin was led to conclude that work was not a "central life interest" of industrial workers. Chinoy found that almost four-fifths of the auto workers he studied had at some time contemplated leaving; they dreamed of escape into their own small business. They emphasized leisure and consumption, as women are said to do, rather than work. There is other evidence that the "interrupted career" pattern is true for men as well as women; blue-collar men leave organizations to start small businesses (but leaving to run a family is like gaining the independence of a small business, too), then return when, as is statistically likely, the business fails.[6]

As measured on my Indsco sales force survey, commitment was unrelated to salary or organizational status. (Appendix I describes the derivation of the commitment measure.) Respondents with the highest grade positions and in the highest salary category were found in nearly equal numbers in the highest and lowest quartiles of the sample on commitment. But commitment did show some relationship to years of company service, when we compare those above and below the median with respect to their commitment scores, as Table 6–3 indicates. Although the data are cross-sectional rather than longitudinal, they constitute some evidence that people might go through a cycle of responses to

TABLE 6–3

Commitment to Indsco of Sales Force Sample, by Years of Company Service

Years Served:	½–1 (N = 12)	1–2 (N = 20)	2–5 (N = 27)	5–10 (N = 35)	10–20 (N = 61)	more than 20 (N = 22)
Proportion above median on commitment	58.4%	60%	29.6%	45.7%	52.5%	63.7%
Proportion below median on commitment	41.6%	40%	70.3%	52.4%	47.6%	36.3%

the corporate environment, responses bearing a plausible relationship to opportunity. It is possible to speculate that people allow a certain amount of time after joining the organization before they develop strong feelings pro or con; after about a year of service, opportunities are perceived and commitment rises accordingly; but then, when approaching five years, commitment falls sharply, reflecting disillusionment and violated expectations. After the five-year period, those with low commitment may have left the company; those who remain may have made peace with their opportunity, settling for whatever they have, and their average commitment scores go up.

To the extent that commitment is a function of opportunity, there were signs of lower work involvement among people at dead ends in Indsco. For one thing, they tended to talk more often and more openly about life outside. A personnel specialist who had gone as far as he could in a staff job, with no prospects of moving into management, talked about giving priority to his wife's career and leaving the company if she got a good job, to go anywhere, insisting that he would like a more independent life as a free-lance consultant anyway. A senior salesman on the low-opportunity professional sales ladder advised a group of younger people to make sure they had exciting lives outside the company. One manager said he thought that people with "career frustrations" looked for recognition outside the company, in community affairs, family, neighborhood, golf, the bottle. And in the sales force survey, a higher proportion of those who were above the median age for their position (an indication that they were stuck) reported that they had frequently considered leaving the company.

Another example from the sales force survey shows that job characteristics that can be taken as indications of having opportunity might also be related to commitment, although the items reflect prospects in the present job, rather than mobility, and the data are only suggestive of possible trends. Respondents who fell into the low commitment quartile felt they had *less* of some opportunity-enhancing job features (prestige within the company, responsibility over others, influence and power, chance to make autonomous decisions, chance to learn new things) than did those respondents high in their commitment, as Table 6–4 shows; the only thing the people low in commitment felt they had more of was the chance to be left alone, i.e., ignored by the corporation.

The responses of one man on the professional sales ladder whose commitment score was among the lowest of all respondents also exemplified the decreasing involvement with decreasing opportunity. At age forty-one, and after seventeen years with the company, he was still a relatively junior salesman, anticipating movement over the next ten years only to more prestigious accounts but not to managerial positions or to an increased rank. Family and

TABLE 6–4

Commitment to Indsco by Sales Force Sample as a Function of
Having Opportunity-Linked Job Characteristics

(*Question: Here are some things people often say they want from their jobs. For each*
item, indicate how much of this you have now, using the following scores:
1 = *I have all I want now.*
2 = *I have some; want more.*
3 = *I have none to speak of.*)

Item	Mean score of High Commitment quartile (N = 47)	Mean score of Low Commitment quartile (N = 47)
prestige within the company	2.00	2.23
responsibility over others	2.49	2.70
chance to make autonomous decisions	2.13	2.40
chance to learn new things	1.89	2.06
fun and excitement	1.85	2.06
influence, power	2.22	2.60
exercise of my skills	1.96	2.06
to be left alone	2.16	1.72

friends were much more important to him than his job. He had often considered leaving the company, as recently as a few months before, but his advanced age and the fact that his family was settled in a good town held him back. He felt he had no security, no influence and power, no chance to make autonomous decisions, and no opportunity to grow and learn—and he had ranked all of these as top priorities for what he wanted from his job. His other priorities (money, prestige outside the company, and working closely with others) were only partially met. And he said there was *no* way to meet his goals of personal growth and self-expression within the company.

This salesman's scores on the commitment indicators reflecting involvement and trust were similarly very low. (These items were rated from 1 to 5, with 1 representing the maximum and 5 the minimum of commitment. For the overall sample, the mean of individual item scores on thirty of the thirty-four ranged from 1.8 to 2.9; the remaining items had mean scores of 3.1. Thus, much higher scores than this reflected an unusually low degree of commitment.) First, trust that his interests were reflected in company decisions was minimal. Though he reported he tried hard to get his ideas heard higher up (a 2 rating), he had little sense that company policy was in his best interest (4); he would not trust his peers on a committee to represent him (4); he considered his manager only partly willing to listen to what was on his mind (3); and trust for a superior's decisions in terms of his interests was only slightly better than trust for peers (3). His boss made promotion and salary decisions without consulting him, and he found these decisions only somewhat fair (3). On a list of twelve factors possibly important in promotions, he ranked first "an 'in' with management"; as we saw in Table I, Chapter 3, this factor was ranked *eighth* by the overall sample. This is consistent with studies of alienation; belief in the fairness of the system is shaped by one's own chances to advance. In one survey of nearly 2,000 office workers, the attitude that it "takes pull to get ahead" was associated with low promotion rates or low expectations of promotion.[7]

Belief in the company's goals and values was also minimal; this salesman had little stake in Indsco's future, was cynical about whether the company "really cares about its people," and thought many people in it, in turn, were likely to "try to cheat the company when they can." His own sense of contribution was practically nonexistent. Asked whether he contributed to the overall success of the company, he indicated that he felt he made very little difference (5), had only a small amount to offer the company (3), and received only moderate recognition for achievement and skills (3). A sense of distance and non-involvement was also reflected in the man's relatively low valuing of Indsco people and minimal contact with them outside of routine business dealings.

Non-Responsibility

Disengagement was behaviorally reflected in the tendency for some people at dead ends to withdraw from responsibility. Indsco culture had a name for people who were in the "write it off" stage of their careers; they were known as "mummies" or "zombies" or "mystery men in the office." They walked around doing only what they were told, taking no initiative, and responded only to crises, if then. Sometimes they stopped participating in office social functions. An executive complained about some "zombies" he had to work with, "They tend to get into a blaming thing if they are told they're not motivated, like, 'How can I be motivated after what the company has done to me?' " Another one reported, "Some people reach the stage where the challenge they once had from their work no longer exists. They get into a job-oriented depressed state. They mope around. I think the company *could* change the atmosphere for people like that, help turn them on, if they could only be given a growth move."

Some people seemed lost to the company as effective performers. A marketing manager in his early fifties, in a dead end job, was virtually unable to follow through on projects; he was always beginning things that somehow never went anywhere, using the latest involvement to justify dropping out of the previous project. A middle manager who had once had "prospects," and whose hopes for an officer slot were cut short by a change of management team to people antagonistic to him, disguised his loss of interest in the company by appearing busy; he used the office to do his work for outside involvements and always seemed to be going to meetings. The greater motivation, commitment, and responsibility of people on the move compared with those who were stuck was recognized subtly in Indsco's folk wisdom: "If you want a job done right, give it to the busiest person" (a managerial maxim); "You're better off with a boss who is going places" (a secretarial maxim).

Substitute Social Recognition

When they are blocked from organizational recognition, people may substitute a variety of forms of "social recognition," finding ways to look good in the eyes of at least some other people. It is low-opportunity people who seem to find their greatest satisfactions at work through connections with others. I do not mean to sound critical of this concern with relationships by calling it a "substitute" form of recognition; after all, communities are founded on such valuing of social ties, and this may be a better place for the investment of human energy in the long run than individual career success. But in the corporate context a concern with interpersonal involvements as the *highest* reward in work is appropriately viewed as a substitute. Though managers are rewarded for getting along well socially, as shown in Chapter 3, and the managers I interviewed had needs to be with people, their primary sense of worth at work came through good job performance. Additionally, the focus here is on those ways people actually use it as a substitute way to meet needs for status, dignity, or value that they have been blocked from meeting through the organization's mobility channels.

There is a body of theory, survey and laboratory research that contrasts the interpersonal orientations of people in high- and low-mobility situations and demonstrates the degree to which peer-group solidarity as a value and a fact develops most among those low in opportunity. People on the move seem to be too busy climbing or figuring out how to relate to those upward in the hierarchy to pay much attention to social relationships, the argument runs (although the stereotypical argument ignores the warm, humanistic types among the mobile), and in any event, they hardly stay put long enough to form close ties. The stuck are also stuck with each other for much longer. Some of this contrast is exaggerated, in that many low-mobility workers do not care much whether they have a peer group at work or not, and among the comers at Indsco were those who had close friendship groups and manifested many signs of caring about people. But the evidence is worth considering for the light it sheds on the different kinds of social concerns that can be aroused by differences in opportunity.

Previous research has found that high-mobility situations tend to foster rivalry, instability in the composition of work groups, comparisons upward in the hierarchy, and concern with intrinsic aspects of the job. Low-mobility situations, by contrast, tend to foster camaraderie, stably composed groups, and more concern with extrinsic rewards—both social and monetary. In a classic piece of sociological analysis, Robert Merton argues that the amount of upward mobility, as an institutionalized characteristic of a social system, generated either vertical or horizontal orientations. When people face favorable advancement opportunities, they compare themselves upward in rank, with one foot already out of the current peer group, in the process Merton called "anticipatory socialization." But unfavorable advancement prospects lend themselves to comparison with peers and concern with peer solidarity. One study provided empirical confirmation of Merton's propositions by showing that the importance attached by workers to intrinsic aspects of the job—to the nature of the job itself as opposed to such external factors as relationships with co-workers—varied with promotion rates out of that job; when there was a greater probability of promotion, there was more concern with the job and less with sociability. In another study among relatively low-level employees, work-group solidarity was a prime factor in identification with the organization.[8]

A laboratory study of communication in experimentally created hierarchies offered supportive evidence for the relationship between the structure of opportunity situations and the development of work and peer orientations. Arthur Cohen put male subjects into high-power (management-like) or low-power (subordinate-like) task groups, varying the opportunity structure for the two low-power groups.[9] One condition offered no opportunities for mobility into the high-power group; the other created the possibility for mobility during the experimental situation. The mobile groups showed greater concern with the task, suppressed irrelevant communications, were less critical of the upper groups, and were more oriented toward the high-power groups than toward members of their own peer group. They were careful about criticism, stayed more with the task, and tended to be less attracted to members of their own group than to the high-power people.

The non-mobiles, on the other hand, centered their affect and attention on the members of their own group, neglecting the high-power people because "for them, communication and interaction cannot be instrumental to mobility." The non-mobiles were also significantly more likely to feel that their "social validity" was received from their own rather than the upper group, to send "cohesiveness-building content" to their own group, and to be openly critical of the upper group—like the men in the bank wiring room in the classic experiments at Western Electric, who created a strong peer group that restricted work output.[10]

A laboratory experiment like this one adds an extra note of validity to field observations of the relation between opportunity and work concerns. In every real-life organization the questions of self-selection and initial channeling remain unanswerable. Did people who opt out of the ambitious climb select, or find selected for them, the low-opportunity situations? Was their other-directed focus a *cause* rather than a consequence of low mobility in the first place? Were they just not that ambitious to begin with? The Cohen experiment suggests otherwise, that opportunity does indeed shape behavior, because, for one thing, the subjects were placed randomly in the various conditions. High-achievement orientations were found among men in both groups, but the high achievers in the two groups faced different situations, coping with them differently. Achievement-oriented subjects in the non-mobile groups handled the contradiction between their drives and their objectively limited opportunities by a kind of "vicarious achievement," conjecturing about the job of the high-power group and projecting themselves into the role. This was a form of substitute upward movement through identification with power holders, and it is characteristic of the attitudes of some clerical workers, or secretaries who identify the chief's success as their own.

In short, the evidence would predict that people whose opportunity to achieve through movement is blocked are likely to try to meet any needs for recognition through social groups other than the powerful people upward in the hierarchy. At Indsco, several forms of substitute social recognition were observed beyond the concern with peer solidarity noted in the literature. The social group of peers was important for some people who were stuck; others became "social professionals," turned to work-related people outside the company, or looked downward for respect, as I indicated in Figure 6–1.

Anti-"Success" Peer Solidarity

Tom Burns was among the first to describe the kind of countersystem that could be developed by people who are shut out of opportunity, in order to protect themselves and each other from feelings of failure. He observed a factory in an uncertain, changing environment, but his descriptions could apply to Indsco people. Younger and still mobile men oriented themselves around power, and when they developed peer groups, it was to plot mutual political advantage; but the older men, considered "over the hill" and in positions outside of the main career advancement ladders, formed "cliques" oriented toward protection and reassurance, which Burns thought were organized retreats from occupational status into the realm of intimacy. The clique permitted the maintenance of face and self-esteem, a declaration of choice, and an assertion of human dignity. As Burns commented:

> Sometimes an individual fails or is doubtful about his success or has rejected his occupational role because it has become devalued or because it is a second choice anyway. The failure will seek to opt out of his occupational role in collusion with others—he will want to present the occupational role as being less important to

him. . . . In this way, by putting success, so to speak, in quotation marks, the greater intimacy and "naturalness" prevailing in the clique affords a status to its members that can be regarded as more desirable than the occupational status from which the individual retreats; it is indeed superior in that wider tolerances for conduct and the securities of friendship endow the status with a higher "reality" value.[11]

Co-worker groups can be a route to either protection and support or power, depending on the structure of opportunity.[12] The less advantaged in opportunity regardless of organizational level, dead end managers as well as clerical and production workers, may develop a countersystem built around peer relations instead of ladder-climbing. Such countersystems may find some of their solidarity in open rejection and criticism of those who dominate the hierarchy, but the stuck and disadvantaged have not usually been a revolutionary force. Their rebellion is more likely to take the form of passive resistance, as in the Hawthorne plant bank wiring room's informal quotas. Or it could be gossip, joking, and ridicule at the expense of the advantaged. The ringleader of such a group is likely to be a good resister or a "comic" or a person with a sassy tongue well placed in a gossip network. Peer groups of those with blocked mobility generally do not plot to confront the system for more mutual gain, as do the "cabals" of the more advantaged. This is one of the explanations for the historical view of the lesser interest of working women in unions—although this is true only when women are in low-opportunity jobs. In one Canadian investigation of male and female white-collar workers, there was some relationship between mobility expectations and union potential. Those most supportive of unions were those with some expectation of promotion short of a management position. This was true for women as well as men, but women were also much more scarce among the ranks of those with realistic mobility hopes.[13] In short, it takes some opportunity to feel there are any benefits in developing a group that can confront and try to change the system. Low opportunity can depress self-image as well as aspirations, reducing feelings of efficacy.

If peer groups formed by those low in opportunity tend to focus on group solidarity and internal group culture more than confrontation or action outward, they can also become quickly closed. Members have redefined success, have built their own status system and signals of membership, and have little reason to look for any other relationships, for there is little to gain.[14] These groups, typical among secretaries and other clerical workers, were the office equivalents to adolescent gangs, developing norms of mutual aid and loyalty. Women could count on one another to "cover" if they had something else to do and even to cover-up, when that was possible. Indsco men were likely to comment on the "cattiness" of women toward one another, reporting that they had overheard the secretaries' gossip, but the secretaries themselves reported a great deal of solidarity and support.

As a member of such a closed peer group, a person is under pressure to remain loyal to the immediate group of workmates and to see leaving the group, even for a promotion, as an act of "disloyalty"—an act, indeed, that poses an uncomfortable challenge to the group's rejection of success in the hierarchy. It would belie the countersystem. There have been many comments on the ambivalences associated with hierarchical advancement out of a low-opportunity situation with high peer-group solidarity. Indsco's folk wisdom had it that it was only women who would be concerned about taking a promotion because it would mean "leaving friends." But in actuality, this reaction was likely to occur wherever closed anti-"success" peer groups had formed. Though in a different context, William Foote Whyte's classical portrayal of group life among young men in *Street Corner Society* posed the issue poignantly. A slum boy could leave his environment and go to college only if he saved money; but his peers expected that extra money would be shared with friends, since relationships in the group were considered the highest value and it was thought that the fortunate should help the less lucky. So an equation was imposed: getting ahead meant forsaking those you loved best.[15]

For women in clerical and secretarial jobs at Indsco, the dilemma was probably more severe—and not because women could be supposed to "naturally" care more about relationships. But mobility was so rare and the chance for social contact so great in office jobs that strong peer networks easily developed. It was also easier for the women to support a culture devaluing hierarchical success because of tradition and because they had few women upward in the hierarchy with whom to identify. Then, the distribution of men and women throughout the organization also shaped the psychological filter through which these women viewed promotion. As a woman rose in Indsco, she was likely to find fewer and fewer female peers, whereas men found a male peer group at every level of the system. So concern about "leaving friends" and the social discomforts of a promotion were often expressed by women in the clerical ranks; men in management had no such problem. One secretary said to another who had recently been promoted, "*I* don't want to get promoted. Then I'd have to eat with the men." (Accusingly): "*You* eat with the men." And another: "I wouldn't get promoted into an inside office. You don't have as nice an office as I do. I'd stay an executive secretary." These were typical comments, for almost identical statements were reported by other women who moved out of nonexempt jobs; many of them made a point of going back to have lunch with the old "girls." And a woman manager who had been a nonexempt employee commented that "the social part of a promotion *is* difficult. New managers need to make dates, to set meetings, to call people for lunch. It is more difficult for a woman to do. Even I hesitate to call other managers in other departments. I'm concerned that if I invite them for lunch, they'll feel they have to pay. And there were new things to learn. One man noticed that I didn't have a credit card, because he asked me why I didn't sign for lunch, and then he made sure I got it. But I can see why some women don't want to leave the safety of their group. They don't have all these awkward social things to contend with."

A key to understanding the anti-hierarchical-success culture developed by close-knit peer groups of the stuck lies in the impossibility of untangling two statements: "I don't want to_____" (achieve or advance or move) and "You can't_____." Starting with either tends to produce the other, and it is sometimes impossible to tell which was prior in time. When a system tells some people they cannot advance, they may respond with a culture that declares, "We wouldn't want to anyway." At the same time, when people opt out of ladder-climbing and reduce their mobility aspirations, for reasons that may include an alternative set of values or a critical assessment of the weaknesses of the system, others respond to their statement of "I don't want to" with "You can't; you're not able to." And sometimes people who are told they "can't," internalize the message that they can't (they lack some critical skills or abilities) and adopt the banner of "I don't want to" as a means of self-protection. Some of the secretaries who declared defiantly they would never want to be promoted may have been concerned that they couldn't handle it if it came their way, for a number of women who left clerical for exempt jobs reported great initial fears, concerns, and self-doubts.

Social Professionals

There was another social means for coping with blocked opportunity that tended to be an individual rather than a group response. Some people became "social professionals," achieving renown and recognition through having the best gossip and latest inside information or telling the best jokes or being the most compatible on the golf course. (One can find here ironic echoes of the "Miss Congeniality" award in the Miss America contest, going to the loser everyone likes best.) The office storyteller, who was the best source of gossip for that particular segment and would be willing to spend the time to relay it, was often someone who was stuck. Gossip was, of course, one of the tools for control that secretaries wielded, and it could also be used to gain prestige by people with few alternatives.

One man was typical of the "old pro salesman" who had become a social expert now that career progress was stopped. People liked to be around him because he was so smooth and easygoing and had such good stories. He had been with the company twenty-five years. He told good jokes, lots of them.

He made people feel at ease. He dressed casually but in a dapper fashion, always immaculately. To people around him, he belonged on a golf course. He was friendly, smiled a great deal, and always tried to be helpful. In a sales meeting, he introduced himself by talking about his twenty-fifth anniversary, and in conversations usually focused on how long he had been with the company, his history with the company. He participated enthusiastically in everything, and willingly answered the younger people's questions.

There were two subgroups among the social professionals: those who focused outward, on work-related people outside the company; and those who focused downward, on subordinates or more junior personnel.

Sociability Outward

Salespeople could most easily specialize in work-related social relations outside the company, since this was considered part of their job. However, there was known to be a fine line between pleasing customers enough to sell them on Indsco and turning into a "customers' man." Customers' men spent their time entertaining customers, to the point that they were absent from the office more than usual and identified with customers rather than with the corporation. Their attitude toward company decisions was based on answering the question: Is it good for my friends (the customers)? Along with Indsco scientists, who had an outside professional group, salesmen could go on what was known as the "banquet tour." Here the front persons were removed from day-to-day business. Instead, they went to sales meetings, customer golf outings, dinners, association meetings, professional society conventions—always accepting invitations. One manager wryly commented, "People could make a career out of this. It disguises for a time that their job isn't needed. They look very busy, but they're not writing reports or figuring out ways to improve the organization. They can get away with it longer if they were once a good performer but lost out through politics." One satisfaction for such people lay in the fact that outsiders did not know their true position. They could still be treated with respect, they could still be seen as prestigious insiders in a major corporation. And their affability won them acceptance.

Social Recognition Downward

Some people turned to younger or more junior people for recognition. For example, they could capitalize on a technical base and set up an advice shop for younger people. In a few cases, this stance had been institutionalized, with people being asked to spend some of their time teaching new hires about the technical aspects of their work. Some men in sales whose career was at an endpoint adopted an avuncular manner and spent their time in training programs or in the office trying to tell everyone "the secrets." It was a sure sign that someone was at a dead end when he or she could be found regularly eating lunch or having a drink with less experienced, more junior, young people to the exclusion of peers, for it was likely that they were using that occasion to derive some respect they felt they lacked elsewhere. Men sometimes used their secretaries or women in the office for such ego boosts.

It was critical for such people that there *did* exist a group of people below them to whom they could feel superior and who were called upon to recognize their superiority. Maintaining dignity and self-esteem in the face of non-success required that the stuck still have some basis for value that their years of service had earned them. But it seemed to be especially threatening to this group to see young people—who should have been looking up to them—go whizzing by them on a fast track upward. During a promotion freeze period, when practically everyone in the organization was stuck, there was particular resentment of "water walkers" or "boy wonders" who were being moved anyway. One employee relations official predicted dire consequences: "When the older guys, in their forties, see themselves passed over because a young guy, thirty-six, has been promoted beyond them, even in the freeze, I'd put money on it that he is going to be undermined from below." It also seemed to be this group of the stuck who resented bitterly any attention given to the upward mobility of women and minorities. Affirmative action appeared to erode away a large segment of the population those stuck in the exempt ranks could see as below them. Whereas a number of high-opportunity managers actively favored upgrading women and minorities (sometimes because of values, sometimes because they saw a personal advantage to them of showing that they could manage such a challenging situation, and certainly because there was no personal threat), low-opportunity people often expressed grave concerns. A group of non-mobile older salesmen could be heard venting their rage about the situation at coffee breaks during task force meetings, when they thought none of the bosses were around.

There were also two less Machiavellian forms of downward sociability that sometimes occurred among people in their terminal job or with low opportunity to advance. The first was to genuinely identify with subordinates, deciding that if one could not advance any further, at least one could get the satisfaction of helping them to advance. This choice was extremely rare, for reasons that will be explored in the next chapter; it took a degree of security and a strong people-orientation that a competitive corporation was not likely to breed. But once in a while, such a person emerged with dignity from a stuck situation.

The last kind of downward sociability involved identification with groups several levels below a person's own peers, and it could be found most often among those who had themselves come up from that lower-level group. They might retain a sense of connection with that group, and they might also be un-sure of their acceptance among people closer to their own level. Sometimes also this stance came out of strong values and concerns about injustice. A black man who moved into a technical supervisory job in a financial accounting department in the marketing division, without enough background to go fur-ther, was genuinely interested in the situation of nonexempt employees and ate lunch with them at least three days a week. He also had a large friendship network and many outside ties. In his case, there was a congruence between values and personal needs, for his social connections offered him a status and reward that he would never have received from his job *per se;* he was known as a very poor businessman. In another instance, a woman administrative as-sistant who was stuck in a rather routinized job found herself empathizing with the situation of nonexempts. She had the same feelings of being trapped, the same personal self-doubts and inner insecurities. So it was more comfortable for her to continue her relationship with friends from her former nonexempt job. They provided a real ego boost for her, because they were impressed by a job she found so boring and they were always pleased that someone of her new stature would bother to come to see them.

CONSERVATIVE RESISTANCE

Some people also coped with their lack of opportunity by criticism of those who *had* made it and were occupying the rungs above them (as research reported earlier also demonstrated). They resisted innovations and new ideas that came from higher levels and behaved as though they were "keepers of the faith," who would protect the organization against disruptive new-fangled in-fluences.[16] Criticism and resistance to change served several functions: It carved out an area of control for those who were not going into larger decision-making arenas, reminding the people above that they were still a force to be reckoned with, still had to be taken into account. It was often the only alterna-tive to having to lose face by admitting that upper-level management really did know best—and thus had perhaps made a good decision by not promoting the stuck. Criticism of the short-sighted or ignorant decisions made by higher-ups carried with it the implication that the same wrong-headedness had been involved in blocking the speaker's mobility. Sometimes it made the speaker look smart—that the critic knew more than higher officials. Criticism and resistance, too, could be ways to create a certain swagger—an air of power and independence—in the eyes of peers, junior, or outsiders. Such behavior rep-resented a prime form of retaliation against those who had blocked a person, by undermining their plans and objectives. And, finally, there was also a self-protective aspect to a stand of conservative resistance. The stuck were often not secure in their own job tenure and sometimes felt that they could be replaced by the mobility squeeze from below if they made a mistake. Some proportion of all new plans and policies did not work out (in a time of recession, often a large proportion), and the stuck did not want to be caught by a wrong move. So, in not wanting to jump onto a rickety bandwagon that might cause them to be dumped, they became automatically conservative.

Chronic Criticism

Indsco managers could identify a style they called the "chronic complainer." Such a person was likely to resist change by appearing as an "old hand" who had been through it all before. "When policy changes are proposed, or we get asked for a certain effort, guys who are at endpoints in their careers react with, 'We've tried it before, and it hasn't worked. I wish those idiots in headquarters would read the papers from before.' Or they say, 'When is Indsco going to wise up? They don't know the market like I do. . . .' " Such reactions also occurred among low-mobility workers like secretaries, who were often very suspicious of new policy proposals. Ironically, resistance to change also served to perpetuate the organization that complainers were so critical of, because they offered no *new* ideas—just threats to the implementation of others' ideas. And unlike the active politicking of people on the move, the form discontent took on the part of those low in opportunity was passive: griping from the sidelines.

Too much resistance, of course, could be risky. Troublemakers ran the risk of termination. Negativity represented more than just a source of annoyance or inconvenience; it also violated the norms of an organization that considered itself "people-conscious" and valued "nice," easygoing behavior. So some people adopted more subtle resistance stances. This involved taking a "know-it-all," "wait and see" attitude of distance toward proposals, changes, or new ideas—not criticizing them overtly, but also not rushing in to try them or implement them. Foot-dragging, especially by claiming a work overload, could effectively undermine proposals without making the resister too vulnerable, because he or she could always point out that the other work and the old way were also "ordered" (clerical workers could use this form of resistance very well). In training programs, the stuck could sometimes be distinguished from the moving by their more distant and disdainful stance. Whereas younger people and people still on the move often plunged themselves into activities with enthusiasm and were helpful to the staff, the stuck more often implied by their behavior that there was nothing there for them and nothing that they could be taught or benefit from. (In some sense, they were right, of course. People who were as far as they could go and could not hide it any longer from themselves or from peers often had nothing to gain, at least in the purely instrumental sense, by getting more training.)

Low-risk Conservatism

"Playing it safe" was a strategy of some dead-enders. Not only might they be resistant to changes proposed by others, they were also reluctant to do anything innovative themselves. Over and over again, I found that people who were most cautious about "rocking the boat" or experimenting with new ideas were those whose opportunity was blocked or who were stuck in a terminal job. A rising young manager, known as a mover, who had worked under a man at a dead end and was sensitive to his boss's dilemma, put it this way: "A person who has stabilized [going nowhere] feels less secure. You price yourself out of a job soon because you reach the top of your level. You know no one is watching out for you. So you won't take risks. When you set goals for your department, you set them low. You won't put your neck on the block. If you find out you did something wrong, you panic and try to cover your tracks." A personnel specialist also commented about the pressures from a static hierarchy, when people feel they are not moving: "Managers aren't developing people, they are expecting of them. They won't try anything new, even if it might mean an improvement. All they want are enough results to prove they've met their targets. If they can't get results, then they sharpen their pencils so they can get them on paper."

Unlike the chronic critics, the low-risk brand of conservative resistance to change was carried out by people who did everything they could to make sure they offended no one. Approval for a simple project involving very few people could take months if the manager involved felt he had to proceed through every possible organizational channel, checking with everyone (whether officially necessary or not) who might possibly object to any part of the content. By the time this procedure was completed, everything risky or controversial about the project had been eliminated—as well as a large part of what made it valuable in the first place. Many ideas or targets would be squashed completely or slowly disappear. And because the low risk-takers were spending a great deal of their time on the phone or in meetings getting approval, finding out what their own managers wanted, explaining and apologizing, or covering their tracks, they hardly had much time left to develop new and better approaches.

At one meeting discussing the state of Indsco as an organization, a group of rising managers complained about the tendency for the company to lag behind its competitors in innovation. Perhaps a part of the explanation lay in a distribution of opportunity that made too many people feel stuck.

OPPORTUNITY AS A SELF-FULFILLING PROPHECY:

CYCLES OF ADVANTAGE AND DISADVANTAGE

Opportunity structures shape behavior in such a way that they confirm their own prophecies. Those people set on high-mobility tracks tend to develop attitudes and values that impel them further along the track: work commitment, high aspirations, and upward orientations. Those set on low-mobility tracks tend to become indifferent, to give up, and thus to "prove" that their initial placement was correct. They develop low-risk, conservative attitudes, or become complaining critics, demonstrating how right the organization was not to let them go further. It is graphically clear how cycles of advantage and cycles of disadvantage are perpetuated in organizations and in society. What the clerical worker with low motivation to be promoted might need is a promotion; what the chronic complainer might need is a growthful challenge. But who would be likely to give it to them?

One place the cycles of advantage and disadvantage function clearly is in the relationship of individual mobility to peer-group culture. We have already seen that peer culture in low-opportunity situations can develop an anti-hierarchical-"success" orientation to protect members against their lack of advancement prospects. How cliques treat upwardly mobile members, how much pressure they impose and conflict they engender, shapes the future relationship of people who rise to their former peers and accounts for whether that mobility eventually helps the group as a whole. If the peer group makes it hard to leave and threatens group sanctions against a mover, that person may resolve discomfort and ambivalence by giving up identification with the old group and by taking on a new identity as part of the higher-level cohort. The mover is then much less likely to advance the interests of the old group or to use the perquisites of the new position to help former clique members get ahead; indeed, a mover may even turn against the old group for its lack of support. Those who advance out of a blocked-mobility peer group, then, may be highly unlikely to take care of the old network. People who "escape" disadvantaged situations—rare blacks or women who rise from the ranks to prestigious positions, poor youths who make it out of slums, rare workers promoted into management—have frequently been criticized for not acting as advocates for former peers, with little recognition of the mobility conflicts such people may face. Those most likely to be remembered and rewarded when a mover rises are peers that supported the move. Yet, paradoxically, peers supportive of mobility are also likely to be already relatively advantaged. As frequently happens in social life, "those that have" get more. Low-mobility peer groups need to actively encourage the mobility of at least some of their members if those members are to first gain influence and then use it to help the group. However, the very lack of opportunity the group faces creates a self-defeating cycle and puts pressure on members to limit their aspirations. This, coupled with the other tendency we have seen for people who move up via a "wrong" path to get stuck early themselves, sheds grave doubts on a strategy of individual mobility—giving a few people among the disadvantaged a chance to rise—to improve the situation for a disadvantaged group. Opportunities must be opened up for the social category as a whole. Finding a few places for clerical workers in professional jobs, giving a few individuals a crack at moving up, will not improve the situation of such low-opportunity people; only changing the advancement picture for clerical work as a whole could interrupt the cycle.

Tracking occurs, of course, even before people enter organizations as adult workers,[17] and this can affect initial placement decisions. Individual characteristics and the nature of external social ties also play a part. But even so, there is striking flexibility in people to adapt to their situations, and there is striking power in organizations to raise or dash hopes. The structure of organizations plays a powerful role in creating work behavior. Women in low-mobility organizational situations develop attitudes and orientations that are sometimes said to be characteristic of those people as individuals or "women as a group," but that can more profitably be viewed as more universal *human* responses to blocked opportunities.

Beyond Sex Differences

This analysis should thus lead to a reinterpretation of familiar findings about sex differences in work behavior: that men are more ambitious, task-oriented, and work-involved, and women care more about relationships at work.[18] When women seem to be less motivated or committed, it is probably because their jobs carry less opportunity. There is evidence that in general the jobs held by most women workers tend to have shorter chains of opportunity associated with them and contain fewer advancement prospects. This is true in production as well as clerical jobs. One study looked at industries employing about 17 percent of the U.S. work force (motor vehicles and parts, basic steel, communications, department and variety stores, commercial banking, insurance carriers, and hotels and motels). It was found that as the amount of progression possible in non-supervisory jobs increased (the number of steps of opportunity they contained), the proportion of women declined markedly.[19] Though women represented nearly half of all non-supervisory workers, they constituted 64 percent of workers in the "flattest" jobs (least advancement opportunities) and 5 percent of workers in the highest opportunity jobs. (See Table 6–5.) A recent Canadian study examined 307 white-collar work-

TABLE 6–5

Percentage of Men and Women in Jobs with Long and Short Opportunity Structures in Eleven Industries

	Number of non-supervisory workers	% Male	% Female	% of workers to total
1. Craft or craft type progression	1,350,000	95	5	19
2. Long, narrow pyramid progression—at least 6 steps normally	1,235,000	68	32	18
3. Moderate pyramid progression—3 to 5 steps normally	2,045,000	39	61	29
4. Flat pyramid progression—at most, 2 steps normally	2,390,000	36	64	34
	7,020,000	54% (average)	46% (average)	100%

Source: William J. Grinker et al., Climbing the Job Ladder, *New York: E. F. Shelley and Co., 1970, page 13.*

ers in twenty firms, half of them women. The women were clustered in the jobs with less control, more machine work, lower incomes, less job security, and less chance to be promoted into management. Thirty percent of the women, compared with 21 percent of the men, felt they had little or no chance of promotion; 60 percent of them, compared with 45 percent of the men, had had no promotions of any kind in the previous year. Only 5 percent of the women, versus nearly a third of the men, expected management jobs in the future. This low female expectation was confirmed by a management sample that predicted *no promotions* for 21 percent of the women (compared with 6 percent of the men).[20] Surveys have also shown that women are more likely to exhibit "normlessness": a perception that ability has little to do with getting ahead.[21]

Two sociological studies in particular bring an ironic twist to the popular picture of women as less intrinsically work-committed than men. One demonstrated that work is not a "central life interest" of factory workers by using a sample of *men*. The second showed that work *is* a central life interest of professionals by studying an all-women sample of nurses,[22] women who did have opportunity. Interestingly enough, these women found personal satisfaction but not necessarily personal friendships at work. In another study of teachers and nurses, the women were more committed to their organizations than the men (perhaps because the fields were defined as offering strong opportunities for women), and those with "sponsors" to aid their mobility had the highest commitment. Women can also be more committed than men at upper levels when they have had to work harder to overcome barriers; effort helps build commitment. [23] At the same time, *men with low opportunity look more like the stereotype of women in their orientations toward work*, as research on blue-collar men has shown; they limit their aspirations, seek satisfaction in activities outside of work, dream of escape, interrupt their careers, emphasize leisure and consumption, and create sociable peer groups in which interpersonal relationships take precedence over other aspects of work. [24]

OPPORTUNITY VERSUS JOB SATISFACTION

It is important to distinguish the effects of opportunity from what is usually measured when social scientists study "job satisfaction." Job satisfaction studies usually involve the content of work and characteristics of the work environment. Measurements tend to consider present-time issues only and look at jobs independent of their relationship to the larger organizational structure in which they are embedded. But opportunity is a more dynamic concept, in which it is the relationship of a present position to a larger structure and to anticipated future positions that is critical. Job satisfaction may reflect day-to-day comfort, whereas opportunity affects a person's overall mode of work involvement. A person could feel reasonably satisfied with the content of a job but frustrated about growth through it or movement from it, and thus depress aspiration and look to other realms for opportunity.

For example, in a number of surveys, a surprisingly low percentage of workers expresses direct job dissatisfaction; yet a very high percentage tends to report that they would seek another occupation if they had a chance. [25] Perhaps one reason for this discrepancy is the effects that work has on self-image. Those who lack opportunity but fear challenging the system may rationalize their situation by assuming that they are doing just what they should be, just what they are suited for. Disadvantage depresses self-evaluation as well as aspirations. The textile workers Robert Blauner described in *Alienation and Freedom* are a good example. A high proportion of the production workers in this industry are women. The jobs characteristically pay low wages and offer little freedom, and women tend to be concentrated especially in low-involvement jobs where workers can let their minds wander. There are very limited opportunities for advancement—few skilled jobs, a narrow wage spread, and a limited occupational ladder. Yet the objective alienation is not matched by subjective dissatisfaction because the women's self-image fits the job. They have low estimates of their own abilities and possibilities and don't feel that the jobs are too simple for their own best abilities. [26] The women clerical workers surveyed at Indsco seem to demonstrate the same thing. Hierarchy activates the achievement drives of only those with opportunity for mobility, for advancement, and for growth. The disadvantaged, those whose mobility is limited or blocked, can develop a self-image that matches their situation. This is true not only of workers at the bottom, those with the lowest-status jobs, for, as we have seen at Indsco, people can find themselves on dead-end tracks at any level of an organization.[27]

Expectation effects also have to be taken into account. The results of one study of 545 manual and clerical workers can be interpreted as evidence that opportunity is related to reported satisfaction with the present job through its effect on expectations. Those who were high in opportunity relative to others of similar status tended to show higher job satisfaction. The low in opportunity who saw that no one else of their kind had it either also showed high job satisfaction. That is, those who perceived rigid stratification were more satisfied than those who perceived a mobile system in which they personally were not mobile.[28] At the same time, when the content of a job is changed in ways that should be theoretically "more satisfying" (e.g., more use of employees' skills), expectations also shape satisfaction. Feelings on the part of job-holders in the enlarged jobs that they are worth more and deserve more because more is demanded of them can result in dissatisfaction if opportunity does not change to match the raised expectations.[29] Finally, as others have similarly pointed out, job satisfaction is also not the same as commitment, which refers to *overall* attachment to the organization and is shaped in a major way by opportunity.[30] Under some circumstances, commitment may override dissatisfaction with a specific job, as in the case of people who know that a job with uninteresting content is a stepping-stone to better things and important to do in order to move on.

Thus, studies of "job satisfaction" based on just the job and its immediate setting are too narrow; they would not pick up, nor be able to explain, the variety of effects that are associated with degrees of opportunity.

DILEMMAS OF OPPORTUNITY STRUCTURES
IN LARGE, HIERARCHICAL ORGANIZATIONS

The costs to those low in opportunity, and the loss to the organization, are clear. What is not always so clear are the costs of too *much* opportunity, too much emphasis on mobility to the top. A number of human and humane values tend to be developed in the absence of opportunity: an emphasis on peer solidarity, a sense that work isn't everything, a questioning of the meaning of "success." (Perhaps this is why radicals often look to the less privileged for standards of morality.) But great opportunity—the promise of ever-increasing status and power—can breed competitiveness, an instrumental orientation toward relationships, a politically generated focus upward in the organization, and an excessive absorption in work that can threaten such outside institutions as the family. Some people call this a "male" style, but, like the reactions of the disadvantaged, it seems to be a set of responses set in motion by the way large hierarchical organizations are structured. The challenge for contemporary organizations involves simultaneously opening opportunities for the disadvantaged and also reducing the emphasis on mobility for the advantaged, substituting other rewards and values, and making them real through organizational design.

The differentiated structure of opportunity in a large system like Industrial Supply Corporation and the value placed on hierarchical "success" present a number of organizational dilemmas:

—One goal of a organization's opportunity structure is to motivate performance in the job. But the hierarchical organization in which mobility is the reward ends up defeating its own goal. Those who are winning become so hooked on movement that they are less interested in the actual job than where they can go from it. Those who are losing are more disaffected than they would have been if the promise of movement had never been held out. And at every point at which the hierarchy is static and people are stuck, dysfunctional responses like non-responsibility, low commitment, and conservative resistance may be engendered.

—A form of organizational inflation sets in. Once movement is promised, people must be kept moving. But this then tends to reduce the value of the earlier jobs and make the people in them more dissatisfied, so they push even more for movement.

—The higher-status jobs can usually be the ones that take a long time to get good at. Yet those are the ones that tend to contain opportunity. People rarely stay long enough in them to master them fully, and they are not rewarded by the system if they do. Good technical people do not stay in jobs maximizing their skills but move on to a higher rung, where they might be less valuable to the organization, because only "flow-through" is valued. Yet people stay very long in more routine, lower-status jobs with little opportunity—jobs that it takes no time to get good at and where the costs of allowing rapid movement in and out of them would be minimal.

Such dilemmas are difficult to resolve within the present structure of large, hierarchical bureaucracies. Trying to create more opportunities by opening up more levels of hierarchy, as some organizations try to do, only makes the problems worse. New forms of organizational structure must be designed.

7

Power

"The level of decision-making is way up. The level of accountability is
way down. That's a problem."
                    —First line manager at Industrial Supply Corporation

Powerlessness corrupts. Absolute powerlessness corrupts absolutely.
                    —Variation on Lord Acton's comment

Organizational politics was an endlessly fascinating topic of conversation for
the people who carried out the day-to-day administration of Industrial Supply
Corporation. They watched for the signs of favor and inclusion. They talked
over the interesting new people. They speculated about the effects of changes
in senior management. They chuckled over the real story behind certain
decisions (but were never sure of the truth). A young manager amused himself
by starting a rumor about the name of the replacement for a fired vice-
president, and then heard the word come back to him "on substantial authority." One day, a fairly new sales worker from the field went into the cafeteria at
headquarters, and, because all the other tables were filled, he sat down at one
where an older man was eating alone. He introduced himself, but the other's
name did not register. It was the corporate president. All heads turned. The
talk started: "Who's that young guy with Peter Farrell?"

Somewhere behind the formal organization chart at Indsco was another,
shadow structure in which dramas of power were played out. An interest in
corporate politics was a key to survival for the people who worked at Indsco.
This had both a narrower, more personal meaning (how individuals would do
in the striving for hierarchical success) and an important job-related meaning
(how much people could get done and how satisfying they could make their
conditions of work). First, individual careers rose and fell, and people found
the "top" more or less open to them, through dealings in power. Sometimes,
crossing the wrong person could be dangerous. There was the story of the
powerful executive who was angry at the president of a supplier and wanted to

make it difficult for that supplier to sell to Indsco, even though its products were an important manufacturing component. A slightly junior manager—let's call him X—created an arrangement for buying from the supplier that was acceptable to the executive, and that firm's dealings were processed separately. Then another manager—Y—looked over the figures with his subordinate and asked why things were done differently. The subordinate replied, "It's always been like that. That's how it comes down from X." Y said he didn't understand it and asked the subordinate to check into it. The subordinate came back with the story and the word that the arrangement could not be changed, but Y had the manufacturing area in his business plan and wanted to change the situation. He elected to fight, against the advice of his subordinate. Y lost. The situation stayed the same, and he was pushed out of the line of ascent. For the next four or five years, he remained in limbo in a dead-end job. As an observer commented, "He blew it with one move."

However, it was not only individual competition and jockeying for position that made power dynamics important. Sometimes, people could only do their work effectively and exercise whatever competence gave them personal satisfaction if they knew how to make their way through the more cumbersome and plodding official structure via the shadow political structure underneath. Since the labyrinthine complexities of the large, fairly centralized organization reduced everyone's autonomy of action and made every function dependent on every other, politics was automatically necessitated by the system in order for people to gain some control over the machine. Politics was a way of reducing something too large, incomprehensible, and unmanageable to something smaller, more human, and more familiar. For some people, certainly, the concern with power represented individualistic striving for competitive advantage and a lion's share of scarce resources. For others, however, power was a necessary tool for living or surviving in the system at all, and they cared primarily about having a share (a sphere of autonomy and a right to call on resources) rather than monopolizing it.

For the people called "leaders," power was supposedly an automatic part of their functioning. They were given the formal titles of leadership (director, manager, supervisor), and they were expected to aid the mobilization of others toward the attainment of objectives. They had responsibility for results, and they were accountable for what got done; but as everyone knew, power did not necessarily come automatically with the designation of leaders, with the delegation of formal authority. People often had to get it not from the official structure but from the more hidden political processes.

A DEFINITION OF POWER

"Power" is a loaded term. Its connotations tend to be more negative than positive, and it has multiple meanings. Much has been written in the attempt to distinguish power from related concepts: authority, influence, force, dominance, and others. William Gamson has differentiated the forms of power that contribute something to another person in exchange for compliance (inducements) from those that only remove a threat (constraints).[1] There have been many debates about whether power exists in fixed quantities, in a zero-sum sense, so that one person's amount of power inherently limits another person's, or whether power refers to expansible capacities that could grow, synergistically, in two people simultaneously. Because the hierarchical form of large organizations tends to concentrate and monopolize official decision-making prerogatives and the majority of workers are subject to "commands" from those above, it would be natural to assume that any use of the term "power" must refer to this sort of scarce, finite resource behind hierarchical domination.

However, I am using "power" in a sense that distinguishes it from hierarchical domination. As defined here, power is the ability to get things done, to mobilize resources, to get and use whatever it is that a person needs for the goals he or she is attempting to meet. In this way, a monopoly on power means that only very few have this capacity, and they prevent the majority of others from being able to act effectively. Thus, the *total* amount of power—and total system effectiveness—is restricted, even though some people seem to have a great deal of it. However, when more people are empowered—that is, allowed to have control over the conditions that make their actions possible—then more is accomplished, more gets done. Thus, the meaning of power here is closer to "mastery" or "autonomy" than to domination or control over others. Power does refer to interpersonal transactions, the ability to mobilize other people; but if those others are powerless, their own capacities, even when mobilized, are limited. Power is the ability to *do*, in the classic physical usage of power as energy, and thus it means having access to whatever is needed for the doing. The problems with absolute power, a total monopoly on power, lie in the fact that it renders everyone else powerless. On the other hand, empowering more people through generating more autonomy, more participation in decisions, and more access to resources increases the total capacity for effective action rather than increases domination. The powerful are the ones who have access to tools for action.

THE IMPORTANCE OF POWER FOR LEADERSHIP FUNCTIONS

What makes leaders effective in an organization? What transforms people into effective bosses, managers, supervisors, team leaders? Trying to answer these questions has, of course, long engaged the energies of a large number of social scientists, especially psychologists, and their answers have filled volumes. After an early emphasis on leader "traits," stemming from characteristics of individuals, a more social perspective took hold, one that saw leadership as consisting of transactions between leaders and followers. The leader was presented as a kind of "super-follower," serving through follower designation and follower consent, and able to inspire because first able to respond to the needs, concerns, wishes, and desires of the group. Attention shifted away from the cataloging of individual attributes to the cataloging of behaviors and resources: a series of functions needed by a group that could be called "leadership," a series of resources useful in interpersonal exchanges. Tuning in to other people was considered very important. For a time in the 1960s, in fact, the belief that sensitive human relations skills held the key to success as a leader achieved almost cult-like proportions in American organizations, and Industrial Supply Corporation was no exception in instituting sensitivity training for managers—made acceptable under blander labels like "organizational skills" or "management awareness."

Yet research attempts to distinguish more effective and less effective leadership styles based on a human relations emphasis have generally failed, in part because there are trade-offs associated with one or another form of supervision. As early studies comparing authoritarian, democratic, and laissez-faire leaders showed, there were advantages and disadvantages in group productivity and morale associated with each emphasis. Although most theorists today would conclude that human relations skills are important if coupled with a production emphasis, the evidence is mixed enough to permit few conclusions about leader behaviors alone.[2] Two researchers tried to differentiate instrumental and expressive exchanges between superiors and subordinates in several Michigan businesses as a way to predict interactions and group process. The distinction was ultimately not very useful. Subordinates reported getting about equally as much job-related information, whether the leaders emphasized task or human relations matters, and the researchers found very little relationship between style of leadership behavior and subordinate group process.[3] This is one of a number of studies demonstrating that choices about how to relate to other people (listen to their problems? offer praise?) fail to make much, if any, difference in effective management—at least by themselves.

What does make a difference is *power*—power outward and upward in the system: the ability to get for the group, for subordinates or followers, a favorable share of the resources, opportunities, and rewards possible through the organization. This has less to do with how leaders relate to followers than with how they relate to other parts of the organization. It has less to do with the quality of the manager-subordinate relationship than with the structure of power in the wider system. Early theory in organizational behavior assumed a direct relation between leader behavior and group satisfaction and morale, as if each organizational subgroup existed in a vacuum. However, Donald Pelz, in a study at Detroit Edison in the early 1950s, discovered that perceived influence *outside* the work group and upward in the organization was a significant intervening variable. He compared high- and low- morale work groups to test the hypothesis that the supervisor in high-morale groups would be better at communicating, more supportive, and more likely to recommend promotion. Yet when he analyzed the data, the association seemed to be nonexistent or even reversed. In some cases, supervisors who frequently recommended people for promotion and offered sincere praise for a job well done had *lower* morale scores. The differentiating variable that Pelz finally hit upon was whether or not the leaders had power outside and upward: influence on their own superiors and influence over how decisions were made in the department as a whole. The combination of good human relations *and* power produced high morale. Human relations skills coupled with low power sometimes had negative effects on morale.[4] What good is praise or a promise if the leader can't deliver? As other research discovered, both women and men attach more importance to having a competent, rather than a nice, boss—someone who gets things done. A classic study of first-line supervisors showed that more secure (and hence effective) foremen were those who had closer relationships upward in the hierarchy; they had the most frequent exchanges with superiors.[5]

Power begets power. People who are thought to have power already and to be well placed in hierarchies of prestige and status may also be more influential and more effective in getting the people around them to do things and feel satisfied about it. In a laboratory experiment, subordinates were more likely to cooperate with and to inhibit aggression and negativity toward leaders of higher rather than lower status. In a field study of professionals, people who came into a group with higher external status tended to be better liked, talked more often, and received more communications. The less powerful, who usually talked less, were often accused of talking *too much*. There was a real consensus in such groups about who was powerful, and people were more likely to accept direct attempts to influence them from people they defined as among the powerful. Average group members, whether men or women, tended to engage in deferential, approval-seeking behavior toward those seen as higher in power.[6] Thus, people who look like they can command more of the organization's resources, who look like they can bring something that is valued from outside into the group, who seem to have access to the inner circles that make the decisions affecting the fate of individuals in organizations, may also be more effective as leaders of those around them—and be better liked in the process.

Twenty Indsco executives in a sample of managers reached the same conclusion when asked to define the characteristics of effective managers. The question of the relative importance of "people sensitivity," as they put it, provoked considerable debate. Finally, they agreed that "credibility" was more important than anything else. "Credibility" was their term for competence plus power—the known ability to get results. People with credibility were listened to, their phone calls were answered first, because they were assumed to have something important to say. People with credibility had room to make more mistakes and could take greater risks because it was believed that they would produce. They were known to be going somewhere in the organization and to have the ability to place their people in good jobs. They could back up their words with actions. Thus, the ultimate in credibility in the corporate bureaucracy was "the guy who doesn't have to make recommendations; he comes out with a *decision* and all supporting material. Everyone else just says yes or no. . . ."

Credibility upward rather than downward—that is, wider-system power—rendered managers effective, they thought. To have it downward, with subordinates, they must first have it upward, with their own superiors and the people with whom their tasks were interwoven in the matrix. Credibility downward was based on subordinates' belief in their managers' importance, which in turn was based on their political position. People-sensitivity could be an added bonus, but it was considered much less important than power. "Some managers are very successful and very tough," an executive commented. "John Fredericks is as tough as they come but also sensitive to people. His people have gone far, but is that because he's sensitive or because he has clout? It's impossible to untangle." "You can get people to do nearly anything for you if they think you have their interest at heart and will fight for them. They must see that you can produce for them, that the fighting will pay off." And lack of system power could undermine the best of human relations: "Fred Burke came in as an outsider to manage his department, so he didn't know the business and he didn't have the right connections in the company. When he tried to get things from headquarters, he had no clout. Headquarters wanted to talk to the people *under* him because they knew the answers. But sensitive, yes! Christ, I don't know anyone more sensitive than Fred Burke.

You've never seen a more sensitive guy; but his people turned against him anyway. They had no respect for him." "What we're saying, I guess," someone tried to summarize the discussion, "is that you need a combination of both—people-skills and credibility." "No," others disagreed. "It's the need to take action that distinguishes effective managers. Having some results at the end of all that people-sensitivity. What good is it if you can't get anything done in Indsco?"

The preference for association with the powerful and the degree to which this preference motivates member of organizations is a function of the degree of dependency built into the organization itself. Where people can do their work rather independently, where they can easily get the things they need to carry out their tasks, where they have a great deal of latitude in decision-making, and where rewards are not so contingent on career mobility, then there need not be the same concern with appropriate political alliances. However, the large, complex hierarchical corporation fosters dependency. Emile Durkheim, in *The Division of Labor in Society,* called this "interdependence": the way specialization had created bonds of "organic solidarity" between people who needed each other for the completion of complex tasks. However, an uncomfortable feeling of *dependency* is often the psychological result when the problems of getting approval, being recognized, or moving resources through multiple checkpoints make people see one another as threats, roadblocks, or hindrances rather than as collaborators. A manager known as highly competent made these revealing comments about himself: "I had psychological tests a few years ago. They showed that the weakest point I had was lack of independence, inability to make independent decisions. I bet it would be true of a lot of people in this company. We don't make a decision alone; we are always consulting other people. Because we are not allowed to make decisions without going through too many channels. And that's the other problem as a manager in this company. You don't really have a lot of authority when you come right down to it." In the context of such organizationally fostered dependency, people seem willing to work very hard to reduce it. One way to do this is by allying themselves with the powerful, with people who can make them more independent by creating more certainty in their lives.

Power in an organization rests, in part, on the ability to solve dependency problems and to control relevant sources of uncertainty.[7] This can be true with respect to the system as a whole as well as around individuals. For the system, the most power goes to those people in those functions that provide greater control over what the organization finds currently problematic: sales and marketing people when markets are competitive; production experts when materials are scarce and demand is high; personnel or labor relations specialists when labor is scarce; lawyers, lobbyists, and external relations specialists when government regulations impinge; finance and accounting types when business is bad and money tight.[8] There is a turning to those elements of the system that seem to have the power to create more certainty in the face of dependency, to generate a more advantageous position for the organization.

There is a wide range of dependencies faced by individuals in large corporations, varying in kind and degree with specific organizational location. Weber considered a virtue of rationalized bureaucracies that they rendered power impersonal through the development of rules, thereby reducing one sort of uncomfortable dependency: the need to be subject to the arbitrary and unpredictable whim of rulers. Michel Crozier echoed the Weberian proposition: bureaucracies are built because people are "trying to evade face-to-face relationships and situations of personal dependency whose authoritarian tone they cannot bear." [9] However, ironically, as one source of dependency on other people is reduced, others spring up. People become dependent on those who can help them make their way through the system or who provide the means to bypass rules that are behaviorally constraining or inappropriately applied. They become dependent on those with discretion over necessary resources; and to the extent that the system cannot be perfectly rationalized, with pockets of uncertainty remaining, those who control important contingencies retain a strong basis for personal power.

The uncertainty inherent in managerial roles has already been discussed. This uncertainty makes pre-selection and automatic movement in careers, or reduced discretion in performance, highly unlikely. It means that people who can influence promotion and placement decisions have a source of power to the extent that people feel dependent because of the uncertainties in their careers. Other sources of dependency derive from the size of giant corporations like Indsco. Beyond the people in the most routine of functions, no one has within a small domain all of the things he or she needs to carry out his or her job. Everyone must get things done through others who are not part of the same face-to-face group in which personal agreements and informal understandings develop. There must be power tools to use in bargaining with those others who are not bound with the person in any form of communal solidarity, or else those others can keep the person in a state of dependency that renders both planning and autonomous action impossible. What makes this more bearable is that others are in the same situation, equally dependent. So as long as dependencies are relatively symmetrical, people can agree to cooperate rather than trade on each other's vulnerabilities. Problems arise as asymmetry grows.

James Thompson developed a set of propositions about the kinds of political processes that develop when organizations contain interdependencies among discretionary jobs; that is, positions that are not completely routinized, where decisions are possible and can affect outcomes: (1) Individuals in highly discretionary jobs seek to maintain power equal to or greater than their dependence on others in the organization. (2) When power is less than dependency, people seek a coalition. Depending on the function, the coalition may be formed inside or outside of the organization. Coalitions with people in the external environment that is relevant for the organization's success may increase power. (3) The more sources of uncertainty or contingency for the organization, the more bases there are for power and the larger the number of political positions in the organization.[10] Thus, more complicated organizations have more politics than less complicated ones, and power is a much more relevant concern for the people who must function within large, complex, hierarchical systems.

To see power as a dominant issue around people in leadership positions in organizations, then, is not the same as positing individual motives such as "needs for power" or "achievement motivation." It is not a characterological but a social structural issue. Critics sometimes assume that a defect in the American character makes people (such as followers or subordinates) prefer winners to losers, or that some excessive striving for status makes people seek vicarious identification with success. However, this should also be seen as a survival mechanism for people who live in the typically American organizational worlds created in the twentieth century: to know that one is better off, less dependent and uncertain, when in league with people who are powerful in the dependency-creating systems that one must somehow make one's way through. There are real as well as symbolic payoffs in working for someone who is powerful in systems where resources are scarce and there is constant scrambling for advantage. Powerful authorities can get more for their subordinates. They can more effectively back up both promises and threats; they can more easily make changes in the situation of subordinates. They offer the possibility of taking subordinates with them when they move, so that the manager's future mobility may help others' prospects. Subordinates as well as peers may indeed capitalize on the success of a "comer" in the organization, as Barry Stein has pointed out.[11]

That is not all. There can also be something more immediately empowering about working under a powerful person. Opportunity and power both have structural impact on managers' authority styles. Bernard Levenson suggested that the fact of promotability itself shapes style of supervision. Mobile managers are likely to behave like "good" leaders *because* of their opportunity, whereas nonmobile managers behave in the rigid, authoritarian way characteristic of the powerless, as I show later. *Promotable* supervisors, he argued, are more likely to adopt a participatory style in which they share information, delegate authority, train subordinates for more responsibility, and allow latitude and autonomy. They do this, first, to show that they are not indispensable in their current jobs—to show that someone else could indeed take over when they advance. They also find it in their political interest to delegate control as a method of training a replacement, so that the vacancy created by their promotion will be filled with someone on their team. Unpromotable supervisors, on the other hand, may try to retain control and restrict the opportunities for their subordinates' learning and autonomy. The current job is their only arena for power, and they anticipate no growth or improvement for themselves. Moreover, they have to keep control for themselves, so that it will be clear that no one else could do their job. Subordinates must be forced to exercise their skills as narrowly as possible, for a capable subordinate represents a serious replacement threat.[12]

For people at Indsco, having a powerful boss was considered an important element in career progress and the development of competence, just as lack of success was seen as a function of working under a dead-ender. People wanted to work for someone on the move who had something to teach and enough power to take others along. A secretary recalled, "I came in looking for a place to stake out my career. I was first assigned to work for a man who was a dowdy dresser and never cleaned his shoes. (I have a thing about men and shoes. How they take care of their shoes is a good sign of other things.) The whole atmosphere in the group made it clear that people were going nowhere. It was not businesslike. So I said to myself, 'He's going nowhere. I'd better change.' And he did go nowhere." One of Indsco's highest ranking women said, "I had to learn everything myself. So did men. Lots of people go into managerial jobs without any training. I had to model myself after my boss. If the boss is good, okay. If not, that can be terrible. It's better to get a boss who is successful in the organization's terms." In response to a question about what is "helpful" in a manager, a sales worker wrote, "He sees a subordinate's growth as in his interest. He is confident, capable, and conveys a sense that he will be promoted. Clichés like 'being on a winner's team' have taken on new meaning for me. . . . Unhelpful managers are uncertain of themselves, their abilities, present position, or future." An older executive commented, "It's a stroke of luck to get an opportunity to work for someone who's a mover and demonstrate performance to him because astute managers look for good workers and develop them." There was much agreement among managers that people were more likely to emerge with "manager quality" if they worked for the right boss. "Right" meant high credibility. Credibility meant power.

ORGANIZATIONAL POLITICS AND THE SOURCES OF POWER

There have been a number of useful classifications of the bases of social power. John R. P. French and Bertram Raven proposed five: reward power (controlling resources that could reward), coercive power (controlling resources that could be used to punish), expert power (controlling necessary knowledge or information), reference power (being personally attractive to other people, so that they are likely to identify or seek a relationship), and legitimate power (authority vested in a position or role and accepted by others as appropriate).[13] Each of these certainly plays a part in determining who becomes powerful in an organization; personal characteristics and background combine with the way an organization distributes scarce resources through positions to give people differential opportunities to become influential.

However, there are also a number of bases of power that are specifically organizational. The French and Raven typology and others of its kind are most useful for understanding one-on-one exchanges or the exercise of influence in rather small-scale interpersonal situations. The politics of a large-scale system are more complex and often do not seem reducible to such simple elements, even though the actual wielding of influence in any one instance may seem to rest on one or another of those five bases of power. This is the familiar problem of system levels in social science. Whereas there are many ways in which human systems are similar, regardless of level, more complex systems also add elements and problems not characteristic of simpler systems. However, social psychology has often treated power as though its operation in the small group were directly analogous to its operation in the large organization, thereby missing some of the more important dynamics of the latter.

The accumulation of power in a corporation is closely tied to the overall state of the system. At Indsco, formal position in the hierarchy was very important, and competence within the position was also a major factor. (Competence, indeed, is often a neglected side of power.) However, rank and decision-making authority alone were sometimes no more than a formal confirmation of already accumulated power; and getting into such a position was not enough to keep a person there, even though the position often provided the means for the consolidation of power. The size of the system and the complexity of its problems meant that even those with advantageous formal positions had to work with and through many others who had similar bases for power—what Thompson signified when he proposed that the number of power bases in an organization increase with the number of uncertainties or contingencies it faces. Finally, as I have already argued, the relative importance of functions reflected in formal positions shifted with shifting organizational problems and priorities. Though up-the-ladder managerial jobs supposedly became less tied to function, in reality, identification in terms of functional specialties remained. This was even truer lower down the management hierarchy, where people often promoted their function in order to promote themselves and could get trapped when their function was suddenly seen as less critical to financial success or other goals than some other one. A changing business climate was known to shift the relative position of functions with respect to one another and to account for the balance of power between people who depended on each other across functions. The relative centralization or decentralization of decision-making within each function and product area accounted for the relative power that lower-level representatives of an area brought to their task interactions with each other. In addition, whether a person was one of few or one of many in a position to bring pressure on a worker in a related function also affected relative amounts of power.

These abstractions came to life at Indsco in the relationships of field sales managers to product line managers in headquarters. Field sales managers directed the activities of sales workers over a number of product lines in a specific geographic territory; they were concerned with the performance of their people and the kinds of deals that could be made with customers. They responded to the exigencies of a competitive market situation and wanted to be in a favorable position on such things as price, quantity (especially during a time of material shortages), and shipping arrangements. Product line managers had a different set of priorities; they were the "business types" with responsibility, responsible for the profitability of their products across all geographic areas. They controlled price and allocation of product lines. The arrangements actually offered to customers were derived from the negotiations of sales people and line managers. There could be a great deal of tension between the people in these two positions. They had few face-to-face contacts, relating primarily by telephone or by telegram and mail, and their views from their locations differed. Field sales managers would insist that the product people were out of touch with the market, that they had no idea of the competitive scene out there, that they didn't know the customers. Product line managers, on the other hand, complained that the sales force was parochial and lacked knowledge of the overall business picture, that salespeople became too involved with their own special customers and forgot about the fate of Indsco as a whole.

The relative power of the people in these two jobs was determined by a number of system issues. In a growing economy several years earlier, when the corporation was also more decentralized, field managers were considered very powerful, running their "own little business." As the recession emerged and business fell off, and as the corporation began to centralize more and more decisions, the importance of the product line managers grew. Hierarchical position and departmental organization also had an effect. Depending on the department, many of the product managers held grade 16 positions; field managers were more typically at grade 12 or 14. Where this discrepancy in rank occurred, the field managers felt more dependent on the evaluations of product managers for their own career progress, and winning credibility with product managers was more important than the reverse ("They have the power to make or break our careers"), creating an asymmetry in power when the time for negotiations occurred. This asymmetry was reinforced by the typical form of interactions: field managers requested, product managers responded. If a product manager could not be reached by phone, field managers often could not act because they lacked important information. This infuriated them, but often there was nothing they could do without jeopardizing their relationship with the product manager. (A field manager once became so frustrated when he called a product manager several times one day, only to be told that he was in a meeting, then at lunch, then at another meeting, that he finally called the other's boss to say that he was needed right away. "He'll return my messages faster next time." However, he knew that this "kamikaze move" was risky. "With credibility you can get away with it. It depends on your relative position.") So field managers were generally much more concerned with winning favor with product managers, since they were functionally often more dependent, and they were much more effective managers of their own people when they had credibility with headquarters people. Finally, the relative numbers of field managers or product managers interfacing with each other could also affect the balance of power. Dealing with many made it easier for a person to retain some independence and to play them off against one another. One field sales manager related to seven different product line managers, and "with that many, there's no way I'm going to see them as my boss. If one isn't responsive, we'll just work harder on the other products, that's all."

There was thus a formal organizational component of power that was often out of the hands of individuals to determine. However, there were also a number of ways in which people could use the organization or operate through it that could increase the power available to them. These involved both activities and alliances.

ACTIVITIES AS A ROUTE TO POWER

Power could be accumulated as a result of performance—the job-related activities people engaged in. The organization itself could be used as a source of power. (This is a side of power that political scientists consider more often with respect to the public arena than do social psychologists and sociologists of organizations.) However, for activities to increase the power of the persons engaging in them, they have to meet three criteria: (1) they are extraordinary, (2) they are visible, and (3) they are relevant—identified with the solution to a pressing organizational problem.

Extraordinary Activities

Not everyone in an organization is in a position to accumulate power through competent performance because most people are just carrying out the ordinary and the expected—even if they do it very well. The extent to which a job is routinized fails to give an advantage to anyone doing it because "success" is seen as inherent in the very establishment of the position and the organization surrounding it. Neither persons nor organizations get "credit" for doing the mandatory or the expected. Excellent performance on tasks where behavior is more or less predictable may be valued, but it will not necessarily add to power. Most factory workers and lower participants in organizations have been rendered powerless not only by the managerial monopoly on decision-making but also by the routinization of tasks that reduces, if not eliminates, the opportunity to show enterprise or creativity, or ever do anything out of the ordinary or larger than life. This is a stronger and obverse version of Thompson's proposition that performance requiring discretion is more likely to be noticeable, and noticeability increases power. Crozier, too, theorized that the edge in a bargaining relationship is held by the person whose behavior is not predictable.[14]

There were several ways people at Indsco did something extraordinary: by being the first in a new position, by making organizational changes, or by taking major risks and succeeding. The rewards go to innovators, not to the second ones to do something; "the first to volunteer for extra work exhibits 'leadership,' " a quality anyone after that seems to lack.[15] A cycle could be observed around new functions and new positions in the corporation. The first time certain jobs were filled, fast track people were attracted. One of the inducements was the chance to step out of the ordinary and to participate in the development of a new function. The second cycle of people started to get trapped, and in one case a job that had been given a high grade when it was new (and required a person with sophisticated skills) was downgraded on the five-year reviews, so that it was seen to require a less senior manager. It became more and more difficult to fill the job as the function became more and more established. It was almost paradoxical: the success of the function as a whole made it less and less possible for the people running it to seem successful as individuals.

It becomes clear why some organizations seem to be continually changing, why new proposals and procedures are always under development. New managers must make changes or handle crises to demonstrate their abilities. If everything was running smoothly before and continues to run smoothly along the same track, what has the leader done? The "builder's complex" may emerge. Each leader needs his or her monument, which can be a physical structure or a redesigned organization chart. Crozier wrote about the plant directors whose ability to initiate action was curtailed by routinization of their functions—except in the case of planning and guiding the construction of new buildings or new physical layouts for shops. So people had a stake in finding reasons to undertake construction.[16] Very top executives at Indsco similarly became identified with the building of new field offices or proposed corporate moves. They would look for businesses to acquire or businesses to divest. They would have pet projects with which they were heavily identified, especially sweeping proposals such as taking the entire sales force off for a week-long meeting. There were definite costs if such plans did not work well—such single events were behind a number of firings—but enhanced power if they did.

Reorganizations were a common way to manipulate the structure to increase power. One new top executive at Indsco quickly established his position by making two power plays: firing the person in a key position under him and bringing in someone from outside the organization to fill the post, and creating a new division from a subgroup of the largest division, putting in someone he had worked with as its general manager. Another head of a function removed levels of the hierarchy; when he was promoted, his replacement put it back in. On a smaller scale, the manager of a personnel staff unit created two new levels of hierarchy in his nine-person group, putting in an assistant and developing two levels of the remaining people by upgrading some. (The people left on the lowest rung maintained their former position in the organization, retaining their "downward anchoring" and distance from the bottom, but they suddenly felt less powerful because when they looked up, they felt more junior.) Reorganizations were a frequent and important power move, for they served several functions at once. They ensured leaders that their own teams were well placed; opposition could be removed or rendered less effective. They provided leaders with rewards to dole out in the form of new opportunities and job changes. They enhanced the leader's power by creating new uncertainties in a situation that had been relatively routinized, making people more dependent on central authorities while they learned the new system. They were highly visible and difficult not to notice. In addition, because the question of the "best way to organize" was always relevant at Industrial Supply Corporation, reorganizations could always be presented as a problem-solving innovation.

Pulling off extraordinary risks was also power-enhancing—a classic source of the awe inspired by charismatic leaders. Very few people dared, but those who did became very powerful, for both organizational and social reasons. Organizationally, they had indicated their task-related value: they could perform in the most difficult of circumstances. Socially, they developed charisma in the eyes of the less daring. This was true of Indsco's most noted charismatic leader, an executive who had died prematurely, in Kennedy-like fashion. I heard about the devotion he inspired at many different levels of the organization and from many different kinds of people: "If we had him still with us, he'd shoot from the hip and say, 'Do it.' We'd all fall all over ourselves to do it, no matter whether it was logical or not. Unfortunately, he's gone; but where this thing might be were he still here! . . ." It was assumed that he could do anything, that no problem would be as bad if he were in charge. His rise to the top and the power he consolidated once he got there, was based almost entirely on one extraordinary risk: he took over a very unproductive plant and turned it around, staking his career on the outcome. When he finally became a division president, he continued to assume personal responsibility for events, to seek relationships and information far down the line, and to make himself available for criticism or blame if employees were unhappy with company decisions.

Visibility

For activities to enhance power, they have to be visible, to attract the notice of other people. Jobs that straddle the boundaries between organizational units or between the organization and its environment tend to have more noticeable activities, for example, than those that are well within a unit. These often become "power positions" because of their visibility. The chance to be noticed is differentially distributed in organizations, especially one that is so large that personal knowledge of everyone in even one's own function is impossible. It was also possible to gain visibility through participation on task forces or committees.

People who looked like "comers" seemed to have an instinct for doing the visible. A new marketing manager found that there was a communications gap around his function; no one seemed to know what was going on in other relevant corners of the unit, so he put out a report every other week. He netted a great deal of appreciation—and visibility. However, in other cases the things that were done for the sake of visibility seemed less beneficial. There were numerous complaints about certain managers who were more interested in choosing those programs that would be visible than those that represented high priorities to other people for reasons of organizational effectiveness or social value.

There were also some games played around "risks" because of the high costs of failure in an organization not set up to reward innovation: "Here when someone takes a chance, he strikes out on his own. If that sucker fails, he's got no place back at home. Nobody's got a string on my ass that's going to pull me back into this thing if I take a chance and try something new. Even the vice-president of the new business department says, 'If you come into this department, I can't give you a string to get back with. I don't have that much authority yet.' So we're saying to that guy that it's a total-risk, no-win situation. It's safer to be part of a group. The whole group can't fail. You learn to take a calculated risk, to be 90 percent sure. That's the game to play. The thing to do is to make it *look* like a risk but have it in your back pocket. You need the attention that comes from taking a risk but the security of knowing you can't fail." In short, public appearance was more important than substance.

Relevance

Finally, even extraordinary and visible activities would not necessarily build power if they failed the relevance test: whether or not they could be identified with the solution to pressing organizational problems. Relevance is similar to what other theorists have termed "immediacy." [17] As I have indicated, reorganizations can always demonstrate some relevance in systems where there can be no such thing as the "perfect" way to organize, but the relevance of other kinds of activities will be dependent on larger system issues, such as a current set of pressures upon the organization, and on how the actor presents his or her activities. Activities could not be engaged in for their own sake, even if brilliantly performed; wider system goals and ideology always had to be honored.

The importance of relevance in organizational politics was made very clear at Indsco in the case of a highly talented and very promising executive who became involved with the design of some new programs for employee relations. He was personally charismatic, and the people under him were highly devoted. He was also highly innovative; the programs he developed were very successfully received, and the organizational model he built represented a highly effective use of resources. His strategy for extending the applicability of his programs ran from the bottom up: first junior people would be involved, then they would pass the word on to their bosses, who would get a personal invitation to attend "briefing sessions" to learn what their subordinates were getting. All of this fit the organization development textbook picture of how to develop a new program. However, the manager became trapped in his own over-investment in his territory; his primary interest was in "drumming up business" so that he could create an even larger and more widespread set of programs. He was such a zealous advocate of his programs and his function that at a time when the company was having financial trouble, he began to be seen as "out to lunch." Questions were raised about his business sense, if he was still pushing development of people when the company might have to lay off people. Those who were against such activities in the first place found their excuse for criticism in declaring them irrelevant or saying that they might be a good thing but that the timing was off. Then the manager also had problems with his own alliances. The people who usually backed him were no longer in positions of power. He had one strong supporter at a high corporate level who saw that his next job was at least a lateral move, but developing the new function did not produce the career advance the manager had originally anticipated and seemed to decrease rather than increase his power.

Another staff unit was more aware of the relevance problem, if less creative in its programs. There the major strategy was to "sell things by finding an already acceptable label and an organization need to hang it on."

ALLIANCES: POWER THROUGH OTHERS

The informal social network that pervades organizations can be very important, as many theorists have pointed out. In a large, complex system, it is almost a necessity for power to come from social connections, especially those outside of the immediate work group. Such connections need to be long-term and stable and include "sponsors" (mentors and advocates upward in the organization), peers, and subordinates.

Sponsors

Sponsors have been found to be important in the careers of managers and professionals in many settings. In the corporation, "sponsored mobility" (controlled selection by elites) seems to determine who gets the most desirable jobs, rather than "contest mobility" (an open game), to use Ralph Turner's concepts.[18] At Indsco, high-level sponsors were known as "rabbis" or "godfathers," two colorful labels for these unofficial bestowers of power.

Sponsors are often thought of as teachers or coaches whose functions are primarily to make introductions or to train a young person to move effectively through the system. However, there are three other important functions besides advice that generate power for the people sponsored. First, sponsors are often in a position to *fight* for the person in question, to stand up for him or her in meetings if controversy is raised, to promote that person for promising opportunities. When there are large numbers of personnel distributed across wide territories, as in Industrial Supply Corporation, there was much advantage to being the favorite of a powerful person who could help distinguish a person from the crowd and argue his or her virtues against those of other people. ("They say the rabbi system is dead," commented a young manager, "but I can't believe we make promotion decisions without it.") Despite a rating system that tried to make the system more open and equitable at lower levels, sponsors could still make a difference. Indeed, one of the problems with not having a powerful manager, Indsco workers thought, was that the manager would not be strong enough to stand up and fight for subordinates in places where they could not fight for themselves.

Second, sponsors often provided the occasion for lower-level organization members to *bypass the hierarchy:* to get inside information, to short-circuit cumbersome procedures, or to cut red tape. People develop a social relationship with a powerful person which allows them to go directly to that person, even though there is no formal interface, and once there, a social interchange can often produce formal results. This could be very important to formal job success in Indsco, to the ability to get things done, in a system where people could easily get bogged down if they had to honor official protocol. One salesman with a problem he wanted to solve for a customer described Indsco as "like the Army, Air Force, and Navy—we have a formal chain of command." The person who could make the decision on his problem was four steps removed from him, not in hierarchical rank but according to operating procedure. Ordinarily, he would not be able to go directly to him, but they had developed a relationship over a series of sales meetings, during which the more powerful person had said, "Please drop by anytime you're at headquarters." So the salesman found an occasion to "drop by," and in the course of the casual conversation mentioned his situation. It was solved immediately. A woman manager used her powerful sponsors in a similar way. Whenever her boss was away, she had lunch with her friends among the corporate officers. This provided an important source of information, such as "secret" salary information from a vice-president. In fact, the manager revealed, "much of what I get done across groups is based on informal personal relations through the years, when there is no formal way to do it."

Third, sponsors also provide an important signal to other people, a form of *"reflected power."* Sponsorship indicates to others that the person in question has the backing of an influential person, that the sponsor's resources are somewhere behind the individual. Much of the power of relatively junior people comes not from their own resources but from the "credit" extended to them because there appears to be a more powerful set of resources in the distance. This was an important source of the power of "comers" at Indsco, the "water walkers" and "high fliers" who were on fast tracks because they were high performers with powerful backing. A manager in that position described it this way: "A variety of people become impressed with you. You see the support at several levels; someone seems comfortable with you although he's a vice-president, and he looks you in the eye. You get offered special jobs by powerful people. You're pulled aside and don't have to go through channels. If you can sustain that impression for three to four years, your sphere of influence will increase to the point where you have a clear path for a few miles. You can have anything you want up to a certain level, where the power of the kingpins changes. Here's how it happens. A manager who is given a water walker, knowing that the person is seen as such from above and from below, is put in a no-win situation. If the person does well, everyone knew it anyway. If the person doesn't do well, it is considered the manager's fault. So the manager can only try to get the star promoted, move him or her out as fast as possible; and the manager wants to help accelerate the growth of water walkers because someday the manager might be working for them. All of this promotes the star's image." Another rising executive commented, "Everyone attempts to get on the heels of a flier. Everyone who does well has a sponsor, someone to take you on their heels. In my case, I had three managers. All of them have moved but continue to help me. A vice-president likes me. I can count on getting any job up a level as long as he remains in favor."

Those seen as moving accumulated real power because of their connections with sponsors, but they also had to be careful about the way they used the reflected power of the sponsor: "It's an embryonic, gossamer-type thing because four levels up is *far* away, and the connection is very tenuous. It's only a promise of things to come. You can't use it with your own manager, or you get in trouble. The rabbis are not making commitments right now. One guy tried to use his connections with his manager, to cash in his chips too early. The axe fell. He had to go back to zero." Handling relationships with sponsors could be tricky, too. "It's scary because you have to live up to others' expectations. There is great danger if you go up against a godfather. It becomes a father/son issue as well as business. God help you if you are not grateful for the favors given." And, of course, fast trackers can also fall when their sponsors fall if they have not developed their own power base in the interim.

If sponsors are important for the success of men in organizations, they seem absolutely essential for women. If men function more effectively as leaders when they appear to have influence upward and outward in the organization, women need even more the signs of such influence and the access to real power provided by sponsors. Margaret Cussler's and Margaret Hennig's studies of those few women in top management positions in U.S. corporations showed dramatically the importance of sponsorship. A British study concluded that "office uncles" were important in the careers of women in organizations because they offered behavioral advice and fought for the women to be promoted.[19] Ella Grasso, the first woman elected to a state governorship on her own, had a sponsor in John Bailey, who was chairman of the Democratic National Committee from 1961 to 1968. He first spotted her as a political "comer" in the 1950s. Since then he has provided advice, campaign help, and introductions to certain circles.[20] At Indsco the same pattern emerged. One woman was brought into her management position at Indsco by a sponsor, a vice-president for whom she had worked as an executive secretary. Her relation to him and the connections she had already made through him made her reception into management quite different from that of other former secretaries. Another secretary who was promoted without sponsorship felt ignored, isolated, and resented after her move, but the first woman's experience was different. Male peers immediately made her one of the gang. During her first week in the new position, she remembered, she was deluged with phone calls from men letting her know they were there if she had any questions, making sure she had a lunch date, and inviting her to meetings.

If sponsors are more important for women, they can also be harder to come by. Sponsorship is sometimes generated by good performance, but it can also come, as one of Indsco's fast trackers put it, "because you have the right social background or know some of the officers from outside the corporation or look good in a suit." Some people thought that higher-ups decided to sponsor particular individuals because of identification and that this process almost automatically eliminated women. (There is, indeed, much research evidence that leaders choose to promote the careers of socially similar subordinates.) [21] Men could not identify with women, and very few women currently held top positions. Identification was the issue in these remarks: "Boy wonders rise under certain power structures. They're recognized by a powerful person because they are very much like him. He sees himself, a younger version, in that person. . . . Who can look at a woman and see themselves?" This was a good question. When women acquired sponsors, the reasons were often different from the male sponsor-protégé situation. In one case, officers were looking for a high-performing woman they could make into a showpiece to demonstrate the organization's openness to good women. In another instance, an executive was thought to have "hung his hat on a woman" (decided to sponsor her) to demonstrate that he could handle a "tricky" management situation and solve a problem for the corporation.

Peers

More often neglected in the study of the accumulation of organizational power is the importance of strong peer alliances, although Barry Stein has written about the ways groups can capitalize on the success of a "comer." [22] At Indsco high "peer acceptance," as managers put it, was necessary to any power base or career success. "Individual performers" found their immediate accomplishments rewarded, but their careers stuck as we saw in Chapter 3, because they had not built, nor were seen as capable of building, the kinds of connections necessary for success in ever more interdependent higher-level jobs. "The group needs each other," a sales manager remarked. "To become powerful, people must first be successful and receive recognition, but they must wear the respect with a lack of arrogance. They must not be me-oriented. Instead of protecting their secrets in order to stand taller than the crowd, they are willing to share successes. They help their peers. . . . This is 'leader quality.' "

Strong alliances among peers could advance the group as a whole, as Stein noted in commenting on the fact that certain cohorts sometimes seem to produce all of the leaders in an organization.[23] However, a highly competitive situation could also imbue peer relations with politics and pitfalls. A star performer just promoted to his first management position told me quite proudly how he had just handled his first political battle with a counterpart in his position. One reason he was telling me at such length, he explained, was because he had no one he could tell within the organization. He had decided to take care of the issue by going directly to the other man and working it out with him, then promising him it would go no further. My informant had been the one who was wronged, and he could have gone to his boss or the other person's boss, but he decided that in the long run he was wiser to try to honor peer solidarity and try to build an ally out of the person who had hurt him. "I didn't want to create enemies," he commented. "Some peers look to you for help, to work with you for mutual gain, but others wait for you to stumble so they can bad-mouth you: 'Yeah, he's a sharp guy, but he drinks a lot.' If I had gone against the other guy now, even if I had won, he would have had a knife out for me sometime. Better to do him a favor by keeping quiet, and then he'll be grateful later."

Peer alliances often worked through direct exchange of favors. On lower levels information was traded; on higher levels bargaining and trade often took place around good performers and job openings. In a senior executive's view, it worked like this: "A good job becomes available. A list of candidates is generated. That's refined down to three or four. That is circulated to a select group that has an opportunity to look it over. Then they can make bargains among themselves." A manager commented, "There's lots of 'I owe you one.' If you can accumulate enough chits, that helps you get what you need; but then, of course, people have to be in a position to cash them in."

Subordinates

The accumulation of power through alliances was not always upward-oriented. For one thing, differential rates of hierarchical progress could mean that juniors or peers one day could become a person's boss the next. So it could be to a person's advantage to make alliances downward in the hierarchy with people who looked like they might be on the way up. There was a preference for "powerful" subordinates as well as powerful bosses. Just in the way Bernard Levenson proposed, a manager on the move would try to develop subordinates who could take over, keeping a member of "his team" in place. Professionals and executives needed more junior people loyal to them as much as they needed the backing of higher-level people. Especially higher up, the successful implementation of plans and policies depended heavily upon the activities of those people lower down in the hierarchy who were responsible for the carrying out of day-to-day operations or the translation into specifics of general guidelines. So alliances with subordinates often developed early in careers, anticipating the time when managers would need the support of "their team." There was often a scrambling by managers to upgrade the jobs reporting to them so that they could attract more powerful subordinates. Also, as I have indicated, managers could benefit from speeding up the career of a person already on a fast track.

However, if power was something that not everyone could accumulate, what happened to the powerless?

ACCOUNTABILITY WITHOUT POWER:
SOURCES OF BUREAUCRATIC POWERLESSNESS

People who have authority without system power are powerless. People held accountable for the results produced by others, whose formal role gives them the right to command but who lack informal political influence, access to resources, outside status, sponsorship, or mobility prospects, are rendered powerless in the organization. They lack control over their own fate and are dependent on others above them—others whom they cannot easily influence—while they are expected by virtue of position to be influential over those parallel or below. Their sense of lack of control above is heightened by its contrast with the demands of an accountable authority position: that they mobilize others in the interests of a task they may have had little part in shaping, to produce results they may have had little part in defining.

First-line supervisors in highly routinized functions often are functionally powerless. Their situation—caught between the demands of a management hierarchy they are unlikely to enter because of low opportunity and the resistance of workers who resent their own circumstances—led classic writers on organizations to describe them as "men in the middle." [24] (However, they are also often "women in the middle.") They have little chance to gain power through activities, since their functions do not lend themselves to the demonstration of the extraordinary, nor do they generate high visibility or solutions to organizational problems. They have few rewards to distribute, since rewards are automatically given by the organization; and their need for reliable performance from workers in order to keep their own job secure limits the exercise of other forms of power. "I'm afraid to confront the employees because they have the power to slack, to slouch, to take too much time," a supervisor of clerical workers said, "and I need them for results. I'm measured on *results*—quantitative output, certain attendance levels, number of reports filed. They have to do it for me." Another one said, "When I ask for help, I get punished because my manager will say, 'But it's your job. If you can't do it, you shouldn't be in that job.' So what's *their* job? Sending me notes telling me it's unacceptable? They're like teachers sending me a report card." First-line supervisors also felt powerless because their jobs were vulnerable during times of recession, while people farther up in the hierarchy seemed secure. They resented the fact that their peers were let go, while higher managers were not. "Why us? Aren't they running the show? Shouldn't they be the ones to suffer if business isn't going well?" And supervisors of secretaries, as we saw in Chapter 4, were also rendered powerless by the secretary's allegiance to a boss with more status and clout in the organization.

Occupants of certain staff jobs were similarly organizationally powerless.[25] They had no line authority and were dependent on managers to implement their decisions and carry out their recommendations. Staff programs that managers saw as irrelevant to their primary responsibilities would be ignored. Affirmative action and equal employment opportunity officers often found themselves in this position. Their demands were seen by line people as an intrusion, a distraction from more important business, and the extra paperwork that EEO entailed was annoying. Personnel staff who tried to introduce more rational, universalistic, and equitable systems for job placement for nonexempts also had difficulty selling their programs, as Chapter 4 indicated. These staff activities were seen as destroying a managerial prerogative and interfering with something managers preferred to do for themselves. The aims of personnel people in sending out certain candidates for jobs could conflict with the desires of the manager who would be using the candidate, and when battles resulted, it was often the more prestigious line manager who prevailed.

Regardless of function, people could also be rendered powerless if their own management did not extend opportunities for power downward—if their situations did not permit them to take risks, if their authority was undercut, or if their sphere of autonomous decision-making was limited. There seemed to be a consensus at Indsco that superiors who solved problems themselves or tried to do the job themselves disempowered the managers or professionals under them. Considered ideal, by contrast, was the manager who "never gave anyone an answer; but when you walked out of his office, you had it because he asked you the questions that made you think of it." Many women thus objected to the "protectiveness" that they perceived in their managers, protection that "encased" them "in a plastic bubble," as one put it, and rendered them ineffectual. Anyone who is protected loses power, for successes are then attributed to the helpful actions of others, rather than the person's own actions. Women complained about the "people who want to move walls for me instead of saying, 'Hey, here's a wall. Let's strategize working through it.'" Another said, "You need a lot of exposure to get ahead, a broad base of experience. I don't want to be protected, given the easy management situations, the easy customers, the sure-fire position." And being in a position where decisions were reviewed and authority could be undercut also created powerlessness. A customer service representative faced a situation where she had to tell a customer that she couldn't ship to him because the materials were not available; this was an order that had come down to her. The customer said he would call the immediate manager. The manager backed up the representative, indicating that he would call headquarters but that the rep was right and had the information. So the customer went one step higher in the hierarchy, calling headquarters himself. This time he managed to get a change. Everyone lost credibility, but especially the woman. Nothing diminishes leaders' power more than subordinates' knowledge that they can always go over their heads, or that what they promise has no real clout. A management recruiter advised companies that wanted to ensure the success of new women managers not to inadvertently encourage resistance to the new manager; even seemingly innocuous requests, such as a higher manager asking to be kept informed, could encourage subordinates to bypass the woman and do their reporting higher up.[26]

Powerlessness, finally, was the general condition of those people who could not make the kinds of powerful alliances that helped to manage the bureaucracy. People without sponsors, without peer connections, or without promising subordinates remained in the situation of bureaucratic dependency on formal procedures, routine allocations of rewards, communication that flowed through a multi-layered chain of command, and decisions that must penetrate, as Robert Presthus put it, "innumerable veto barriers."[27] People who reached dead ends in their careers also rapidly lost power, since they could no longer promise gains to those who followed them and no longer had the security of future movement. Powerlessness was also the psychological state of people who, for whatever reason, felt insecure in their functioning as leaders and anticipated resistance rather than cooperation from those whom they were to lead. Indeed, the structural characteristics of modern organizational life tend to produce the symptoms of powerlessness in more and more lower-to-middle managers, supervisors, bureaucrats, and professionals. The chance to engage in the non-routine, to show discretion, to take risks, or to become known, are all less available in the large bureaucracy.

BEHAVIORAL RESPONSES TO POWERLESSNESS

Controlling Behavior and Close Supervision

Psychoanalyst Karen Horney, in *The Neurotic Personality of Our Time*, described people's neurotic attempt to dominate when they feel anxious or helpless, inferior or insignificant. As a protection and a defense, the psychologically powerless turn to control over others. They want to be right all the time and are irritated at being proven wrong. They cannot tolerate disagreement.[28] In short, they become critical, bossy, and controlling. Some degree of power, in the sense of mastery and control over one's fate, is necessary for feelings of self-esteem and well-being, as Rollo May has indicated.[29] When a person's exercise of power is thwarted or blocked, when people are rendered powerless in the larger arena, they may tend to concentrate their power needs on those over whom they have even a modicum of authority. There is a displacement of control downward paralleling displacement of aggression. In other words, people respond to the restrictiveness of their own situation by behaving restrictively toward others. People will "boss" those they can, as in the image of the nagging housewife or old-maid schoolteacher or authoritarian boss, if they cannot flex their power muscles more constructively and if, moreover, they are afraid they really are powerless.

One example of this syndrome comes from research on the leadership style of low-power male Air Force officers. Officers of lower status and advancement potential favored more directive, rigid, and authoritarian techniques of leadership, seeking control over subordinates. Subordinates were their primary frame of reference for their own status assessment and enhancement, and so they found it important to "lord it over" group members. They also did not help talented members of the group get ahead (perhaps finding them too threatening) and selected immediate assistants of mediocre rather than outstanding talent.[30] Similarly, in a French bureaucracy technical engineers in an isolated position with low mobility and low power with respect to directors were, in turn, extremely authoritarian and paternalistic with *their* subordinates.[31]

When people expect to be successful in their influence attempts, in contrast, they can afford to use milder forms of power, such as personal persuasion. Even a little bit of influence is likely to work, and it is so much more pleasant to avoid conflict and struggle. But when people anticipate resistance, they tend to use the strongest kind of weapon they can muster. As Frantz Fanon proposed in *The Wretched of the Earth,* the powerless may come to rely on force, first and foremost.[32] In a series of laboratory studies simulating supervision of three production workers, male subjects who lacked confidence in their own abilities to control the world or who thought they encountered resistance from the mock subordinates used more coercive than persuasive power, especially when resistance stemmed from "poor attitude" (a direct threat to their power) rather than ineptness.[33] We know from other laboratory studies that people are more automatically obedient toward the organizationally powerful than the powerless, regardless of formal position. Subordinates inhibit aggression in the face of power, but they direct more intense aggression to the relatively powerless. Indeed, it can be argued, as a number of other theorists have also done, that a controlling leadership style is a *result* rather than a *cause* of hostile, resistant, or noncompliant behavior on the part of subordinates.[34]

Thus, the relatively powerless in positions of organizational authority also have reason to be more controlling and coercive. If they have less call on the organization's resources, less backup and support from sponsors and managers, less cooperative subordinates, and less influence in the informal power structure, people can only use the strongest tools at their disposal: discipline or threats or maintaining tight control over all of the activities in their jurisdiction. If managers or supervisors who encounter resistance from those they are trying to direct tend to become more coercive in their power tactics, it is a vicious cycle: powerless authority figures who use coercive tactics provoke resistance and aggression, which prompts them to become even more coercive, controlling, and behaviorally restrictive.

At Indsco relatively powerless managers who were insecure about their organizational status tended to give the least freedom to subordinates and to personally control their department's activities much more tightly. (I used formal job characteristics, other people's perceptions, and my own observations to decide who was relatively powerless.) These managers made all of the decisions, did an amount of operating work themselves that others in the organization would consider "excessive," and did not let subordinates represent them at meetings or on task forces. They tried to control the communication flow in and out of their department, so that all messages had to pass through them. One manager in a low-power situation, who was considered "tough to work for—too tight," jumped on a subordinate for calling a vice-president directly to ask a question, saying, "*I'm* the one who represents this function to v.p.'s." Another manager with good people working for him wanted to see that all the credit went to him. He wrote a report of his unit's activities that made it seem as though he, and not the salespeople involved, had generated an increase in sales: "By negotiating with the profit center, I saw to it that. . . ."

Sometimes low-power managers and supervisors took over the task and tried to do or direct closely the work of subordinates instead of giving them a free hand, because technical mastery of job content was one of the few arenas in which they *did* feel powerful. Often people get to first-line managerial jobs, for example, because they are good at the operating tasks. Trying to do the job themselves or watching over subordinates' shoulders to correct the slightest deviation from how the supervisors themselves would do it represents a comfortable retreat into expertise from the frustrations of trying to administer when organizational power is low. People can still feel good knowing that they could do the job well—or better than their subordinates. Thus, they are tempted to control their subordinates, keep them from learning or developing their own styles, jump in too quickly to solve problems, and "nitpick" over small things subordinates do differently. All of these things were considered characteristics of ineffective managers at Indsco. However, the temptation to take over the work of the next level down instead of engaging in more general leadership—a temptation that always existed, even for people at the very top, as one of them told me—was succumbed to especially by the powerless.

Conditions of work could intersect with low organizational power to reinforce a tendency toward closeness of supervision. Departments of women clerical workers run by powerless women managers were a case in point. The supervisors were, in turn, managed by men, who gave them detailed orders and little discretion, and the supervisors tended to be in a terminal job and poorly connected to informal power alliances. At the same time, the office setup encouraged a restrictive, controlled atmosphere. The clerical workers were confined to banks of desks in large offices virtually under the nose of the supervisor. These departments were considered among the most tightly run in the corporation. They had the least absenteeism and a decided "schoolroom" atmosphere. In contrast, the conditions of work in sales made it more difficult for even the most control-prone manager to supervise as tightly, since salespeople under one manager were often scattered throughout several field offices, and sales workers were legitimately out of the office a great deal of the time. Field sales managers, similarly, operated away from the direct view of their own managers. So the greater freedom of the sales function was empowering all down the line. However, the setting for clerical workers and their bosses made it easier for them to remain powerless.

Rules-Mindedness

The powerless inside an authority structure often become rules-minded in response to the limited options for power in their situation, turning to "the rules" as a power tool. Rules are made in the first place to try to control the uncontrollable; invoking organization rules and insisting on careful adherence to them is a characteristic response of the powerless in authority positions. For one thing, "the rules" represent their only safe and sure legitimate authority, the place where higher-ups are guaranteed to give them backing, because higher-ups wrote or represent the rules. They have few other means to use in bargaining with subordinates for cooperation. As Crozier wrote, "If no difference can be introduced in the treatment given to subordinates, either in the present definition of the job or in the fulfillment of their career expectations, hierarchical superiors cannot keep power over them. Superiors' roles will be limited to controlling the application of rules." [35]

Second, powerlessness coupled with accountability, with responsibility for results dependent on the actions of others, provokes a cautious, low-risk, play-it-safe attitude. Getting everything right is the response of those who lack other ways to impress those above them or to secure their position; and in turn they demand this kind of ritualistic conformity from subordinates, like school-teachers more concerned about neatness of a paper than its ideas. Secretarial supervisors at Indsco tended to be known for these traits: a concern with proper form rather than a good outcome. Or, as someone else said, "You don't give freedom or experiment with procedure when you're a first-liner. You try to cover your ass and not make a mistake they can catch you on."

Overconformity to the rules and ritual concern with formalities are characteristics of the "bureaucratic personality" identified in Robert Merton's classic essay. Bureaucratic organizations, by their very structures, exert constant pressures on employees to perform reliably within prescribed and predictable behavioral limits. At the same time, routinization of careers within a bureaucracy—the provision of planned, graded, incremental promotions and salary increases—offers incentives for disciplined action and conformity to official regulations. These features taken together, Merton concluded, produced the bureaucrat's substitution of means (the rules, the forms, the procedures) for ends (goals, purposes, underlying rationales). [36]

Melville Dalton also recognized that the powerless hang on to rules, contrasting the "strong" and the "weak" as models of managerial tendencies.

> The weak are fearful in conflict situations and absorb aggressions to avoid trouble. . . . They hesitate to act without consulting superiors and take refuge in clearly formulated rules, whether adequate or not for their footing at the moment. Following their fairy-tale image of the organization as a fixed thing, they suffer from

their experience that it is not. This, of course, aggravates their difficulty in grasping the tacit expectations that associations do not want to spell out, when events are troublesome. . . . As they seek to escape dilemmas, their unfitness to act outside the haven of understood rules invites aggression from the strong who are searching for shortcuts in the network of official routes.[37]

Thus, it is those lower in power who become rules-minded, but it is a bit too simple to attribute the concern with rules only to a reactive stance—a general bureaucratic world view. For those with relatively little organizational power but who must lead or influence others, *their control of "the rules" can represent one of their few areas of personal discretion.* They can exchange a bending of the rules for compliance; they can reward their favorites with a lighter application of the rules. However, first the rules must be experienced and honored. Subordinates or clients or workers must know what the formalities are like before they can be grateful for a bit of special treatment. They must see that the manager or supervisor or official has the right to invoke the full measure of the rule. So the persons who concern themselves with the rules both have something that *must* command obedience and have the basis for a form of power through differential application of those same rules. Staff officials without the power or credibility to persuade people in other departments to carry out the *spirit* of new programs (like affirmative action or centralized secretarial hiring) could fall back on their *letter,* burying uncooperative departments in mounds of paperwork.

One Indsco manager who was particularly concerned about protocol, formalities, and proper procedure had come up the ranks the hard way and was still not in a very influential position. He was upset that perquisites and privileges that had taken him long to earn were now automatically given out to younger people. He felt that they took liberties and behaved much too casually. One time, a young person introduced himself to the manager at a company function and then called to make a lunch date. The manager turned him down and then phoned his boss to complain that the young person was trying to get into the executive dining room. However, there were hints of the true feelings behind the manager's complaints. The manager was someone whose only source of power and respect came through the organizational formalities. He counted on being able to control his subordinates by carefully doling out privileges or offering small deviations from the formal rules. If the rules did not mean much anymore, what did he have left?

Territoriality and Domain Control

Merton went on to argue that bureaucrats adopt a domineering manner because whenever they use the authority of their office with clients or subordinates, they are acting as representatives of the power and prestige of the entire structure.[38] Vicarious power—power through identification—Merton seemed to say, breeds bossiness. However, if we look more closely at the organizational structures he described, we can see that this aspect of the "bureaucratic personality" reflects a response to *powerlessness* rather than to power, delegated or otherwise. The organization's concern with regulations reduces administrators' spheres of autonomy, limits their influence and decision-making power. The very provision of graded careers stressing seniority, in which incremental advances are relatively small and all must wait their turn, fosters dependency on the organization, which always holds back some rewards until the next advance. It removes incentives for assertion and reduces people to a common denominator—one in which they did not participate in defining. Unless people can accumulate power through activities or alliances, they face a sense of helplessness and insignificance.

In response to organizational insignificance, officials turn to their own small territory, their own little piece of the system—their subordinates, their function, their expertise. They guard their domain jealously. They narrow their interests to focus exclusively on it. They try to insulate and protect it and to prevent anyone else from engaging in similar activities without their approval or participation as "the experts." Another organizational cycle is set in motion. As each manager protects his or her own domain, the sense of helplessness and powerlessness of other administrators in intersecting units increases. They, in turn, may respond by redoubling their domination over their territory and their workers. The result can be "sub-optimization": each subgroup optimizing only its own goals and forgetting about wider system interests. For example, a worker in Crozier's clerical agency described this territoriality of supervisors. Supervisors were squeezed by higher management, which blamed them for poor morale and delivered speeches and written instructions advising them to pay more attention to leadership. In the worker's view, "They worry too much about their career and the possibility of promotion. They are jealous and awfully competitive. They are also sectarian. Often there is a lot of hostility between sections. . . . Each one of them wants to have his little kingdom." [39]

At Indsco, territoriality seemed more often a response of relatively powerless staff than of line officials. Line officials could turn to close supervision or rules application, but staff had only whatever advantage they could gain through specialized knowledge and jurisdiction over an area of expertise. This was especially clear around personnel functions. The organization was so large that personnel training, management development, and organization development responsibilities were divided up among many different units, some attached to divisions, some attached to the corporation, and some attached to specific functions. Such units often prevented each other from acting by claiming territorial encroachments. The result was that nearly all of them remained narrowly specialized and highly conservative. It was enough to kill a proposal with which other units would have to cooperate if the idea originated in one that was looking temporarily more powerful. There was a parallel problem on the wider system level, where one division was much larger and more powerful than others. Organizational and personnel innovations developed by the major division were rarely adopted by any of the others, even if they proved highly effective, because the other units were trying to protect their own territory as an independent domain.

There were also reflections of territoriality among low-power staff people on the individual level. The tendency was to hang on to a territory that provided legitimacy, even when inappropriate. One staff women, hired to run affirmative action programs, tended to bring up the women's issue wherever she was, as though she would have no right to participate unless she dragged in her "expertise." Yet, on one occasion she had been invited to join a group of managers because of what she might contribute to general discussions of organizational issues. But she could not let go of her domain, and the managers were sorry they had included her. Similarly, sometimes staff people clung to whatever might help solve their future power issues, regardless of its relevance to present tasks. One manager asked a personnel staff official to send him an older, experienced woman for a position as his administrative assistant. Instead, the man in the personnel department insisted on sending him three ambitious, rather inexperienced younger women, making it clear that personnel matters, such as the decision about which candidates were appropriate, were his domain. However, perhaps there was something else underneath. The three women were ambitious and on the move. If he placed them fast, they owed him a favor, and because they were going to seek to move, they would have to keep coming back to him. Therefore, they were "his" candidates and represented possible future alliances.

Territorial control and domain concerns were also behind much of the treatment of secretaries at Indsco, as we saw in Chapter 4; but now it also becomes clear that relatively powerless bosses are likelier to be the ones who try to keep strong personal control over secretaries. Those secretaries who were encouraged by their bosses to seek promotions out of the secretarial ranks tended to work for the more powerful bosses.

The behavioral responses of powerless "leaders" to their situations, then, in controlling behavior, rules-mindedness, and territoriality, could make the conditions of work less satisfying for subordinates. To seek a more powerful leader could also be a way of seeking a more empowering, freedom-enhancing environment.

CYCLES OF POWER AND POWERLESSNESS

Power rises and falls on the basis of complex exigencies: the organizational situation, environmental pressures, the simultaneous actions of others. However, in terms of individual behavior at least, power is likely to bring more power, in ascending cycles, and powerlessness to generate powerlessness, in a descending cycle. The powerful have "credibility" behind their actions, so they have the capacity to get things done. Their alliances help them circumvent the more restricting aspects of the bureaucracy. They are able to be less coercive or rules-bound in their exercise of leadership, so their subordinates and clients are more likely to cooperate. They have the security of power, so they can be more generous in allowing subordinates power of their own, freedom of action. We come full circle. The powerful are not only given material and symbolic advantage but they are also provided with circumstances that can make them more effective mobilizers of other people. Thus they can accomplish and, through their accomplishments, generate more power. This means they can build alliances, with other people as colleagues rather than threats, and through their alliances generate more power.

The powerless are caught in a downward spiral. The coping mechanisms of low power are also those most likely to provoke resistance and further restriction of power. The attitudes of powerlessness get translated downward, so that those under a low-power leader can also become ineffective. There was this vicious circle at Indsco: A young trainee was assigned to a "chronic complainer" of a manager, who had had organizational problems and had fallen well below the level of peers in his cohort. The trainee was talented but needed to be channeled. The manager's negativism began to transfer down to the trainee, and the young man started to lose his motivation. Nothing was done to correct the atmosphere. He became less motivated and more critical of the organization. He vented his hostility in nonconformist ways (long hair, torn clothes, general disrespect for people and things). Then people began to reinforce his negativity by focusing on what they observed: he's a "wise guy." They observed the symptoms but never looked at the real problem: the manager's situation. Finally, the trainee resigned just before he would have been terminated. Everyone breathed a sign of relief that the "problem" was gone. The manager lost even more credibility. This just reinforced his negativity and his coerciveness.

Since the behavioral responses of the powerless tend to be so ineffective as leadership styles, it would be the last rather than the first solution of most organizations to give such ineffective people more power or more responsibility. Yet all the indicators point to the negative effects of behavior that come from too little power, such as rules-mindedness and close supervision. Chris Argyris has noted that alienation and low morale accompany management's praise for the reliable (rules-obedient) rather than the enterprising (risk-taking) worker. Studies have shown that turnover varies with the degree to which supervisors structure tasks in advance and demand compliance, absenteeism with the tendency of supervisors to be "directive" and maintain close and detailed control. Yet when supervisors at Sears, Roebuck had responsibility for so many people that they could not watch any one person closely, employees responded to this greater latitude with greater job satisfaction.[40] So perhaps it is meaningful to suggest interrupting the cycle of powerlessness: to empower those in low-power situations by increasing their opportunities and their latitude rather than to continue to punish them for their ineffectiveness, reinforcing their powerless state of mind.

"Power" in organizations, as I am using the term, is synonymous with autonomy and freedom of action. The powerful can afford to risk more, and they can afford to allow others their freedom. The bureaucratic machinery of modern organizations means that there are rather few people who are really powerful. Power has become a scarce resource that most people feel they lack. Although the scramble for political advantage still distinguishes relative degrees of power, the organization places severe limits on everyone's freedom of action. The powerful get more, but they still share some of the mentality of powerlessness.

And women, in large hierarchical organizations, are especially often caught in the cycles of powerlessness.

WOMEN AND POWER IN ORGANIZATIONS

My analysis of the importance of power in large organizations and the behavioral consequences of powerlessness for management styles can help to explain some familiar clichés about women's lack of potential for organizational leadership: "No one wants to work for a woman"; and "Women are too rigid and controlling to make good bosses anyway."

Preference for Men = Preference for Power

There is considerable evidence for a general cultural attitude that men make better leaders. A large number of studies have concluded that neither men nor women want to work for a woman (although women are readier to do so than men). In a 1965 survey of 1,000 male and 900 female executives, among *Harvard Business Review* readers, over two-thirds of the men and nearly one-fifth of the women reported that they themselves would not feel comfortable working for a woman. Very few of either sex (9 percent of the men and 15 percent of the women) thought that *men* felt comfortable working for a woman, and a proportion of the male respondents said that women did not belong in executive positions at all. A total of 51 percent of the men responded that women were "temperamentally unfit" for management, writing in gratuitous comments such as, "They scare male executives half to death. . . . As for an efficient woman manager, this is cultural blasphemy. . . ." [41] In the survey of nonexempts at Indsco, these workers, too, overwhelmingly agreed with the statement that "men make better supervisors." And they did so while also rejecting the idea that it was "unacceptable" or "unfeminine" for a woman to be a manager, as Table 7–1 indicates. Women managers were aware of this attitude. One woman at Indsco showed me a poster which she considered indicative; it was large and painted in dark, rather foreboding tones. Most of the poster was taken up by the head of a man wearing a workman's cap; he was saying furtively into a telephone, "I just quit. The new boss is a woman."

Yet when it comes to evaluating concrete leadership styles, as used by men or by women outside of organizations, research has found that there is no strong preference for men or general tendency to perceive men and women differently. In one study subjects were asked to make judgments about male and female leaders exhibiting a variety of styles. The evaluations of men and women did not differ significantly on most variables, including such critical ones as "production emphasis," but there was a tendency to give higher ratings to men than to women when they "initiated structure" and higher ratings to women than men when they showed "consideration," demonstrating some propensity for raters to "reward" people for sex-stereotypical behavior. Another study used a different set of categories but had nearly identical results.

TABLE 7–1

Attitudes of Nonexempt Employees at Indsco about Women as Supervisors

	Mean rating of agreement with statement on 9-point scale, with 1 = strongly disagree 9 = strongly agree	
	Men (N = 23)	Women (N = 88)
1. "Men make better supervisors."	7.92	6.50 *
2. "It is acceptable for a man to be competitive, but not a woman."	3.51	3.22
3. "A woman cannot be a supervisor and feminine as well."	3.30	3.10

* The difference between the ratings of men and women on this statement was statistically significant (p < .05).
(Figures reported with the permission of G. Homall)

Students and bank supervisors judged stories involving male and female leaders using four different styles. The "reward" style was rated somewhat more effective when used by men, but the "friendly-dependent" style (which the researchers hoped would capture a female stereotype) was rated high for *either* sex when used with the opposite sex. The use of "threat" was considered ineffective for both sexes, though there was a slight but not significant tendency to let men get away with it more than women. It has also been found that people who have once worked for a woman boss are more likely than those who never have to be favorably disposed toward women leaders.[42] And women, as Table 7–1 above showed, are slightly more accepting of the idea of women supervisors and managers than are men. Thus, sex preferences in general seem to play only a very small role, if any, in responding to the style of any specific leader.

Theories saying that women handle power differently from men, that men are the instrumental leaders, oriented toward competition and domination through nature or childhood training, also do not match the realities of adult life in organizations. By the age of ten, for example, leadership in groups does not reflect the use of different strategies of persuasion by females and males. Nor does either sex seem more naturally cooperative or susceptible to social influence from peers.[43] There is as yet no research evidence that makes a case for sex differences in either leadership aptitude or style. A wide variety of investigations, from field studies of organizations to paper-and-pencil tests, indicates that the styles of men and women vary over the same range and that there are no conclusive sex-related strategies.[44] (See Appendix II for some examples of field observations.) In an organizational simulation using college students, Kay Bartol found that sex of the leader did not by itself affect follower satisfaction, even when female leaders were characterized by high dominance, a trait most likely to "offend" male subordinates.[45] In fact, if sex stereotypes were true, then an argument could be made for the greater capacity of women for leadership roles in organizations, given socialization experiences emphasizing "people-handling" skills. One study showed that members of a business school class ranking high on "masculine" interests, power seeking, and aggressiveness met with less success in large organizations than those with more "feminine" interests in interpersonal relations.

If the much greater desire for men as leaders in organizations does not reflect real sex differences in style and strategy, what does it reflect? As we have seen, people often prefer the *powerful* as leaders. As the Pelz studies at Detroit Edison showed, good human relations skills and sensitivity but low power (a likely combination for women leaders in sexist organizations) could have negative effects on morale.[46] Thus, a *preference for men is a preference for power,* in the context of organizations where women do not have access to the same opportunities for power and efficacy through activities or alliances.

As in the old cliché, everyone likes a winner; in large organizations at least, people would rather work for winners than losers. Perhaps a preference for male managers reflects a "bet" that men are more likely to emerge as winners and power-holders than women. One clever social psychological experiment offers suggestive evidence. Judges were asked to rate paintings supposedly produced by either a man or a woman, with sex of artist varied for different judges. In one condition the paintings were presented as entries in a contest; in a second they were the winning paintings. The women presented as attempting to accomplish were judged less favorably than the men, but those whose paintings had succeeded were evaluated just as favorably.[47] In the great corporate contest, then, subordinates may be "betting" on who is going to be a winner when they respond differently to the idea of women or men as bosses. It is as though followers extend "credit" in the present for imagined future payoffs. This is reminiscent of the Mark Twain tale of the Englishman with the million-pound note. He made a bet with a wealthy man that he could live well forever just on the strength of the note and without using it. Credit was given to him; people vied with each other to supply his wants; and they graciously picked up the bills. He became wealthy and successful—and he never had to cash in the million-pound note. The power that devolved on star performers backed by sponsors at Indsco worked in much the same way. The problem with women was that, first, there were doubts about how far they could go in the corporation, and second, a widespread belief that women could only be individual "movers"—i.e., even if they moved, they could not take anyone else with them.

But power wipes out sex. A woman who does acquire power stops arousing the same level of concern about whether or not she will be wanted as a leader. People who want to attach themselves to power may not even notice sex. On one occasion, a senior Indsco salesman told a long story to colleagues about a problem with a "very, very smart, tough-minded" president of a small company. The president had made good friends among a number of senior Indsco people and therefore managed to get all kinds of concessions. The salesman had to bring this to an end, as well as tell this very powerful client that there would be no credit for the material that had failed when her customers, in turn, used it. . . . It took a long time for the audience to this story to realize that the salesman was saying "she." Some even interjected comments using "he." The salesman presented the story with such awe of the powerful customer that sex made no difference. He said later that she was someone he would eagerly work for.

The "Mean and Bossy Woman Boss" Stereotype

The other issue around women as organizational leaders also turns out to be a power issue. Perhaps the most blatant picture of the negative American stereotype of a woman boss appeared on the cover of *MBA* magazine in March 1972. *MBA*, distributed to business school students and faculty, devoted this issue, as its blurb indicated, to "Women in Business!" Shown on the cover is a Roy Lichtenstein-style comic-cartoon head of a sultry blond woman with blue eyes, bright red lips, and a low-cut, cleavage-revealing dress. Head thrown back snottily, she is saying, "You're fired!" [48]

And that's what women bosses supposedly do with their authority. No wonder no one wants one.

Abuse of power is only the first in a long list of negative characteristics attributed to women managers over the last few decades by those who don't want them. One survey of 521 young working women just before World War II uncovered so much hostility toward women bosses that even the author, Donald Laird (who thought women belonged behind a typewriter), had to conclude that there was overreaction. [49] Of the women workers, 99.81 percent said they preferred a male boss for reasons such as the following:

1. Women bosses are too jealous. Their positions go to their heads. They boss for the mere sake of bossing, to remind you they are in charge.
2. Women bosses take things too personally. They are not businesslike.
3. Women bosses are overly concerned with efficiency and routine details. They are slaves to the system. They bother about small, petty things.
4. Women bosses supervise too closely. They delegate only superficially.
5. Women bosses find more fault. They are too critical.
6. Women bosses scream to impress people with their importance.

One less prejudiced woman, who had worked for both men and women, reflected on her experiences:

> The two women bosses I've had were very lovely people and were good bosses so far as women bosses go . . . but most women bosses have [this fault, which I call] "old-maid thinking." It is eternally thinking in terms of details, not in terms of the big thing—more interested in the details of the means than in the general significance of the results. A man [gives] me a job to do, and he'll let me do it and not ask how and why and did I check with an "x" or a "v"—which is wasting time and makes me want to yell. Further, a woman boss is so everlastingly curious about my personal business: "when, how many, how late, and who" about my own social affairs. A man doesn't give a hoot just as long as I'm on the job and on my toes when I'm on it. [50]

Laird himself concluded that women make poor supervisors in factories, offices, and even at home because of their tendency to "henpeck" and become too bossy. For evidence he cited, without specific reference, a study showing that being "too dictatorial" was a fault in twice as many women as men in the general population.

Burleigh Gardner, a human relations expert also writing during the war, when women entered formerly closed jobs, found similar complaints by both men and women about women bosses, although he felt that the system forced women into positions where they were likely to fail. His respondents said that women were too emotional, unfriendly, critical, strict, and petty. The National Manpower Council's report on "Womanpower" in the 1950s concluded that women supervisors were said to be more demanding and controlling of subordinates as well as guilty of partiality and discrimination. British surveys show the same thing.[51] And this refrain echoed through my interviews at Indsco.

Stereotypes persist even in the face of evidence negating them. The *real* extent of bossiness among women in authority in organizations may have little to do with the persistence of the stereotype, but this particular portrait has one very important characteristic: *It is a perfect picture of people who are powerless. Powerlessness tends to produce those very characteristics attributed to women bosses.*

A careful look at comparisons between men and women supposedly in the same position shows that what looks like sex differences may really be power differences. It has been hard to test this directly, partly because there are so few women managers, especially in the same organizational positions as men. (Rarity itself, as we see in the next chapter, creates a very different situation for the person who is rare.) One recent investigation, however, did find an organizational setting in which women leaders were more common: high school departments in Florida public schools. The research covered 205 teachers and 40 department heads (25 male and 15 female) in small departments with a roughly equal sex distribution. The first interesting finding was that on the usual measures of leadership style (like taking action, providing emotional support, and so forth), operating styles could not be distinguished by sex. However, there was one statistically significant sex-linked difference in group climate: there was a slightly greater tendency for women leaders to be perceived as generating a tight and controlled atmosphere. Departments headed by men were perceived as slightly higher in "esprit and intimacy"—a good indicator of morale; those headed by women, in "hindrance"—an indicator that the leader was thought to get in the way, to intrude too much, rather than to promote subordinates' autonomy and flexibility.[52] In short, the research uncovered a watered-down version of the bossiness complaint. Where could it have come from?

The difference in atmosphere in the woman-run departments can be traced directly to differences in organizational power of the men and women leaders, although the author of the research did not see this. Mobility prospects, the likelihood that department heads would be moving up in the system, were strikingly different for the men and women in this set of high schools. For one thing, there were no women *above* the level of department head in the whole county. Second, the women seemed to have moved to their last position. They had risen into the headship more slowly than the men; they were older, had put in more time teaching, and had spent a longer time in their previous jobs. At the same time, they had more limited aspirations; one-seventh of the women, in contrast to half of the men, expressed a desire for further promotions. Thus, the men and the women managers were not really in comparable positions. The women were much less mobile and much more powerless. And the powerless are handicapped in leadership.

Women at Indsco in exempt positions where they had organizational accountability or leadership responsibilities were differentially in the most powerless situations. They were primarily first-line supervisors of secretaries or clerical workers or they held staff jobs in personnel or public relations functions. There were no other women with line responsibilities and no women above grade 14, with the exception of a senior researcher. They were more likely to lack powerful alliances, and they reported constantly having to fight off the tendency for the organization to "protect" them by encapsulating them in safe situations. Statistics on the distributions of men and women in organizational functions, reported in Chapter 1, make clear how common this situation is. Women, when they do achieve managerial or leadership positions, are clustered in the low-power situations. It should not be surprising if they adopt the behavior of the powerless.

It is not only their own relative power that determines the behavior of managers but also the behavior and feeling of powerlessness of those above and below. The relationship with their own superiors is important in shaping the responses of those who supervise too closely. One such generalization about where most women bosses are found is that they are located in tightly supervised and rules-conscious hierarchies. The "female" professions, like nursing, social work, and primary school teaching, all feature close supervisory hierarchies and concern with detail. Government agencies, where more women managers are found than in private business, epitomize bureaucracy in civil service structure, endless red tape, and concern with rules and regulations. Women managers in these settings are likely to themselves be subject to bossy bosses and may take this restriction of their power out on their own subordinates, perpetuating the style downward. Simultaneously, they learn bossiness as a leadership style from their own role models. In corporations like Indsco, where women managers are so rare as to be tokens (as we see in the next chapter), they themselves may be watched more closely, so that again the restriction of their own latitude of conduct may be transmitted to subordinates.

Simultaneously, powerless feelings of subordinates are translated upward to leaders. Most women managers are likely to manage relatively powerless subordinates: clerical workers, women factory workers, low-level personnel. Powerless subordinates may take out their own frustration in resistance to their managers, provoking them to adopt more coercive styles. The powerless may also resent a boss's advantage, particularly if they think that they could just as easily be the boss. One woman at Indsco who had not attended college was forthright about her hostility toward "credentialed" women brought in to manage her department as a result of affirmative action efforts, while she was still held back. She resented the special treatment they were getting. Women who are jealous of another woman's promotion and try to let her know she's really no better than they may instead provoke her to try to demonstrate her superiority and her control. This is the "lording it over us" behavior some women have complained of in women bosses. From the subordinate's perspective, it is hard to be generously happy about the success of someone getting a chance denied to you. From the boss's perspective, it is hard to share power with people who resent you. The combination of these two viewpoints produces controlling, directive bosses.

Furthermore, people who feel vulnerable and unsure of themselves, who are plunged into jobs without sufficient training or experience, regardless of the official authority they are given, are more likely to first adopt authoritarian-controlling leadership styles. The behavior attributed to women supervisors is likely to be characteristic of new and insecure supervisors generally. Gardner saw this in his World War II studies, when the demands of war production brought inexperienced women into formerly all-male positions. He observed that many people complained about the bossiness of women supervisors but concluded that newly promoted men given supervisory jobs without sufficient training also showed these tendencies.

> Any new supervisor who feels unsure of himself, who feels that his boss is watching him critically, is likely to demand perfect behavior and performance from his people, to be critical of minor mistakes, and to try too hard to please his boss. A woman supervisor, responding to the insecurity and uncertainty of her position as a woman, knowing that she is being watched both critically and doubtfully, feels obliged to try even harder. And for doing this she is said to be "acting just like a woman." [53]

Without the experience or confidence to permit the minor deviations from the rules that in fact make the system work and without enough knowledge and faith in outcomes to loosen control, new managers may be prone to be too directive, controlling, and details-oriented.

In a variety of ways, then, powerlessness stemming from organizational circumstance breeds a particular leadership style caricatured in the stereotype of the bossy woman. This style reflects the situation more than sex, however— if the stereotype carries even a grain of truth—for men who are powerless behave in just the same ways. As Elizabeth Janeway pointed out, "The *weak* are the second sex." [54]

The problem of power thus is critical to the effective behavior of people in organizations. Power issues occupy center stage not because individuals are greedy for more, but because some people are incapacitated without it.

8

Numbers: Minorities and Majorities

The token woman stands in the Square of the Immaculate Exception blessing pigeons from a blue pedestal. . . . The token woman is placed like a scarecrow in the long haired corn: her muscles are wooden. Why does she ride into battle on a clothes horse?
—Marge Piercy, *Living in the Open* *

Up the ranks in Industrial Supply Corporation, one of the most consequential conditions of work for women was also among the simplest to identify: there were so few of them. On the professional and managerial levels, Industrial Supply Corporation was nearly a single-sex organization. Women held less than 10 percent of the exempt (salaried) jobs starting at the bottom grades—a 50 percent rise from a few years earlier—and there were no women at the level reporting to officers. When Indsco was asked to participate in a meeting on women in business by bringing their women executives to a civic luncheon, the corporate personnel committee had no difficulty selecting them. There were only five sufficiently senior women in the organization.

The numerical distributions of men and women at the upper reaches created a strikingly different interaction context for women than for men. At local and regional meetings, training programs, task forces, casual out-of-the office lunches with colleagues, and career review or planning sessions with managers, the men were overwhelmingly likely to find themselves with a predominance of people of their own type—other men. For men in units with no exempt women, there would be, at most, occasional events in which a handful of women would be present alongside many men. Quite apart from the content of particular jobs and their location in the hierarchy, the culture of corporate administration and the experiences of men in it were influenced by this fact of numerical dominance, by the fact that men were the *many*.

* Copyright © 1976 by Marge Piercy. Reprinted by permission of Alfred A. Knopf, Inc.

Women, on the other hand, often found themselves alone among male peers. The twenty women in a three hundred-person sales force were scattered over fourteen offices. Their peers, managers, and customers were nearly all men. Never more than two women at a time were found in twelve-person personnel training groups. There was a cluster of professional women on the floor at corporate headquarters housing employee administration and training, but all except three were part of different groups where they worked most closely with men.

The life of women in the corporation was influenced by the proportions in which they found themselves. Those women who were few in number among male peers and often had "only woman" status became tokens: symbols of how-women-can-do, stand-ins for all women. Sometimes they had the advantages of those who are "different" and thus were highly visible in a system where success is tied to becoming known. Sometimes they faced the loneliness of the outsider, of the stranger who intrudes upon an alien culture and may become self-estranged in the process of assimilation. In any case, their turnover and "failure rate" were known to be much higher than those of men in entry and early grade positions; in the sales function, women's turnover was twice that of men. What happened around Indsco women resembled other reports of the experiences of women in politics, law, medicine, or management who have been the few among many men.

At the same time, they also echoed the experiences of people of any kind who are rare and scarce: the lone black among whites, the lone man among women, the few foreigners among natives. Any situation where proportions of significant types of people are highly skewed can produce similar themes and processes. It was rarity and scarcity, rather than femaleness *per se*, that shaped the environment for women in the parts of Indsco mostly populated by men.

The situations of Industrial Supply Corporation men and women, then, point to the significance of numerical distributions for behavior in organizations: how many of one social type are found with how many of another.[1] As proportions begin to shift, so do social experiences.

THE MANY AND THE FEW: THE SIGNIFICANCE

OF PROPORTIONS FOR SOCIAL LIFE

Georg Simmel's classic analysis of the significance of numbers for social life argued persuasively that numerical shifts transform social interaction, as in the differences between two-person and three-person situations or between small and large groups.[2] But Simmel, and then later investigations in this tradition, dealt almost exclusively with the impact of absolute numbers, with group size as a determinant of form and process. We have no vocabulary for dealing with the effects of *relative* numbers, of *proportional* representation: the difference for individuals and groups that stem from particular numerical distributions of categories of people.

Yet questions of how many and how few confound any statements about the organizational behavior of special kinds of people. For example, certain popular conclusions and research findings about male-female relations or role potentials may turn critically on the issue of proportions. One study of mock jury deliberations found that men played proactive, task-oriented leadership roles, whereas women in the same groups tended to take reactive, emotional, and nurturant postures—supposed proof that traditional stereotypes reflect behavior realities. But, strikingly, *men far outnumbered women in all of the groups studied.* Perhaps it was the women's scarcity that pushed them into classical positions and the men's numerical superiority that encouraged them to assert task superiority. Similarly, the early kibbutzim, collective villages in Israel that theoretically espoused equality of the sexes but were unable to fully implement it, could push women into traditional service positions because there were *more than twice as many men as women.* Again, relative numbers interfered with a fair test of what men or women can "naturally" do, as it did in the case of the relatively few women in the upper levels of Indsco. Indeed, recently Marcia Guttentag has found sex ratios in the population in general to be so important that they predict a large number of behavioral phenomena, from the degree of power women and men feel to the ways they cope with the economic and sexual aspects of their lives.[3]

To understand the dramas of the many and the few in the organization requires a theory and a vocabulary. Four group types can be identified on the basis of different proportional representations of kinds of people, as Figure 8–1 shows. *Uniform* groups have only one kind of person, one significant social type. The group may develop its own differentiations, of course, but groups called uniform can be considered homogeneous with respect to salient external master statuses such as sex, race, or ethnicity. Uniform groups have a typological ratio of 100:0. *Skewed* groups are those in which there is a large preponderance of one type over another, up to a ratio of perhaps 85:15. The numerically dominant types also control the group and its culture in enough ways to be labeled "dominants." The few of another type in a skewed group can appropriately be called "tokens," for, like the Indsco exempt women, they are often treated as representatives of their category, as symbols rather than individuals. If the absolute size of the skewed group is small, tokens can also be solos, the only one of their kind present; but even if there are

FIGURE 8–1

*Group Types as Defined by Proportional Representation of
Two Social Categories in the Membership*

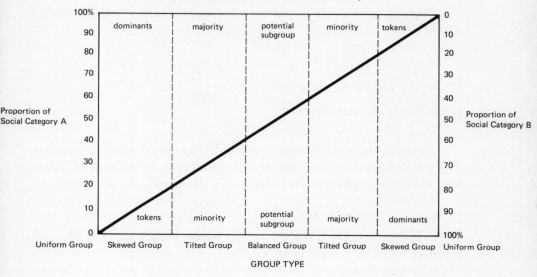

two tokens in a skewed group, it is difficult for them to generate an alliance that can become powerful in the group, as we shall see later. Next, *tilted* groups begin to move toward less extreme distributions and less exaggerated effects. In this situation, with ratios of perhaps 65:35, dominants are just a "majority" and tokens become a "minority." Minority members have potential allies among each other, can form coalitions, and can affect the culture of the group. They begin to become individuals differentiated from each other as well as a type differentiated from the majority. Finally, at about 60:40 and down to 50:50, the group becomes *balanced*. Culture and interaction reflect this balance. Majority and minority turn into potential subgroups that may or may not generate actual type-based identifications. Outcomes for individuals in such a balanced peer group, regardless of type, will depend more on other structural and personal factors, including formation of subgroups or differentiated roles and abilities.

It is the characteristics of the second type, the skewed group, that underlay the behavior and treatment of professional and managerial women observed at Indsco. If the ratio of women to men in various parts of the organization begins to shift, as affirmative action and new hiring and promotion policies promised, forms of relationships and peer culture should also change. But as of the mid-1970s, the dynamics of tokenism predominated in Indsco's

exempt ranks, and women and men were in the positions of token and dominant. Tokenism, like low opportunity and low power, set in motion
self-perpetuating cycles that served to reinforce the low numbers of women
and, in the absence of external intervention, to keep women in the position of
token.

VIEWING THE FEW: WHY TOKENS
FACE SPECIAL SITUATIONS

The proportional rarity of tokens is associated with three perceptual tendencies: visibility, contrast, and assimilation. These are all derived simply
from the ways any set of objects are perceived. If one sees nine X's and one 0:

$$X \quad X \quad x \quad x \quad X \quad X \quad 0 \quad X \quad x \quad X$$

the 0 will stand out. The 0 may also be overlooked, but if it is seen at all, it will
get more notice than any X. Further, the X's may seem more alike than different because of their contrast with the 0. And it will be easier to assimilate
the 0 to generalizations about all 0's than to do the same with the X's, which
offer more examples and thus, perhaps, more variety and individuation. The
same perceptual factors operate in social situations, and they generate special
pressures for token women.

First, tokens get attention. One by one, they have higher visibility than
dominants looked at alone; they capture a larger awareness share. A group
member's awareness share, averaged over other individuals of the same social
type, declines as the proportion of total membership occupied by the category
increases, because each individual becomes less and less surprising, unique,
or noteworthy. In Gestalt psychology terms, those who get to be common
more easily become "ground" rather than "figure"; as the group moves from
skewed to tilted, tokens turn into a less individually noticed minority. But for
tokens, there is a "law of increasing returns": as individuals of their type represent a *smaller* numerical proportion of the overall group, they each potentially
capture a *larger* share of the awareness given to that group.

Contrast—or polarization and exaggeration of differences—is the second
perceptual tendency. In uniform groups, members and observers may never
become self-conscious about the common culture and type, which remain
taken for granted and implicit. But the presence of a person or two bearing a
different set of social characteristics increases the self-consciousness of the
numerically dominant population and the consciousness of observers about
what makes the dominants a class. They become more aware both of their

commonalities and their difference from the token, and to preserve their commonality, they try to keep the token slightly outside, to offer a boundary for the dominants. There is a tendency to exaggerate the extent of the differences between tokens and dominants, because as we see next, tokens are, by definition, too few in numbers to defeat any attempts at generalization. It is thus easier for the commonalities of dominants to be defined in contrast to the token than in tilted or balanced groups. One person can be perceptually isolated and seen as cut off from the core of the group more than many, who begin to represent too great a share of what is called the group.

Assimilation, the third perceptual tendency, involves the use of stereotypes, or familiar generalizations about a person's social type. The characteristics of a token tend to be distorted to fit the generalization. Tokens are more easily stereotyped than people found in greater proportion. If there were enough people of the token's type to let discrepant examples occur, it is eventually possible that the generalization would change to accommodate the accumulated cases. But in skewed groups, it is easier to retain the generalization and distort the perception of the token. It is also easier for tokens to find an instant identity by conforming to the preexisting stereotypes. So tokens are, ironically, both highly visible as people who are different and yet not permitted the individuality of their own unique, non-stereotypical characteristics.

All of these phenomena occurred around the proportionally scarce women in Indsco, but there was, of course, no way to compare these same women's behavior and treatment when they were not in the token position. However, a clever and suggestive laboratory experiment showed that the same person may be perceived differently depending on whether he or she is a token in a skewed group or one of many in a balanced group. (Because the categories used in the experiment were black-white rather than male-female, it also demonstrated the generality of such perceptual tendencies beyond token women.) Shelley Taylor and Susan Fiske played a tape of a group discussion to subjects while showing them pictures of the "group," and then asked them for their impressions of group members on a number of dimensions. The tape was the same for all subjects, but the purported composition of the group varied. The pictures illustrated either an otherwise all-white male group with one black man (the "token" condition) or a mixed black-white male group. In the token condition, disproportionate attention was paid to the token, his prominence in the group was overemphasized, and his attributes were exaggerated. Similarly, the token was perceived as playing out special roles in the group, often highly stereotypical ones. By contrast, in "integrated" groups, subjects recalled no more about blacks than whites, and their attributes were evaluated about the same.[4]

Visibility, contrast, and assimilation are each associated with particular forces and dynamics that, in turn, generate typical token responses. These dynamics are, again, similar regardless of the category from which the tokens come, although the specific kinds of people and their history of relationships with dominants provide cultural content for specific communications. Visibility tends to create *performance pressures* on the token. Contrast leads to heightening of *dominant culture boundaries,* including isolation of the token. And assimilation results in the token's *role encapsulation*.

The experiences of exempt women at Industrial Supply Corporation took their shape from these processes.

PERFORMANCE PRESSURES: LIFE IN THE LIMELIGHT

Indsco's upper-level women, especially those in sales, were highly visible, much more so than their male peers. Even those who reported they felt ignored and overlooked were known in their immediate divisions and spotted when they did something unusual. But the ones who felt ignored also seemed to be those in jobs not enmeshed in the interpersonal structure of the company: for example, a woman in public relations who had only a clerical assistant reporting to her and whose job did not occupy a space in the competitive race to the top.

In the sales force, where peer culture and informal relations were most strongly entrenched, everyone knew about the women. They were the subject of conversation, questioning, gossip, and careful scrutiny. Their placements were known and observed through the division, whereas those of most men typically were not. Their names came up at meetings, and they would easily be used as examples. Travelers to locations with women in it would bring back news of the latest about the women, along with other gossip. In other functions, too, the women developed well-known names, and their characteristics would often be broadcast through the system in anticipation of their arrival in another office to do a piece of work. A woman swore in an elevator in an Atlanta hotel while going to have drinks with colleagues, and it was known all over Chicago a few days later that she was a "radical." And some women were even told by their managers that they were watched more closely than the men. Sometimes the manager was intending to be helpful, to let the woman know that he would be right there behind her. But the net effect was the same as all of the visibility phenomena. Tokens typically performed their jobs under public and symbolic conditions different from those of dominants.

The Two-Edged Sword of Publicity

The upper-level women became public creatures. It was difficult for them to do anything in training programs, on their jobs, or even at informal social affairs that would not attract public notice. This provided the advantage of an attention-getting edge at the same time that it made privacy and anonymity impossible. A saleswoman reported: "I've been at sales meetings where all the trainees were going up to the managers—'Hi, Mr. So-and-So'— trying to make that impression, wearing a strawberry tie, whatever, something that they could be remembered by. Whereas there were three of us [women] in a group of fifty, and all we had to do was walk in and everyone recognized us."

But their mistakes or their intimate relationships were known as readily as other information. Many felt their freedom of action was restricted, and they would have preferred to be less noticeable, as these typical comments indicated: "If it seems good to be noticed, wait until you make your first major mistake." "It's a burden for the manager who gets asked about a woman and has to answer behind-the-back stuff about her. It doesn't reach the woman unless he tells her. The manager gets it and has to deal with it." "I don't have as much freedom of behavior as men do; I can't be as independent."

On some occasions, tokens were deliberately thrust into the limelight and displayed as showpieces, paraded before the corporation's public but in ways that sometimes violated the women's sense of personal dignity. One of Indsco's most senior women, a staff manager finally given two assistants (and thus managerial responsibilities) after twenty-six years with the company, was among the five women celebrated at the civic lunch for outstanding women in business. A series of calls from high-level officers indicated that the chairman of the board of the corporation wanted her to attend a lunch at a large hotel that day, although she was given no information about the nature of the event. When she threatened not to go unless she was given more information, she was reminded that the invitation had come down from the chairman himself, and of course she would go. On the day of the luncheon, a corsage arrived and, later, a vice-president to escort her. So she went, and found she was there to represent the corporation's "prize women," symbolizing the strides made by women in business. The program for the affair listed the women executives from participating companies, except in the case of Indsco, where the male vice-presidential escorts were listed instead. Pictures were taken for the employee newsletter and, a few days later, she received an inscribed paperweight as a memento. She told the story a few weeks after the event with visible embarrassment about being "taken on a date. It was more like a senior prom than a business event." And she expressed resentment at being singled out in such a fashion, "just for being a woman at Indsco, not for any real achievement." Similar sentiments were expressed by a woman personnel manager who wanted a pay increase as a sign of the company's appreciation, not her picture in a newspaper, which "gave the company brownie points but cost nothing."

Yet the senior woman had to go, the personnel manager had to have her picture taken, and they had to be gracious and grateful. The reaction of tokens to their notice was also noticed. Many of the tokens seemed to have developed a capacity often observed among marginal or subordinate peoples: to project a public persona that hid inner feelings. Although some junior management men at Indsco, including several fast trackers, were quite open about their lack of commitment to the company and dissatisfaction with aspects of its style, the women felt they could not afford to voice any negative sentiments. They played by a different set of rules, one that maintained the split between public persona and private self. One woman commented, "I know the company's a rumor factory. You must be careful how you conduct yourself and what you say to whom. I saw how one woman in the office was discussed endlessly, and I decided it would be better to keep my personal life and personal affairs separate." She refused to bring dates to office parties when she was single, and she did not tell anyone at work that she got married until several months later—this was an office where the involvement of wives was routine. Because the glare of publicity meant that no private information could be kept circumscribed or routine, tokens were forced into the position of keeping secrets and carefully contriving a public performance. They could not afford to stumble.

Symbolic Consequences

The women were visible as category members, because of their social type. This loaded all of their acts with extra symbolic consequences and gave them the burden of representing their category, not just themselves. Some women were told outright that their performances could affect the prospects of other women in the company. In the men's informal conversations, women were often measured by two yardsticks: how *as women* they carried out the sales or management role; and how *as managers* they lived up to images of womanhood. In short, every act tended to be evaluated beyond its meaning for the organization and taken as a sign of "how women perform." This meant that there was a tendency for problematic situations to be blamed on the woman—on her category membership—rather than on the situation, a phenomenon noted in other reports of few women among many men in high-ranking corporate jobs. In one case of victim-blaming, a woman in sales went to her manager to discuss the handling of a customer who was behaving seductively.

The manager jumped to the assumption that the woman had led him on. The result was an angry confrontation between woman and manager in which she thought he was incapable of seeing her apart from his stereotypes, and he said later he felt misunderstood.

Women were treated as symbols or repesentatives on those occasions when, regardless of their expertise or interest, they would be asked to provide the meeting with "the woman's point of view" or to explain to a manager why he was having certain problems with his women. They were often expected to be speaking for women, not just for themselves, and felt, even in my interviews, that they must preface personal statements with a disclaimer that they were speaking for themselves rather than for women generally. Such individuality was difficult to find when among dominants. But this was not always generated by dominants. Some women seized this chance to be a symbol as an opportunity to get included in particular gatherings or task forces, where they could come to represent all women at Indsco. "Even if you don't want *me* personally," they seemed to be saying to dominants, "you can want me as a symbol." Yet, if they did this, they would always be left with uncertainty about the grounds for their inclusion; they were failing to distinguish themselves as individuals.

Women also added symbolic consequences to each other's affairs. Upper-level women were scrutinized by those on a lower level, who discussed the merits of things done by the higher-ranking women and considered them to have implications for their own careers. One woman manager who was passed over for a promotion in her department was the subject of considerable discussion by other women, who felt she should have pushed to get the opening and complained when she did not.

The extension of consequences for those in token statuses may increase their self-consciousness about their self-presentation and about their decisions, and can change the nature of the decisions that get made. Decisions about what to wear and who to sit with at lunch are not casual. One executive woman knew that her clothing and leisure choices would have impact. She deliberately wore pants one day as she walked through an office—not her own—of female clerks supervised by a man who wanted them to wear dresses, and she noted that a few women cautiously began to wear pants occasionally. She decided to let it be known that she was leaving at four p.m. for ballet lessons once a week, arguing that the men at her level did the same thing to play golf, but also knowing that ballet was going to have a very different meaning from golf. Her act was a gesture performed with an audience in mind as much as an expression of preference. The meaning of "natural" in such situations is problematic, for in doing what they might find natural as private beings, tokens as public personae are also sending messages to the organization.

Business as well as personal decisions were handled by tokens with an awareness of their extended symbolic consequences. One woman manager was faced with the dilemma of deciding what to do about a woman assistant who wanted to go back to the secretarial ranks from which she had recently been promoted. The manager felt she jeopardized her own claims for mobility and the need to open the system to more women if she let her assistant return and had to admit that a woman who was given opportunity had failed. She spent much more time on the issue than a mere change of assistants would have warranted, going privately to a few men she trusted at the officer level to discuss the situation. She also kept the assistant on much longer than she felt was wise, but she thought herself trapped.

Sometimes the thought of the symbolic as well as personal consequences of acts led token women to outright distortions. One was an active feminist in a training staff job who, according to her own reports, "separated what I say for the cause from what I want for myself." Her secret ambition was to leave the corporation within a year or two to increase her own professional skills and become an external consultant. But when discussing her aspirations with her own manager in career reviews or with peers on informal occasions, she always smiled and said, "Chairman of the board of Industrial Supply Corporation." Every time a job at the grade level above her became vacant, she would inquire about it and appear to be very interested, making sure that there was some reason at the last minute she could not take it. "They are watching me," she explained, "to see if women are really motivated or if they will be content to stay in low-level jobs. They are expecting me to prove something one way or the other."

The Tokenism Eclipse

The token's visibility stemmed from characteristics—attributes of a master status—that threatened to blot out other aspects of a token's performance. Although the token captured attention, it was often for her discrepant characteristics, for the auxiliary traits that gave her token status. The token does not have to work hard to have her presence noticed, but she does have to work hard to have her achievements noticed. In the sales force, the women found that their technical abilities were likely to be eclipsed by their physical appearances, and thus, an additional performance pressure was created. The women had to put in extra effort to make their technical skills known, and said they worked twice as hard to prove their competence.

Both male peers and customers could tend to forget information women provided about their experiences and credentials while noticing and remembering such secondary attributes as style of dress. For example, there was this report from a salesman: "Some of our competition, like ourselves, have women sales people in the field. It's interesting that when you go in to see a purchasing agent, what he has to say about the woman sales person. It is always what kind of a body she had or how good-looking she is or "Boy, are you in trouble on this account now." They don't tell you how good-looking your competitors are if they're males, but I've never heard about a woman's technical competence or what kind of a sales person she was—only what her body was like." And a saleswoman complained in an angry outburst, "There are times when I would rather say to a man, 'Hey, listen, you can have our bodies and look like a female and have the advantage of walking in the room and being noticed.' But the noticeability also has attached to it that surprise on the part of men that you can talk and talk intelligently. Recognition works against you as well as for you." And another: "Some of the attention is nice, but some of it is demeaning to a professional. When a man gets a job, they don't tell him he's better looking than the man who was here before—but they say that to me." The focus on appearance and other non-ability traits was an almost direct consequence of the presence of very few women.

Fear of Retaliation

The women were also aware of another performance pressure: not to make the dominants look bad. Tokenism sets up a dynamic that can make tokens afraid of being too outstanding in performance on group events and tasks. When a token does well enough to "show up" a dominant, it cannot be kept a secret, since all eyes are upon the token, and therefore, it is more difficult to avoid the public humiliation of a dominant. Thus, paradoxically, while the token women felt they had to do better than anyone else in order to be seen as competent and allowed to continue, they also felt, in some cases, that their successes would not be rewarded and should be kept to themselves. They needed to toe the fine line between doing just well enough and too well. One woman had trouble understanding this and complained of her treatment by managers. They had fired another woman for not being aggressive enough, she reported; yet she, who succeeded in doing all they asked and brought in the largest amount of new business during the past year, was criticized for being "too aggressive, too much of a hustler."

The fears had some grounding in reality. In a corporate bureaucracy like Indsco, where "peer acceptance" held part of the key to success in securing promotions and prized jobs (as Chapters 3 and 7 showed), it was known how people were received by colleagues as well as by higher management. Indeed, men down the ranks resented the tendency for some top executives to make snap judgments about people after five minutes' worth of conversation and then try to influence their career reviews and create instant stars. So the emphasis on peer acceptance in performance evaluations, a concept known to junior managers, was one way people lower down the managerial hierarchy retained some control over the climbing process, ensured themselves a voice, and maintained a system they felt was equitable, in which people of whom they approved had a greater chance for success. Getting along well with peers was thus not just something that could make daily life in the company more pleasant; it was also fed into the formal review system.

At a meeting of ten middle managers, two women who differed in peer acceptance were contrasted. One was well liked by her peers even though she had an outstanding record because she did not flaunt her successes and modestly waited her turn to be promoted. She did not trade on her visibility. Her long previous experience in technical work served to certify her and elicit colleague respect, and her pleasant but plain appearance and quiet dress minimized disruptive sexual attributes. The other was seen very differently. The mention of her name as a "star performer" was accompanied by laughter and these comments: "She's infamous all over the country. Many dislike her who have never met her. Everyone's heard of her whether or not they know her, and they already have opinions. There seems to be no problem with direct peer acceptance from people who see her day-to-day, but the publicity she has received for her successes has created a negative climate around her." Some thought she was in need of a lesson for her cockiness and presumption. She was said to be aspiring too high, too soon, and refusing to play the promotion game by the same rules the men had to use: waiting for one's turn, the requisite years' experience and training. Some men at her level found her overrated and were concerned that their opinions be heard before she was automatically pushed ahead. A common prediction was that she would fail in her next assignment and be cut down to size. The managers, in general, agreed that there was backlash if women seemed to advance too fast.

And a number of men were concerned that women would jump ahead of them. They made their resentments known. One unwittingly revealed a central principle for the success of tokens in competition with dominants: to always stay one step behind, never exceed or excell. "It's okay for women to have these jobs," he said, "as long as they don't go zooming by *me*."

One form peer retaliation against success took was to abandon a successful woman the first time she encountered problems. A dramatic instance involved a confrontation between a very dignified woman manager, the only woman in a management position in her unit, who supervised a large group of both male and female workers, and an aggressive but objectively low-performing woman subordinate, who had been hired by one of the other managers and was unofficially "sponsored" by him. The woman manager had given low ratings to the subordinate on her last performance appraisal, and another review was coming up; the manager had already indicated that the rating would still be low, despite strong protests of unfairness from the worker. One day after work, the manager walked through a public lounge area where several workers were standing around, and the subordinate began to hurl invectives at her, accusing her of being a "bitch, a stuck-up snob," and other unpleasant labels. The manager stood quietly, maintaining her dignity, then left the room, fearing physical violence. Her feelings ranged from hurt to embarrassment at the public character of the scene and the talk it would cause. The response over the next few days from her male peers ranged from silence to comments like, "The catharsis was good for X. She needed to get that off her chest. You know, you never *were* responsive to her." A male friend told the manager that he heard two young men who were passed over for the job she was eventually given commenting on the event: "So Miss High-and-Mighty finally got hers!" The humiliation and the thought that colleagues supported the worker rather than her was enough to make this otherwise-successful woman consider leaving the corporation.

Tokens' Responses to Performance Pressures

A manager posed the issue for scarce women this way: "Can they survive the organizational scrutiny?" The choices for those in the token position were either to over-achieve and carefully construct a public performance that minimized organizational and peer concerns, to try to turn the notoriety of publicity to advantage, or to find ways to become socially invisible. The first course means that the tokens involved are already outstanding and exceptional, able to perform well under close observation where others are ready to notice first and to attribute any problems to the characteristics that set them apart—but also able to develop skills in impressions management that permit them to retain control over the extra consequences loaded onto their acts. This choice involved creating a delicate balance between always doing well and not generating peer resentment. Such dexterity requires both job-related competence and political sensitivity that could take years to acquire. For this reason, young women just out of college had the greatest difficulty in entering male domains like the Indsco sales force and were responsible for much of the high turnover among women in sales. Women were successful, on the other hand, who were slightly older than their male peers, had strong technical backgrounds, and had already had previous experiences as token women among male peers. The success of such women was most likely to increase the prospects for hiring more women in the future; they worked for themselves and as symbols.

The second strategy, accepting notoriety and trading on it, seemed least likely to succeed in a corporate environment because of the power of peers. A few women at Indsco flaunted themselves in the public arena in which they operated and made a point out of demonstrating their "difference," as in refusing to go to certain programs, parading their high-level connections, or by-passing the routine authority structure. Such boldness was usually accompanied by top management sponsorship. But this strategy was made risky by shifting power alliances at the top; the need to secure peer cooperation in certain jobs where negotiation, bargaining, and the power of others to generate advantage or disadvantage through their use of the rules were important; and the likelihood that some current peers would eventually reach the top. Furthermore, those women who sought publicity and were getting it in part for their rarity developed a stake in not sharing the spotlight. They enjoyed their only-women status, since it gave them an advantage, and they seemed less consciously aware than the other women of the attendant dangers, pressures, psychic costs, and disadvantages. In a few instances, they operated so as to keep other women out by excessive criticism of possible new-hires or by subtly undercutting a possible woman peer (who eventually left the company), something that, we shall see later, was also pushed for by the male dominants. Thus, this second strategy eventually kept the numbers of women down both because the token herself was in danger of not succeeding and because she might keep other women out. This second strategy, then, serves to reinforce the dynamics of tokenism by ensuring that, in the absence of external pressures like affirmative action, the group remains skewed.

The third choice was more often accepted by the older generation of corporate women, who predated the women's movement and had years ago accommodated to token status. It involved attempts to limit visibility, to become "socially invisible." This strategy characterizes women who try to minimize their sexual attributes so as to blend unnoticeably into the predominant male culture, perhaps by adopting "mannish dress," as in reports by other investigators. Or it can include avoidance of public events and occasions for performance—staying away from meetings, working at home rather than in the office, keeping silent at meetings. Several of the saleswomen deliberately took such a "low profile," unlike male peers who tended to seize every opportunity to make themselves noticed. They avoided conflict, risks, or controversial situations. They were relieved or happy to step into assistant or technical staff jobs such as personnel administration or advertising, where they could quietly play background roles that kept men in the visible forefront—or they at least did not object when the corporation put them into low-visibility jobs, since for many years the company had a stake in keeping its "unusual" people hidden.

Those women preferring or accepting social invisibility also made little attempt to make their achievements publicly known or to get credit for their own contributions to problem-solving or other organizational tasks, just like other women reported in the research literature who have let men assume visible leadership or take credit for accomplishments that the women really produced—the upper corporate equivalent of the achieving secretary. In one remarkable laboratory experiment, women with high needs for dominance, paired with a man in a situation where they had to choose a leader, exercised their dominance by *appointing him* the leader.[5] Women making this choice, then, did blend into the background and control their performance pressures, but at the cost of limited recognition of their competence. This choice, too, involved a psychic splitting, for rewards for such people often came with secret knowledge—knowing what they had contributed almost anonymously to an effort that made someone else look good. In general, this strategy, like the last, also reinforces the existence of tokenism and keeps the numbers of women down, because it leads the organization to conclude that women are not very effective: low risk-takers who cannot stand on their own.

The performance pressures on people in token positions generate a set of attitudes and behaviors that appear sex-linked, in the case of women, but can be understood better as situational responses, true of any person in a token role. Perhaps what has been called in the popular literature "fear of success in women," for example, is really the token woman's *fear of visibility.* The original research that identified the fear of success concept created a hypothetical situation in which a woman was at the top of her class in medical school—a token woman in a male peer group. Such a situation is the kind that exacts extra psychic costs and creates pressures for some women to make themselves and their achievements invisible—to deny success. Replication of this research using examples of settings in which women were not so clearly proportionately scarce produced very different results and failed to confirm the sex-linked nature of this construct. Seymour Sarason also pointed out that minorities of any kind, trying to succeed in a culturally alien environment, may fear visibility because of retaliation costs and, for this reason, may try to play down any recognition of their presence, as did Jews at Yale for many years.[6] Fear of visibility, then, is one response to performance pressures in a token's situation. The token must often choose between trying to limit visibility—and being overlooked—or taking advantage of the publicity—and being labeled a "troublemaker."

BOUNDARY HEIGHTENING AND MEMBERSHIP COSTS:
TOKENS IN DOMINANTS' GROUPS

Contrast, or exaggeration of the token's differences from dominants, sets a second set of dynamics in motion. The presence of a token or two makes dominants more aware of what they have in common at the same time that it threatens that commonality. Indeed, it is often at those moments when a collectivity is threatened with change that its culture and bonds become exposed to itself; only when an obvious "outsider" appears do group members suddenly realize aspects of their common bond as insiders. The "threat" a token poses is twofold. First, the token represents the danger of challenge to the dominants' premises, either through explicit confrontation by the token or by a disaffected dominant who, through increased awareness, sees the culture for what it is and sees the possibility of alternatives. Second, the self-consciousness created by the token's presence is uncomfortable for people who prefer to operate in casual, superficial, and easygoing ways, without much psychological self-awareness and without the strain of reviewing habitual modes of action—a characteristic stance in the corporate environment.

Furthermore, as Everett Hughes pointed out, part of the hostility peer groups show to new kinds of people stems from uncertainty about their behavior when non-structured, non-routine events occur. Tokens cannot be assumed to share the same unspoken understandings that the rest of the members, share because of their common membership in a social category, one basis for closing ranks against those who are different, as Chapter 3 argued. For smooth interaction, groups require both discretion (the ability to put statements in their proper perspective) and a shared vocabulary of attitudes (the ability to take feelings and sentiments for granted) so that they can avoid the time-consuming process of translation. At best, then, members of the dominant category are likely to be uncomfortable and uncertain in the presence of a member of a different category. Other analysts have also shown that people with "incongruent statuses," like women in male jobs, strain group interaction by generating ambiguity and lack of social certitude.[7] It is not only the first of a kind that arouses discomfort. People who are usually not found in that setting and come from a category with a history of special forms of interaction with the numerical dominants, as rare women among men, are also potentially disruptive of peer interaction.

The token's contrast effect, then, can lead dominants to exaggerate both their commonality and the token's "difference." They move to heighten boundaries of which, previously, they might even have been aware. They erect new boundaries that at some times exclude the token or at others let her in only if she proves her loyalty.

Exaggeration of Dominants' Culture

Indsco men asserted group solidarity and reaffirmed shared in-group understandings in the presence of token women, first, by emphasizing and exaggerating those cultural elements they shared in contrast to the token. The token became both occasion and audience for the highlighting and dramatizing of those themes that differentiated her as the outsider. Ironically, tokens, unlike people of their type represented in greater proportion, are thus instruments for under*lining* rather than under*mining* majority culture. At Indsco, this phenomenon was most clearly in operation on occasions that brought together people from many parts of the organization who did not necessarily know each other well, as in training programs and at dinners and cocktail parties during meetings. Here the camaraderie of men, as in other work and social settings,[8] was based in part on tales of sexual adventures, ability with respect to "hunting" and capturing women, and off-color jokes. Other themes involved work prowess and sports, especially golf and fishing. The capacity for and enjoyment of drinking provided the context for displays of these themes. They were dramatized and acted out more fervently in the presence of token women than when only men were present.[9] When the men were alone, they introduced these themes in much milder form and were just as likely to share company gossip or talk of domestic matters such as a house being built. This was also in contrast to more equally mixed male-female groups in which there were a sufficient number of women to influence and change group culture and introduce a new hybrid of conversational themes based on shared male-female concerns.[10]

Around token women, then, men sometimes exaggerated displays of aggression and potency: instances of sexual innuendos, aggressive sexual teasing, and prowess-oriented "war stories." When a woman or two were present, the men's behavior involved "showing off," telling stories in which "masculine prowess" accounted for personal, sexual, or business success. They highlighted what they could do, as men, in contrast to the women. In a set of training situations for relatively junior salespeople, these themes were even acted out overtly in role plays in which participants were asked to prepare and perform demonstrations of sales situations. In every case involving a woman, the men played the primary, effective roles, and the women were objects of sexual attention. Sexual innuendos were heightened and more obvious and exaggerated than in all-male role plays, as in these two examples:

1. Two men and a woman simulated a call on a buyer; the woman was introduced as the president of the company, but the sales manager and his assistant did all the talking. The company was in the business of selling robots. The sales manager brought in a male "robot" to demonstrate the product. The sales manager leered at him, saying, "Want a little company?" He then revealed that the woman introduced as the president was actually one of the female robots.

2. The two-man, one-woman team was selling wigs; the woman was the wig stylist. The buyer on whom they were calling adopted an exaggerated homosexual caricature, which broadened considerably during the "sales call." Toward the end of the role play, one of the men, trying to wrap up the sale, said, "We have other special services along with wigs. Other women who work with our stylist will come to

your store to work for you." The buyer's response made it clear that he would be interested in those women sexually (though he was simulating homosexuality). Said the seller, "They'll be on your payroll; you can use them any way you want." Said the buyer, leering, "*Any* way I want?" The seller answered, "We might offer other services like a massage along with the wig." Said the buyer, "That sounds interesting. Can I have one right now?"

After these role plays, the group atmosphere seemed quite tense, and the women especially appeared highly uncomfortable.

The women themselves reported other examples of "testing" to see how they would respond to the "male" culture. They said that many sexual innuendos or displays of locker-room humor were put on for their benefit, especially by the younger men. (The older men tended to parade their business successes.) One woman was a team leader at a workshop (and the only woman), when her team decided to use as its slogan, "The [obscenity] of the week," looking at her for a reaction. By raising the issue and forcing the woman to choose not to participate, the men in the group created an occasion for uniting against the outsider and asserting dominant group solidarity. Such events, it must be pointed out, were relatively rare and occurred only at those informal occasions outside of the business routine in which people were unwinding, letting themselves go, or, as in the training role plays, deliberately creating unreal situations. Most behavior at Indsco was more businesslike in tone. But the fact that such interaction ever occurred, even infrequently, around women served to isolate them and make them uncomfortable at those very moments when, ironically, people were supposed to be relaxing and having fun.

A sales meeting at Indsco provided an interesting example of how the dominant culture could simultaneously acknowledge the presence of tokens and retain its own themes and flavor. It was traditional for salesmen to tell traveling salesman/farmer's daughter jokes at informal gatherings. On this occasion, four years after women first entered the sales force, a raunchy traveling sales*woman*/farmer's *son* joke was told, a story currently going around the company. The form was the same, but the content reflected the presence of women.

Tokens' functions as audience for dominant cultural expressions also played a part in the next set of processes.

Interruptions as Reminders of "Difference"

On more formal occasions, as in meetings, members of the numerically dominant category underscored and reinforced differences between tokens and dominants, ensuring that tokens recognized their outsider status, by making the token the occasion for "interruptions" in the flow of group events. Dominants prefaced acts with apologies or questions about appropriateness directed at the token; they then invariably went ahead with the act, having placed the token in the position of interrupter or interloper, of someone who took up the group's time. This happened often in the presence of the saleswomen. Men's questions or apologies represented a way of asking whether the old or expected cultural rules were still operative—the words and expressions permitted, the pleasures and forms of release indulged in. (Can we still swear? Toss a football? Use technical jargon? Go drinking? Tell "in" jokes?) [11] Sometimes the questions seemed motivated by a sincere desire to put the women at ease and treat them appropriately, but the net effect was the same regardless of dominants' intentions. By posing these questions overtly, dominants made the culture clear to tokens, stated the terms under which tokens enter the relationship, and reminded them that they were special people. It is a dilemma of all cross-cultural interaction that the very act of attempting to learn what to do in the presence of the different kind of person so as to integrate him can reinforce differentiation.

The answers about conduct almost invariably affirmed the understandings of the dominants. The power of sheer numbers means that an individual rarely feels comfortable preventing a larger number of peers from engaging in an activity they consider normal. Most women did not want to make a fuss, especially about issues they considered trivial and irrelevant to their job status, like saying "goddamn" or how to open doors. Their interest in not being signaled out for special treatment made them quickly agree that things should proceed as they would if women were not present, and to feel embarrassment about stopping the flow of conversation. None wanted to be a "wet blanket"! As one said, "They make obscene suggestions for slogans when kidding around, looking to me for a reaction. Then they jump on me for not liking it."

Secondly, the tokens have been put on notice that interaction will not be "natural," that dominants will be "holding back," unless they agree to acknowledge and permit (and even encourage) majority cultural expressions in their presence. (It is important that this be stated, of course, for one never knows that another is holding back unless the other lets a piece of the suppressed material slip out.) At the same time, tokens have also been given the implicit message that majority members do *not* expect those forms of expression to be "natural" to the tokens' home culture; otherwise, majority members would not need to raise the question. (This is a function of what Judith Long Laws called the "double deviance" of tokens: deviant first because they are women in a man's world and second because they inappropriately aspire to the privileges of the dominants.) [12] Thus, the saleswomen were often in the odd position of reassuring peers and customers that they could go ahead and do

something in the women's presence, like swearing, that the women themselves would not be permitted to do. They listened to dirty jokes, for example,
but reported that they would not dare tell one themselves. In fact, whether or
not to go drinking or tell jokes was a major question for women: "You can't tell
dirty jokes. Clean jokes would go over like a lead balloon. So I sit there like a
dummy and don't tell jokes."

Via difference-reminding interruptions, then, dominants both affirm
their own shared understandings and draw the cultural boundary between
themselves and tokens. The tokens learned that they caused interruptions in
"normal" communication, and that their appropriate position was more like
that of audience than that of full participant. But the women also found the audience position frustrating or wearying, as these statements indicated: "I felt
like one of the guys for a while. Then I got tired of it. They had crude mouths
and were very immature. I began to dread the next week because I was tired
of their company. Finally, when we were all out drinking, I admitted to
myself, this is not me; I don't want to play their game." And: "I was at a dinner
where the men were telling dirty jokes. It was fun for a while; then it got to
me. I moved and tried to have a real conversation with a guy at the other end
of the table. The dinner started out as a comrade thing, but it loses its flavor,
especially if you're the only woman. I didn't want them to stop on my account,
but I wish I had had an alternative conversation."

Overt Inhibition: Informal Isolation

In some cases, dominants did not wish to have tokens around all the time;
they had secrets to preserve or simply did not know how far they could trust
the women, especially those who didn't seem to play by all the rules. They
thus moved the locus of some activities and expressions from public settings to
which tokens had access to more private settings from which they could be
excluded. When information potentially embarrassing or damaging to dominants is being exchanged, an outsider-audience is not desirable, because dominants do not know how far they can trust the tokens. As Hughes and Chapter
3 pointed out, colleagues who rely on unspoken understandings may feel uncomfortable in the presence of "odd kinds of fellows" who cannot be trusted to
interpret information in just the same way or to engage in the same relationships of trust and reciprocity.[13] There was a sense that it was not possible
to level with a woman or be real with her, as one could with other men.

The result was sometimes "quarantine"—keeping tokens away from some
occasions. Informal pre-meeting meetings were sometimes held. Some topics
of discussion seemed rarely raised by men in the presence of many of their
women peers, even though they discussed them among themselves: admis-
sions of low commitment to the company or concerns about job performance,

ways of getting around formal rules, political plotting for mutual advantage, strategies for impressing certain corporate executives. Many of the women did not tend to be included in the networks by which informal socialization occurred and politics behind the formal system were exposed, as researchers have found in other settings. One major project found that people with incongruent statuses, like the Indsco exempt women, were likely to become isolates in peer groups and to have less frequent interaction with the group than other members, outside of formally structured occasions.[14] Toward the upper levels of the corporation, any tendency for peer groups to quarantine women was reinforced by men-only social establishments; a senior personnel administrator committed to placing more women in top executive jobs was concerned about whether they could overcome the limitation on their business effectiveness placed by exclusion from informal exchanges at male clubs.

In a few cases, overt inhibition worked directly against women in their jobs. They missed out on important informal training by peers.[15] There were instances in which women trainees did not get direct criticism in time to improve their performance and did not know they were the subjects of criticism in the company until told to find jobs in other divisions. They were not part of the buddy network that uncovered such information quickly, and their managers were reluctant to criticize a woman out of uncertainty about how she would receive the information. (One man put quite simply how he felt about giving negative feedback to a woman: "I'm chicken.") Here feelings that it was impossible to level with a different kind of person stood in the way.

Loyalty Tests

At the same time that tokens may be kept on the periphery of colleague interaction, they may also be expected to demonstrate loyalty to their dominant peers. Failure to do so could result in further isolation; signs of loyalty, on the other hand, permitted the token to come closer to being included in more of the dominants' activities. Through loyalty tests, the group sought reassurance that the tokens would not turn against the dominants or use any of the information gained through their viewing of the dominants' world to do harm to the group. In the normal course of peer interactions, people learn all sorts of things about each other that could be turned against the other. Indeed, many colleague relationships are often solidified by the reciprocal knowledge of potentially damaging bits of information and the understanding that they both have an interest in preserving confidentiality. Tokens, however, pose a different problem and raise uncertainties, for their membership in a different social category could produce loyalties outside the peer cadre.

This was a quite rational concern on occasion. With government pressures and public interest mounting, Indsco somen were often asked to speak to classes or women's groups or to testify before investigating committees. One woman was called in by her manager before her testimony at hearings on discrimination against women in business; he wanted to hear her testimony in advance and have censorship rights. She refused, but then made only very general and bland statements at the hearing anyway.

Peers seek reassurance about embarrassing as well as damaging disclosures. There is always the possibility that tokens will find some of what the dominants naturally do silly or ridiculous and will insult them where they feel vulnerable. Dominants also want to know that tokens will not use their inside information to make the dominants look bad or turn them into figures of fun to members of the token's category outside with whom they must interact. The joking remarks men made when seeing women colleagues occasionally eating with the secretaries (e.g, "What do you 'girls' find so interesting to talk about?") revealed some of their concerns.

Assurance could be gained by asking tokens to join with or identify with the dominants against those who represented competing loyalties; in short, dominants pressured tokens to turn against members of their own category, just as occurred in other situations where women were dominants and men tokens.[16] If tokens colluded, they made themselves psychological hostages to the majority group. For token women, the price of being "one of the boys" was a willingness to occasionally turn against "the girls."

There were three ways token women at Indsco could demonstrate loyalty and qualify for a closer relationship with dominants. First, they could let slide (or even participate in) statements prejudicial to other members of their category. They could allow themselves to be viewed as "exceptions" to the "general rule" that others of their category have a variety of undesirable or unsuitable characteristics; Hughes recognized this as one of the "deals" token blacks might make for membership in white groups.[17] Women who did well were sometimes told they were "exceptions" and exceptional, not like a "typical woman." It is an irony of the token situation that women could be treated as both representatives of their type and exceptions to it, sometimes by the same people.

At meetings and training sessions, women were occasionally the subjects of ridicule or joking remarks about their incompetence. Some of the women who were insulted by such innuendos found it easier to appear to agree than to start an argument. A few accepted the dominants' view fully. One of the first saleswomen denied in interviews having any special problems because she was a woman, calling herself "skilled at coping with a man's world," and said the company was right not to hire more women. Women, she said, were unreliable and likely to quit; furthermore, young women might marry men who would not allow them to work. (She herself quit a few years later.) In this case, a token woman was taking over "gatekeeping" functions for dominants, letting them appear free of prejudice while a woman acted to exclude other women.[18]

Tokens could also demonstrate loyalty by allowing themselves and their category to provide a source of humor for the group. Laughing with others, as Rose Coser indicated, is a sign of a common definition of the situation; to allow oneself or one's kind to be the object of laughter signals a further willingness to accept the others' culture on their terms.[19] Just as Hughes found that the initiation of blacks into white groups might involve accepting the role of comic inferior,[20] Indsco women faced constant pressures to allow jokes at the expense of women, to accept "kidding" from the men around them. When a woman objected, the men denied any hostility or unfriendly intention, instead accusing the woman, by inference, of "lacking a sense of humor." In order to cope, one woman reported, she "learned to laugh when they try to insult you with jokes, to let it roll off your back." Tokens could thus find themselves colluding with dominants through shared laughter.

Thirdly, tokens could demonstrate their gratitude for being included by not criticizing their situation or pressing for any more advantage. One major taboo area involved complaints about the job or requests for promotion. The women were supposed to be grateful for getting as far as they had (when other women clearly had *not*) and thus expected to bury dissatisfaction or aspirations.

Responses of Tokens to Boundary Heightening

The dilemma posed here for tokens was how to reconcile their awareness of difference generated by informal interaction with dominants with the need, in order to belong, to suppress dominants' concerns about the difference. As with performance pressures, peer group interaction around the tokens increased the effort required for a satisfactory public appearance, sometimes accompanied by distortions of private inclinations.

Of course, not all men participated in the dynamics noted. And some tokens managed to adapt very well. They used the same kind of language and expressed the same kinds of interests as many of the men. One woman loved fishing, she said, so when she came on as a manager and her office was concerned that that would end fishing trips, she could show them they had nothing to fear. Another had a boat on which she could take customers (along with her husband and their wives). A professional woman joined the men on "woman hunts," taking part in conversations in which the pro's and con's of particular targets were discussed. There were women known to be able to "drink the men under the table." It was never clear what the psychic toll of such accommodation was—whether, for example, such people would have made different choices in a balanced context—for they were also unlikely to talk about having any problems at all in their situation; they assumed they were full members.

Numerical skewing and polarized perceptions left tokens with little choice about accepting the culture of dominants. There were too few other people of the token's kind to generate a "counterculture" or to develop a shared intergroup culture. Tokens had to approach the group as single individuals. They thus had two general response possibilities. They could accept isolation, remaining only an audience for certain expressive acts of dominants. This strategy sometimes resulted in friendly but distant peer relations, with the risk of exclusion from occasions on which informal socialization and political activity took place. Or they could try to become insiders, proving their loyalty by defining themselves as exceptions and turning against their own social category.

The occurrence of the second response on the part of tokens suggests a reexamination of the popularized "women-prejudiced-against-women" hypothesis, also called the "Queen Bee syndrome," for possible structural (numerical) rather than sexual origins. Not only has this hypothesis not been confirmed in a variety of settings,[21] but the analysis offered here of the social psychological pressures on tokens to side with the majority provides a more compelling explanation for the kinds of situations most likely to produce this effect. To turn against others of one's kind (and thus risk latent self-hatred) can by a psychic cost of membership in a group dominated by another culture.

ROLE ENCAPSULATION

Tokens can never really be seen as they are, and they are always fighting stereotypes, because of a third tendency. The characteristics of tokens as individuals are often distorted to fit preexisting generalizations about their category as a group—what I call "assimilation." Such stereotypical assumptions about what tokens "must" be like, such mistaken attributions and biased judgments, tend to force tokens into playing limited and caricatured roles. This constrains the tokens but is useful for dominant group members. Whatever ambiguity there might be around a strange person is reduced by providing a stereotyped and thus familiar place for tokens in the group, allowing dominants to make use of already-learned expectations and modes of action, like the traditional ways men expect to treat women. Familiar roles and assumptions, further, can serve to keep tokens in a bounded place and out of the mainstream of interaction where the uncertainties they arouse might be more difficult to handle. In short, tokens become encapsulated in limited roles that give them the security of a "place" but constrain their areas of permissible or rewarded action.

Status Leveling

Tokens were often initially misperceived as a result of their numerical rarity. That is, an unusual woman would be treated as though she resembled women on the average—a function of what has been called "statistical discrimination" rather than outright prejudice.[22] Since people make judgments about the role being played by others on the basis of probabilistic reasoning about what a particular kind of person will be doing in a particular situation, such misperceptions are the result of statistical mistakes. Thus, women exempts at Indsco, like other tokens, encountered many instances of "mistaken identity"—first impressions that they were occupying a *usual female* position rather than their *unusual* (for a woman) job. In the office, they were often taken for secretaries; on sales trips on the road, especially when they traveled with a male colleague, they were often taken for wives or mistresses; with customers, they were first assumed to be temporarily substituting for a man who was the "real" salesperson; with a male peer at meetings, they were seen as the assistant; when entertaining customers, they were assumed to be the wife or date. (One woman sales trainee accompanied a senior salesman to call on a customer, whose initial reaction was laughter: "What won't you guys think up next? A woman!" She had the last laugh, however, for that company's chief engineer happened to be a woman with whom she had instant rapport.)

Mistaken first impressions can be corrected, although they give tokens an extra burden of spending more time untangling awkward exchanges and establishing accurate and appropriate role relations. But meanwhile, status leveling occurs. Status leveling involves making adjustments in perception of a token's professional role to fit with the expected position of the token's category—that is, bringing situational status in line with what has been called "master status," the token's social type. Even when others knew that the women were not secretaries, for example, there was still a tendency to treat them like secretaries or to make secretary-like demands on them. In one blatant case, one woman was a sales trainee along with three men, all four of whom were to be given positions as summer replacements. The men were all assigned to replace salesmen; the woman was asked to replace a secretary— and only after a long and heated discussion with the manager was she given a more professional assignment. Similarly, when having professional contacts with customers and managers, the women felt themselves to be treated in more wife-like or date-like ways than a man would treat another man, even though the occasion was clearly professional. A professional woman at Indsco asked for a promotion and talked about looking for a better job; her manager's first assumption was that she did not feel "loved" and it was his fault for failing to give love to a woman. (She wanted challenge and more money as did many of the secretaries in Chapter 4.) In all these instances, it was easier for others to fit the token woman to their preexisting generalizations about women than to change the category; numerical rarity provided too few examples to contradict the generalization. (Instances of status leveling have also been noted around other kinds of tokens, such as male nurses; [23] in the case of tokens whose master status is higher than their situational status, leveling can work to their advantage, as when male nurses are called "Dr.")

The Woman's Slot

There was also a tendency to encapsulate women and to maintain generalizations by defining special roles for women, even on the managerial and professional levels, that put them slightly apart as colleagues. Again, it was easy to do this with a small number and would have been much harder with many more women spilling over the bounds of such slots. A woman could ensure her membership by accepting a special place but then find herself confined by it. Once women began to occupy certain jobs, those jobs sometimes gradually came to be defined as "women's slots." One personnel woman at Indsco pointed this out. In her last career review, she had asked to be moved, feeling that, in another six months, she would have done and learned all she could in her present position and was ready to be upgraded. "They [the managers] told me to be patient; if I waited a year or two longer, they had just the right job for me, three grades up. I knew what they had in mind. Linda Martin [a senior woman] would be retiring by then from a benefits administration job, and they wanted to give it to me because it was considered a place to put a woman. But it had no *real* responsibilities despite its status; it was all routine work."

Affirmative action and equal employment opportunity jobs were also seen as "women's jobs." Many women, who would otherwise be interested in the growth and challenge they offered, said that they would not touch such a position: "The label makes it a dead end. It's a way of putting us out to pasture." There was no way to test the reality of such fears, given the short time the jobs had been in existence, but it could be observed that women who worked on women's personnel or training issues were finding it hard to move out into other areas. These women also found it hard to interest some other, secretly sympathetic managerial women in active advocacy of upward mobility for women because of the latter's own fears of getting too identified with a single issue. (Others, though, seized on it as a way to express their values or to get visibility.)

Committees, task forces, and other ad hoc events had a tendency, too, to develop a woman's slot for those women selected to participate. Sometimes it would take the form of giving the women areas of responsibility that were stereotypically "female" concerns, or, as mentioned earlier, giving them the role in the group of "expert on women." This posed major dilemmas for the women seriously interested in being women's advocates but who were also aware of how the role encapsulation process could undercut their effectiveness and limit their organizational mobility. They had to carefully balance the time spent as woman-symbols with other activities and with attention to the technical/professional aspects of their jobs.

Stereotyped Informal Roles

Dominants can incorporate tokens and still preserve their generalizations by inducting tokens into stereotypical roles that preserve familiar forms of interaction between the kinds of people represented by the token and the dominants. In the case of token women in colleague groups at Indsco, four informal role traps were observed, all of which encapsulated the tokens in a category the men could respond to and understand. Each was formed around one behavioral tendency of the token, building this into an image of the token's place in the group and forcing her to continue to live up to the image; each defined for dominants a single response to the token's sexuality. Two of the roles are classics in Freudian theory: the "mother" and the "seductress." Freud wrote of the need for men to handle women's sexuality by envisioning them either as "madonnas" or "whores"—as either asexual mothers or overly sexual, debased seductresses, perhaps as a function of Victorian family patterns, which encouraged separation of idealistic adoration toward the mother and animalistic eroticism.[24] The others, termed the "pet" and the "iron maiden," also have family counterparts in the kid sister and the virgin aunt.

Mother

A token woman sometimes found that she became a "mother" to men in the group. One by one, they brought her their private troubles, and she was expected to comfort them. The assumption that women are sympathetic, good listeners and easy to talk to about one's problems was common, even though, ironically, men also said it was hard to level with women over task-related issues. One saleswoman was constantly approached by her all-male peers to listen to their problems with their families. In a variety of residential training groups, token women were observed acting out other parts of the traditional nurturant-maternal role: doing laundry, sewing on buttons for men.

The mother role was comparatively safe. A mother is not necessarily vulnerable to sexual pursuit (for Freud it was the very idealization of the madonna that was in part responsible for men's ambivalence toward women), nor do men need to compete for her favors, since they are available to everyone. However, the typecasting of women as nurturers can have three negative consequences for the woman's task performance: (1) The mother is rewarded primarily for service and not for independent action. (2) The dominant, powerful aspects of the maternal image may be feared, and thus the mother is expected to keep her place as a non-critical, accepting, "good mother" or lose her rewards. Since the ability to differentiate and be critical is often an indicator of competence in work groups, the mother is prohibited from exhibiting this skill. (3) The mother becomes an emotional specialist. This provides her with a place in the life of the group and its members. Yet, at the same time one of the stereotypically "feminine" characteristics men in positions of authority in industry most often criticize in women is excess "emotionality," as I indicated in Chapter 1. Although the mother herself might not ever cry or engage in emotional outbursts in the group, she remains identified with emotional matters. As long as she is in the scarce position of token, however, it is unlikely that nurturance, support, and expressivity will be valued or that a mother can demonstrate and be rewarded for critical, independent, task-oriented behaviors.

Seductress

The role of seductress or sexual object is fraught with more tension than the maternal role, for it introduces an element of sexual competition and jealousy. The mother can have many sons; it is more difficult for the sexually attractive to have many swains. Should the woman cast as sex object (that is, seen as sexually desirable and potentially available—seductress is a perception, and the woman herself may not be consciously behaving seductively) share her attention widely, she risks the debasement of the whore. Yet, should she form a close alliance with any man in particular, she arouses resentment, particularly so because she represents a scarce resource; there are just not enough women to go around.

In several situations I observed, a high status male allied himself with the seductress and acted as her "protector," partly because of his promise of rescue from sex-charged overtures of the rest of the men as well as because of his high status *per se*. The powerful male (staff member, manager, sponsor, etc.) could easily become the "protector" of the still "virgin" seductress, gaining through masking his own sexual interest what the other men could not gain by declaring theirs. However, this removal of the seductress from the sexual marketplace contained its own problems. The other men could resent the high-status male for winning the prize and resent the woman for her ability to get an "in" with the high-status male that they could not obtain as men. Although the seductress was rewarded for her femaleness and insured attention from the group, then, she was also the source of considerable tension; and needless to say, her perceived sexuality blotted out all other characteristics.

Men could adopt the role of protector toward an attractive woman, regardless of her collusion, and by implication cast her as sex object, reminding her and the rest of the group of her sexual status. In the guise of "helping" her, self-designated protectors may actually put up further barriers to the solitary woman's full acceptance by inserting themselves, figuratively speaking, between the woman and the rest of the group. A male management trainer typically offered token women in management assessment groups extra help and sympathetic attention to the problems their male peers might cause, taking them out alone for drinks at the end of daily sessions. But this kind of "help" also preserved the sex object role.

Pet

The "pet" was adopted by the male group as a cute, amusing little thing and symbolically taken along on group events as mascot—a cheerleader for shows of prowess. Humor was often a characteristic of the pet. She was expected to admire the male displays but not to enter into them; she cheered from the sidelines. Shows of competence on her part were treated as special and complimented just because they were unexpected (and the compliments themselves can be seen as reminders of the expected rarity of such behavior). One woman reported that when she was alone in a group of men and spoke at length on an issue, comments to her by men after the meeting often referred to her speech-making ability rather than the content of what she said (e.g., "You talk so fluently"), whereas comments the men made to one another were almost invariably content- or issue-oriented. Competent acts that are taken for granted when performed by males were often unduly "fussed over" when performed by exempt women, considered precocious or precious—a kind of look-what-she-did-and-she's-only-a-woman attitude. Such attitudes on the part of men encouraged self-effacing, girlish responses on the part of solitary women (who, after all, may be genuinely relieved to be included and petted) and prevented them from realizing or demonstrating their own power and competence.

Iron Maiden

The "iron maiden" is a contemporary variation of the stereotypical roles into which strong women are placed. Women who failed to fall into any of the first three roles and, in fact, resisted overtures that would trap them in a role (such as flirtation) might consequently be responded to as "tough" or dangerous. (One woman manager developed such a reputation in company branches throughout the country.) If a token insisted on full rights in the group, if she displayed competence in a forthright manner, or if she cut off sexual innuendos, she could be asked, "You're not one of those women's libbers, are you?" Regardless of the answer, she was henceforth regarded with suspicion, undue and exaggerated shows of politeness (by inserting references to women into conversations, by elaborate rituals of *not* opening doors), and with distance, for she was demanding treatment as an equal in a setting in which no person of her kind had previously been an equal. Women inducted into the "iron maiden" role were stereotyped as tougher than they are (hence the name) and trapped in a more militant stance than they might otherwise take. Whereas seductresses and pets, especially, incurred protective responses, iron maidens faced abandonment. They were left to flounder on their own and often could not find peers sympathetic to them when they had problems.

Responses of Tokens to Role Encapsulation

The dynamics of role entrapment tended to lead tokens to a variety of conservative and low-risk responses. The time and awkwardness involved in correcting mistaken impressions led some tokens to a preference for already-established relationships, for minimizing change and stranger-contact in the work situation. It was also often easier to accept stereotyped roles than to fight them, even if their acceptance meant limiting the tokens' range of expressions or demonstrations of task competence, because they offered a comfortable and certain position. The personal consequence for tokens, of course, was a measure of self-distortion. John Athanassiades, though not taking into account the effects of numerical representation, found that women in organizations tended to distort upward communication more than men, especially those with low risk-taking propensity, and argued that many observed work behaviors of women may be the result of such distortion and acceptance of organizational images. Submissiveness, frivolity, or other attributes may be feigned by people who feel they are prescribed by the dominant organizational culture.[25] This suggests that accurate conclusions about work attitudes and behavior cannot be reached by studying people in the token position, since there may always be an element of compensation or distortion involved.

The analysis also suggests another way in which tokenism can be self-perpetuating: acceptance of role encapsulation and attendant limitations on demonstration of competence may work to keep down the numbers of women in the upper ranks of the organization, thus continuing to put people in token positions. Role encapsulation confirms dominants' stereotypes and proves to them how right they were all along. On the other hand, some women try to stay away from the role traps by bending over backwards not to exhibit any characteristics that would reinforce stereotypes. This strategy, too, is an uneasy one, for it takes continual watchful effort, and it may involve unnatural self-distortion. Finally, token women must steer a course between protectiveness and abandonment. Either they allow other people to take over and fight their battles for them, staying out of the main action in stereotypical ways, or they stand much too alone. They may be unable by virtue of scarcity even to establish effective support systems of their own.

HOW MANY ARE ENOUGH?: THE TWO-TOKEN SITUATION

The examination of numerical effects leads to the additional question of tipping points: How many of a category are enough to change a person's status from token to full group member? When does a group move from skewed to tipped to balanced? What is the impact for a woman of the presence of another?

In the exempt ranks of Indsco, there were a number of instances of situations in which two rather than one woman were found among male peers, but still constituted less than 20 percent of the group. Despite Solomon Asch's classic laboratory finding that one potential ally can be enough to reduce the power of the majority of secure conformity,[26] in the two-token situation in organizations, dominants several times behaved in ways that defeated an alliance between the two women. This was done through setting up invidious comparisons. One woman was characteristically set up as superior, and the other as inferior—exaggerating traits in both cases. One was identified as the success, the other as the failure. The one given the success label felt relieved to be included and praised, recognizing that alliance with the identified failure would jeopardize her acceptance. The consequence, in one office, was that the identified success stayed away from the other woman and did not give her any help with her performance, withholding criticism she had heard that might have been useful, and the second woman soon left. In another case, a layer of the hierarchy was inserted between two women who were at the same level: one was made the boss of the other, causing great strain between them. Dominants also could defeat alliances, paradoxically, by trying to promote them. Two women in a training group of twelve were treated as though they were an automatic pair, and other group members felt that they were relieved of responsibility for interacting with or supporting the women. The women reacted to this forced pairing by trying to create difference and distance between them and becoming extremely competitive. Thus, structural circumstances and pressures from the majority could further produce what appeared to be intrinsically prejudicial responses of women to each other. There were also instances in which two women developed a close alliance and refused to be turned against each other. Strong identification with the feminist cause or with other women was behind such alliances. Allied, two tokens could reduce some of the pressures and avoid some of the traps in their position. They could share the burden of representing womankind, and they could each be active on some pieces of "the woman's slot" while leaving time free to demonstrate other abilities and interests. Two women personnel trainers, for example, on a six-person staff, could share responsibility for programs on women without either of them becoming over-identified with it.

A mere shift in *absolute* numbers, then, as from one to two tokens, could potentially reduce stresses in a token's situation even while *relative* numbers of women remained low. But two were also few enough to be rather easily divided and kept apart. It would appear that larger numbers are necessary for supportive alliances to develop in the token context.

EFFECTS ON TOKENS AS INDIVIDUALS:

STRESSES AND COSTS IN THE TOKEN SITUATION

The point is not that all of these things happen to token women, or that they happen only to people who are tokens. Some young men at Indsco complained that as new-hires they, too, felt performance pressures, uncertainties about their acceptance, and either over-protected or abandoned. But these issues were part of a transitional status out of which new-hires soon passed, and, in any event, men did not so routinely or dramatically encounter them. Similarly, age and experience helped women make a satisfactory accommodation, and over time, many women settled into comfortable and less token-like patterns. Some said that there was no problem they could not handle with time and that the manifestations of discrimination in their jobs were trivial. But still, the issues stemming from rarity and scarcity arose for women in every new situation, with new peers, and at career transitions. Even successful women who reported little or no discrimination said that they felt they had to "work twice as hard" and expend more energy than the average man to succeed. It is also clear that not all women in the token situation behave alike or engender the same responses in others. There was variety in the individual choices, and there were alternative strategies for managing the situation. But a system characteristic—the numerical proportion in women and men were found—set limits on behavioral possibilities and defined the context for peer interaction.

The token position contains a number of dilemmas and contradictions: [27]

—Tokens are simultaneously representatives and exceptions. They serve as symbols of their category, especially when they fumble, yet they also are seen as unusual examples of their kind, especially when they succeed.

—They are made aware of their differences from the numerical dominants, but then must often pretend that the differences do not exist, or have no implications.

—Tokens are among the most visible and dramatized of performers, noticeably on stage, yet they are often kept away from the organizational backstage where the dramas are cast.

—Tokens are the quintessential "individuals" in the organization, since they stand apart from the mass of peer group members; yet they lose their individuality behind stereotyped roles and carefully constructed public personae that can distort their sense of self.

—Those situations in which organizational peers are supposedly "relaxing" (after-work drinks, celebratory dinners, sports events) are often the most stressful for tokens, for on such occasions the protection of defined positions and structured interaction disappears. So tokens, paradoxically, may be most relaxed and feel the most "natural" during the official parts of the business day when other people are the most constrained by formal roles.

—Tokens suffer from their loneness, yet the dynamics of interaction around them create a pressure for them to seek advantage by dissociating themselves from others of their category and, hence, to remain alone.

—As long as numbers are low, disruptions of interaction around tokens (and their personal problems) are seen by the organization as a huge deflection from its central purposes, a drain of energy, leading to the conclusion that it is not worth having people like the tokens around. Yet the disruptions are primarily a function of the numbers being low and could be remedied by proportional increases.

In short, organizational, social, and personal ambivalence surrounds people in token situations. It is likely that the burdens carried by tokens in the management of social relations take their toll in psychological stress, even if the tokens succeed in work performance. Research on people with inconsistent or poorly crystallized statuses has identified a number of psycho-social difficulties, including unsatisfactory social relationships, unstable self-images, frustration from dealing with contradictory demands (from others as well as the self), and insecurity. More serious physical and mental stress has also been found to be associated with status incongruities and from role pressures at work.[28]

Even the best coping strategy is likely to have some internal repercussions, ranging from inhibition of self-expression to feelings of inadequacy and, perhaps, self-hatred. Sidney Jourard hypothesized that one of the "lethal" aspects of the male role (that literally kills men off at an early age) is the inhibition of self-disclosure.[29] Self-repression and refraining from certain kinds of expressiveness are, as we have seen, part of the culture in large organizations. But tokens of any kind are especially in a position where true disclosure to peers is not possible, and tokens may not even easily join work peers in their characteristic modes of tension release. Finally, to the extent that tokens accept their exceptional status, dissociate themselves from others of their category, and turn against them, tokens may be denying parts of themselves and engaging in self-hatred. This can produce inner tension.

There is a small positive psychological side to tokenism: the self-esteem that comes from mastering a difficult situation and from getting into places that traditionally exclude others of one's kind. If the token can segregate conflicting expectations and has strong outside support groups with which to relax, then perhaps a potentially stress-producing situation can be turned into an opportunity for ego enhancement. Indeed, one study showed that people whose racial ethnic statuses were "lower" than their occupational ranks on social prestige scales (the upwardly mobile) did not report the physical symptoms otherwise associated with inconsistent statuses.[30] But, on balance, token situations seem more stressful than beneficial.

EXTENSIONS AND ORGANIZATIONAL IMPLICATIONS

What have been identified as the major issues in the situation of the numerically few at Industrial Supply Corporation are also characteristic of the token position in general. The same pressures and processes can occur around people of any social category who find themselves few of their kind among others of a different social type, as a few examples indicate. Bernard Segal studied the male token situation in a hospital in which 22 out of 101 nurses were men. He found that male nurses were isolates in the hospital social structure—not because the men dissociated themselves from their women peers but because the women felt the men were out of place and should not be nurses. The male and female nurses had the same objective rank, but people of both sexes felt that the men's subjective status was lower. The women placed the men in stereotypical positions, expecting them to do the jobs the women found distasteful or considered "men's work." [31] One male nursing student whom I interviewed reported that he thought he would enjoy being the only man in a group of women. Then he found that he engendered a great deal of hostility and that he was teased every time he failed to live up to a manly image—e.g., if he was vague or subjective in speech. The *content* of interaction when men are tokens may appear to give them an elevated position, but the process is still one of role encapsulation and treating tokens as symbols. Deference can be a patronizing reminder of difference, too.

Similarly, a blind man indicated that when he was the only blind person among sighted people, he often felt conspicuous and attended to more than he would like, creating pressure for him to work harder to prove himself. In the solo situation, he was never sure that he was getting the same treatment as other members of the group (first fellow students, later fellow members of an academic situation), and he suspected that people tended to protect him. When he was a token, compared with balanced situations in which other blind people were present, sighted people felt free to grab his arm and pull him along and were more likely to apologize for references to visual matters, reinforcing his sense of being different and being cast in the role of someone who is more helpless than he, in fact, perceived himself to be.

People's treatment, then, is not automatically fixed by inflexible characteristics but depends on their numbers in a particular situation. Change in the behavior and treatment of women in token positions is strongly tied to shifting proportions. But to argue for the importance of numbers smacks of advocacy of quotas, and many Americans object to quotas. Quantitative limits on expansion (which is how quotas are seen: not as more jobs for women, but fewer for men) have always seemed objectionable to some in the United States, especially when "individual rights" for the advantaged are involved, as shown in concerns over gasoline rationing or income ceilings. Yet, it seems clear that numbers, especially relative numbers, can strongly affect a person's fate in an organization. This is a *system* rather than an individual construct—located not in characteristics of the person but in how many people, like that person in significant ways, are also present. *System phenomena* require *system-level intervention* to make change.

In the absence of external pressures for change, *tokenism is a self-perpetuating system.* Tokens of Type O who are successful in their professional roles face pressures and inducements to dissociate themselves from other O's, and thus they may fail to promote, or even actively block, the entry of more O's. At the same time, tokens who are less than successful and appear less than fully competent confirm the organization's decision not to recruit more O's, unless they are extraordinarily competent and not like most O's. And since just a few O's can make the X-majority people feel uncomfortable, X's will certainly not go out of their way to include more O's. In short, outside intervention is required to break the cycles created by the social composition of groups.

Most arguments made in favor of numerical guidelines in hiring and job placement limit their own effectiveness by making only part of the case. They say that *equality of opportunity* is the goal, but that this goal is hard to measure without *proof of outcome*. Therefore, numbers hired serve as a shorthand for, a measure of, non-discrimination in selection. However, there is also a strong case that can be made for number-balancing as a worthwhile goal in itself, because, inside the organization, relative numbers can play a large part in further outcomes—from work effectiveness and promotion prospects to psychic distress.

Part IV

Understanding and Action

9

Contributions to Theory: Structural Determinants of Behavior in Organizations

The highest wisdom has but one science, the science of the whole.
—Leo Tolstoy, *War and Peace*

There is nothing so practical as a good theory.
—Attributed to Kurt Lewin

In coming to understand the people of Industrial Supply Corporation, I wanted to focus on the observable regularities in behavior and attitudes that arose from common situations, that represented responses to particular places in a highly complex organization. Each separate study that I conducted was analyzable in and of itself, of course, but I also wanted to discover the overarching dimensions of the person-organization relationship. Without a comprehensive and integrated theory, any policy suggestions or programs for change would be limited and perhaps ineffective. They would be limited by a less than full understanding of how organizations impact upon the people in them, and how those people, in turn, come to reflect their situations in their behavior.

As I pulled together and looked for meaning in information from varied sources (objectified survey questions, official company forms, formal interviews, group meetings, and idle comments made in passing in casual conversations), I identified three variables as central explanatory dimensions: the structure of opportunity, the structure of power, and the proportional distribution of people of different kinds (the social composition of peer clusters). These variables contain the roots of an integrated structural model of human behavior in organizations, one that builds on but enlarges other frameworks, one that can point out dilemmas and guide change efforts. In this chapter, I examine this approach in the context of some of its potential contribution to theory; the next chapter applies the three variables to the problems of equal employment opportunity and improving the quality of work life, suggesting practical policies.

ORGANIZATIONAL BEHAVIOR AND
ITS STRUCTURAL DETERMINANTS

Opportunity, power, and relative numbers (proportions and social composition) have the potential to explain a large number of discrete individual responses to organizations. Indeed, except for factors more properly located outside of an organization's boundaries, there appear to be few instances of important aspects of individual behavior and attitudes that do not bear a relation to one or more of these variables. They also represent a link between the overall organizational context—not just the job or the work group or the subunit but the overarching system—and concrete, observable behaviors and statements of individuals. Many hypotheses can be derived from this approach, based on the case study of Indsco and a large number of discrete findings in the social scientific literature. These hypotheses lend themselves to direct empirical test.[1]

Opportunity

Opportunity refers to expectations and future prospects. The structure of opportunity—of mobility and growth—is determined by such matters as promotion rates from particular jobs, ladder steps associated with a position, the range and length of career paths opening from it, access to challenge and increase in skills and rewards, and, as a variable matter for each person, the individual's prospects relative to others of his or her age and seniority (in turn shaped in part by route into the job). On the basis of the differentiation of opportunity in complex organizations, we can hypothesize that: people *low in opportunity* would tend to:

—limit their aspirations, not hoping for mobility in general, not valuing more responsibility, more participation;

—have lower self-esteem, value their competence less than adequately;

—seek satisfaction in activities outside of work, dream of escape, and "interrupt" their careers (sometimes as a function of insecurity in the job itself);

—have a "horizontal" orientation, compare themselves with peers;

—be critical of high power people, of management, or at least, fail to identify with them;

—but be less likely to protest directly or seek change; rather to channel grievances into griping or output restriction rather than direct action;

—orient peer groups toward protection and reassurance, with strong loyalty demands; and hence, discourage members of the group from seeking mobility;

—find ways to create a sense of efficacy and worth through personal relationships (as in the case of secretaries) or doing well socially, rather than in terms of task accomplishment;

—be more attached to the local unit than to the larger organization, and, hence, be more parochial;

—resign themselves to staying put;

—be concerned with basic survival and extrinsic rewards: the economic or social payoff of the job.

People *high in opportunity* would tend to:

—have high aspirations;

—have high self-esteem, value or overrate their competence;

—consider work a more central life interest;

—be more committed to the organization, willing to sacrifice for it and believe in its goals;

—be competitive, oriented toward rivalry;

—have a "vertical" orientation, compare themselves upward;

—be more attracted to high power people, seek validation from them, identify with them;

—create power and action-oriented informal groups;

—when dissatisfied, engage in active change-oriented forms of protest: collective action, formal meetings, suggestions for change;

—consider themselves members of the larger organization rather than the local unit;

—become impatient or disaffected if they don't keep moving;

—be concerned with the job as an instrument for mobility and growth, and hence with intrinsic aspects such as its potential for learning.

Power

Power refers to the capacity to mobilize resources. The structure of power—the capacity for the person to act efficaciously within the constraints of the wider organizational system—is determined by both formal job characteristics and informal alliances. Factors include the routinization or the discretion embedded in the job, the visibility of the function, relevance of the function to current organizational problems, approval by high status people, the mobility prospects of subordinates, and as a variable individual matter, the existence of sponsors or favorable alliance with peers. We can hypothesize that:

People *low in organizational power* would tend to:

—foster lower group morale;

—behave in more directive, authoritarian ways;

—try to retain control, restrict opportunities for subordinates' growth or autonomy, supervise too closely;

—use subordinates as their frame of reference for status assessment and enhancement;

—try to hold back talented subordinates, thereby reducing the threat of replacement;

—use more coercive than persuasive power;

—be more insecure and thus more controlling, critical;

—be very concerned about controlling a territory, and hang on to that territory, even when inappropriate;

—be less well liked, less talkative in meetings with high power people.

People *high in organizational power* would tend to:

—foster higher group morale;

—have subordinates who inhibit their negativity and agressiveness, behaving in more cooperative and less critical ways, thereby reducing the need to exercise strong controls;

—behave in less rigid, directive, authoritarian ways, to delegate more control and allow subordinates more latitude and discretion;

—provide opportunities for subordinates to move along with them, find talented subordinates and groom them for better things;

—have their actions seen more often as helping than hindering;

—be better liked, talk more often, and receive more communications in meetings.

Proportions

This variable refers to the social composition of people in approximately the same situation. It is a simple quantitative matter of how many people there are of what relevant social types in various parts of the organization—e.g., the proportion of women, men, blacks, ethnic minorities. Being "different" is a matter of how many similar people compose the work force. We can hypothesize that:

People whose type is represented in *very small proportion* would tend to:

—be more visible, be "on display";

—feel more pressure to conform, to make fewer mistakes;

—try to become "socially invisible," not to stand out so much;

—find it harder to gain "credibility," particularly in high uncertainty positions such as certain management jobs;

—be more isolated and peripheral;

—be more likely to be excluded from informal peer networks, and hence, limited in this source of power-through-alliances;

—have fewer opportunities to be "sponsored" because of the rarity of people like them upward;

—face misperceptions of their identity and role in the organization and hence, develop a preference for already-established relationships;

—be stereotyped, be placed in role traps that limit effectiveness;

—face more personal stress.

People whose type is represented *in very high proportion* would tend to:

—be easily seen as one of the group, as fitting in;

—be preferred for high-communication managerial jobs;

—find it easier to gain "credibility" for high uncertainty positions, such as some management jobs;

—be more likely to join the informal network, form peer alliances, learn the ropes from peers;

—be more likely to be sponsored by higher status organization members;

—be accurately perceived, have a congruent identity and ease in self-presentation;

—face less personal stress.

Cycles and Feedback Loops

Though the hypothesized associations between each variable and its correlates can be identified, cause and effect are difficult to untangle, because structure and behavior are related in an interacting, rather than a static, way. (Does low opportunity produce low commitment, for example, or do those with low commitment get channeled into low opportunity positions?) Feedback loops connect position and response. Those with opportunity are thereby induced to behave in ways that generate more opportunity, which, in turn, produces further inducement for the behavior. Such a feedback loop is behind such phenomena as "power begets power." The feedback between structure and behavior can produce upward cycles of advantage, or downward cycles of disadvantage. And it is hard for a person to break out of the cycle, once begun. To some extent, low opportunity, powerlessness, and tokenism constitute self-perpetuating, self-sealing systems, with links that can be broken only from outside.

ASSUMPTIONS ABOUT THE PERSON-ORGANIZATION
RELATIONSHIP

The three variables are the building blocks of a structural approach to the problems of women and men in organizations. This book has explored the nature of situations as the critical constraint on organizational behavior. We have seen that organizational roles carry characteristic images of the kinds of people that should occupy them, thus encouraging incumbents to turn into those kinds of people. Positions carry a particular structure of rewards. These rewards may or may not be related to formal tasks in the narrower sense, but they emerge because of the human issues with which people must grapple as they live in large organizations. The structures of rewards, in turn, channel behavior, setting people on a course which ties them further into their roles, makes them even more a product of their situations. Each position in an organization carries with it a set of constraints and limits on the possibilities for occupants to achieve recognition and autonomy. People are confronted with dilemmas: how to garner rewards and reduce dependency using the restricted set of tools their position makes available. For some people, their solutions sometimes trap them in self-defeating cycles that bind them and limit them even further. For others, an advantageous organizational location, possession of the "right" social attributes, and a favorable position with respect to opportunity and power make success almost inevitable.

There are five major underlying assumptions in this model:

1. Work is not an isolated relationship between actor and activity. What happens to people in the course of their work is determined by the larger setting in which it takes place, and that setting, in contemporary society, is likely to be an organization. Jobs and the relations of people to them cannot be understood without reference to the organized systems in which the contemporary division of labor operates. Understanding organizations and how they function is the key to discovering the ways in which people manage their work experiences. Here lie the answers to questions about success (what it means and who gets access to it), about influence seeking (why political bargaining is such an important requirement inside organizations), and about the choices made by people at various stages in their careers. Thus, analysis of a job alone is not enough, without considering where it and its occupant stand in organizational distributions of opportunity and power, on ladders and tracks and spheres of influence. The nature of the total system is important in determining the relationship of any individual worker to his or her work.

There is a future thrust to this relationship, a structure through time as well as space. Unfortunately, most analyses of the person in his or her relation to the organization are highly static, as though the only relevant consideration is the nature of the present-time position and present set of relationships. "Once a sales representative, always a sales representative; once a secretary, always a secretary" seem to be the kind of assumption behind much research on organizational behavior. But organizations and people's connections to them are dynamic, not static. In a larger sense, the structure as a whole may be in constant flux, as it was at Indsco, with jobs and functions and units frequently reshuffled, and managerial relocations common. And in the narrower sense, individuals may move through a sequence of positions in the course of their work lifetime; this is the very meaning of "career." When people give power to a "comer," they do it in terms of bets about future prospects. Thus, the person-organization relationship must be put in dynamic rather than static terms. There must be room in the theory for movement.

Here opportunity is a critical variable, for movement itself is a factor differentiated in modern organizations. Jobs—and their superstructure in career lines—can be distinguished in terms of the amount of movement potential they contain, in terms of their future prospects for reward and growth. Plateaus and dead ends are perceived very differently from high mobility positions, even if the actual work content, status, and compensation level is the same. To be "stuck" is a very different work experience from being on the move, from being "up and coming." This relationship of one point in time to the overall possibilities inherent in the organization has many consequences. Too little opportunity, for example, may result in rapid decay of whatever interest or excitement is contained in a particular position, just as the uplifting effect of a raise may decline if no further raises appear to be forthcoming. Too much mobility, on the other hand, may result in a lack of interest in the present job content, since today's job is only a stopping-off point in a longer process of flow-through and exit. In short, people relate to the present in part in terms of their expectations and prospects for the future. Any position, then, must be viewed in the larger organizational context.

2.   Behavior in organizations is, when all is said and done, adaptive. What people do, how they come to feel and behave, reflects what they can make of their situation, limited though it might be, and still gather material rewards and preserve a modicum of human dignity. Dignity requires a sense of value (that one has worth according to a shared standard) and a sense of mastery or autonomy (that one is able to retain some control over life conditions). (The second has been called, "reduction of dependency." [2]) Some people are given dignity automatically with their jobs in the degree of recognition, reward, status, autonomy, and control made possible. For others, however, recognition and autonomy must be sought within narrower constraints. This is what

Michel Crozier meant when he stressed that managers did not have a monopoly on "rationality," even though workers sometimes appeared to be behaving in ways that would not advance their careers or guarantee their economic security. "Subordinates," he wrote, "can be considered as free agents who can discuss their own problems and bargain about them, who do not only submit to a power structure but also participate in that structure. Of course, their degree of freedom is not very great, and their conduct, when viewed from outside, may seem to a large extent to be determined by non-rational motivations. But one must never forget that to them it is rational, i.e., adaptive." [3] Perhaps the word "strategic" is a better term than "rational"; people's choices reflect strategic approaches to managing a situation.

3.   If behavior reflects a "reasonable" response to an organizational position, it is not thereby seen as mechanically inevitable. In the interaction of person and situation, the person still has a degree of latitude in deciding how to combine latent possibilities into action. Only the most constrained and routinized job has no degrees of freedom for choice about approach. Social structure does not *control* so much as it *limits*—restricts the range of options, narrows the tools, and confronts the individual with a characteristic set of problems to solve. These problems often come in the form of dilemmas: seemingly unreconcilable pulls that make every choice bear its load of costs as well as benefits. We have seen in every corner of Indsco how many dilemmas are inherent in organizational roles and structures. My view, then, sees behavior as the result of a sense-making process involving present experiencing and future projecting rather than of psychological conditioning in which the dim past is a controlling force.

4.   Behavior is also directly connected to the formal tasks set forth in a job's location in the division of organizational labor. As an overreaction to mechanistic models which assumed that the *only* important thing about organizations was the official definition of a job and official authority delegated through the hierarchy, some social psychological writers began to imply the opposite: that the formal structure counted for little and that the organization was nothing more than a setting for a vast interpersonal game. The behavior of people inside organizations was reduced to political bargaining or abstracted social psychological dynamics or, in some popularized writings like Anthony Jay's *Corporation Man,* to the acting out of traditional tribal hunting rituals and warrior games. [4] The fact that people also had jobs, jobs with real content and a connection to the tasks the organization was supposedly performing, seemed lost in the shuffle. Wilbert Moore, in *The Conduct of the Corporation,* was one of a number of theorists who helped bring back the reality of the organization when he wrote that when all is said and done, the content of

the job a person is supposed to be doing is the best predictor of his or her behavior.[5]

The job content is very important here, too. Certain social psychological pressures are seen as arising out of the formal constraints placed on people trying to do their jobs. The fact that secretaries spend most of their time typing becomes the starting point for seeing how the authority relationship between bosses and secretaries is managed. The squeeze that first-line supervisors are caught in accounts for their tendency to try to keep control over the job, even to the extent of jumping in to do it themselves. The amount of communication that takes place in a manager's day leads managers to avoid problematic communications, translated into an avoidance of people who are "different." The relative hierarchical levels and formal job constraints of people in different functions who depend on one another to get their jobs done account for the balance of power in the relationship when the time comes to bargain for resources or attention. The actual promotion opportunities leading from a particular job have a large amount to do with how engaged people are in their work. And so forth.

5. An interest in the relationship of formal task, formal location, to behavioral responses also leads to an emphasis on competence—ability to do the job—more than it is often stressed in social psychological analyses. Sheer competence often plays the most important part in distributing people over positions, but competence is not equally easily *measured* in all kinds of functions, as we saw in Chapter 3. Social factors (such as sex or background or conformity to similar values) become more important in direct relation to the difficulty and uncertainty of evaluating competence. Furthermore, the opportunity to *demonstrate* competence is not distributed equally over all jobs, as Chapter 7 argued. Some are so routinized that they fail to allow individuals to show talent; others provide ongoing opportunities to engage in extraordinary acts or succeed at risky challenges.

Thus, organizational behavior is produced in the interaction of individuals, seeking to meet their own needs and manage their situations, with their positions, which constrain their options for the ways they can act. The total interaction is a dynamic one: certain responses touch off others and provide the moving force behind cycles and chains of events.

ENLARGING OTHER PERSPECTIVES

The structural model proposed here puts together a number of elements that appear only in fragments in other writings, as well as offers some new hypotheses, especially around tokenism and the effects of relative numbers. Many separate pieces of the model, many individual connections, may certainly be known already to organizational analysts—as is shown by the large amount of social scientific literature cited throughout the book. And a structural approach is highly compatible with some current thought in the field, especially of those interested in hierarchy effects. But the intention here is to add those new pieces that are needed for completeness, and then to put all of the fragments together in a way that has conceptual clarity, coherence and unity, and can be translated directly into action suggestions. In these ways, the approach here helps enlarge on the critical views of people in organizations embodied in social psychological and contemporary Marxist perspectives.

Social Psychological Schools

There have been two major intellectual strands in American theories of the person-organization relationship. Though occasionally analysts have worked in both traditions or attempted to bridge them (Chris Argyris is a good example), and though similar conclusions are sometimes reached, their key premises can be distinguished. In focusing on different issues and seeing less than the total picture, each has also led to very different sets of policy suggestions for improving the human functioning of the organization and the quality of work life. They are the cognitive-motivational school and the social school.

The tradition that can loosely be termed "cognitive" developed around work motivation and the nature of incentives: how people weigh the factors that enter into their decisions to participate, to contribute, to be satisfied with their work. The critical factor is the immediate and direct relationship between person and job. Representative American examples include Chester Barnard, Herbert Simon, and James March, in their concern with the "inducements-contributions" balance, and Frederick Herzberg, with his still-controversial dual-factor theory of motivation. (A slightly different British strand focusing on "socio-technical systems" is found in the work of Eric Trist and associates and the Tavistock Institute of Human Relations.) This tradition has led to efforts to identify those aspects of the job itself (and sometimes its material compensation) that act as incentives or disincentives. Much recent research has attempted to distinguish those critical elements of jobs that are associated with work motivation and satisfaction; a variety of diagnostic tools have been developed to measure such variables as task variety, autonomy, feedback, responsibility.[6] Such efforts seem to begin with a Taylorian assumption that there are optimal ways to divide labor and assign tasks, but they stand scientific management on its head in emphasizing job *enlargement* rather than simplification and increased worker responsibility and control. Job enlargement or job enrichment, indeed, are the central intervention strategies and organizational policy alternative to emerge from this tradition. Proponents argue that work redesign *directly* changes behavior, rehumanizes the person, and can help initiate other organization changes.[7]

The other strand is "social," seeing the person's relationship to the organization mediated not by the job itself but by the group, by interpersonal factors. The style of leadership, the forms of membership, the norms and culture reflected in the face-to-face group—these are the critical issues in this tradition, beginning with the Hawthorne studies and continuing through Kurt Lewin's research on group dynamics and that of numerous social psychologists centered around the University of Michigan. Attitudes and behavior in the organization, in this view, are shaped by the fact that the person has varying kinds of interpersonal relationships and varying degrees of membership (and hence, involvement) in particular groups; the consequences of the notion can be seen, for example, in Rensis Likert's proposal that overlapping membership ("linking-pins" between groups) could increase organizational effectiveness.[8] The early concerns with leadership and influence, with communication and participation, have evolved into a more direct interest in power. But still, the key word in this tradition is "participation." Intervention strategies and policy alternatives have focused on a variety of mechanisms for ensuring "membership" in the organization's interests, through team-building efforts and other means for giving employees a voice—though the role of unions and collective bargaining as participation vehicles has often been ignored. The quality of work life will be improved, it is assumed, with the advent of more democratic, more participatory, more team-centered organizations.

Both of these approaches have some value and, under some conditions, have had positive effects on job satisfaction, commitment, self-esteem, and even occasionally on productivity—although here the evidence is much more tenuous.[9] I would certainly agree that, all other things being equal, more participation is better than less, and redesigning boring, meaningless jobs to make them more challenging and meaningful has to have human value. However, problems exist with both of these approaches, both in theory and application, because their views of the-person-and-the-organization are limited; they could each benefit from an enlarged, total system, structuralist theory. A number of recent commentators on work and organizations have come to a similar conclusion—that whole systems must be taken into account, rather than small elements of them— [10] but they have not necessarily developed concepts to pinpoint what is critical about the structure of the total system for individual outcomes.

The things that need to be taken into account in job enrichment (and more broadly, in systematic work redesign) are not confined to aspects of the work itself and its immediate supervisory context; they require attention to structures of opportunity and power. Chapter 6 reviewed some of the evidence for the proposition that "job satisfaction" measures tied to job attributes may miss the most critical element shaping people's relationships to their work and commitment to the organization: the opportunity structure. As others have also indicated, commitment, in the sense of overall attachment to the organization, is not the same as more narrowly defined satisfaction with elements of a job, and in some circumstances, can override immediate job dissatisfaction; [11] commitment seems clearly tied to the increasing rewards and chance for growth implied in high opportunity. But many job satisfaction studies and job enrichment schemes leave out these critical elements. Though there is currently more awareness that the nature of immediate material rewards affects job satisfaction, less often is opportunity, with its sense of expectations for future rewards, taken into account. Employees may not just need more interesting jobs and higher material rewards *now*, they may also need to have their opportunities for mobility, for growth, for increasing status stretched.

There are many indications that job enrichment and work redesign stand or fall in practice by their effects—or lack of them—on opportunity and power structures. Results can be negative when changing employee expectations through the enlarged job conflicts with more limiting organizational structures (such as the lack of chance for mobility); they can also be negative when workers are not very motivated or involved to begin with, as people tend to be in low opportunity jobs. [12] "Job enrichment" can sometimes be perceived as adding to workers' burdens rather than to their prospects, as Richard Balzar found in a factory, where work was supposed to be made more interesting by giving workers variety—i.e., a greater number of boring tasks. [13] Finally, there seems to be excitement and positive results from enriched jobs with flexible work arrangements as long as there remain more prospects for skill increase, especially in those systems where pay increases are geared to employee mastery [14]—that is, as long as *opportunity* remains; but the positive effects seem to fall off when people reach the limits of opportunity.

Furthermore, the structure of power also needs to be taken into account. Richard Walton commented that work redesign may be inadequate and ineffective without other organizational changes; many of the other changes he suggested can be translated, in my terms, into broadening power. For example, work teams must be given enough information to act appropriately, if their greater control is to work; there must be overall disclosure of information about the state of the system.[15] This means that the managerial monopoly on information needs to be reduced, and work teams given more control over the use to make of information. Furthermore, giving more discretion and autonomy to workers and work groups in formally hierarchical systems creates questions about the role of their immediate supervisors and, eventually, questions about the operation of power in management up the whole line. Job enrichment can either be *empowering* (as supervisors give up downward control, they in turn take on some of the planning or external relations tasks of their superiors, which then requires a more decentralized, discretion-delegated management structure), or it can merely make the most vulnerable people in the supervisory chain even more powerless, leaving the structure of upper management intact. First-line supervisors and other low-level managers are usually hardest hit and most threatened by changes anyway, especially if they lose pieces of their job that they may feel best about doing (such as their own mastery of the work itself). Inadequate attention to the effects of power distribution in work redesign can result in much discontent among the people "in the middle" and also great resistance to change, as supervisors find their only claims to efficacy and their one influential domain threatened.

Similarly, ideas about participation need to be enlarged by conceptions of power and opportunity; and, under some circumstances, the numerical effects of social composition would also have to be taken into account to see if participation "works." Participatory systems, by themselves, do not always have positive results, unless the structures of opportunity and power are also affected by the increase in shared influence over decisions.[16] (Whether the *decisions* generated through participatory methods are better is another matter, not directly connected to the personal effects.) For some people in some situations, "participation" can increase the *burden* of work rather than the *options* available or the *power* over outcomes—through the extra time that must be put in at meetings or spent collecting information, the time thinking about issues, the burden of mounting and waging arguments. Those people who appear to have little desire for the increased responsibility of participation—a common research finding identifies some such individuals—might be responding, instead, to the fact that they are being asked to do extra work without changes in the objective structures of opportunity and material rewards or without shifts in their actual autonomy and discretion. One of the factors accounting for the group commitment and productivity in the Relay Assembly Test Room of the Hawthorne experiments was the fact that a woman who emerged as group leader saw in the experiments a chance to improve her objective situation, increase the opportunity factor in her career, by showing her talents to management.[17] Present thinking holds that participation works only when people's rewards are increased. It is plausible to conclude that participation has positive effects through its impact on opportunity or power, but not necessarily only as a process in and of itself.

There are scholars who argue that participation does not always increase the power of those participating and is a poor substitute for truly empowering whatever population is at issue. Critics have attacked some proposals for increased participation as manipulative, saying that they allow subordinates only the choice between limited options, with the options themselves set by some other process. When used in this way, participation does a great deal for the parties *offering* it (who gain the power associated with democratic leaders whom followers like and trust), but not much for the parties *receiving* it. A British study of board-level participation by worker representatives in the British Steel Corporation (one of a number of much-heralded European innovations in participatory democracy) found that the impact of worker-directors was likely to be limited by a number of factors: social pressures at board meetings; the fact that workers had to play by management's rules; the managerial monopoly on knowledge, language, and authority; and workers' lack of opportunity for informal influence over other board members through informal social networks.[18] (In all fairness, the presence of worker-directors did ensure that issues would be raised and considered that the board might otherwise find easy to ignore. So again, some participation is better than none, but without other organizational changes, its value is limited.)

Philip Selznick has also criticized the participation model for its failure to truly empower, writing: "Although human relations has emphasized participation, the latter has had a psychic, interpersonal and *private* cast. The important thing is to 'clue the man [sic] in,' to make him feel wanted and appreciated, to allay his fears, to offer him vehicles of personal fulfillment. These efforts may be humane and gratifying. They may mitigate authoritarian administration. But they do not necessarily presume that the individual can make up his own mind to pursue his rightful ends through a public process. One might treat a slave humanely, with due regard to good 'human relations.' . . . But this would still leave the slave a dependent 'unperson,' incapable of asserting his own will save privately and by indirection. The political perspective asks that this basic dependency and incompetence be transformed; it blends into a legal perspective as the transition is made to orderly process for the invocation of rights and the redress of grievances." [19] Thus, it is possible to see some forms of participation as mechanisms for adjustment, not justice—unless affecting the structure of opportunity and power. The issue is to establish participation that truly empowers.

Marxist Theorists of the Labor Process

Contemporary Marxists have also commented on the person-organization relationship, in analyzing the labor process under corporate capitalism. Harry Braverman and others focused on differentiation of tasks, with a consequent deskilling and "proletarianization" of workers, a process that is seen to affect more and more occupations, including technical personnel and even lower-level managers. Explanations for the division of the work process contained in the modern Marxist literature include three kinds of advantages for capitalism: managerial control (minute specialization makes workers dependent on managers—e.g., for determining work conditions and integrating the products of labor—and makes the labor force more controllable); capitalist-manager legitimation (the division of labor gives capitalists and managers an essential role in the production process and provides a justification for their superior rewards and privileges); and economic advantage (centralized planning and control is a vehicle for necessary capital accumulation and division of tasks into routinized parts is a way to lower the price of labor, since dividing a craft into component parts tends to cheapen each).[20] Such theories provide a critical view and an alternative set of explanations of routinization and job simplification in the corporate bureaucracy.

In this case, too, the analysis needs a fuller view of the ways in which organizational structure impacts on individuals. The conceptions of how to organize embedded in bureaucratization and scientific management not only removed skill, control, and challenge from the employee, they also brought with them a highly differentiated and hierarchized structure of movement possibilities and career pathways. The growth of vertical as well as horizontal differentiation is critical; hierarchy effects are as important as routinization of tasks. While writers in the Marxist tradition occasionally mention the development of job ladders as a concomitant of the new job structures, they do not give sufficient weight to a differentiated structure of opportunity as a determinant of the person-organization relationship. Some critical economists do consider the division of opportunity in their conceptions of internal labor markets and dual labor markets; this is a promising approach. (The "secondary" sector of the labor market, for example, is said to be characterized by little chance for advancement and low employment security, along with low wages, poor working conditions, and harsh supervision.[21]) Still, how hierarchy more specifically divides opportunity, and how this, in turn, affects the person's present behavior and future prospects, is generally not a central theme, even though it deserves more attention.

Furthermore, in emphasizing horizontal differentiation, with hierarchy and vertical differentiation relegated to the background as a vague control mechanism, the new Marxist critics do not pay much attention to the ways in which a formal and informal structure of power overlays an organization. The worker-manager split is too simple. To understand where control lies, and to understand how person and organization are connected, more fully developed theories of power are necessary, theories that take into account the overall structure of the organization, its environmental situation, and the prospects for power accumulation embedded in both the formal nature of tasks and access to informal alliances. On the whole, though there are exceptions, contemporary Marxist critics of the labor process do not offer much guidance to the development of alternative organizational arrangements.

If the structural approach, with its three central concepts, is a useful addition to human relations and Marxist theories, such a model is absolutely critical for dealing with problems of sex discrimination and the place of women in organizations. Here again the contribution to theory also provides background for practice.

THE WOMEN'S ISSUE: "INDIVIDUAL" MODEL AND ITS DEFECTS

It was many years after women's employment in industry was firmly entrenched that the idea of equality between the sexes at work took root as a value. The first concerns about women's work outside the home were protective. In 1875 Azel Ames, a physician, writing about the deleterious effects of industrial occupations on women's health, called working women "a noble army of martyrs." [22] Several decades later, however, protective legislation had been enacted, and the concerns of social scientists had shifted. After World War I, observers began to document inequities and discrimination against women in work organizations and professional life. In 1929 a special issue of the *Annals of the American Academy of Political and Social Science* was devoted to women's activities and the factors keeping them from full equality at work. [23] During World War II, there was another wave of interest. The demands of war production brought large numbers of women workers into male-dominated territories, and experts on human relations in industry could not fail to note the difficulties and discriminatory treatment women faced. In 1957 the National Manpower Council published a' major report of conferences and interviews with employers throughout the country. The conclusions about matters ranging from wage discrimination to unfair stereotyping anticipated in detail findings about women's places at work produced fifteen years later. [24]

The nature of the "problem" is well known then. Solutions are quite another matter. Despite attention to the women's issue, change has been slow to nonexistent. The occupational distributions of men and women have shifted remarkably little over the decades since the situation has been made clear to policy-makers and the general public. Stereotypes about women's work behavior and why women cannot manage men that were uttered in 1942 [25] must still be countered. Change agents must argue the case for women's equality armed with statistics that could have been collected, with minor modifications, thirty years earlier, and they must address themselves to the same myths and over-generalizations. In fact, there is some evidence that occupational segregation has been increasing. [26]

Something has been holding women back. That something was usually assumed to be located in the differences between men and women as individuals: their training for different worlds; the nature of sexual relationships, which make women unable to compete with men and men unable to aggress against women; the "tracks" they were put on in school or at play; and even, in the most biologically reductionist version of the argument, "natural" dispositions of the sexes. Conclusions like these have become standard explanations for familiar statistics about discrimination. They form the basis for the "individual" model of work behavior. Whether one leans toward the more social or the more biological side of the argument, both add up to an assumption that the factors producing inequities at work are somehow carried inside the individual person. [27]

By the 1970s a combination of government decrees, women's movement activism, and large numbers of educated women entering or re-entering the labor force had produced pressures for change in organizations. Policies of "affirmative action" and "equal employment opportunity" were established, with varying degrees of good faith, to "guarantee" women more places in the parts of organizations closed to them.

These efforts will not work any better than yesterday's, as long as individual models of behavior and change remain in full force. In fact, many change programs in organizations are *not* working. They are using the wrong model and drawing the wrong conclusions. Use of versions of the individual model inevitably leads to the conclusion that "women are different" and serves to reinforce the present structure of organizations and the one-down position of women within them. Individual model-thinking leads women to believe that the problem lies in their own psychology, and it gives organizations a set of excuses for the slow pace of change. But the whole thrust of this book is to present an alternative model, one that demonstrates that responses to work are a function of basic structural issues, such as the constraints imposed by roles and the effects of opportunity, power, and numbers. Attention to *these* issues would require organizations—not people—to change.

It is easy to get hooked on the individual model in America. It is tempting to locate at least some of the causes of injuries in the actions of the injured.[28] It can be plausible to blame the poor for their poverty and applaud the powerful for their "deserved" privileges. We pat ourselves on the back for our successes and internalize our failures as a sign of personal unworthiness. And we invent self-improvement programs, often under the banner of "social change," that exhort people to lift themselves up by the bootstraps and do better next time.

Repair programs for women who recognize their personal "deficiencies" in job-market terms constitute a currently profitable industry: how to be more assertive, how to be a manager, how to communicate more effectively, how to make decisions. These programs certainly meet a felt need, and some of the offerings do good. They boost self-esteem; they offer useful skills; they provide a language and insights into the functioning of work situations; they sometimes provide support systems or peers who can serve as allies.

None of them guarantees anyone a job. Some of them even make women less satisfied with the jobs open to them: being a secretary when a program had awakened visions of being a vice-president. One company is currently re-viewing its programs to identify and train female talent, because officials feel they may be hurting morale more than helping it; there are simply not enough "quality" openings for women yet to go around. The title of a recent *Wall Street Journal* article is revealing: "Many Seminars Are Held to Aid Women in Firms; Then What Happens? Some People Say Workshops Raise False Hopes." [29] And none of the personal improvement courses attacks root causes of inequality in the system. Far from it. They offer a subtle and insidious system-maintaining message. They confirm the old American notion that money and time is best spent remaking the person. If the current generation is too far gone to be remade, then early education must be changed, and we must wait for the next generation to come along and do better. The personal improvement strategy for change reinforces stereotypes about women's need for compensatory education to remedy their deficiencies before they are fit to compete with men. The existence of theories and self-improvement tech-niques based on analysis of women's psychology and socialization permits decision-makers in organizations with a male leadership tradition to put a label on their discomfort with the idea of women's equality: "So *that* is why women have not been able to make it as managers." The system remains uncriticized.

What individual models of change also ignore is the range of differences among women and the great overlap between men and women in their work behavior and attitudes.[30] Every statement that can be made about what women typically do or feel holds true for some men. As we have seen through-out this book, what appear to be "sex differences" in work behavior emerge as responses to structural conditions, to one's place in the organization. But it is hard to explain this overlap in individual models. There is no theory about how common situations give rise to common attitudes. Instead, the model sees people as predisposed to strike certain characteristic postures— programmed in advance to respond as they do, with sex one of the major pieces of the program.

This view creates another problem. Individual models absolve the system of responsibility for manufacturing the psychology of their workers. They assume that organizations take people as they find them; the making and molding has all occurred before the workers enter the door. The slots exist for the kinds of people pre-designed to fit them. This view is highly misleading. Certainly people are prepared beforehand for careers set on tracks, and to some extent even develop the appropriate mind-set in advance. But to a very large degree, organizations make their workers into who they are. Adults change to fit the system. It would be interesting to discover just how many people find themselves on career paths dramatically different from anything they envisioned before a good opportunity came their way. Yet organizations often act as though it is possible to predict people's job futures from the characteristics they bring with them a recruiting interview. What really happens is that predictions get made on the basis of stereotypes and current notions of who fits where in the present system; people are then "set up" in positions which make the predictions come true.[31]

If women themselves are not considered the architects of their own fate in the individual model, then men as individuals are blamed for discrimination and oppressions. The equivalent of self-improvement programs for women are "self-examination" programs for men in organizations, in which their sexism and ignorance about women is unmasked. This strategy, too, is doubtful as an effective change technique, even though some men undeniably gain insights into their behavior that can affect the ways they treat the women close to them. As a political tactic alone, questions can be raised. Such approaches are likely to arouse great resistance among men and antagonize those who may be allies. They also treat the world too simply. The possibilities men see are limited by their work roles as much as women's. Men at the top, who may have never thought about a woman as a peer and feel vaguely uneasy about it, are not necessarily part of a conspiratorial plot to keep women from power. They may be responding to the world as they see it, to the system pressures shaping their jobs, and to the organizational relations they have with women. The dynamics of tokenism—the effects of limited numbers of women—make the women who do enter "men's worlds" operate at a disadvantage. We saw in Chapter 3 that uncertainty pressures tend to create exclusive socially homogeneous management groups. And what men think about women's potential as workers and leaders may be honestly based on the women they know best:

their secretaries and their wives. That these women may be limited in their behavior by the constraints of their own roles—as in Chapters 4 and 5—is an issue that never crosses the minds of the men who deal with them. Making change, then, depends not on accusations but on understanding—reaching and seeing the underlying causes of behavior: how organizations systematically make some people "look good" and others "look bad."

Feminists and men in dead-end jobs both have a stake in seeing that organizations change to open opportunity channels and decentralize power, just as both whites and blacks have a stake in better education. Yet, use of individual models of change are likely to prevent people from seeing their joint interests in system-change; rather, they pit groups against one another in the competitive struggle for advantage in situations of scarcity. Accepting the terms of the present situation and improving oneself within it helps the system to maintain itself. Energy is spent in self-scrutiny and struggle with others who appear to be competing for the same scarce resources. Hierarchical systems of organization are often successful in fragmenting groups and leading them to believe that their interests lie in opposition, so that they blame each other for their problems rather than uniting to change the system. Attempting to keep the other group out, while ferociously improving oneself in the hopes that more advantage will follow, is a characteristically American approach to the problems stemming from inequality, an approach rooted in individual models. But the structural approach used here can turn attention away from inter-group competition and toward the real problem: the ways systems of work are organized, and how these systems themselves can be modified to provide more opportunity, more power, and a better balance of numbers, for all of the kinds of people whose work lives are spent there.

Understanding more fully the structural conditions that impact on human behavior in organizations, we can then choose more appropriately policies and programs to improve the quality of work life and promote equal employment opportunity. Understanding guides action. And action on women's work issues may be critically important for the future of American society as a whole.

10

Contributions to Practice: Organizational Change, Affirmative Action, and the Quality of Work Life

The reasonable man adapts himself to the world; the unreasonable one persists in trying to adapt the world to himself. Therefore, all progress depends on the unreasonable man.
— George Bernard Shaw, *Man and Superman*

A long habit of not thinking a thing *wrong* gives it the superficial appearance of being *right*.
— Thomas Paine, *Common Sense*

The workplace has long been dominated by the rule of the carrot and the stick—as if we were a nation of donkeys. But the carrot—the lure of material well-being as defined by money and possessions—is subtly losing its savor. And the stick—once a brutal club labelled "economic insecurity"—has thinned down to a flaccid bundle of twigs.
— Daniel Yankelovich, "The Meaning of Work"

Three important concerns converge around the need to change the structures of organizations. First is a growing recognition that improving the quality of work life and considering the human consequences of organizational arrangements are as important a measure of a system's "effectiveness" as economic indicators. This movement reflects a demand on the part of the working population. Opinion polls, though themselves not always the best indicators, have shown a steady erosion in the satisfaction expressed with work since the early

1960s. Daniel Yankelovich points to a cultural *Zeitgeist* in which ever greater numbers of people expect work to involve challenge and meaning as well as opportunities for self-expression.[1] An American Management Association survey of middle management discovered that over half of the respondents found their work "at best, unsatisfying." There is evidence that blocked opportunity and powerlessness affect the work life quality of managers and professionals along with other workers; in one report, dissatisfaction was growing in middle management as a function of job insecurity, "boxed in" feelings, and responsibility without authority.[2] Remedies clearly involve organizational changes.

Equal employment opportunity for women and minorities is another currently pressing issue, and one that cannot be solved without attention to the structures of opportunity, power, and numbers. Effective strategies of affirmative action must be based on examination of the design of jobs and their settings. Since women and blacks have legal remedies that disadvantaged white men may lack, the levers are at hand, via this issue, to encourage policymakers to reconsider organizational design; equal employment opportunity is a stated policy of the United States government and practically all major organizations. Furthermore, there is a need for change models that do not merely improve the situation of one group at the cost of another, as is often the case now, but rather create more generally satisfying as well as more equitable arrangements. As I have argued earlier, the problem of equality for women cannot be solved without structures that potentially benefit all organization members more broadly.

Finally, organizations themselves should have an interest in effective behavior. Blocked opportunity, powerlessness, and tokenism tend to generate employees who, among other things, have low aspirations, lack commitment to the organization, become hostile to leaders, behave ineffectively in leadership roles themselves, take few risks, or become socially isolated and personally stressed. Aside from the cost to such individuals—often women, but also men—organizations are wasting a large measure of their human talent. Systems that are more generally opportunity- and power-constraining are not developing the resources of either their men or their women to the fullest. Such problems of limited opportunity, limited power, and unbalanced numbers arise especially in large hierarchical organizations. Where rewards and status become increasingly scarce closer to the top, where the gap between "professionals" or administrators and other workers is particularly large, and where rigid bureaucratic models of task organization prevail, there is also likely to be a large group of disadvantaged and underemployed workers. This group can be the source of behavioral blockages and recurrent organizational problems.

What can be done, in policy and practice, about these critical social issues? The analysis of opportunity, power, and numbers provides guidelines for the kinds of programs and arrangements that will broaden access to favorable positions in organizations. The theoretical framework can be used to suggest new structural alternatives, on the one hand, and to provide a conceptual underpinning for better-known strategies, on the other hand—strategies which are currently being applied to some managerial personnel but rarely below. Policies are useful, in this regard, if they *enhance opportunity, empower,* and *balance* the *numbers* of socially different kinds of people.

Elements of structural change are outlined in this chapter. Systematic application of these principles, with supporting arrangements in the organization as a whole, has the potential to make a big difference. For example, people who seem to be uncommitted or at the limit of their abilities might take on greater challenge and be more productive, with beneficial consequences to both person and organization. People who seem to be rigid, rules-minded, and hostile to change might, with greater access to power, become more effective and more innovative. But to reap such benefits, thoroughgoing revision of much present organizational practice is required, including job redefinition and redesign, modifications of the hierarchy, and much more flexibility of opportunity structures. In some instances, this means developing new strategies, but it also involves the systematic application of much of what is already known about structural change in organizations. We can combine the integrated approach to organizational behavior contained in the three-variable model with practical policies based on experiences in innovating organizations to suggest some of the elements of opportunity-enhancing, empowering, and number-balancing strategies.

OPPORTUNITY-ENHANCING EFFORTS

Whenever people are concentrated in low-opportunity and low-mobility jobs with few prospects for growth in skills or advancement and few open pathways out and up, their full participation in the organization is constrained and their involvement in work is limited. While some jobs offer high mobility prospects to their occupants (a high probability of advancement, a short time-span between advances, the chance for increasing challenge, and eventual access to the most rewarded jobs), other positions systematically block opportunity: promotion rates are low, there is a long time-span between moves, tasks do not change, skill and mastery do not increase, and there is no route out of the job into rewarded positions. Internal allocation of personnel, in a complex organization, is governed by hiring, promotion, and layoff rules within separate "labor markets" or kinds of workplaces (office work, professional areas, management, public relations, etc.). Each workplace also formulates its own definition of "suitability" for its jobs. Thus, one issue is not only to provide advancement for some individuals but also to decrease the gap between labor markets so as to raise the stature of low-mobility occupations as a whole.[3]

To enhance opportunity, the nature of such internal labor markets must first be uncovered and then modified; a thorough review of job ladders and an effort to open new ladders is required. Organizations can also more routinely operate in ways that increase skills and competences required for advancement. At the same time, opportunity can be broadened in other, less hierarchical ways that taken into account the imperatives of economic efficiency: that not everyone can be (or wants to be) at the "top," that some undesirable jobs must be done, that monetary rewards may not be infinitely expandable. New structures can reinforce alternatives to definitions of success-as-upward-mobility. Organizations can make more widely available enhancement of skills, movement into new situations, or continuing challenge backed up by recognition.

Opening opportunity for clerical workers is one structural change issue. Because the labor markets and advancement ladders for clerical and managerial personnel are often so different, personnel strategists may have difficulty even in deciding what paths and channels can be opened between these two distinct worlds. What path can a secretary take that would put her on an administrative ladder other than toward clerical supervisor? What kinds of jobs can serve as the links? A system's size and complexity can make such questions difficult to answer. The first requirement is a clear picture of the skills and training required by different jobs, so that it is possible to see whether Job B is an appropriate next step from Job A, despite how different their titles and content areas might make them sound; *bridges between job ladders* can be identified. But even before opportunities can be created, then, the organization must acquire information and find a way to make comparisons across technical, clerical, and lower-management jobs. If, as is often the case, many clerical positions have no job descriptions or non-ad hoc way of discovering or evaluating what the skills of people in those positions actually are, a first step might involve diagnosis: sending a team of people into the field to interview clerical or other low opportunity workers and write *job descriptions*. These descriptions should include a list of the actual tasks performed and, therefore, identification of *competences* needed rather than a title for the overall function, and they should outline the special content knowledge acquired in the job. They should particularly include any special opportunities offered by the job to move beyond the limits of the formal title (such as typist) and exercise special skills (such as budget-writing).

A next step is the establishment of good feedback and encouragement for learning, as in a *performance appraisal system* in which managers and subordinates or groups of work peers and colleagues would periodically meet to review the individuals' performances, suggest areas for improvement, note areas that were outstanding, and record any changes in the skill levels of the employees since the last meeting, such as new proficiencies or educational experiences. Some analysts recommend frequent *work-planning and review meetings* as an alternative to less frequent performance appraisals.

Both of these steps have some opportunity-enhancing aspects by themselves. The people involved are encouraged by such processes to see themselves and their jobs in a different way. Going through the process can boost self-esteem and build people's sense of their own skills. Some can see that they did not just occupy a particular niche for which they were suited in some general and vague way, but rather that they possessed a number of quite specific competences that resembled the skills called for in jobs up the ladder. Where the appraisal interaction between manager and subordinate or within a peer group works as it is planned, *managers* can be seen *as counseling resources*, helping employees decide how to improve their skills and transform "just a job" into a step in a conscious career. This requires managers who are trained in "people-development skills," as discussed below, and who are rewarded by the organization for the development of talent rather than such usual bureaucratic outcomes as conformity to rules.

The opportunity-enhancing features of performance appraisal appear to require formal planning, for there is evidence that even those who think it is a good idea would rarely undertake it on their own.[4] Assessment of competence is certainly an emotionally charged issue, for all parties involved. And performance appraisal can also be abused: when it is used for control (e.g., to justify low pay or firings) rather than to increase opportunity; when bosses who are ineffective communicators evaluate judgmentally rather than analyze capacities in a helpful way, focus on personality rather than performance, or fail to report performance accurately out of fears that their own competence as a manager will be called into question; or when the data are used for peer comparisons, to determine how to distribute a scarce pool of rewards, and people are inappropriately fitted to a curve.[5] But as part of a program to increase the development of human talent and, hence, boost opportunity, systems of performance appraisal can be useful.

At the same time that women and other typically low mobility workers can come to see themselves, through the job description and performance appraisal process, as more mobile and "marketable" than they had thought, the organization itself will now have a *pool of information* on the skills and talents of employees to whom little attention had previously been paid. Some of the information can be surprising, revealing a suitability for promotion or more challenging responsibilities that might not become known otherwise. In addition to the increase of information, the employees themselves might be increasing in skill as a result of the changed context of opportunity. At this point, *career review* processes can be helpful. Managers and subordinates, or employees and personnel specialists, or colleague groups, discuss employees' ultimate career goals and help them to map a series of steps by which they can (a) improve current performance; (b) acquire the additional skills, education, or training necessary to meet their career goals; and (c) look for the appropriate pathway—the sequence of jobs—that will move them toward their goal. Sometimes this can involve inventing a job that does not yet exist, and it can be an important source of innovation for an organization.

Change should not stop here. To lengthen some ladders for blocked-opportunity people on paper and to identify the hidden talent among employees while encouraging them in their learning still does not guarantee that opportunity has really been opened or that the "next step" does not itself turn out to be a dead end. *Job posting* provides one form of insurance: a system by which openings are announced publicly and employees are free to bid on any job. But the nature of certain jobs and their role relations should also be reexamined.

Since women are often concentrated in dead-end secretarial positions, secretarial work is one example of a fruitful area for *job redesign,* in a number of ways. If a secretary's status is based on that of her boss, these statuses should be decoupled so that secretaries are rewarded for what they actually do and not for how senior the boss is. Secretaries could also become apprentices to their bosses, and part of bosses' responsibilities (for which they themselves would be evaluated) would be to teach secretaries enough over a period of time that they could move ahead on management ladders. Again, managers could be officially rewarded for developing talent and losing good secretaries in contrast to their present systematic stake in keeping one as long as possible in the same position. If more work in large organizations begins to take place in project teams and committees, secretaries could more readily be viewed as part of the team rather than a note-taking adjunct, especially when they could have as much as or more information than managers by virtue of reading correspondence and talking with other secretaries. This sometimes occurs informally at present, but there are several problems with informal arrangements. They continue to leave secretaries dependent on the whim and approval of bosses to get training or team membership, they do not permit official recognition of what secretaries are learning and doing, and they do not include such opportunities as regular features of the job so that the next role occupant lacks comparable opportunities. However, to formalize an apprentice or assistant status for secretaries and then enlarge also the training and autonomy of pool typists in preparation for apprenticeships would increase mobility prospects associated with secretarial jobs. It would increase the number of men seeking them. It would also reduce some of the typical "office wife" features of the job. There would be better uses of secretarial time. Secretaries would have to be chosen for intellectual and managerial abilities. They would have opportunities to demonstrate competence and win the respect of a wider audience. And bosses would have to see them as potential peers.

In addition to the redesign of typical jobs for women to add more opportunity to them, it is important to *develop new jobs* that close the gap between different internal labor markets. Wherever the gap between a higher-status category of work and lower-status function is great, so that there is rarely any movement from the lower to the higher, or from one internal labor market to another, the gap needs to be bridged by a sequence of ever more highly skilled jobs that could gradually move employees in the lower-status positions into eligibility for the higher status. For example, this could involve gradually adding functions and competence to clerical workers until they were operating like managers and seen as capable of taking on the higher-level job. The development of paraprofessionals to work with highly trained professionals is one instance of the design of new jobs. Such intermediate positions act as bridges as well as ensure a fuller utilization of human talent.

A second set of opportunity-related problems occurs for higher-level as well as lower-level employees. Blocked opportunity is an almost inevitable problem for some people in pyramidal, hierarchical organizations, where the scarcity of places on mobility ladders increases with each step up and where there is a demand for large numbers of low-paid personnel at the bottom. In other words, there is not enough room for everyone at the top. Some people have to do the less desirable jobs, and some of those in the desirable jobs reach dead ends, too. In an extreme instance of a new organization model, the Israeli kibbutzim have tried to solve such problems by rotating all management positions so that after a certain number of years at the top, people give up their places and go back to lower-level positions.[6] There are variants of this practice in American business and professional organizations: temporary assignments, "flow-through" jobs, academic departments that rotate the chair, loans of managers to outside organizations.

Job rotation could be increased and extended throughout the system, and creative plans could be worked out by innovative organizations willing to experiment. Job rotation helps break down the parochialism of many bureaucrats, such as those in dead-end or powerless positions prone to concern with territorial control, and it builds commitment to the organization as a whole, as I found in my studies of long-lived utopian communities.[7] And, of course, many executives already "rotate" jobs. Even if it is unrealistic to imagine in the corporate or governmental context that job rotation schemes could really work to reduce the opportunity gap between high-mobility and low-mobility jobs, they could help to redefine opportunity as involving lateral as well as vertical moves, as a change in territory offering new potential for growth and learning rather than only a change in status or span of authority. Although hierarchy restricts the number of vertical opportunities, the number of lateral prospects remains high. One company appears to have successfully avoided layoffs (thus enhancing job security as well as opportunity) through a program of encouraging "career bends": posting job openings and offering extensive retraining for people to move into new fields.[8]

Project management, an organizational strategy that involves the creation of temporary teams for particular tasks, teams that cut across departments and even hierarchical levels, is one already viable option. Although much routine work might need to be permanently assigned in fixed departments, non-routine work can be given to short-term project teams whose members spend part of their time on their ongoing tasks and part on the project. (Consulting organizations typically work in this fashion.) Even if the routine tasks do not change, the opportunity to make lateral moves—that is, to be involved in a series of challenging projects—can create a definition of success as consisting in ever-increasing learning experiences and new fields to master—an expansion of personal horizons. Opportunity can mean access to growth and learning as well as promotions. Project organization offers the option of a view of the rewards in work stemming from new adventures and new challenges rather than the long climb to the "top." And it is clear that alternative definitions of success are long overdue. Careerism is not everything, and it contains its own dysfunctions in overwork and family neglect. Organizations must learn other ways to reward people and provide a sense of growth, movement, progress, and value. This is especially important when, as I saw at Indsco, an organization appears to promise more promotions than it can deliver.

One useful alternative to Western definitions of "success" as vertical mobility exists in Japan. Large Japanese organizations distinguish between individual rank (seniority) and hierarchical position (status), an arrangement that permits continuing growth in recognition and rewards (as seniority increases) even when the individual's vertical mobility is low and promotion infrequent.[9] Of course, unions do a somewhat similar thing in the United States by tying certain benefits and raises to seniority rather than performance, but the Japanese model includes a wider range of rewards, including increased respect and privileges with age and rank regardless of job status.

At the same time, jobs could be viewed in terms of advances in skill rather than in status and "level," a growth-orientation like that of crafts people. "Mobility" can mean becoming more skilled, getting better at what one is doing, and being rewarded appropriately for the increase in competence. For this meaning of opportunity to make a difference, however, jobs need to be designed so as to involve creativity and skills—a task for programs of *job enrichment*.[10] It is hard to take pride in dull, routine work, or to gain a sense of mastery and growth when no challenge is involved. Adding a succession of *challenges* as signs of "promotion" or "advance," instead of jumps in privilege and control, could be a way of opening opportunity for women and others at the bottom and redefining it more humanely for those at the top. Richard Walton reported successful experiments in several plants in which *pay increases were geared to employee mastery*, with no limit set; people were encouraged to learn and to teach each other.[11] One key here is that the learning opportunity was associated with material opportunity as well. As I have already pointed out, a *sense of new future prospects* opening up may be as or more important than change in the tasks themselves in accounting for the value of job encroachment or job enlargement. At Cummins Engine, for example, the redesign of jobs to include higher order tasks led, in effect, to promotions, because the increased responsibility brought a higher grade designation and pay, transforming what had been seen as a "dead-end job" with poor pay and no chance for advancement into a position with opportunity.[12]

There is another way to approach the problem of scarcity of opportunity in hierarchical systems. *Decentralization* of large organizations could open more leadership positions. To create more units, to break larger structures into smaller ones, would not necessarily increase the number of workers, but it could very easily increase the number of opportunities and "managerial" openings. The Hutterites, a set of over one hundred communal villages in the American and Canadian Great Plains, offer a striking example. When a colony gets to be over a certain size (much more than a hundred people), tensions increase—in part because there are only so many leadership positions in a colony, and some people's alienation grows in response to opportunity blockage, even in this society of alternative values. So at this point, the colony divides in two, perhaps along the lines of contending power blocs, with half the members going off to found a new colony.[13] Leadership opportunities are also doubled in the process. In this sense, then, decentralization reverses the bureaucratic trend toward putting more and more people under the control of fewer and fewer. It requires countering the concentration of power that is part of oligarchic development. Yet, more decentralization is possible than most organization planners usually assume. (Decentralization also enters later as an aspect of empowering.)

A final opportunity-enhancing organization design strategy is addressed to two issues especially relevant to women: (a) helping people acquire more skills and competences on the job itself; and (b) helping people meet outside family responsibilities while still receiving equal treatment inside the organization. This is an innovation originally developed in Germany but gradually spreading worldwide, in the public sector as well as the private: *flexible working hours*. Under flex-time systems, employees control the exact hours they work (out of a full-time week) within limits specified in advance—for example, everyone might be required to be present between 10 A.M. and 2 P.M. [14]

Flex-time represents more than a rearrangement of working hours, although just in this aspect alone it is helpful to women with family responsibilities. (It should come as no surprise that one piece of research found married women with children to be the most satisfied with flex time of any group studied.) Time control can bring with it many other opportunity-enhancing modifications of the organization of work. It is difficult to maintain certain kinds of limiting hierarchical structures, such as supervisors' total control of decision-making, when people have the freedom to choose when they work and how to make sure that their job is covered. A sense of belonging to a team with responsibility for an overall effort, rather than a feeling of being just an isolated worker with limited responsibility, is created in people, because they must be able to act as replacements for one another when someone is not at work. Members of work teams come to train one another and serve as teachers as well as fellow workers, as they do in many organizations using *autonomous work groups*. [15] All these conditions can improve the prospects for people under flex-time to gain self-esteem and a sense of personal efficacy, along with work satisfaction, motivation, and learning—all very important for women in low-mobility and low-power jobs. Employees under flex-time are, in effect, increasing their own competences and learning decision-making and "managerial" skills.

Organizational officials also need to be reeducated to provide the necessary backup for opportunity-enhancing structural interventions. The first involves *counseling* or *"people-development skills" for managers*. Many of the structural innovations suggested require the support and active participation of managers in helping low-mobility employees get assessments of competence, guidance about further education or improvement, and help in mapping out a future career plan. This means transforming the managerial role from tyrant to teacher. The organization, of course, must back up such innovations with rewards to managers for their subordinates' mobility (especially those managers who feel powerless or are understandably reluctant to lose good employees), making "human resource development" a critical part of a manager's own "performance appraisal." But, in addition, managers will need to be taught how to be effective counselors. This is particularly important in cultures where (a) a deference barrier exists between superiors and subordinates, or (b) where norms of politeness interfere with a manager's ability to offer criticisms, or (c) where men in authority positions do not know how to talk honestly to women about their jobs, or (d) where the ideas of evaluation of competence, goal-setting, and future planning are not prominent. Managers could be taught how to give and receive feedback, how to evaluate the elements entering into a job, and how to collaborate with another person in setting mutually agreed-upon objectives. These skills would also be useful to managers in their own career development, especially as "management by objectives" spreads to more systems.

In general, organizations with enhanced opportunity would be, I propose, more alive and exciting places. There would be fewer people indifferent to work or considered "dead wood." There would be more enthusiasm for innovation and less dysfunctional conservative resistance. And there would be structural supports for more equal treatment of women, minorities and disadvantaged classes.

EMPOWERING STRATEGIES

The second set of issues face those in leadership roles who are expected to mobilize others and are held accountable for decisions and results. Their effectiveness is shaped by their relative power or powerlessness, which affects their desirability as leaders, the morale and satisfaction of their subordinates, and their supervisory style. Low system power has both organizational impacts—in the person's ability to gain cooperation and do the job—and social psychological effects—in a feeling of powerlessness that often promotes rigid-controlling behaviors. Power, we saw in Chapter 7, has both a job-related and a social component. It is associated with the exercise of discretion, the chance to demonstrate out-of-the-ordinary capacities in the job, handling uncertainties rather than routine events; with access to visibility; and with the relevance of the job to current organizational problems. As is well known, organizations also have an informal power structure coexisting alongside of the formal delegation of authority, which is influenced by formal arrangements but may or may not correspond to official hierarchical distinctions. Thus, power is also accumulated through alliances with sponsors, successful peers, and up-and-coming subordinates. To empower those women and others who currently operate at a disadvantage requires attention to both sides of power. It is always hard to get at real power issues or make impactful changes in a power structure, since, almost by definition, those with power have a stake in keeping it for themselves. However, with this limitation in mind, it is still possible to try to structurally improve the power position of more people.

Just as opportunity-enhancement begins with change in the formal structure of the organization (career paths and job ladders), empowerment must also start with, and rest fundamentally on, modification of official structural arrangements. *Flattening the hierarchy*—removing levels and spreading formal authority—is among the more general and important strategies. It has the virtues of adding to the power component of jobs (the non-routine, discretionary, and visible aspects) along with increasing contact among managers, at the same time that it can speed up decisions and improve communication.

Some executives I interviewed felt that flattening managerial hierarchies is a good idea, for a number of reasons worth quoting. Too many levels of managers were seen as detracting from the power of each of them. It was considered hard, with an extra layer and thus fewer people reporting directly to any one manager, to avoid "over-managing"—either supervising too closely or jumping in to do the job oneself. Typical comments included: "Our steep hierarchy prevents effective communication; everyone puts his own interpretation on vital messages. It makes me doubt the validity of some communications." "It's so hard to get a decision that I think of this as a glass, forty-story graveyard. Impediments in the decision-making process affect the morale of the whole organization. It's hard to bridge levels." "People don't take risks, because things get reviewed more critically in a deeper organization—there are more channels to pass through. . . . So I think the best thing we can do is to have as flat an organization as possible. In a flat organization, people underneath become better managers. They are more autonomous, and they feel more powerful."

Evidence about the relative effectiveness of flat and tall organizations on overall performance measures is mixed, but one research team, reviewing in depth five studies with moderately dependable results, concluded that job satisfaction, at least, is associated with flatter organizations; job satisfaction goes up as number of levels of the hierarchy goes down.[16] Flat organizations appear to increase satisfaction, in part, through the greater power they provide—greater exercise of authority at lower levels, more control over organizational goals and strategies, and a greater feeling of mastery and esteem.[17] In one carefully researched case, a level of management was eliminated and replaced by project teams and downward delegation; gains were derived in job satisfaction, commitment, and personal and group productivity (though not in overall organizational effectiveness or satisfaction with superiors). In another case, the hierarchy in a plant was flattened from seven to four levels of supervision; among other things, this helped supervisors become more participatory.[18] This association of flatter hierarchies with participation is not surprising. In general, there is an association, holding across many cultures, between an organization's degree of participation and the gradient defining the sharpness of differentiation of hierarchical levels; more participatory organizations have flatter gradients.[19]

In all of these instances, what should be noted are the effects on those holding authority and accountability, as well as the effects on workers. According to my analysis, many of the positive effects of flatter organizations would be phenomena associated with power, mediated by the empowerment of remaining managers. When lower levels have the chance to accumulate more power upward and outward, they can become more participatory downward (less controlling, less closely supervising, more supportive of the autonomy and discretion of subordinates or clients), thus increasing the "job satisfaction" of those below. If job enrichment or flex-time, for example, turn the supervisor from watchdog to long-range planner, they can serve to *empower* that supervisor—if they reduce the routine component of the job, provide more access to the chance for non-ordinary and visible acts, perhaps link the supervisor more closely to top power-holders, and so forth. Some theorists of sociotechnical systems have recognized this.[20] Yet many writers seem to imply that the supervisors, in these cases, are becoming *less* powerful, because they are less controlling. Sometimes they are rendered powerless, but here is where my theory differs substantially. When such alternatives work it is because they enhance the opportunity of those below while *simultaneously* empowering those above.

Decentralization can empower as well as enhance opportunity, if it creates more *autonomous work units*. In one study of 656 sales workers in 36 offices of a national firm, the most effective offices—those with above average performances by salespeople, among other features—were characterized by greater power and autonomy. There were high levels of interpersonal influence inside the office and high levels of control over office operations by local managers and sales staff.[21]

Any structural change that *increases an official's discretion and latitude* and reduces the number of veto barriers for decisions is, in general, then, empowering. (Note that increasing latitude does not mean increasing the number of subordinates.)[22] Overly bureaucratized organizations that limit and box in a decision-maker's domain tend to produce the mentality of powerlessness, and women, in particular, may be crowded into supervisory or professional slots where their exercise of authority is restricted. But wider latitude for risk and innovation can be provided, along with more opportunity to design options for the conduct of the affairs of the unit over which authority is supposedly given. In one case at Xerox, increasing responsibility, discretion, and areas for autonomous decision-making among customer representatives resulted in better employee attitudes and service performance.[23] (The company calls this "job enrichment" but it would be better labelled "empowerment.") By cutting out some channels and veto barriers, the organization gave people more power and improved their effectiveness. In other instances, giving foreman, supervisors, and/or workers more discretion over budgets and more latitude for implementing their own decisions, has led to technical improvements in equipment and work design associated with increased output.[24]

Adding decision-making rights and increasing professional responsibilities for the powerless can thus improve an organization's functioning in several ways. First, most organizations cannot really afford the waste of talent that is involved every time people are put into empty positions with lofty-sounding titles but no right to make changes or invent new ways to conduct a unit's affairs. Secondly, empowerment can turn a manager's attention from control over others to more organizationally relevant matters as planning and innovation, unlocking hidden capabilities. This suggests a dramatically different *role for managers* of the future: as *planners and professionals* rather than watchdogs. There will be more room for those with expertise and less room for "bosses" in the traditional sense. (Radicals are not the only ones to wonder whether old-fashioned "bosses" are really necessary.) Organization planners, then, should identify those areas where decision-making power can be distributed more widely. *Team concepts* and the carrying out of work by *task forces* and *project groups* with control over the total process encourage the sharing of power by more and more people.

While the other side of power, the informal alliance-based side, is more difficult to tackle, it is still possible to suggest organizational alternatives. Strategies can also be developed to provide *access to the power structure* for people like women, who are the most likely to be excluded. They might include *opening communication channels* and making *system knowledge* (such as budgets, salaries, or the minutes of certain meetings) more routinely available for everyone. In many large organizations, people at the lower end of management ladders often lack even basic system knowledge that seems to be hidden for no very good reason—the salary range for certain job grades, for example, or who made particular kinds of decisions. Some may not know the names or faces of senior officials or the organization of positions at the top. Women are perhaps more likely than men to lack system knowledge or understanding of the ins and outs of fringe benefits and perquisites because they more often lack well-connected peers or sponsors who would make informal introductions or educate them about the *real* workings of the system. So information and communication can be a first step toward empowerment. *Access to operating data* and formerly restricted information is a must, furthermore, for any decentralized or team-oriented system. Often the effectiveness of behavior in organizations is hampered by lack of valid information, in Chris Argyris' terms. And, as Philip Selznick has pointed out, *full disclosure* of corporate information may be demanded by employees as a right in the future.[25] It is also possible that "organizational civil rights" such as information access will increasingly be backed by legal guarantees.

Second, since *sponsorship* is an important vehicle for accumulating power, it is possible to conceive of ways in which it might be extended to more people. Now it occurs informally, but it could be a formal part of a management- or talent-development system. Indeed, superiors could be officially rewarded for the number of successful subordinates they produce, for developing the young people under them, particularly women or minorities who do not usually "make it." Managers would be encouraged to sponsor their subordinates for better jobs and would have a stake in seeing that they do well, even to the extent of helping them in the new position. *"Artificial sponsorship"* can also be created for women, through connections with senior people other than their immediate managers. We saw in Chapter 7 how subtle the sponsorship relationship is, but there is still some benefit to trying to create formal mentors. Such people are in a position to help ease women into the system and, hopefully, to provide a continuing link to power over time. Organizations should also routinely schedule meetings and events which give women an opportunity to come into contact with power-holders.

Orientation programs for new women or people in new jobs offer an ideal time for empowering interventions. Both "foster sponsors" and the communication of system information could be a routine part of the introduction of women, for example, to new positions. Procedures that do this would help solve a lingering question: Even if women are hired, how can their success be reasonably guaranteed? The government can set down guidelines, and the organization hires the requisite number of female bodies. But what do they do then? What happens next? What sorts of training are offered, how are women introduced to the organization? Are networks created? The network issue is of special concern for women in fields where they are still numerically scarce. And how are the women to be integrated with their male peers in empowering ways?

One useful model can be derived from a management-training program I designed that prepared both women and men for a job held formerly only by men. Women as well as men were about to be supervising a largely male, blue-collar work force, and they would be the first woman ever to hold such jobs. This design was intended to address all of the structural issues that often defeat women entering formerly all-male jobs. In this case, politics was considered more important than skills; management skills would be included, of course, but some "system" power would also be provided for the trainees.

First, team feeling was created among the men and women being trained so that the women in the group would have sponsorship and support later from male peers who would be more initially acceptable to their subordinates. Joint participation in training programs is often a source of powerful *peer alliances*.[26] Higher-level supervisors were brought into the program, and the links of communication to them were opened. They got to know the women trainees better than any previous group of new managers. Other managers in the field (expecially men) were involved and made to feel part of the project so that they, too, would be motivated to help introduce the women later. A cycle of field placements in between training activities was developed, so the women could get to meet a wide variety of personnel and would be, in turn, less mysterious to those who loved to gossip. They were sent out to "interview" the few senior women managers in the system, in the hope that sponsor-protégé relationships would develop there. In short, the program tried to offer *role models, potential sponsors,* and *allies.* It tried to lay the groundwork for a support system and a power base that would help the women as well as the men succeed as managers. (But note that we also did not force anyone into relationships; we merely provided opportunity and access.)

Empowering can proceed through *training for managers* as well. Managers must be routinely educated to *provide power buckup* for decisions made by those under them (always short of catastrophe, of course) and to eliminate behaviors that disempower women. Managers can learn about their own behavior and see how much power they offer to subordinates. They could be encouraged to eliminate any practices creating the appearance that women or other subordinates have less than full authority to make decisions on their own. Such negative practices often include: watching women more closely than men, thinking of women managers or professionals as an "experiment" that must be monitored, or reviewing the decisions of women more frequently than usual. "Protective" actions that prevent women from solving their own problems should also be discouraged. It makes a woman look weak and powerless to have a man take over for her in emergencies or crises. The message that gets communicated is: "She's only capable of handling routine matters. She cannot be counted on when the crunch comes." Other forms of power-defeating protection include oversolicitous treatment, giving women the easiest assignments, and making fewer demands on women than on men, letting them slide by without ever having to prove themselves on the firing line.

Education for managers on traditional male behaviors toward women would help ensure that women are given challenges and full opportunity to handle crises on their own. Men in the system could learn to check any tendency to rush in and save a woman; if they slow down, she can save herself—and contribute to a more powerful image in the process. Managers have a role to play in empowering women. They should let others know that women managers or professionals under them have the power of the system behind them, and that they will not keep on peering over the woman's shoulder to make sure everything is all right. They should routinely refuse to listen to people who try to come directly to them, circumventing the woman. They should communicate, "She is in charge of her area," with every gesture. Since so much of management revolves around trust, around delegation of authority to people with the legitimate right to make decisions that commit parts of the system, organizations need to find official ways to let members and client populations know that women, too, are trusted, and that women, too, can be powerful. Particularly in cultures where paternalism and attitudes of chivalry prevail, there is a need for men to learn how their behavior affects the prospects for women's work effectiveness.

Organizations which empower larger numbers of people would be more effective on a number of dimensions. They would reduce the dysfunctional consequences of powerlessness: low morale, bureaucratic rules-mindedness, and tight territorial control. They would benefit from speedy decisions and ability to take advantage of innovations. And they would develop better leaders, even among members of groups who have not traditionally become organizational leaders.

NUMBER-BALANCING STRATEGIES

The third structural constraint requiring change is particularly relevant to affirmative action. It stems from the numerical proportion of people of minorities or women in the organization. In any job category or peer level where men vastly outnumber women, for example, so that women are virtually alone among all-male peers, the problems of "tokenism" arise, and those women operate at a disadvantage in the organization. Tokenism is not unique to women, of course. It is a situation that handicaps members of any racial or ethnic minority who find themselves working nearly alone among members of another social category.

Tokenism is not a problem for the majority of women in organizations, because by definition they tend to be concentrated in typically "female" jobs, where they are likely to constitute the bulk of employees. But it becomes an increasing problem for those women who occupy jobs most frequently held by men, generally closer to the top of the organization. And it is a problem that must be overcome in efforts to reduce occupational segregation, for the first women to enter a formerly "male" field are likely to encounter the dynamics of tokenism. It is here that the informal factors and subtle behaviors identified as "sex discrimination" come into play, for they are elicited by a situation of unequal numbers. The constraints to equal participation brought about by tokenism can occur even if it was *not* the organization's intent to put a woman into an "empty" job for display purposes (the conventional meaning of tokenism).

Some policy implications are obvious in this area. Tokenism is to be avoided, if at all possible. *Batch* rather than one-by-one *hiring* of women for top positions should be the rule. More than one or two women at a time should be placed in every unit where women are scarce. Secondly, when a number of women are brought into positions where they are numerically rare, *clustering* rather than spreading is useful. Women should be clustered in groups in sufficient numbers to be no longer identifiable as tokens, even if it means that some groups or departments or units or locales have none at all. Many organizations currently disperse the available women and spread them over every possible group, as though they were a scarce resource of which each office or group should have at least one. However, this policy may be counterproductive for the organization as well as potentially damaging to the person who is thus forced into the position of token.

Role models are especially important for women in token positions, who are likely to feel alone. They have little idea of what forms of behavior are most appropriate, since their only sources of information are the men with whom they work, and, as discussed earlier, sometimes majority group members would rather see tokens as stereotypes than equally competent peers. It can be very useful for tokens to learn about the strategies and coping mechanisms of successful women. Organizations can schedule meetings and public lectures, or they can make information about successful women in the system available through employee newsletters.

The development of a *women's network* should also be considered. Women can offer each other feedback and support that it is difficult for those in token positions to get from immediate colleagues. These networks are more effective when they are task-related and have a meaningful function to perform for the organization, instead of more peripheral social clubs (which reinforce stereotypes about women's greater interest in talk than tasks). One useful format is a series of women's task forces to aid in the recruitment and orientation of other women. The network then grows automatically, and women are also empowered and collaborating in the process.

Less obvious is the need for more *flexible organization structures*. Clustering is not always possible; sometimes women (or other potential tokens) are not found in the organization in sufficient numbers with the right jobs or skills to permit groupings of substantial size; furthermore, members of other groups, including the majority category itself, might be disadvantaged by some forms of clustering. However, if the organization is sufficiently flexible that in the course of their jobs people belong to more than one group, have contact with more than one leader, move from place to place or unit to unit, then they also have the opportunity to come together with enough others of their own category for task-related purposes so that they can begin to transcend the effects of tokenism, gain personal support, and demonstrate to the others the inaccuracy of stereotypes. With a flexible organization structure permitting such continual grouping and regrouping (as in *project management* or *job rotation*), the culture of any one group becomes more permeable to the effects of the presence of minority people, and it becomes more difficult for a group to maintain an insulated, and thus excluding, culture. So flexible structures that enchance opportunity help balance numbers.

Until there are enough women or minorities in place, *leaders* themselves need to be *educated about tokenism.* While waiting for structures to readjust to the numerical transformations, organization leaders can help ease the transition away from tokenism and help present tokens cope with their situation. Training for managers, supervisors, and other administrators or leaders ought to consider the dynamics of tokenism along with other kinds of group dynamics. They can then come to see that many of the problems faced by tokens stem from the *structure of the situation* rather than the personal characteristics of the tokens as individuals (or category members). If leaders become aware of their own stereotypes, they can help to model a different kind of behavior to other employees. They can also begin to see the longer time involved for tokens to demonstrate their competence or establish good working relationships because of the additional things tokens must overcome; with this insight, perhaps leaders could treat tokens with enough patience to allow their competence to surface.

Support programs for women can also be useful. Such programs offer an alternative to clustering or network development. They would encourage women to help each other gain insight into any problems of their current job situation, thus fostering a collaborative attitude among women who might otherwise be tempted to side with men and turn against women. These programs should also discuss the dynamics of tokenism and work toward sharing solutions to the problems of unequal numbers. They could also be a component in other training programs.

But number-balancing should be the ultimate goal. Organizations with a better balance of people would be more tolerant of the differences among them. In addition to making affirmative action a reality, there would be other benefits: a reduction in stress on the people who are "different," a reduction in conformity pressures on the dominant group. It would be more possible, in such an organization, to build the skill and utilize the competence of people who currently operate at a disadvantage, and thus to vastly enhance the value of an organization's prime resource: its people.

THE LIMITS OF REFORM?

All of these concrete strategies represent modifications of work organizations as most of them are presently constituted. Such changes could help solve the "affirmative action" problems faced by employers. They could make life easier for present incumbents of organizational positions, and they could give more people, women and men alike, a fair chance to experience a greater sense of opportunity, power, and acceptance in their jobs. But as valuable as strategies of reform may be in theory, they are limited in practice by serious barriers to change, as well as problems of intervention and implementation. The very process of introducing a new program itself requires careful attention. Change efforts can fail for a number of reasons that have little to do with the ultimate value of the new policy: insufficient support from the top *or* the bottom, inadequate prior diagnosis of the actual state of the system where the change is launched, insufficient attention to the effects of a program beyond the local area where it is introduced. And there is the problem of time for a change to prove itself or take hold. Sometimes this time is not allowed because crises occur, such as economic downturns; when threatened, the organization may fall back on accepted procedures and hierarchical control. Progressive as well as reactionary organizations succumb in times of crisis.[27]

It is also unfortunately common that innovations are introduced on an experimental basis in large systems, and then, even if they prove worthwhile, they never move beyond their first base. The organization attempts to create an insulated, protected territory as a testing ground, and then the innovation is never diffused further. Inter-unit rivalries play a role here; sometimes one division refuses to touch any rearrangement originating in another department. This is a dilemma of the large system: bigness means that innovations must often start small and locally, but then the complex system dynamics associated with bigness can make it difficult for anything small and local to be accepted on a larger scale. Furthermore, there are equity problems when one group in an organization is given benefits—even on an experimental basis—that are not available to others. This gives the organization the costly, and often impossible, choice of starting big (doing it everywhere at once) or not doing it at all.

In addition, as many commentators have noted, no one specific structural innovation by itself (job redesign or job rotation or flexible work hours alone) is likely, over time, to significantly improve work life quality or equity for disadvantaged groups. Indeed, there may even be problems, as I indicated in Chapter 9, if a program is introduced without other, supporting, organizational changes. More comprehensive approaches are thus needed, using an integrated combination of methods (e.g., job redesign along with a changed pay structure, career opportunities, a new view of the manager's role and flexible work hours). Yet this conclusion, reached by Harvard Business School researchers as well as radical critics of human relations programs, implies widespread system change—virtually the construction of an entirely new system. Such comprehensive change has inherent difficulties and complexities, as well as posing the greatest threat to the greatest number of entrenched power groups and those who like the security of what currently exists. Raymond Katzell and Daniel Yankelovich asked a sample of managers and labor leaders how they felt about programs to improve the quality of work life. There were negative reactions on both sides. One manager said, "Why should I preside over an activity that may well succeed in undermining management's prerogatives?" And a union official said, "Why should I cooperate when the results may undermine the authority of this union just to play management's game?" [28]

For all of these reasons, the possibilities for reform in large organizations may be inevitably limited. And many bureaucratic binds would remain. The problems created by large size and its seemingly inevitable companion, steep hierarchy, would be left to plague people in organizations. Inequities of opportunity and rewards would not disappear, and the power of large organizations over economic life in general would continue.

Thus, organizational reform is not enough. It is also important to move beyond the issues of whether or not concrete individuals get their share to questions of how shares are determined in the first place—how labor is divided and how power is concentrated. The solutions to such questions are clearly beyond the scope of this book, but they form the backdrop that places an ultimate limit on how much can be accomplished by changing organizational structure alone. There are growing numbers of scholars and writers, from all branches of the social sciences as well as business life itself, who have come to the conclusion that large organizations cannot be made effective any more than they can be fully humanized; such systems appear to be economically efficient only because of their power over markets and other aspects of the environment. [29]

A variety of criticisms has been leveled against very large organizations:

that communication becomes so sluggish it is not possible to deal effectively with inputs from the environment; that they are wasteful of resources, especially in increased coordination and administrative costs; that they have so much power that their actions can create vast imbalances for society; and that a pervasive sense of powerlessness is generated in most members. The larger the organization, the greater the need for coordination and the more limited the possibilities for local decision-making and independent action—necessary for empowerment—as Barry Stein has pointed out.[30] Furthermore, as long as the steep multi-leveled hierarchies that tend to accompany large size remain, it is impossible to remedy many inequities of compensation or opportunity, let alone empower more people or share decision-making more widely. When the model is hierarchical rather than collegial, there would also appear to be real limits on the extent to which it is possible to expand anyone's power, other than for those people who already have the managerial monopoly. With unemployment an issue and economic growth in question, there may be real limits on the opportunity to move ahead, let alone hold a desirable job at all. And finally, it is difficult to conceive of opportunity-enhancing reforms in large organizations that do not constitute further bureaucratization (and along with it, powerlessness): an increase in procedures and systems, a growth of paperwork. (These complaints already exist around affirmative action programs in many organizations.) But also, something human is lost when personal discretion—limiting though it may be in some senses for those subject to it—is replaced by bureaucratic rationalization.

These issues about the realistic problems of change must be addressed, but they do not render reform any less necessary. We must go ahead, even with imperfect knowledge, and even in the full awareness that further dilemmas will follow action.

Although I believe that the best solutions ultimately lie in the development of viable alternatives to large, overly hierarchical organizations, I also think that considerable improvement is possible in the organizations we have now. Organizational reform can immediately affect the prospects for millions of workers and fundamentally change their relationship to their work, while at the same time models of smaller, more egalitarian, and more manageable organizations can be put forth and tested. A good revolutionary would not agree, for reform is seen as counter to the goals of fundamental social change, especially if fundamental social change is required to reduce the dominance of giant organizations, break up managerial monopolies on decision-making, and redistribute material rewards. So the revolutionary would argue against strategies that temporarily alleviate distress, emphasizing the positive value of present suffering in heightening radical consciousness.

But who bears the burden of the waiting? Not the well-off. No, it is the people without advantage who continue to lose out: the women who find doors closed to them in certain jobs; the people stuck in dead-end positions, whose lack of opportunity depresses their aspirations and sense of self; the powerless who bear the frustrations of trying to manage without any real resources or influence; the token women or token minorities who suffer from their isolation.

The costs to organizations in productivity and effectiveness of routinely producing such people are considerable, in the sheer waste of potential human talent. Even more serious—and harder to measure—are the costs to those people as individuals. Work, which should be energizing and enlivening, which can be a vehicle for discovering and testing the limits of one's capabilities, for contributing and being recognized, becomes instead a source of strain or dependency or limitation.

It is the people caught in such situations—and the people who cannot even find a job—women and men alike, that make me unwilling to wait.

Appendices
Notes
Bibliography
Index

APPENDIX I

Field Study Methodology and Sources of Data

This study represents primarily a search for explanation and theory rather than just a report of empirical research. I was interested in understanding a complex social reality and its impact on the people who experienced it. I wanted to develop concepts that would make sense out of the actions of people located in different parts of organizational worlds. With Michel Crozier, I wanted to demonstrate that everyone is rational,[1] that everyone within an organization, no matter how silly or irrational their behavior seemed, was reacting to what their situation made available, in such a way as to preserve dignity, control, and recognition from others. Throughout the hierarchy, people had in common the fact of being limited by their organizational circumstance. Finally, I wanted to develop concepts with a dynamic flavor: how processes and cycles were set in motion which bounded and limited people's options.

I also had a series of normative interests. I wanted to further the cause of equality for women in organizations, but I wanted to see the nature of organizations, not men or women as individuals, as the villain of the piece, for I was convinced that men were just as much bound and limited by organizational systems that existed to the present time as were women. I hoped to provide further evidence of the inevitability of binds and dilemmas in which organizations find themselves as long as they are structured the way they typically are: too large, too hierarchical, not democratic enough, not justifying either the number or power of managers, inequitable in their distribution of rewards and opportunities, fostering one view of success as vertical mobility, and not conscious enough or taking responsibility enough for their impact on the family. The current division of labor in organizations has seemed to me, as it has seemed to a large number of others, neither functional nor inevitable. I wanted to explain dysfunctional behavior in organizations—common organizational problems—in such a way that decision-makers could see the benefits to them of developing what I considered more humane, more equitable, and smaller-scale solutions to problems. I was interested in offering practical insight and suggestions that would both be useful to individuals in making sense out of their situations, especially in helping women understand the traps that organizations held out for them, as presently structured, and that would help decision-makers and program planners think more innovatively about new policies and procedures in organizations. Thus, I felt that the merit of this study would stand or fall not on specific details of findings but on the whole it presents: a comprehensive ordering of the experiences and reactions of men and women in organizations, seen as a function of properties of their situations.

However, I am a firm believer in the necessary interplay between theory and empirical observation. This book is thus empirically grounded in a case study of a single organization, composed of multiple projects. The case provided material out of which to generate the concepts and flesh for giving meaning to the abstract propositions I was developing. Periodically, over a five-year period, I was a consultant, participant-observer, and researcher at Industrial Supply Corporation, primarily within one division. Changes that took place in Indsco or its people during the five-year period that affect material I report are mentioned in the text.

I have disguised Indsco's identity as best I could, and I have occasionally changed details of numbers and stories, for a variety of ethical and legal reasons. I promised confidentiality and anonymity to everyone with whom I came into contact; this was an important part of the surveys, and I also felt that I would not want to violate the confidences of many people who gave me information that could potentially have negative impact on their own jobs. I also felt that the validity of the observations reported here would not be affected by disguising the identity of Indsco. After my initial formulations were developed, I held conversations with informants in three other large corporations where I also had consulting relationships in order to satisfy myself that Indsco, although containing its own culture, was not particularly unique in the relationships I observed. I learned that Indsco, indeed, was typical, and its story could be that of many large organizations. Furthermore, I was often a "guest" at Indsco and a confidante to many of its people, and I owed something to my hosts. Some of the research I conducted was initiated or invited by people at Indsco who wanted more insight into their own functions.

On other occasions, however, I was on my own and followed only my own agenda; many people were aware that I was writing a book but were not aware of what specific use I would be making of the information I gathered. I spent most of my time at headquarters, supplemented by trips to a number of field locations; I visited foreign offices, and I saw a number of informants in their homes.

The following sources of information were utilized in developing concepts and drawing conclusions; they provided the basis for both quantitative and qualitative analysis:

1. A mail survey I designed, taking two to three hours to complete, of 205 sales workers and sales managers out of a population of 350. The sample was all men, for there were no women in the sales force when the survey was conducted. The sample size reflected the number of those to whom questionnaires were sent who chose to return them. It was slightly underrepresentative of the oldest age group in sales. The survey was preceded by open-ended interviewing of thirty people in sales and related functions, including officers, staff people, and new hires. The purpose of these interviews was to elicit from the respondents the kinds of questions they thought ought to be included in the survey. Then there was a pretest group of eight. The core of the survey was a thirty-four-item measure of commitment derived from questions about attitude toward the company based on a theory of commitment that I developed in my previous research on utopian communities.[2] The measure consisted of one general question about overall loyalty and eleven questions on each of three dimensions of commitment: sense of long-term investment in the organization, willingness to put in extra effort and continue to participate (instrumental or continuance commitment); sense of belonging, sense of membership in a collectivity, ties with other people (affective or cohesion commitment); belief in the goals and purposes of the organization, in its worth and moral virtue (moral or control commitment). There were also a series of questions about the immediate work setting, decision-making, and reward systems; personal priorities and perceived skills; and training opportunities within the company. Table I-1 describes the sample in age, present position, length of time with Indsco, length of time in present position, and salary.

2. Interviews with the first twenty women to enter the sales force, both individually and in groups. These women were questioned about their personal background; route to the company; experiences with orientation and training; experiences with peers, managers, and customers; sources of support or discomfort; and attitudes about the company. Eight left the Indsco sales force subsequently.

3. Access to a survey of 111 nonexempt employees on attitudes toward promotion. This was not a sample because it was dependent on volunteers who chose to attend a meeting where they were asked to fill out the survey. Respondents were roughly representative of the total population in sex, although women at the lower end of the nonexempt scale were somewhat overrepresented. Table I-2 describes characteristics of this group.

4. A content analysis I conducted of 100 performance appraisal forms turned in on nonexempt clerical personnel, largely secretaries, as part of a consulting project to help personnel staff develop a satisfactory program. Interviews with secretaries and bosses were held in conjunction with this project.

5. Group discussions, recorded verbatim. Such meetings were explicitly defined as data collection. One consisted of twenty-two men and women in a number of dif-

TABLE I–1

Distribution of Sales Workers and Sales Managers
Sample on Background Factors

(N = 205; Sex = 100% Male)

Variable	Percentage
AGE	
Under 25	7.3
25–30	33.3
31–40	37.9
41–50	16.9
Over 50	4.0
PRESENT POSITION	
Sales Worker	66
Manager	26.1
Account Executive	8.0
(Professional Sales Ladder)	
YEARS WITH COMPANY	
Under 1 year	6.8
1–2 years	11.3
2–5 years	15.3
6–10 years	19.8
11–20 years	34.5
Over 20 years	12.4
YEARS IN PRESENT POSITION	
Under 1 year	34.1
1–2 years	26.7
2–5 years	29.5
6–10 years	6.3
11–20 years	2.8
Over 20 years	0.6
SALARY (as of 1970) *	
Less than $10,000	0.6
$10,000–$14,999	43.5
$15,000–$19,999	37.5
$20,000 and over	8.1

* As of 1976, salaries for exempt grades had increased by at least 75%.

ferent jobs, from managers through secretaries, together for four days, discussing career concerns and relations between men and women in the company. Another consisted of three sets of discussions among twenty executives and five personnel specialists on topics such as managerial skills, career pathways and preparation for their present job, and sources of frustration; these discussions were held in conjunction with task force meetings and professional conventions. Twelve husbands and wives met for two days to discuss work/family issues as they occurred in the large corporation.

6.   Participant-observation in meetings. Sometimes these were set up to provide people in Indsco with feedback from earlier projects or data collection efforts.

TABLE I–2

Distribution of Nonexempt Sample on Background Factors

Variable	% Female (N = 88)	% Male (N = 23)	% Total (N = 111)
AGE			
Under 25	30	44	32
25–40	37	22	34
Over 40	33	34	33
YEARS WITH COMPANY			
Under 5	40	65	45
5–15	35	22	32
15–30	22	9	19
Over 30	3	4	4
NO. OF PREVIOUS JOBS WITH COMPANY			
0	27	26	27
1	19	39	23
2	20	13	19
3	14	9	13
4	7	9	7
More than 4	12	4	11
YEARS OF SCHOOLING			
Less than 11	1	0	1
11	1	4	2
12	57	13	48
13	20	13	19
14	14	35	18
15	1	4	2
16	3	22	7
More than 16	2	8	4
TOTAL ANNUAL FAMILY INCOME (as of 1974)*			
$5,000–$10,999	53	43	50
11,000– 15,999	24	35	26
16,000– 20,999	12	22	14
$21,000 and over	9	0	9

* To properly interpret these figures, it should be kept in mind that 83% of the men reported that they were the sole breadwinner, whereas 53% of the women combined their incomes with their husbands' to arrive at this family total.

(Figures reported with the permission of G. Homall)

Sometimes they were meetings discussing new programs or the application of research findings that I was allowed to attend because my experience might be relevant. In one or two cases I was invited to meetings by Indsco managers who were interested in having an outsider present with whom they could later discuss the events of the meeting. Often beforehand, an informant or the person who invited me would describe the participants to me: their career stage, their present position, and their characteristic style. Such descriptions and accompanying anecdotes were often a very valuable source of concepts, ideas, and material.

7. Personal participant-observation in training programs or interviews with staff. I paid attention both to official events and to informal interaction that took place before and after sessions and at social events.

8. A large set of documents. The bulk of these were public documents such as company newsletters (corporate, divisional, field locations), newspapers, booklets for new hires, annual reports, and blank forms used in a variety of personnel programs. I also had occasional access to statistical reports, internal memoranda, and reports, but I do not cite or draw from anything confidential in this book.

9. Individual conversations. These were generally on specific topics with anyone I had reason to visit. They occurred in offices, at social gatherings, at lunch, or at people's homes. Usually these were of mutual benefit, since the respondent would know of my interest in organizational behavior and ask me many questions. The "interviews" I could conduct in this fashion broadened my territory and my view of the organization considerably. (Melville Dalton called this the technique of "conversational interviewing.") [3]

10. A small group of people with whom I built close working relationships over the years. These people were largely in functions where they were well placed to see a large number of people in a large number of levels at Indsco. They could tell me about the history of the company and a variety of experiences in the organization as well as provide information about the issues in their own careers. I could also use them to check out stories I gathered elsewhere. These people were especially valuable because they were interested in similar questions, and they wanted to encourage social science attention to the new human problems of the corporation. Some of them were very wise and very insightful. Although occasionally they would seem embarrassed at not being "experts" in social science, I always found that they knew much more than they thought, and my discussions with them were very enjoyable. In some sense, they participated with me as "coresearchers," and our conversations always tended to be characterized by open exchange. I promised them complete confidentiality; otherwise I would thank them publicly for their help here.

Generally, I tried to follow up on people I had seen earlier, and for some people I had career information extending over the entire five-year period, from personal knowledge. I tended to record everything I could that occurred in my presence. I did this almost automatically, even though I had not yet defined the situation as "research," because, as all good consultants know, it is wise to keep complete notes and collect as much system information as possible in order to be maximally helpful to clients. I found even time waiting outside of people's offices valuable. Time designated as "social" in which I engaged in informal discussions with people was perhaps the most valuable of all. When I could, I asked people to describe other people and their situation to me. This is because I found that people were often unable to tell me what I needed to know about their own behavior and attitudes, but other people in their offices served as useful informants.

Much of what I gathered informally was in the form of stories and retrospective accounts of events. I think that the reasons for this were embedded in the nature of large, complex organizations themselves. First, there is not much to observe directly, because I was interested in administration and in what takes place in offices. Unlike studies of plants or clerical workers in large offices, much of what "occurred" at Indsco happened in small, private offices behind closed doors, over the telephone, or at meetings to which outsiders were definitely not invited. Short of taking an inside job, I would not have had access. Yet with a job at Indsco, I would have been much more limited and confined. My roamings as a consultant and outside researcher brought me in touch with many more people, and I could ask questions that insiders would probably not have been able to ask of people in other functions without arousing undue suspicion. Second, many events other than routine daily activities take place over a long time frame, and daily observation would be a very slow way to gather material about such occurrences. Finally, the system was so large as to be almost boundaryless. Since my interest extended to the system as a whole rather than small units within it, I often found that the best way to wander over such a large territory was to ask people to tell me all that they knew rather than try to discover it for myself by personal observation.

On the whole, I would estimate the number of my personal on-site contact days to be over 120 and the number of people with whom I held more than momentary conversations at well over 120. An additional 500 people participated in the written surveys or performance appraisals which were the primary source of the quantitative data I report.

Crozier framed the methodological problems inherent in studies of large-scale organizations well: "Comprehensive studies of human relations problems at the management level are usually hampered by two sets of difficulties. First, the complexity of the role structure in modern organizations causes much ambiguity and overlapping, making it impossible to match really comparable cases and to use rigorous methods meaningfully. Second, the general emphasis on status and promotions gives a crucial importance to the human relations game, thus preventing the researcher from obtaining reliable data on the central problem of power relationships." [4] Thus, a combination of methods such as used in the classical sociological field studies emerges as the most valid and reliable way to develop understanding of such a complex social reality as the corporation. I used each source of data, and each informant, as a check against the others. In this way, consistent tendencies could be noted. Nothing that I report was totally unique or true of only one person. I chose illustrative examples and quotations that were more widely supported (indeed, it was often frustrating not to be able to use all my material), and important exceptions are also mentioned in the text.

The other important base for this study should not be neglected. This was, of course, an extensive review of the sociological, social psychological, psychological, and organizational behavior literatures. I considered this a part of the study critical to its success. I worked back and forth between the literature and the field. I formulated hypotheses and questions from the literature, and I could test the generalizability of my field observations through literature review. With C. Wright Mills, I believe that reading can also be a valid form of research.[5]

APPENDIX II

Some Observations of Women's

Leadership in Organizations

(With the collaboration of Diane Fassel.)

Diane Fassel and I conducted a small observational study of all-female groups and organizations in order to generate hypotheses for comparative analysis of the effects of sex composition on hierarchical arrangements. Since the women in leadership positions in large organizations like Indsco were so few that their behavior was also shaped by tokenism (and often, low opportunity and low power), we were in effect "controlling" for women's disadvantage in male-dominated organizations by looking at all-female groups. We had two principal questions in mind: (1) Were there identifiable "female" styles of leadership that confirmed psychological arguments about sex differences or accounted for the absence of women in leadership roles in mixed-sex settings? (2) Was hierarchical domination less important in all-female settings? (Some people have argued that hierarchy represents a "male" model to be contrasted with the more cooperative "female" model. Indeed, many women's movement organizations—including such a successful business as *Ms.* magazine—have self-consciously adopted highly collectivist-participatory organization structures, where status differences are officially eliminated).

We watched meetings of two professional women's leadership training programs, a task force at a church, an innovative parochial school, an "alternative" service organization, and a traditional service organization. We took field notes and used a variety of coding schemes in meetings, including variations on Bales' "Interaction Process Analysis." Fassel generally recorded who spoke to whom, and whether remarks were addressed to individuals or the group as a whole, and she paid particular attention to non-verbal gestures.

First we saw that structure shaped behavior. The definition of the situation defined how people behaved. When it came to working on a task, there was little that was especially noteworthy about the way women did it, nothing that stood out as particularly "feminine" or seemed different from numerous reports of the behavior of any set of small groups. All of the groups reflected their task focus as well as the variations in their organizational cultures. Fassel had previously tried to replicate a study by Elizabeth Aries that compared all-male, all-female, and mixed groups and found that men's interaction patterns differed from women's.[1] However, Aries' groups were open-ended, informal groups, like sensitivity training groups, that had no task. Fassel found that when she observed an all-female group working on a *task*, the interaction patterns exactly matched Aries' findings for all-male groups. Task orientation, we concluded, wiped out any sex differences that might be found in patterns of sociability alone.

But there were differences in overall interactional style based on the organizational culture of the groups, reinforcing our conclusion that tasks and task organization are important in shaping organizational behavior. The professional groups were very abstract and intellectual, with a tendency to stay away from personal comments or revelations. Staff and leaders at the innovative school made an attempt to be "open," to listen carefully, to acknowledge feelings, and to ask for feedback (at the same time that put-downs crept through in the form of backhanded comments). There was a division of labor among the women: one guarded the task, watched the agenda, and took notes; another tried to get people to state feelings as well as to work on the task; and a third routinely provided information and offered opinions. Leadership styles varied from commanding-affirming (a woman with clear charismatic presence who provided a great deal of affirmation to others for their contributions) to controlling-disabling (one who did not leave others room to participate).

We also saw that men do not have a monopoly on dominance hierarchies or dominance-signaling behaviors. The traditional service organization where Fassel recorded weeks of observations was a traditional bureaucratic hierarchy, in which some women dominated other women the way some men do in rigid organizations and made gestures to each other like those some men make to women. It was said about Barbara, the chief executive, that "she rules with an iron hand, even though she doesn't seem to." To an observer, she seemed to. Meetings at the center were highly task-oriented. They began on time with practically no preliminary chitchat or exchange of pleasantries (less than one minute, if at all), and Barbara's arrival signaled that it was time to get down to business. She spoke the most at all meetings, and when other staff were asked afterwards about who received the most communications, they routinely named her, even though she was not actually the target of most remarks. In general, the biggest talkers were the people with most seniority in the organization, and those who barely talked were part-time workers. The chief controlled interaction, even in one-on-one-meetings, interrupting frequently and offering little affirmation, as in this typical meeting in her office with a subordinate:

> In this meeting Barbara spoke about 50 percent more than Karen. Barbara also spoke in full sentences, and Karen's language was in the form of short answers: "Yes," "Oh, really?" "Okay," etc. At times, the "timing" of the conversation seemed out of joint. By that I mean that Barbara was cutting off Karen in such a way that Karen never seemed to finish sentences. Karen laughed frequently during the interchange. Barbara asked questions that were really statements: for example, "Doesn't that depend on how many schools want to join?" "Should I ask for 1,000 envelopes?" "No big deal about tax-exempt mail?" "And the return address is Donor of the Year award?" I think that most of these questions were really information that Karen should have and probably did know. At the end of the work on the publicity, Barbara said to Karen, "The board chairman says Dorothy is very pleased at how things are going on this."

The chief signaled and maintained her dominance in a variety of ways. She ate at a separate table in the lunchroom from the clerical workers and tried to see that the other professionals did so, too. She made jokes or sarcastic comments at the expense of the staff. (Rose Coser's observations of staff in a psychiatric hospital showed that high-status people often made jokes at the expense of lower-status people, but the lowers could not make jokes about the highers in their presence; and women were often the targets of men's humor.) [2] For example, Barbara made this remark when one of the professionals tried to move a table closer to the clericals: "Aren't you the little group worker?" She touched other people frequently, putting her arms around a subordinate, for example, as she ushered her out of the office, but she avoided letting people touch her. (Nancy Henley had found that high-status people can touch low-status people but do not permit touch in return, and that women touch men more often then the reverse.) [3] One professional remembered, "Last April, right after Barbara became the chief executive, I put my arm around her and congratulated her on getting the job. I could feel her tighten her shoulders when I did." Finally, at meetings she had a tendency to stand up when she wanted to make a point or to move around the room while talking. She would signal conflict by assertive gestures such as pointing, and she put people on the spot by suddenly demanding information they were not prepared to give, even though she was also likely to apologize.

On the other hand, other women leaders behaved in more nurturant-supportive ways while still maintaining a clear task focus, indicating that women *could* exhibit effective and humanistic leadership styles. Some behaved as this woman did in Fassel's observations:

Susan sits at the head of the rectangular table. She is in her mid-forties, wearing a blue pants-suit. She smiles a lot and calls each person by name. It seemed to me that women younger than herself she called by first names, while older women she called by last names. Susan is clearly in control of the meeting. She moves the agenda along; she clarifies situations when clarification is needed; she defers to staff members for information without seeming to appear uninformed; she makes affirming comments after various board members give reports of their activities; she looks at the group as a whole while she talks. All other speakers look to her when speaking, except when they are answering a question put to them by someone else.

The point is this: the women we saw were sometimes very different from each other and sometimes not very different from men, as leaders. Individual differences were more striking than sex differences.

We also looked at some examples of those few successful women managers in mixed-sex organizations to determine what was characteristic about their styles. The largest number of cases were found in retailing, where women have traditionally had more opportunities, as the statistics in Chapter 1 indicate. In each case, those with system power and an interest in empowering subordinates (sharing power with them) were the most successful and effective. (They were also the most collaborative and humane.) Myra R. is a good example. She was known as a "comer" in the large retailing organization for which she has worked since graduating from college. At twenty-eight she was director of executive training (she has also been a line manager) and the subject of considerable interest from executive head hunters, a fact that increased her power in the organization. "The company knows that recruiters have approached me, and that makes a difference," she said. "Management wants to know, 'What did Gimbels' Philadelphia have to say to you? What did Marshall Field offer?' "

Myra began as an executive trainee. Her first career decision was to choose operations, not merchandising, a program with only six people compared with the ninety in merchandising. She was the only woman. At the end of the ten-week program, Myra had the best evaluations in her group, partly, she said, because she knew the store from her experience as a part-time sales clerk during college. Even so, despite a greater acceptance of woman managers in retail fields, the men in her group were placed much more quickly than Myra and given more responsible jobs. They were all made managers; Myra, an assistant manager. "I complained, but I wasn't given good reasons other than a concern that I wouldn't be tough enough. I was very upset, but I didn't make a fuss. I just decided to do such a good job and make myself so known to management that it wouldn't happen again.

"Then I had a lucky break. The manager got sick, and I took over. I worked twice as hard as anyone else, six days a week, nine to nine. I made relationships with other managers and got support from the executive vice-president of personnel. My own boss was right there behind me. I was responsible for fifty to sixty people—nearly a hundred at Christmas time. I called them all together for a meeting and told them I depended on them and needed their help; they could teach me. I learned how to get them to do things for me without pointing and telling them—not forcibly, but still determined. I asked them to submit evaluations to me, and I learned from them. They told me I didn't have to be so friendly and that I should give them a kick in the ass once in a while. So I did. They came through like troopers. In return, I offered good bonuses because I had gotten to known the vice-president so well. After three months I asked for my own area of responsibility, and I was given the managership. Fifteen months later I was promoted again."

The themes in Myra R's experience are echoed in the careers of other women who have become successful leaders. They have political connections in the wider system, and they know how to make subordinates feel powerful in their own right. Jane Evans, who became president of I. Miller, a chain of elegant stores and a subsidiary of Genesco, at the unusual age of twenty-five, said about her relations with her staff: "I expect them to carry the ball by developing their own jobs without my constant supervision. They tell me I'm a great cheerleader. As a result, we have a very cohesive management staff." [4]

The effectiveness of women leaders, then, like that of men, is a response to opportunities for power, to a favorable position in the power structure. Both men and women can exercise their authority more productively and with better response when they have power behind it. This, too, is a standard organizational cycle: power breeds effectiveness at getting results, which enhances power. But psychological "sex differences" seem to play a limited role, if any, once women are given a chance and access to power.

NOTES

Introduction

1. Norman Birnbaum, *The Crisis of Industrial Society* (New York: Oxford University Press, 1969), pp. 57, 68.

2. *Ibid.*, pp. 7, 12.

3. See also Francis X. Sutton et al., *The American Business Creed* (Cambridge, Mass.: Harvard University Press, 1956).

4. This is a rationale used by Samuel Bowles and Herbert Gintis to support their argument for major transformations in the economy in *Schooling in Capitalist America* (New York: Basic Books, 1976).

5. E. F. Schumacher, *Small Is Beautiful* (New York: Harper Torchbooks, 1973).

6. Barry A. Stein, *Size, Efficiency, and Community Enterprise* (Cambridge, Mass.: Center for Community Economic Development, 1974).

7. See Phyllis A. Wallace, ed., *Equal Employment Opportunity and the AT&T Case* (Cambridge, Mass.: MIT Press, 1976). For a negative view of affirmative action in which the degree of remaining controversy is made clear (though in terms of minorities rather than women), see Nathan Glazer, *Affirmative Discrimination* (New York: Basic Books, 1976).

8. Philip Selznick, *Law, Society, and Industrial Justice* (New York: Russell Sage Foundation, 1969), p. 38.

9. *Ibid.*, pp. 174, 260.

10. Beardsley Ruml, "Corporate Management as a Locus of Power," *Social Meaning of Legal Concepts*, No. 3 (New York University School of Law, 1950), p. 220.

Chapter 1

1. U.S. Bureau of Labor Statistics, *Handbook of Labor Statistics, 1975* (Washington, D.C.: Department of Labor, 1976).

2. The latest available figures were for 1967. U.S. Bureau of the Census, *1967 Enterprise Statistics*, Part I, General Report on Industrial Organization, January 1972, pp. 164-65, 124.

3. *Handbook of Labor Statistics, 1975*.

4. Janice N. Hedges, "Women Workers and Manpower Demands in the 1970's," *Monthly Labor Review*, 93 (June 1970): pp. 19-29.

5. Hilda Kahne, with Andrew I. Kohen, "Economic Perspectives on the Role of Women in the American Economy," *Journal of Economic Literature*, 13 (December 1975): pp. 1249-92.

6. U.S. Bureau of the Census, *Occupational Characteristics* and *Occupations of Persons with Higher Earnings* (Washington, D.C.: U.S. Government Printing Office, 1973).

7. *Personnel Policies Forum*, 1971.

8. G. W. Bowman, N. B. Worthy, and S. A. Greyser, "Are Women Executives People?", *Harvard Business Review*, 43 (July-August 1965): pp. 14-30.

9. Calculations based on figures in U.S. Bureau of the Census, *Occupational Characteristics* and *Occupations of Persons with Higher Earnings*.

10. Calculations are based on data in U.S. Census Bureau, *Occupational Characteristics*, 1973; U.S. Bureau of Labor Statistics, *Handbook of Labor Statistics*, 1971.

11. Joseph A. Hill, *Women in Gainful Occupations 1870–1920*, Census Monographs IX (Washington, D.C.: U.S. Government Printing Office, 1929). Reprinted (New York: Johnson Reprint Corp., 1972).

12. Calculations based on figures in *Historical Statistics of the United States: Colonial Times to 1957* (Washington, D.C.: U.S. Government Printing Office, 1960).

13. Despite John Kenneth Galbraith, James Burnham, and others who have argued that control has passed to the managers out of the hands of large capital owners, a considerable recent literature has shown the extent to which a few families still do wield important control over large corporations. See Maurice Zeitlin, "Corporate Ownership and Control: The Large Corporation and the Capitalist Class," *American Journal of Sociology*, 79 (March 1974): pp. 1073–1119.

14. Samuel P. Hays, *The Response to Industrialism, 1855–1914* (Chicago: University of Chicago Press, 1957), p. 49; see also pp. 12, 52. Daniel Nelson presents data on the jumps in size of manufacturing firms between 1870 and 1900. In 1870, there was only a handful of large firms, concentrated in textiles; by 1900, there were 1,063 factories with 500–1,000 workers and 443 with more than 1,000. Nelson, *Managers and Workers: Origins of the New Factory System in the United States, 1880–1920* (Madison: University of Wisconsin Press, 1975), p. 4.

15. Thomas C. Cochran, *Basic History of American Business* (Princeton: D. Van Nostrand, 1959), p. 52.

16. *Ibid.*, p. 141.

17. John A. Garraty, *The New Commonwealth, 1877–1890* (New York: Harper & Row, 1968), p. 102. See also Alfred D. Chandler, *Strategy and Structure: Chapters in the History of American Business Enterprise* (Cambridge, Mass.: MIT Press, 1962). Nelson shows that foremen, who had commonly functioned as independent labor contractors before the change, lost power and autonomy along with workers under the new managerial systems. See Nelson, *Managers and Workers,* especially p. 50.

18. Thomas C. Cochran, *The American Business System: A Historical Perspective, 1900–1955* (Cambridge, Mass.: Harvard University Press, 1957), p. 73. Litterer, furthermore, found only 15 articles relevant to management in U.S. publications between 1870 and 1880; the great wave of interest began in the 1890s. See Joseph A. Litterer, "Systematic Management: Design for Organizational Recoupling, *Business History Review*, 37 (Winter 1963): pp. 369–91.

19. Reinhard Bendix, *Work and Authority in Industry: Ideologies of Management in the Course of Industrialization* (New York: Wiley, 1956), Harper Torchbook edition, 1963.

20. Daniel Bell, "The Breakup of Family Capitalism," in *The End of Ideology*, rev. ed. (New York: Collier Books, 1961). This analysis has also been greatly influenced by Bendix, *Work and Authority in Industry.*

21. Wilbert Moore, *The Conduct of the Corporation* (New York: Random House, 1962), Vintage Books, p. 237.

22. Michel Crozier, *The Bureaucratic Phenomenon* (Chicago: University of Chicago Press, 1964), p. 157.

23. Burton J. Hendrick, *The Age of Big Business: A Chronicle of the Captains of Industry* (New Haven: Yale University Press, 1921), p. 21.

24. Richard M. Abrams, "Brandeis and the Ascendancy of Corporate Capitalism," Introduction to Torchbook edition of Louis D. Brandeis, *Other People's Money, and How the Bankers Use It* (New York: Harper & Row, 1967).

25. Frederick W. Taylor, *Scientific Management* (New York: Harper & Row, 1947). See also Anthony Tillett, Thomas Kempner, and Gordon Wills, eds., *Management Thinkers* (Baltimore, Md.: Penguin, 1970).

26. The quote is from Cochran, *The American Business System: A Historical Perspective, 1900–1955*, p. 68.

27. Zaleznik in Gene W. Dalton, Louis B. Barnes, and Abraham Zaleznik, *The Distribution of Authority in Formal Organizations* (Cambridge, Mass.: MIT Press, 1973).

28. Chester I. Barnard, *The Functions of the Executive* (Cambridge, Mass.: Harvard University Press, 1938). See also Tillett, Kempner, and Wills, eds., *Management Thinkers.*

29. Hans Gerth and C. Wright Mills, eds., *From Max Weber: Essays in Sociology* (New York: Oxford University Press, 1958), pp. 215–16. Weber's notion of the virtues of bureaucracy's exclusion of passion converges interestingly with Freud's argument that women—the bearers of passion and sexuality—must be excluded from the workaday world of men. In *Civilization and Its Discontents* (1930), Freud wrote that women are driven by emotion and incapable of suppressing or sublimating their passions and sexual instincts as men could. Further, since the work of men in civilized societies removed them from their homes and families, women became hostile to the male world of organizations, constantly trying to lure men away from their higher, reasoned pursuits. Economic necessity, Freud declared, made it necessary for men to withdraw energy from sexuality and establish organizations in which the irrational instincts were sublimated; organic repression, he proposed, paves the way to civilization, despite the costs to individuals. Resisting female enticements, men carry on the burdens of government and rational thought; rationality is the male principle, in opposition to the female principle of emotionality. Men master their sexuality, in the Freudian view, whereas women "live dangerously close to the archaic heritage." It would be interesting for a study to be done of the convergences of Weber and Freud, not only on male and female principles in organizational life but also on the origin and nature of authority. See Philip Rieff, ed., *Freud: Sexuality and the Psychology of Love* (New York: Collier, 1963). The material in quotes is from Rieff, p. 203.

30. Elton Mayo, *The Human Problems of an Industrial Civilization* (New York: Macmillan, 1933); F. J. Roethlisberger and William J. Dickson, *Management and the Worker* (Cambridge, Mass.: Harvard University Press, 1939).

31. Mary Parker Follett, *Dynamic Administration* (London: Pitman, 1941).

32. Mayo, *The Human Problems of an Industrial Civilization,* p. 122.

33. Bendix, *Work and Authority in Industry,* p. 332.

34. *Ibid.,* p. 312.

35. Roethlisberger and Dickson, *Management and the Worker;* W. Lloyd Warner and J. O. Low, *The Social System of a Modern Factory* (New Haven: Yale University Press, 1947).

36. Alvin Gouldner noted in a literature review: ". . . the nonrational, traditionalistic orientations of management personnel have been obscured, and informal organization tends to be examined primarily among lower ranking personnel." "Organizational Analysis," *Sociology Today: Problems and Prospects,* R. K. Merton, L. Broom, and L. S. Cottrell, Jr., eds. (New York: Basic Books, 1959), p. 407. There is, of course, a large popular literature about management using analogies including jungles, primitive hunting bands, or medieval city-states, and the classic scholarly examination of informal relations in management in Melville Dalton, *Men Who Manage* (New York: Wiley, 1959).

37. Chris Argyris, "Some Limits of Rational Man Organization Theory," *Public Administration Review* (May-June 1973): pp. 253–67.

38. J. Alan Winter has proposed that there is a new "spirit of managerialism" today which perhaps rests on a more humanistic foundation—in my terms, reducing the "masculine ethic." Winter, "Elective Affinities between Religious Beliefs and Ideologies of Management in Two Eras," *American Journal of Sociology,* 79 (March 1974), pp. 1134–50.

39. Edith M. Lynch, *Executive Suite: Feminine Style* (New York: AMACOM, 1973), p. 64.

40. Perhaps there is an element of "projection" in this. What people are often most concerned about controlling in others reflects those uncontrollable elements in themselves. The *Harvard Business Review* survey: Bowman, Worthy, and Greyser, "Are Women Executives People?" The *Business Week* reference: Berry Yarmon, "Women Executives Gripe Too," *Boston Globe,* January 17, 1973.

41. C. Wright Mills, *White Collar* (New York: Oxford University Press, 1951), pp. 192–93.

42. Calculations are based on data in Hill, *Women in Gainful Occupations 1870–1920,* pp. 39, 56–7, and Table 115; and Margery Davis, "Woman's Place Is at the Typewriter: The Feminization of the Clerical Labor Force," *Radical America,* 8 (July-August 1974): pp. 1–28.

43. Grace D. Coyle, "Women in the Clerical Occupations," *Annals of the American Academy of Political and Social Science,* 143 (May 1929): p. 180.

44. Davies, "Woman's Place Is at the Typewriter"; Judith Smith, "The 'New Woman' Knows How to Type: Some Connections Between Sexual Ideology and Clerical Work, 1900–1930," Paper presented at the 1974 Berkshire Conference of Women Historians, American Civilization Department, Brown University.

45. Information on Katharine Gibbs Schools is from David Gumpert, "Women's Liberation Has All but Bypassed the Katy Gibbs Chain," *Wall Street Journal*, March 15, 1974. The YWCA date is from Robert Smuts, *Women and Work in America* (New York: Columbia University Press, 1951), p. 83.

46. Calculations based on data from U.S. Bureau of the Census, *Occupations of People with Higher Earnings* (Washington, D.C.: U.S. Government Printing Office, 1973). Also Vance Packard, *The Pyramid Climbers* (New York: McGraw-Hill, 1962); John F. Cuber with Peggy Harroff, *The Significant Americans: A Study of Sexual Behavior Among the Affluent* (New York: Appleton Century, 1965). Data on headmasters are from a private survey of wives of headmasters of independent schools, conducted by the wives themselves. I am grateful to Margaret Torrey of Windsor, Connecticut, for making the survey results available, and to Maizie Dolven of Bethel, Maine, for directing me to Torrey.

Chapter 2

1. The rationale for the disguised name, and the ethical-moral concerns that led me to change details and try to keep both the company and my informants anonymous, are provided in Appendix I, along with a description of the methods used in the field study.

2. This is consistent with organization theory. James Thompson proposed that when the core technology is not perfected, it is more likely to be represented in the dominant coalition in an organization—as it was when scientists and engineers were the top leaders in Indsco's early days. But the contemporary dominance of sales confirms another proposition: The more heterogeneous the task-environment, the larger the number of task-environment specialists in the dominant coalition; when competition is brisk, the power of sales executives should rise. Thompson, *Organizations in Action* (New York: McGraw-Hill, 1967), p. 136.

3. For an interesting look at the role of rituals and traditions in the history of General Electric, see George D. Downing, "The Changing Structure of a Great Corporation," in *The Emergent American Society: Large Scale Organizations*, L. W. Warner and D. Unwalla, eds. (New Haven: Yale University Press, 1967), pp. 215–25.

4. The famous example is the large number of words Eskimos have for different kinds of snow. Psycholinguistics deals with these matters. Roger Brown and Eric Lenneberg wrote: "In our professional roles we focus on particular kinds of recurrences and categorize in the way that reveals these recurrences. Similarly, communities as a whole have their different purposes and, accordingly, their different vocabularies." Brown and Lenneberg, "Studies in Linguistic Relativity," in *Basic Studies in Social Psychology*, H. Proshansky and B. Seidenberg, eds. (New York: Holt, Rinehart and Winston, 1965), p. 252.

5. Avoidance of introspection is perhaps a milder form of what Robert Jay Lifton has called psychic numbing: "an incapacity to feel or to confront certain kinds of experience due to the blocking or absence of inner forms or imagery that can connect with such experience." *The Life of the Self* (New York: Simon and Schuster, 1976), p. 27.

Chapter 3

1. Similar propositions are developed by Anthony Downs, *Inside Bureaucracy* (Boston: Little, Brown, 1966), p. 68. The Kerr quote is from Clark Kerr, John T. Dunlop, Frederick H. Harbison, and Charles A. Myers, *Industrialism and Industrial Man* (Cambridge, Mass.: Harvard University Press, 1960).

2. Wilbert Moore, *The Conduct of the Corporation* (New York: Random House, 1962), Vintage edition, p. 109.

3. James D. Thompson, *Organizations in Action* (New York: McGraw-Hill, 1967), p. 159.

4. *Ibid.*, p. 24.

5. Philip Selznick, "Critical Decisions in Organization Development," in *Leadership in Administration*, excerpted in *Complex Organizations*, A. Etzioni, ed. (New York: Holt, Rinehart and Winston, 1961), pp. 355–62.

6. Concerns about abuse of power among the first to lead a new kind of system were as prominent in the Chinese Revolution as they were among the first modern corporations. Communist Party leadership rose to the challenge brilliantly, by asking village officials to confess their "crimes" in front of the people and thus prove their trustworthiness for the future. But there was also care to keep early party membership confined to a relatively small group from similar backgrounds. See William Hinton, *Fanshen: A Documentary of Revolution in a Chinese Village* (New York: Monthly Review Press and Vintage Books, 1966).

7. Oscar Grusky, *The New Military* (New York: Russell Sage Foundation, 1964).

8. Cited in Sidney Pollard, *The Genesis of Modern Management: A Study of the Industrial Revolution in Great Britain* (Cambridge, Mass.: Harvard University Press, 1965), pp. 12–13. Pollard is also the source of the earlier quote.

9. On Britain: Pollard, *Genesis*, p. 14. On insurance: Morton Keller, *The Life Insurance Enterprise, 1885–1910* (Cambridge, Mass.: Harvard University Press, 1963), p. 74.

10. Peter F. Drucker, *Management: Tasks, Responsibilities, Practices* (New York: Harper & Row, 1974), p. 381.

11. Dan Rottenberg, "The Moneyweight Champion," *New York Times Magazine*, February 22, 1976, p. 16.

12. Keller, *Life Insurance*, p. 42.

13. Carl B. Kaufman, *Man Incorporate: The Individual and His Work in an Organized Society*, rev. ed. (Garden City, New York: Doubleday Anchor, 1969), p. 155. There is, of course, a large literature on the time span of control that holds that distributional equity is maximized by rewarding most highly those decisions covering the longest time span, those whose with results are not measurable for the longest time.

14. Rosabeth Moss Kanter, *Commitment and Community* (Cambridge, Mass.: Harvard University Press, 1972), pp. 93–94, 104.

15. General references are the following: James Burnham, *The Managerial Revolution* (New York, John Day, 1941); William Miller, *Men in Business* (New York, Harper & Row, 1962); W. Lloyd Warner and James C. Abegglen, *Big Business Leaders in America* (New York, Harper and Brothers, 1955); Francis X. Sutton et al., *The American Business Creed* (Cambridge, Mass.: Harvard University Press, 1956); C. Wright Mills, "The American Business Elite: A Collective Portrait," in *Power, Politics, and People*, I. L. Horowitz, ed. (New York, Ballantine, 1963). The study of one plant was in Melville Dalton, *Men Who Manage* (New York, Wiley, 1959).

16. William E. Henry, "Executive Personality," in *The Emergent American Society: Large-Scale Organizations*, W. Lloyd Warner and Darab B. Unwalla, eds. (New Haven: Yale University Press, 1967), pp. 241–75; Leonard R. Sayles, *Managerial Behavior* (New York: McGraw-Hill, 1964), p. 27; Tom Burns, "The Direction of Activity and Communication in a Departmental Executive Group," *Human Relations*, 8 (1954): pp. 73–97; D. N. Ulrich, D. R. Booz, and P. R. Lawrence, *Management Behavior and Foreman Attitude* (Boston: Harvard Business School, 1950); Robert Dubin, "Business Behavior Behaviorally Viewed," in *Social Science Approaches to Business Behavior* (Homewood, Illinois: Irwin-Dorsey, 1962), p. 17; A. W. Palmer and R. J. Beishon, "How the Day Goes," *Personnel Management*, 2 (1970): pp. 36–38; and Henry Mintzberg, *The Nature of Managerial Work* (New York: Harper & Row, 1973).

17. Fred Goldner, cited in Thompson, *Organizations*, p. 115.

18. Moore, *Conduct of Corporation*, p. 15.

19. See the section on "Size, Complexity, and Administration" in Wolfe V. Heydebrand, ed.,

Comparative Organizations: The Results of Empirical Research (Englewood Cliffs, New Jersey: Prentice-Hall, 1973).

20. Barry A. Stein, *Size, Efficiency, and Community Enterprise* (Cambridge, Mass.: Center for Community Economic Development, 1974).

21. Stanley Lieberson and John F. O'Connor, "Leadership and Organizational Performance: A Study of Large Corporations," *American Sociological Review*, 37 (April 1972): pp. 117–30.

22. Stephen A. Marglin, "What Do Bosses Do? The Origins and Functions of Hierarchy in Capitalist Production," *The Review of Radical Political Economics*, 6 (Summer 1974): pp. 33–60; Harry Braverman, *Labor and Monopoly Capital* (New York: Monthly Review Press, 1974).

23. Moore, *Conduct of Corporation*, p. 75. Karl Marx saw secrecy as an essential characteristic of bureaucracy.

24. R. L. Kahn, G. R. Gurin, E. Baar, and A. I. Kraut, *Discrimination without Prejudice: A Study of Promotion Practices in Industry* (Ann Arbor: Institute for Social Research, 1964), p. 7.

25. R. P. Quinn, R. L. Kahn, J. M. Tabor, and L. K. Gordon, *The Chosen Few: A Study of Discrimination in Executive Selection* (Ann Arbor: Survey Research Center, 1968).

26. Henry, "Executive Personality," p. 251.

27. Sexton Adams and Don Fyffe, *The Corporate Promotables* (Houston: Gulf Publishing, 1969), p. 87.

28. Moore, *Conduct of Corporation*, p. 114.

29. Kanter, *Commitment and Community*.

30. Moore, *Conduct of Corporation*, p. 134.

31. Margaret Hennig, *Career Development of Women Executives*, Unpublished Doctoral Dissertation, Harvard Business School, 1970.

Chapter 4

1. See Geraldine Homall, *The Motivation to be Promoted among Non-Exempt Employees: An Expectancy Theory Approach*, Unpublished M.S. Thesis, Cornell University, 1974.

2. Reinhard Bendix, *Max Weber: An Intellectual Portrait* (Garden City, New York: Doubleday Anchor, 1960), p. 425.

3. Robert Townsend, *Up the Organization* (New York: Knopf, 1970), pp. 168, 172; Chester Burger, *Survivial in the Executive Jungle* (New York: Macmillan, 1964), p. 219.

4. David Gumpert, "Women's Liberation Has All but Bypassed the Katy Gibbs Chain," *Wall Street Journal*, March 15, 1974.

5. Herbert Marcuse, *One-Dimensional Man* (Boston: Beacon Press, 1964), pp. 74–5. The question of what difference it would make if a secretary were a man cannot be adequately answered. But I can present one intriguing fictional comparison: Della Street and Archie Goodwin, two characters of detective story fame. Both are "confidential secretaries" to well-known detectives, taking shorthand and typing efficiently, and acting as "buffers" for their bosses against all those who might demand access, from possible clients to the police. However, there the resemblance ends. Archie Goodwin is the "leg man" for Nero Wolfe as well as the narrator of the novels, assertively roaming the city to collect clues and taking initiative when necessary, while his boss, who refuses to leave his house on business, remains immobile. Goodwin has a voice in the Wolfe tales, in all senses of that term. Della Street, on the other hand, is usually found in the office in the more traditional immobile and spatially limited position, while her boss, Perry Mason, generates the action elsewhere. Street calls Mason "Chief" and resists doing certain letters without him; he occasionally calls on her to add the "feminine angle" to a case. Goodwin, in contrast, often makes decisions on the spot to act for and commit Wolfe; he is noted for his strength and his power, including the power to attract women. Della Street hovers admiringly in the background, while Mason takes the risks and undergoes the adventures, rewarded occasionally by Mason with a kiss

or a steak dinner; she is the traditional "office wife." Goodwin, instead, is the proactive "assistant to," entering and often controlling the action around Nero Wolfe's cases, and he is the one who wins the romantic prize on *his* terms at the end of the story.

6. The examples of incredulous acts and the quote are from Ellen Goodman, "How Personal Can You Get?" *Boston Globe*, March 25, 1975.

7. In India secretaries tend to be lower caste males.

8. Perhaps this is why many academic departments resist hiring their own students for a first job after graduate school.

9. Harold H. Kelley, "The Warm-Cold Variable in First Impressions of Persons," *Journal of Personality*, 18 (1950): pp. 431–39.

10. Amatai Etzioni proposed that female white-collar workers seem more influenced by normative symbols than male, along with theorizing that the manipulation of esteem and prestige symbols is more effective among white-collar than blue-collar employees. *A Comparative Analysis of Complex Organizations* (New York: Free Press, 1961), pp. 33, 38. But Michel Crozier noted that studies of white-collar workers as a group were generally missing in research on occupations. Citing a 1954 study by Erwin Smigel which found that only 3 percent of the journal articles on occupations were devoted to office workers (versus 38 percent devoted to medicine alone), Crozier concluded that office workers tended to be studied only as instances of subordinate employees and not as an occupational grouping and organizational class in their own right. However, he found many compelling reasons for studying such workers and jobs, including their feminine character, calling the feminization of office jobs "certainly one of the most fundamental phenomena in the evolution of the occupational structure." *The World of the Office Worker*, translated by David Landau (Chicago: University of Chicago Press, 1971), p. 15.

11. Grace D. Coyle, "Women in the Clerical Occupations," *Annals of the American Academy of Political and Social Science*, 143 (May 1929): p. 187. See also Dick Bruner, "Why White Collar Workers Can't Be Organized," *Man, Work, and Society*, S. Nosow and W. H. Form, eds. (New York: Basic Books, 1962), pp. 188–97.

12. Coyle, "Women in Clerical Occupations."

13. Studs Terkel, *Working* (New York: Pantheon, 1974), pp. 55, 56; see also Robert Presthus, *The Organizational Society* (New York: Knopf, 1962), p. 237.

14. Advice book is Chester Burger, *Survival in the Executive Jungle* (New York: Macmillan, 1964), p. 225; Woods quote is Ann Wood, "The Women at the Rim of Power," *Boston Globe*, November 28, 1973.

15. I call the relationship a marriage in form, without implying sexuality as a necessary ingredient. However, even if not a universal attribute, sex could be involved in some relationships. I did not study "office sex" at Indsco, and it was not mentioned by interviewees. Sex is often commented on vis-à-vis secretaries as a way to deflect attention from aspects of the job worthy of intellectual analysis.

16. Mary Kathleen Benet, *The Secretarial Ghetto* (New York: McGraw-Hill, 1973), p. 72.

17. Terkel, *Working*, p. 56. See also John Cuber and Peggy Harroff, *The Significant Americans* (New York: Appleton Century, 1965), p. 150, for similar statements.

18. Wood, "Women at the Rim of Power."

19. Michael Korda, *Male Chauvinism! How It Works* (New York: Random House, 1973), p. 19.

20. Wilbert Moore, *The Conduct of the Corporation* (New York: Vintage, 1962), pp. 97–98.

21. Robert K. Merton, "Bureaucratic Structure and Personality," in *Complex Organizations: A Sociological Reader*, A. Etzioni, ed. (New York: Holt, Rinehart and Winston, 1961), pp. 51, 52.

22. The classic book is C. Wright Mills, *White Collar* (New York: Oxford University Press, 1951). Other research also picks up this theme. Nancy Morse studied the job satisfaction of male and female white-collar workers in *Satisfaction in the White Collar Job* (Ann Arbor, Michigan: Survey Research Center, 1953), and Crozier reported research on office workers in six Parisian insurance companies in *The World of the Office Worker*. Joel Seidman et al. included telephone workers, clerical and otherwise, in *The Worker Views His Union* (Chicago: University of Chicago Press,

1958). Excellent recent investigations include Margery Davies, "Woman's Place Is At the Type-writer; the Feminization of the Clerical Labor Force," *Radical America;* Judith Smith, "The 'New Woman' Knows How to Type: Some Connections Between Sexual Ideology and Clerical Work 1900–1930," presented at the Berkshire Conference on Women's History, 1974, American Civilization Department, Brown University. There are recent journalistic accounts: Barbara Garson, "Women's Work," *Working Papers for a New Society,* 1 (Fall 1973), pp. 5–14; Elinor Langer, "Inside the New York Telephone Company," in *Women at Work,* W. L. O'Neill, ed. (Chicago: Quandrangle, 1972); and Benet, *The Secretarial Ghetto.* See also "The Hidden Proletariat," *Society,* 11 (May/June 1975), pp. 12–14. Roslyn Feldberg and Evelyn Glenn at Boston University have work in progress. And for the effects of automation, see Ida Rossakoff Hoos, "When the Computer Takes Over the Office," in *Man, Work, and Society,* S. Nosow and W. H. Form, eds. (New York: Basic Books, 1962), pp. 72–82; and Jon Shepard, *Automation and Alienation: A Study of Office and Factory Workers* (Cambridge, Mass.: MIT Press, 1971).

Chapter 5

1. At an interview for a high administrative post at a university, a student once asked me, "Our present provost's wife is very active around here and does many things for the college. Would you be bringing somebody like that with *you?*"

2. Robert Seidenberg, *Corporate Wives—Corporate Casualties?* (New York: AMACOM, 1973), p. 129.

3. Evelyn Keene, "Cruising on a Collision Course: Policeman's Wives Vs. Policewomen," *Boston Globe,* November 2, 1974.

4. Samuel A. Culbert and Jean R. Renshaw, "Coping with the Stresses of Travel as an Opportunity for Improving the Quality of Work and Family Life," *Family Process,* 11 (September 1972), pp. 321–22.

5. William H. Whyte, Jr., "The Wives of Management," and "The Corporation and the Wife," *Fortune* (October 1951, and November 1951).

6. Seidenberg, *Corporate Wives;* Harry Levinson, *Emotional Problems in the World of Work* (New York: Harper & Row, 1964); Myrna M. Weissman and Eugene S. Paykel, "Moving and Depression in Women," *Society,* 9 (July-August, 1972): pp. 24–28. See also W. Lloyd Warner and James C. Abegglen, *Big Business Leaders in America* (New York: Harper and Brothers, 1955), p. 125.

7. Associated Press, " 'It's like being a prisoner,' says Trudeau's wife," *Boston Globe,* October 28, 1974; "The Relentless Ordeal of Political Wives," *Time,* October 7, 1974, pp. 15–22; Myra MacPherson, *The Power Lovers: An Intimate Look at Politicians and Their Marriages* (New York: Putnam, 1975).

8. Seidenberg, *Corporate Wives,* p. 94.

9. William E. Henry, "Executive Personality," in *The Emergent American Society: Large-Scale Organizations,* W. L. Warner and D. B. Unwalla, eds. (New Haven: Yale University Press, 1967), p. 270.

10. John F. Cuber with Peggy Harroff, *The Significant Americans: A Study of Sexual Behavior among the Affluent* (New York: Appleton Century, 1965), p. 59; *New York Times,* April 29, 1973, cited in Seidenberg, *Corporate Wives,* p. 79; Whyte, "Wives of Management" and "The Corporation and the Wife"; Helena Z. Lopata, *Occupation: Housewife* (New York: Oxford University Press, 1971), p. 101.

11. Seidenberg, *Corporate Wives,* p. 86.

12. Lewis Coser uses this phrase, although he did not look at corporate wives. See *Greedy Organizations* (New York: Free Press, 1974).

13. Hanna Papanek, "Men, Women, and Work: Reflections on the Two-Person Career," *American Journal of Sociology,* 78 (January 1973), pp. 90, 96. Of course, not all women are in-

volved in the careers of their husbands at all. There are also accounts of pre-1950s corporate marriages in which husbands kept business (and often themselves) as far from the home as possible. See Warner and Abegglen, *Big Business Leaders in America.*

14. This comment also reveals how attuned mobile men are to superiors and peers rather than subordinates. See Chapter 6.

15. Wilbert Moore, *The Conduct of the Corporation* (New York: Random House, 1962), Vintage edition, pp. 84–5; Levinson, *Emotional Problems in the World of Work,* p. 185.

16. Whyte, "The Wives of Management" and "The Corporation and the Wife."

17. Whyte, "Wives of Mangement" and "The Corporation and the Wife." Vance Packard adds these rules: "Don't stand up at the bar to drink. Don't wear a mink coat if the president's wife doesn't have one." Packard, *The Pyramid Climbers* (New York: McGraw-Hill, 1962). And also Alice Lake, "I Hate My Husband's Success," *McCall's* (July 1958); Packard's story about a wife axing another one because she didn't know where Yale was located; her husband lost his job; W. R. Roberts, "Executives, Wives, and Trouble," *Dun's Review* (January 1965); and Cuber and Harroff, *Significant Americans,* p. 82.

18. Seidenberg, *Corporate Wives,* p. 30.

19. "Most bureaucratic structures are capped by a nonbureaucratic elite operating with greater freedom than the lower levels of the organization." Theodore Caplow, *The Sociology of Work* (Minneapolis: University of Minnesota Press, 1954), p. 66.

20. In one well-known commodity-producing company, the wife of the chief executive is now a vice-president of the corporation. Several years earlier she had returned to school to complete a graduate degree. Said her husband, "If you have time to go to school, you have time to come to work for the company." She began to work on the executive level in a financial area where she had little previous experience and then moved to her present position. Now both she and her husband commute with their young daughter, the last child at home, from their family residence in one city to an apartment in the company's headquarters city; graduate student tutors take care of her daughter's education. Or take the case of "Mr. and Mrs. Kleer Pak," a husband-wife team that owns and runs a series of plastic packaging plants. She is responsible for machinery, scheduling, and plant operation; he is responsible for finance and administration. She started working by accident, coming to help out in the office one day when the usual "girl" was absent. "I was the whole office—bookkeeper, telephone operator, saleswoman, and artist," she told a reporter. By 1973 she had moved from her auxiliary status as volunteer to manager, earning $45,000 a year, while the female office workers whose jobs she "helped out" with earned salaries with a ceiling of $12,500. Such mobility would not have occurred had "Mrs. Kleer Pak" not been the boss's wife. (Jean Christensen, "Mr. and Mrs. Kleer Pak, A Smooth Team," *New York Times,* November 11, 1973.) These examples are all from family businesses, however, where such patterns are typical, as they are among some politicians, where widows take over. A similar thing would be rather unlikely and strongly disapproved in large public shareowner corporations.

21. Moore, *Conduct of Corporation,* pp. 84–5.

22. William H. Whyte, Jr., "How Hard Do Executives Work?", in *The Executive Life* (Garden City, New York: Doubleday, 1956), pp. 61–78; Peter Willmott, "Family, Work, and Leisure Conflicts Among Male Employees: Some Preliminary Findings," *Human Relations,* 2 (December 1971), pp. 575–84.

23. Of course, not all volunteer work is so instrumental; it is an important and often altruistic public service. The quote is from Dollie Ann Cole, "New Style of Corporate Wife," *New York Times,* December 2, 1973.

24. *Ibid.*

25. "Relentless Ordeal," *Time,* pp. 15–22.

26. Papanek, "Men, Women, and Work," p. 100.

27. Jessie Bernard, *Women and the Public Interest* (Chicago: Aldine, 1971), pp. 26, 115–116.

28. Differences between organizations in their degree of "wife-absorptiveness" based on these structural issues are dramatically illustrated in the case of headmasters' wives. Their roles are

much more constrained in the boarding schools, which are equivalent to "total institutions" in "company towns," than in day schools. The following table, which I compiled from a survey of 210 headmasters' wives, shows this:

	Percentage of headmasters' wives responding affirmatively to questionnaire item:	
	Boarding school (N = 75)	Day school (N = 135)
Items indicating constraint:		
Feel headmasters' wives' duties are obligatory	73%	36%
Entertain 50 or more times a year	29%	3%
All or some of the entertaining is required	61%	19%
School comes first in home/school conflicts	17%	6%
Feel not very, not at all free to engage in controversial activities	45%	20%
Items indicating lack of constraint:		
Entertain 10 times or less per year	18%	38%
Feel free to engage in controversial activities	20%	26%
Feel free to have on-campus close friends	28%	43%
Can engage in volunteer work outside school	50%	94%

I am grateful to Margaret Torrey of Windsor, Connecticut, for the survey results and permission to use the data.

29. Theoretical issues are raised in Rosabeth Moss Kanter, *Commitment and Community* (Cambridge, Mass.: Harvard University Press, 1972), Chapter 4.

30. A large number of policy issues are raised in Rosabeth Moss Kanter, *Work and Family in the United States* (New York, Russell Sage Foundation, 1976). See also Bill Frupp, "Transfers and the Executive Rebellion," *Boston Globe,* November 13, 1975; and Culbert and Renshaw, "Coping."

Chapter 6

1. Arnold S. Tannenbaum, Bogdan Kavcic, Menachem Rosner, Miro Vianello, and George Wieser, *Hierarchy in Organizations: An International Comparison* (San Francisco: Jossey-Bass, 1974), p. 8. S. M. Miller and Frank Riessman also argue that structure (job conditions) and cognitive factors (such as evaluation of opportunities and risks) are more important in understanding workers than intra-psychic variables such as motivation or affective tendencies. See "The Working Class Subculture: A New View," *Social Problems,* 9 (Summer 1961): pp. 86–97. See also Judith Long Laws, in "Work Aspirations in Women: False Leads and New Starts," *Signs: A Journal of Women in Culture and Society,* 2 (Spring 1976): pp. 33–50.

2. Robert Guest, "Work Careers and Aspirations of Automobile Workers," *American Sociological Review,* 19 (1954): pp. 155–163; Eli Chinoy, *Automobile Workers and the American Dream* (New York: Doubleday, 1955); Robert Blauner, *Alienation and Freedom* (Chicago: University of

Chicago Press, 1964); Theodore V. Purcell, *Blue Collar Man: Patterns of Dual Allegiance in Industry* (Cambridge, Mass.: Harvard University Press, 1960); and Charles M. Bonjean, Bruce D. Grady, and J. Allen Williams, Jr., "Social Mobility and Job Satisfaction: A Replication and Extension," *Social Forces*, 46 (June 1967): pp. 492–501.

3. Geraldine Homall, *The Motivation To Be Promoted among Non-Exempt Employees: An Expectancy Theory Approach*, Unpublished M.S. Thesis, Cornell University, 1974.

4. Using a rigorous expectancy-value approach, Homall calculated an overall motivation score for each respondent by using this formula: Motivation to be promoted = Estimate of overall chances × Mean of desirability ratings for each promotional consequence × Mean of likelihood ratings for each promotional consequence. The overall mean score for men was 896.04; for women, 639.70. This difference was statistically significant at the .05 level. Homall did not, however, analyze the data in terms of the present position (and hence, future prospects) of respondents. I gathered some of this information independently.

5. Tannenbaum et al., *Hierarchy in Organizations*, p. 1; R. C. Stone, "Mobility Factors as They Affect Workers' Attitudes and Conduct Toward Incentive Systems," *American Sociological Review*, 7 (1952): pp. 58–64; James G. March and Herbert A. Simon, *Organizations* (New York, Wiley, 1958), p. 74; Oscar Grusky, "Career Mobility and Organizational Commitment," *Administractive Science Quarterly*, 10 (March 1966): pp. 489–502. But another study offers partially conflicting evidence. In research on TVA employees, Patchen found that subjective reports of promotion prospects bore no relation to identification with the organization, as measured by perception of common interest between management and employees, self-image of oneself as a TVA member, willingness to choose TVA again, etc. Yet the people surveyed were largely lower-level employees whose real job ceilings and absolute advancement prospects were rather low; perhaps they could not be differentiated in terms of opportunity, having objectively so little of it. It is striking that identification with the organization was highly correlated with a feeling of work group solidarity ($r = .45$, $p < .01$, and the partial correlation when other factors related to identification were controlled was reduced but still high and statistically significant). As we see in Note 7, below, placement in the opportunity structure can affect those factors that make people feel good about their work; peer relations seem much more important to those with low overall mobility prospects. Martin Patchen, *Participation, Achievement, and Involvement on the Job* (Englewood Cliffs, New Jersey: Prentice-Hall, 1970).

6. Robert Dubin, "Industrial Workers' Worlds," *Social Problems*, 3 (January 1956): pp. 131–142; Chinoy, *Automobile Workers*. On "drop-outs" to small business: Kurt B. Mayer and Sidney Goldstein, "Manual Workers as Small Businessmen," in *Blue Collar World*, A. Shostak and W. Gomberg, eds. (Englewood Cliffs, New Jersey: Prentice-Hall, 1964), pp. 537–50. See also Seymour Martin Lipset and Reinhard Bendix, *Social Mobility in Industrial Society* (Berkeley: University of California Press, 1962).

7. Jon Shepard, *Automation and Alienation: A Study of Office and Factory Workers* (Cambridge, Mass.: MIT Press, 1971), p. 34.

8. Noel Tichy, "An Analysis of Clique Formation and Structure in Organizations," *Administrative Science Quarterly*, 18 (1973): pp. 194–207; Robert K. Merton, *Social Theory and Social Structure* (New York: Free Press, 1968), p. 233. Study of the effects of promotion rates was J. M. Pennings, "Work-Value Systems of White Collar Workers," *Administrative Science Quarterly*, 15 (1970): pp. 397–405. And Patchen, *Participation* (see Note 5 for details).

9. Arthur R. Cohen, "Upward Communication in Experimentally Created Hierarchies," *Human Relations*, 11 (1958): pp. 41–53. See especially p. 49.

10. F. J. Roethlisberger and William J. Dickson, *Management and the Worker* (Cambridge: Harvard University Press, 1939).

11. Tom Burns, "The Reference of Conduct in Small Groups: Cliques and Cabals in Occupational Milieux," *Human Relations*, 8 (1955): p. 476.

12. Philip Selznick, *Law, Society, and Industrial Justice* (New York: Russell Sage Foundation, 1969), p. 118.

13. Patricia Marchak, "Women Workers and White Collar Unions," *Canadian Review of So-*

ciology and Anthropology, 10 (1973): pp. 134–147. David Lockwood reports, however, after British research, that the stereotype that women are an obstacle to developing white-collar unions is not true to the facts, in *The Blackcoated Worker: A Study in Class Consciousness* (London: Unwin University Books, 1958), p. 151.

14. Tichy, "Analysis of Clique Formation."

15. William F. Whyte, *Street Corner Society* (Chicago: University of Chicago Press, 1943). Tannenbaum commented on this in *Hierarchy in Organizations,* p. 9.

16. Anthony Downs called such people, who have low expectation of promotion, "conservors" and defined a law of increasing conservorism involving sticking to rules and hostility to change. Downs, *Inside Bureaucracy* (Boston: Little Brown, 1966). See also Robert Presthus, *The Organizational Society* (New York: Vintage, 1962) and the section on Powerlessness in Chapter 7 of this book.

17. See James E. Rosenbaum, "The Stratification of Socialization Processes," *American Sociological Review,* 40 (February 1975): pp. 48–54.

18. There are several sets of findings purporting to show that women are more interested in relationships than in the intrinsic nature of tasks. See Keith Davis, *Human Relations at Work* (New York: McGraw-Hill, 1967), pp. 35–36; Joan E. Crowley, Teresa E. Levitan, and Robert P. Quinn, "Seven Deadly Half-Truths About Women," *Psychology Today,* 7 (1973): pp. 94–96; and an Australian study: Ruth Johnston, "Pay and Job Satisfaction: A Survey of Some Research Findings," *International Labour Review,* 3 (May 1975): pp. 441–49. However, a laboratory experiment found that in high-opportunity situations—i.e., a competitive game with uncertainty about the outcome—the female tendency to be more relationship-oriented disappeared. The early studies were: W. Edgar Vinacke, "Sex Roles in a Three-Person Game," *Sociometry,* 22 (December 1959): pp. 343–60; Thomas K. Uesugi and W. Edgar Vinake, "Strategy in a Feminine Game," *Sociometry,* 26 (1963): pp. 35–38. The structural refutation of sex differences was: Sidney I. Lirtzman and Mahmoud A. Wahba, "Determinants of Coalitional Behavior of Men and Women: Sex Role or Situational Requirements?," *Journal of Applied Psychology,* 56 (1972): pp. 406–11.

19. William J. Grinker, Donald D. Cooke, and Arthur W. Kirsch, *Climbing the Job Ladder: A Study of Employee Advancement in Eleven Industries* (New York: Shelley and Co., 1970).

20. Marchak, "Women Workers and White Collar Unions."

21. Shepard, *Automation and Alienation,* pp. 77–89.

22. On blue-collar men: Dubin, "Industrial Workers' Worlds." On professionals: Louis H. Orzack, "Work as a 'Central Life Interest' of Professionals," *Social Problems,* 7 (Fall 1969).

23. On teachers and nurses: J. A. Alutto, L. G. Hrebiniak, and R. C. Alonso, "On Operationalizing the Concept of Commitment," *Social Forces,* 51 (June 1973): pp. 448–54. On commitment as a function of overcoming barriers: Grusky, "Career Mobility," and Rosabeth Moss Kanter, *Commitment and Community* (Cambridge, Mass.: Harvard University Press, 1973), pp. 76–80.

24. Chinoy, *Automobile Workers;* Purcell, *Blue Collar Man;* Mayer and Goldstein, "Manual Workers as Small Businessmen."

25. Harold L. Wilensky, "Varieties of Work Experience," in *Man in a World at Work,* H. Borrow, ed. (Boston: Houghton Mifflin, 1964), pp. 125–54; Ray Wild, "Job Needs, Job Satisfaction, and Job Behavior of Women Manual Workers," *Journal of Applied Psychology,* 54 (1969): pp. 157–62; Nancy C. Morse and Robert S. Weiss, "The Function and Meaning of Work and the Job," *American Sociological Review,* 20 (April 1955): pp. 191–98; J. E. Kennedy and H. E. O'Neill, "Job Content and Workers' Opinions," *Journal of Applied Psychology,* 48 (1962): pp. 372–75; William Form, "Auto Workers and Their Machines: A Study of Work, Factory, and Job Satisfaction in Four Countries," *Social Forces,* 52 (1973): pp. 1–16. In the Form study, for example, only a minority of 100 auto workers in four countries appeared dissatisfied, though there was slightly more dissatisfaction expressed by those in lower-level jobs.

26. Blauner, *Alienation and Freedom,* pp. 81ff.

27. Wilensky included engineers among those with dead-end jobs in "Varieties of Work Experience."

28. William H. Form and James A. Geschwender, "Social Reference Basis of Job Satisfaction: The Case of Manual Workers," *American Sociological Review*, 27 (April 1962): pp. 228–37.

29. See, for example, Floyd C. Mann and Lawrence K. Williams, "Some Effects of the Changing Work Environment in the Office," *Journal of Social Issues*, 18 (July 1962): pp. 90–101.

30. John Van Maanen, Peter Gregg, and Ralph Katz, *Work in the Public Service* (Washington, D.C.: National Training and Development Service, 1974), p. 61.

Chapter 7

1. William A. Gamson, *Power and Discontent* (Homewoood, Illinois: Dorsey, 1968).

2. See Arnold S. Tannenbaum, *Social Psychology of the Work Organization* (Belmont, California: Wadsworth, 1966), pp. 78–79. After a computerized review of a large number of studies, Suresh Srivastva and colleagues concluded that different ways of supervising do affect subordinates' performance and internal states but that the results seem context-determined; in other words, no conclusions can be drawn about style in the absence of situation. Srivastva, et al., *Job Satisfaction and Productivity* (Cleveland: Department of Organizational Behavior, Case Western Reserve University, 1975), p. 44.

3. Philip M. Marcus and James S. House, "Exchange Between Superiors and Subordinates in Large Organizations," *Administrative Science Quarterly*, 18 (1973): pp. 209–22.

4. Donald C. Pelz, "Influence: A Key to Effective Leadership in the First-Line Supervisor," *Personnel*, 29 (1952): pp. 3–11.

5. Joan E. Crowley, Teresa E. Levitan, and Robert P. Quinn, "Seven Deadly Half-Truths About Women," *Psychology Today*, 7 (March 1973); William F. Whyte and Burleigh Gardner, "The Man in the Middle," *Applied Anthropology*, 4 (Spring 1945): pp. 1–28.

6. The study of negativity: John W. Thibaut and Henry W. Riecken, "Authoritarianism, Status, and the Communication of Aggression," *Human Relations*, 8 (1955): pp. 95–120. The study of professionals: Jacob I. Hurwitz, Alvin F. Zander, and Bernard Hymovitch, "Some Effects of Power on the Relations Among Group Members," in *Group Dynamics*, D. Cartwright and A. Zander, eds. (New York: Harper & Row, 1968). See also R. Lippit, N. Polansky, and S. Rosen, "The Dynamics of Power," *Human Relations*, 5 (1952): pp. 44–50; this is a classic study.

7. Michel Crozier, *The Bureaucratic Phenomenon* (Chicago: University of Chicago Press, 1964), p. 164.

8. Charles Perrow has also analyzed the ways in which changing technical requirements affect organizational authority structures in his studies of hospitals. See Perrow, "Hospitals: Technology, Structures, and Goals," in *Handbook of Organizations*, J. G. March, ed. (Chicago: Rand McNally, 1965), and Perrow, "The Analysis of Goals in Complex Organizations," *American Sociological Review*, 26 (1961): pp. 854–66. James Thompson made a similar point with respect to businesses in *Organizations in Action* (New York: McGraw-Hill, 1967).

9. Crozier, *Bureaucratic Phenomenon*, p. 54.

10. Thompson, *Organizations in Action*, pp. 125–29.

11. Barry A. Stein, "Getting There: Patterns in Managerial Success," Working Paper, Center for Research on Women, Wellesley College, 1975. Available through Center for Social and Evaluation Research, University of Massachusetts, Boston.

12. Bernard Levenson, "Bureaucratic Succession," in *Complex Organizations: A Sociological Reader*, Amitai Etzioni, ed. (New York: Holt, Rinehart and Winston, 1961), pp. 362–75.

13. John R. P. French, Jr., and Bertram H. Raven, "The Bases of Social Power," in *Studies in Social Power*, D. Cartwright, ed. (Ann Arbor, Michigan: Institute for Social Research, 1959), pp. 150–67.

14. Thompson, *Organizations in Action*, pp. 107–9; Crozier, *Bureaucratic Phenomenon*, p. 158. Thompson also proposed that since highly routinized jobs are protected from the environ-

ment and employ skills commonly available, they cannot easily become visible outside the organization.

15. Wilbert Moore, *The Conduct of the Corporation* (New York: Random House, 1962), Vintage Books, p. 115.

16. Crozier, *Bureaucratic Phenomenon,* pp. 155–6.

17. One group which used the concept of immediacy proposed that activities generate power when their consequences are close to, rather than remote from, goals. C. R. Hinings, D. J. Hickson, D. M. Pennings, and R. E. Schneck, "Structural Conditions of Intraorganizational Power," *Administrative Science Quarterly,* 19 (March 1974): pp. 22–44.

18. In a system of sponsored mobility, elites or their agents choose recruits early and then carefully induct them into elite status. Ralph H. Turner, "Sponsored and Contest Mobility in the School System," *American Sociological Review,* 25 (December 1960): pp. 855–67.

19. Margaret Cussler, *The Woman Executive* (New York: Harcourt, Brace, 1958); Margaret Hennig, *Career Development for Women Executives,* Unpublished Doctoral Dissertation, Harvard Business School, 1970; Michael Fogarty, A. I. Allen, Isobel Allen, and Patricia Walters, *Women in Top Jobs: Four Studies in Achievement* (London: George Allen and Unwin, 1971).

20. Paul Cowan, "Connecticut's Governor Grasso Remembers How She Made It," *New York Times,* May 4, 1975.

21. The evidence that social similarity and compatibility affects a leader's evaluation of followers or subordinates comes from a variety of situations. Borgatta found that high acceptability to a supervisor at the social level was associated with receiving high ratings from him, in an all-male sample. Edgar Borgatta, "Analysis of Social Interaction and Socio-metric Perception," *Sociometry,* 17 (February 1954): pp. 7–32. A study of staff nurses and their supervisors in three hospitals discovered that friendship with supervisors was a greater determinant of high evaluations than shared work attitudes and values. Ronald Corwin, Marvin J. Taves, and J. Eugene Haas, "Social Requirements for Occupational Success: Internalized Norms and Friendships," *Social Forces,* 39 (1961): pp. 135–40. The cause-effect relationship is not clear in these studies, of course.

22. Stein, "Getting There: Patterns in Managerial Success."

23. *Ibid.*

24. Whyte and Gardner, "Man in the Middle." See also Donald R. Wray, "Marginal Men of Industry, the Foremen," *American Journal of Sociology,* 54 (January 1949): pp. 298–301.

25. See Melville Dalton, "Conflicts between Staff and Line Managerial Officers," *American Sociological Review,* 21 (June 1950): pp. 342–51.

26. Sidney Reynolds, "Women on the Line," *MBA,* 9 (February 1975): pp. 27–30.

27. Robert Presthus, *The Organizational Society* (New York: Knopf, 1962), p. 35.

28. Karen Horney, *The Neurotic Personality of Our Time* (New York: Norton, 1937), pp. 163–70.

29. Rollo May, *Power and Innocence* (New York: Norton, 1972).

30. Stanley A. Hetzler, "Variations in Role-Playing Patterns Among Different Echelons of Bureaucratic Leaders," *American Sociological Review,* 20 (December 1955): pp. 700–706.

31. Crozier, *Bureaucratic Phenomenon,* pp. 122–23.

32. Franz Fanon, *The Wretched of the Earth* (New York: Grove Press, 1965).

33. B. Goodstadt and D. Kipnis, "Situational Influences on the Use of Power," *Journal of Applied Psychology,* 54 (1970): pp. 201–207; B. Goodstadt and L. Hjelle, "Power to the Powerless: Locus of Control and the Use of Power," *Journal of Personality and Social Psychology,* 27 (July 1973): pp. 190–96.

34. Thibaut and Riecken, "Authoritarianism, Status, and the Communication of Aggression." Chow and Grusky, in a laboratory simulation with complicated results, found that worker compliance (the degree of productivity and the degree of aggressiveness) shaped supervisory style, especially closeness of supervision and adoption of a punitive style; there were complex interaction phenomena in the data. Esther Chow and Oscar Grusky, "Worker Compliance and Supervisory Style: An Experimental Study of Female Superior-Subordinate Relationships," Paper presented at the 1973 Meetings of the American Sociological Association. Blau and Scott also pointed out that a

group's low productivity may be a cause of supervisory style, as well as a result. Peter M. Blau and W. Richard Scott, *Formal Organizations* (San Francisco: Chandler, 1962), p. 50.

35. Crozier, *Bureaucratic Phenomenon*, p. 188.

36. Robert K. Merton, "Bureaucratic Structure and Personality," in *Social Theory and Social Structure*, rev. ed. (Glencoe, Illinois: Free Press, 1957).

37. Melville Dalton, *Men Who Manage* (New York: Wiley, 1959), p. 247.

38. Merton, "Bureaucratic Structure and Personality."

39. Crozier, *Bureaucratic Phenomenon*, pp. 40–42.

40. Chris Argyris, *Integrating the Individual and the Organization* (New York: Wiley, 1964); M. Argyle, G. Gardner, and I. Cioffi, "Supervisory Methods Related to Productivity, Absenteeism, and Labor Turnover," *Human Relations*, 11 (1958): pp. 23–40; study by E. Fleishman and E. Harris cited in Charles Hampden-Turner, "The Factory as an Oppressive Environment," in *Workers' Control: A Reader on Labor and Social Change*, G. Hunnius, G. D. Garson, and J. Case, eds. (New York: Vintage, 1973), pp. 30–44. The Sears study was James Worthy, "Organizational Structure and Employee Morale," *American Sociological Review*, 15 (1950): pp. 169–79.

41. G. W. Bowman, N. B. Worthy, and S. A. Greyser, "Are Women Executives People?," *Harvard Business Review*, 43 (July–August 1965): pp. 14–30. The preference for male bosses was also a finding of National Manpower Council, *Womanpower* (New York: Columbia University Press, 1957), pp. 104–6.

42. The first study is Kathryn M. Bartol and D. Anthony Butterfield, "Sex Effects in Evaluating Leaders," Working Paper No. 74–10, University of Massachusetts School of Business Administration, 1974. The second is Benson Rosen and Thomas H. Jerdee, "The Influence of Sex-Role Stereotypes on Evaluations of Male and Female Supervisory Behavior," *Journal of Applied Psychology*, 57 (1973): pp. 44–48.

43. Eleanor Emmons Maccoby and Carol Nagy Jacklin, *The Psychology of Sex Differences* (Stanford, California: Stanford University Press, 1974), pp. 261, 361.

44. Michel Crozier, *The World of the Office Worker*, trans. David Landau (Chicago: University of Chicago Press, 1971); D. R. Day and R. M. Stogdill, "Leader Behavior of Male and Female Supervisors: A Comparative Study," *Personal Psychology*, 25 (1972): pp. 353–60; Cecile Roussell, "Relationship of Sex of Department Head to Department Climate," *Administrative Science Quarterly*, 19 (June 1974): pp. 211–20.

45. Kathryn M. Bartol, "Male Versus Female Leaders: The Effect of Leader Need for Dominance on Follower Satisfaction," *Academy of Management Journal*, 17 (June 1974): pp. 225–33; and "The Effect of Male Versus Female Leaders on Follower Satisfaction and Performance," *Journal of Business Research*, 3 (January 1975): pp. 33–42.

46. Pelz, "Influence."

47. Gail I. Pheterson, Sara B. Kiesler, and Philip A. Goldberg, "Evaluation of the Performance of Women as a Function of Their Sex, Achievement, and Personal History," *Journal of Personality and Social Psychology*, 19 (September 1971): pp. 114–18.

48. *MBA*, 6 (March 1972).

49. Donald A. Laird, with Eleanor C. Laird, *The Psychology of Supervising the Working Woman* (New York: McGraw-Hill, 1942), pp. 175–79.

50. Laird, *The Psychology of Supervising the Working Woman*, p. 31.

51. Burleigh B. Gardner, *Human Relations in Industry* (Chicago: Richard D. Irwin, 1945), pp. 269–71; National Manpower Council, *Womanpower* (New York: Columbia University Press, 1957), p. 106; and the British reference is Fogarty et al., *Women in Top Jobs*, p. 15.

52. Roussell, "Relationship of Sex of Department Head to Department Climate."

53. Gardner, *Human Relations*, pp. 270–71.

54. Elizabeth Janeway, "The Weak are the Second Sex," *Atlantic Monthly*, December 1973, and *In Between Myth and Morning* (New York: William Morrow, 1974).

Chapter 8

1. There are two questions that must be answered, of course, in any analysis of the effects of proportional representation: first, the circumstances under which a given characteristic is "salient" for differentiating group members; and second, the nature of the boundaries defining the extent and limits of the "group" within which proportional representation is measured. Here I am defining ascribed characteristics with a physical manifestation (such as sex) as salient, and the "group" as work peers in equivalent statuses.

2. Kurt H. Wolff, *The Sociology of Georg Simmel* (Glencoe, Illinois: Free Press, 1950).

3. On juries: Fred L. Strodtbeck and Richard D. Mann, "Sex Role Differentiation in Jury Deliberations," *Sociometry*, 19 (March 1956): pp. 3–11; and Fred L. Strodtbeck, Rita M. James, and Charles Hawkins, "Social Status in Jury Deliberations," *American Sociological Review*, 22 (1957): pp. 713–19. On the kibbutz: Lionel Tiger and Joseph Shepher, *Women in the Kibbutz* (New York: Harcourt, Brace Jovanovich, 1975), and my critique in terms of sex ratios, Rosabeth Moss Kanter, "Interpreting the Results of a Social Experiment," *Science*, 192 (14 May 1976): pp. 662–63. "Behavioral demography" as the study of population ratios: Marcia Guttentag, *Too Many Women* (New York: Basic Books, in press).

4. Shelley E. Taylor and Susan Fiske, "The Token in the Small Group: Research Findings and Theoretical Implications," in *Psychology and Politics*, J. Sweeney, ed. (New Haven: Yale University Press, 1976).

5. Margaret Hennig, *Career Development for Women Executives*, Unpublished Doctoral Dissertation, Harvard Business School, 1970, p. vi–21. The experimental study of high-dominance women was Edwin I. Megaree, "Influence of Sex Roles on the Manifestation of Leadership," *Journal of Applied Psychology*, 53 (1969): pp. 377–82. Cynthia Epstein's book is *Woman's Place* (Berkeley: University of California Press, 1970). See also Edith M. Lynch, *The Executive Suite: Feminine Style* (New York: AMACOM, 1973); Margaret Cussler, *The Woman Executive* (New York: Harcourt, Brace, 1958).

6. See Adeline Levine and Janice Crumrine, "Women and the Fear of Success: A Problem in Replication," *American Journal of Sociology*, 80 (January 1975): pp. 967–74. Seymour Sarason's argument is in his "Jewishness, Blackness, and the Nature-Nurture Controversy," *American Psychologist*, 28 (November 1973): pp. 962–71.

7. The Hughes citation is to Everett Hughes, *Men and Their Work* (Glencoe, Illinois: Free Press, 1958), p. 109. See also Hughes, "Dilemmas and Contradictions of Status," *American Journal of Sociology*, 50 (March 1944): pp. 353–59. Judith Lorber came to some similar conclusions in "Trust, Loyalty, and the Place of Women in the Informal Organization of Work," presented at the 1975 Meetings of the American Sociological Association. On "status incongruence" as an explanatory variable in group member behavior, used in many of the same ways I use "tokenism" but without the explicit numerical connotations, see A. Zaleznik, C. R. Christensen, and F. J. Roethlisberger, *The Motivation, Productivity, and Satisfaction of Workers: A Prediction Study* (Boston: Harvard Business School Division of Research, 1958), especially pp. 56–68.

8. Jeane Kirkpatrick, *Political Woman* (New York: Basic Books, 1974), p. 113; Lionel Tiger, *Men in Groups* (New York: Random House, 1969).

9. Clearly I was limited in first-hand observations of how the men acted when alone, since, by definition, if I, as a female researcher, were present, they would not have been alone. For my data here I relied on tape recordings of several meetings in which the tape was kept running even during breaks, and on informants' reports immediately after informal social events and about meetings.

10. For supportive laboratory evidence, see Elizabeth Aries, *Interaction Patterns and Themes of Male, Female, and Mixed Groups*, Unpublished Doctoral Dissertation, Harvard University, 1973. Her work is discussed further in Appendix II.

11. For examples in another context, see Marcia Greenbaum, "Adding 'Kenntnis' to 'Kirch, Kuche, und Kinder,'" *Issues in Industrial Society*, 2 (1971): pp. 61–68.

12. Judith Long Laws, "The Psychology of Tokenism: An Analysis," *Sex Roles*, 1 (1975): pp. 51–67.

13. Hughes, "Men and Their Work" and "Dilemmas and Contradictions of Status"; Lorber, "Trust, Loyalty, and the Place of Women."

14. Zaleznik et al., *Motivation, Productivity, and Satisfaction of Workers;* Hennig, *Career Development for Women Executives;* Epstein, *Woman's Place;* Brigid O'Farrell, "Affirmative Action and Skilled Craft Work," Unpublished Report, Cambridge, Mass., 1973 (available from Center for Research on Women, Wellesley College); Carol Wolman and Hal Frank, "The Solo Woman in a Professional Peer Group," *American Journal of Orthopsychiatry*, 45 (January 1975): pp. 164–71.

15. On secrecy and loyalty to peers in training, see Donald Roy, "Quota Restriction and Goldbricking in a Machine Shop," *American Journal of Sociology*, 57 (March 1952): pp. 427–42; Howard S. Becker and Anselm L. Strauss, "Careers, Personality, and Adult Socialization," *American Journal of Sociology*, 62 (November 1956): pp. 253–63.

16. Bernard E. Segal, "Male Nurses: A Study in Status Contradiction and Prestige Loss," *Social Forces*, 41 (October 1962): pp. 31–38. Personal interviews were used as a supplement.

17. Hughes, "Dilemmas and Contradictions of Status."

18. Laws, "Psychology of Tokenism."

19. Rose Laub Coser, "Laughter Among Colleagues: A Study of the Social Functions of Humor Among the Staff of a Mental Hospital," *Psychiatry*, 23 (1960): pp. 81–95.

20. Everett C. Hughes, "Race Relations in Industry," in *Industry and Society*, W. F. Whyte, ed. (New York: McGraw-Hill, 1946), p. 115.

21. Marianne Abeles Ferber and Joan Althaus Huber, "Sex of Student and Instructor: A Study of Student Bias," *American Journal of Sociology*, 80 (January 1975): pp. 949–63.

22. *Annual Report of the Council of Economic Advisers* (Washington, D.C.: U.S. Government Printing Office, 1973), p. 106.

23. Segal, "Male Nurses," supplemented by my personal interviews.

24. Philip Rieff, ed., *Freud: Sexuality and the Psychology of Love* (New York: Collier Books, 1963); Bryan Strong, "Toward a History of the Experiential Family: Sex and Incest in the Nineteenth Century Family," *Journal of Marriage and the Family*, 35 (August 1973): pp. 457–66.

25. John C. Athanassiades, "An Investigation of Some Communication Patterns of Female Subordinates in Hierarchical Organizations," *Human Relations*, 27 (1974): pp. 195–209.

26. Solomon E. Asch, "Effects of Group Pressure on the Modification and Distortion of Judgment," in *Group Dynamics*, second edition, D. Cartwright and A. Zander, eds. (Evanston, Illinois: Row Peterson, 1960), pp. 189–200.

27. Hughes used this phrase in a slightly different way in "Dilemmas and Contradictions of Status."

28. Gerhard Lenski, "Status Crystallization: A Non-Vertical Dimension of Status," *American Sociological Review*, 19 (August 1954): pp. 405–13; Lenski, "Social Participation and the Crystallization of Status," *American Sociological Review*, 21 (August 1956): pp. 458–64; G. H. Fenchel, J. H. Monderer, and E. L. Hartley, "Subjective Status and the Equilibrium Hypothesis," *Journal of Abnormal and Social Psychology*, 45 (October 1951): pp. 476–79; Elton F. Jackson, "Status Consistency and Symptoms of Stress," *American Sociological Review*, 27 (August 1962): pp. 469–80. On role overload and coronary disease see Stephen M. Sales, "Organizational Roles as a Risk Factor in Coronary Heart Disease," *Administrative Science Quarterly*, 14 (1969): pp. 235–336. For general reviews, see James S. House, "The Effects of Occupational Stress on Physical Health," in *Work and the Quality of Life*, James O'Toole, ed. (Cambridge, Mass.: MIT Press, 1974), pp. 145–70; and Stanislav V. Kasl, "Work and Mental Health," in *Work and the Quality of Life*, James O'Toole, ed. (Cambridge, Mass.: MIT Press, 1974), pp. 171–96.

29. Sidney M. Jourard, *The Transparent Self: Self-Disclosure and Well-Being* (Princeton: D. Van Nostrand, 1964).

30. Jackson, "Status Consistency and Symptoms of Stress."

31. Segal, "Male Nurses."

Chapter 9

1. There are, of course, a large number of methodological questions to be addressed, issues beyond the scope of the present book, but quantitative tests of the hypotheses are already underway.

2. Michel Crozier, *The Bureaucratic Phenomenon* (Chicago: University of Chicago Press, 1964).

3. *Ibid.*

4. Anthony Jay, *Corporation Man* (New York: Random House, 1971).

5. Wilbert Moore, *The Conduct of the Corporation* (New York: Random House, 1962).

6. Arthur N. Turner and Paul R. Lawrence, *Industrial Jobs and the Worker* (Boston: Harvard University Graduate School of Business Administration, 1965); J. Richard Hackman and Edward E. Lawler, III, "Employee Reactions to Job Characteristics," *Journal of Applied Psychology,* 55 (1971): pp. 259–86.

7. J. Richard Hackman, "On the Coming Demise of Job Enrichment," *Technical Report No. 9* (New Haven: Yale University Department of Administrative Sciences, 1974); Robert N. Ford, *Motivation through the Work Itself* (New York: American Management Association, 1969) and "Job Enrichment Lessons from AT&T," *Harvard Business Review,* 51 (January-February 1973): pp. 96–106.

8. Rensis Likert, *New Patterns of Management* (New York: McGraw-Hill, 1961).

9. Raymond A. Katzell and Daniel Yankelovich, *Work, Productivity, and Job Satisfaction: An Evaluation of Policy-Related Research* (New York: The Psychological Corporation, 1975); Suresh Srivastva, et al., *Job Satisfaction and Productivity* (Cleveland: Department of Organizational Behavior, Case Western Reserve University, 1975).

10. Katzell and Yankelovich, *Work, Productivity, and Job Satisfaction;* Richard E. Walton, "Innovative Restructuring of Work," in *The Worker and the Job: Coping with Change,* Jerome M. Rosow, ed. (Englewood Cliffs, New Jersey: Prentice-Hall, 1974), pp. 145–76. Arnold Tannenbaum's interest in the effects of hierarchy on attitudes and behavior is very compatible with this approach.

11. John Van Maanen, Peter Gregg, and Ralph Katz, *Work in the Public Service* (Washington, D.C.: National Training and Development Service, 1974), p. 61.

12. The first finding is in Walton, "Innovative Restructuring of Work," pp. 146–47; the second is from H. M. F. Rush, *Organization Development: A Reconnaissance* (New York: The Conference Board, 1973) and comes out of research on the Internal Revenue Service. See also Linda L. Frank and J. Richard Hackman, "Job Enrichment: The Case of the Change That Wasn't," *Technical Report No. 8,* Department of Administrative Sciences, Yale University, 1974; Clayton P. Alderfer, "Job Enlargement and the Organizational Context," *Personnel Psychology,* 22 (Winter 1969): pp. 418–26.

13. Richard Balzar, *Clockwork* (Garden City New York: Doubleday, 1976).

14. Walton, "Innovative Restructuring of Work."

15. *Ibid.,* p. 160.

16. Participation does not always equalize power. See Mauk Mulder, "Power Equalization through Participation?" *Administrative Science Quarterly,* 16 (March 1971): pp. 31–40.

17. George C. Homans, "The Western Electric Researches," in *Readings on Modern Organizations,* Amatai Etzioni, ed. (Englewood Cliffs, New Jersey: Prentice Hall, 1969), pp. 99–114.

18. Peter Branner, Eric Batstone, Derek Fatchett, and Philip White, *The Worker Directors: A Sociology of Participation* (London: Hutchinson, 1976).

19. Philip Selznick, *Law, Society, and Industrial Justice* (New York: Russell Sage Foundation, 1969), p. 117.

20. Harry Braverman, *Labor and Monopoly Capital* (New York: Monthly Review Press, 1974); Stephen A. Marglin, "What Do Bosses Do? The Origins and Functions of Hierarchy in Capitalist Production," *Review of Radical Political Economics,* 6 (Summer 1974): pp. 33–60; Katherine

Stone, "The Origins of Job Structures in the Steel Industry," *Review of Radical Political Economics*, 6 (Summer 1974): pp. 61–97. Braverman tends to favor the arguments about control and cheapening of labor; Marglin, legitimation and capital accumulation.

21. Michael J. Piore, "Upward Mobility, Job Monotony, and Labor Market Structure," in *Work and the Quality of Life*, James O'Toole, ed. (Cambridge, Mass.: MIT Press, 1974), pp. 73–86.

22. Azel Ames, M.D., *Sex in Industry: A Plea for the Working Girl* (Boston: James R. Osgood and Company, 1875).

23. Viva B. Boothe, Ph.D., *Women in the Modern World* (May 1929 issue of *The Annals of the American Academy of Political and Social Science*) (New York: Arno Press, 1974).

24. National Manpower Council, *Womanpower* (New York: Columbia University Press, 1957).

25. See Donald A. Laird with Eleanor C. Laird, *The Psychology of Supervising the Working Woman* (New York: McGraw-Hill, 1942).

26. Hilda Kahne with Andrew I. Kohen, "Economic Perspectives on the Roles of Women in the American Economy," *Journal of Economic Literature*, 13 (December 1975): p. 1274.

27. Rosabeth Moss Kanter, "The Policy Issues: Presentation VI," *Signs: Journal of Women in Culture and Society*, 1 (Spring 1976): pp. 282–91. See also Judith Long Laws, "Work Aspiration of Women: False Leads and New Starts," *Signs: Journal of Women in Culture and Society*, 1 (Spring 1976): pp. 33–50.

28. This mentality is described very well in William Ryan, *Blaming the Victim* (New York: Random House, 1971).

29. Ellen Graham, "Many Seminars Are Held To Aid Women in Firms," *Wall Street Journal*, September 26, 1973.

30. For a methodological critique that says that overlap is the most relevant issue to study, in any case, see David Tresemer, "Assumptions Made about Gender Roles," in *Another Voice: Feminist Perspectives on Social Life and Social Science*, Marcia Millman and Rosabeth Moss Kanter, eds. (New York: Doubleday Anchor, 1975), pp. 308–39.

31. Ivar Berg, *Education and Jobs: The Great Training Robbery* (Boston: Beacon Press, 1971). A theory of "statistical discrimination" has been developed by some economists, who argue that sex of job applicant is taken as a proxy for interior characteristics of that applicant that are not directly measured because of the high cost that would be entailed. See E. S. Phelps, "The Statistical Theory of Racism and Sexism," *American Economic Review*, 62 (September 1972): pp. 659–61.

Chapter 10

1. Daniel Yankelovich, "The Meaning of Work," in *The Worker and the Job*, Jerome M. Rosow, ed. (Englewood Cliffs, New Jersey: Prentice-Hall, 1974), pp. 19–47.

2. On the AMA study: Sam Zagoria, "Policy Implications and Future Agenda," in *The Worker and the Job*, Jerome M. Rosow, ed. (Englewood Cliffs, New Jersey: Prentice-Hall, 1974), pp. 177–201. On managers' discontents: Emanuel Kay, "Middle Management," in *Work and the Quality of Life*, James O'Toole, ed. (Cambridge, Mass.: MIT Press, 1974), pp. 106–30.

3. Peter B. Doeringer and Michael J. Piore, *Internal Labor Markets and Manpower Analysis* (Lexington, Mass.: D.C. Heath, 1971). On individual mobility versus occupational inequality, see Christopher Jencks, et al., *Inequality* (New York: Basic Books, 1973), pp. 196–99.

4. Herbert H. Meyer, Emanuel Kay, and John R. P. French, Jr., "Split Roles in Performance Appraisal," *Harvard Business Review*, 43 (January-February 1965).

5. Paul H. Thompson and Gene W. Dalton, "Performance Appraisal: Managers Beware," *Harvard Business Review*, 48 (January-February 1970); Alan L. Patz, "Performance Appraisal: Useful but Still Resisted," *Harvard Business Review*, 53 (May-June 1975), pp. 74–80. There are a

variety of other problems with appraisal systems that involve measurement: problems of quantification, ambiguity, validity, reliability across bosses, weighting of performance areas, and "halo effects" whereby generally good or generally bad impressions are generalized to all areas.

6. The kibbutz model is interesting in a number of respects, for it represents a successful attempt to manage industry as well as agriculture on a communal basis. See, for example, Menachem Rosner, "Direct Democracy in the Kibbutz," in *Communes: Creating and Managing the Collective Life*, R. M. Kanter, ed. (New York: Harper & Row, 1973), pp. 178–91. There are also descriptions of the kibbutz organization of work in Arnold Tannenbaum, et al., *Hierarchy in Organizations: An International Comparison* (San Francisco: Jossey Bass, 1974); David French and Elena French, *Working Communally* (New York: Russell Sage Foundation, 1974).

7. Rosabeth Moss Kanter, *Commitment and Community* (Cambridge, Mass.: Harvard University Press, 1972), especially pp. 95–97 and 236.

8. "How IBM Avoids Layoffs through Retraining," *Business Week*, November 10, 1975, pp. 110–12.

9. See Ronald Dore, *British Factory-Japanese Factory: The Origins of National Diversity in Industrial Relations* (Berkeley: University of California Press, 1973).

10. Robert N. Ford, *Motivation through the Work Itself* (New York: American Management Association, 1969) and "Job Enrichment Lessons from AT&T," *Harvard Business Review*, 51 (January–February 1973), pp. 96–106. See also Louis E. Davis and Eric L. Trist, "Improving the Quality of Work Life: Sociotechnical Case Studies," in *Work and the Quality of Life*, James O'Toole, ed. (Cambridge, Mass.: MIT Press, 1974), pp. 246–80.

11. Richard E. Walton, "Innovative Restructuring of Work," in *The Worker and the Job*, Jerome M. Rosow, ed. (Englewood Cliffs, New Jersey: Prentice Hall, 1974), pp. 145–76. The plants were General Foods and Norsk Fertilizer.

12. E. James Bryan, "Work Improvement and Job Enrichment: The Case of Cummins Engine Company," in *The Quality of Working Life: Cases and Commentary*, L. E. Davis and A. B. Cherns, eds. (New York: Free Press, 1975), p. 318.

13. John Hostetler, *Hutterite Society* (Baltimore: Johns Hopkins University Press, 1975).

14. Results are summarized in Barry A. Stein, Allan Cohen, and Herman Gadon, "Flextime: Work When You Want To," *Psychology Today*, 10 (June 1976): pp. 40–43, 80. See also Alvar O. Elbing, Herman Gadon, and John R. Gordon, "Flexible Working Hours: It's About Time," *Harvard Business Review*, 52 (January–February 1974): pp. 18–33; Robert T. Golembiewski, Rick Hilles, and Munro S. Kagno, "A Longitudinal Study of Flexi-Time Effects: Some Consequences of an OD Structural Intervention," *Journal of Applied Behavioral Science*, 10 (October-November-December 1974): pp. 503–32; Virginia H. Martin, *Hours of Work When Workers Can Choose: The Experience of 59 Organizations with Employee Chosen Staggered Hours and Flexitime* (Washington, D.C.: Business and Professional Women's Foundation, 1975).

15. These results are similar to those reported for some experiments in systematic work redesign. See Walton, "Innovative Restructuring of Work." An informant from a large insurance company utilizing flex time very effectively told me that the biggest benefit was the change it forced in management style, away from "babysitting" or "headcounting" ("the visual school of management") to longer-range planning. On semiautonomous work teams, Stephen C. Iman, "The Development of Participation by Semiautonomous Work Teams: The Case of Donnelly Mirrors," in *The Quality of Working Life: Cases and Commentary*, L. E. Davis and A. B. Cherns, eds. (New York: Free Press, 1975), pp. 216–31.

16. Suresh Srivastva, et al., *Job Satisfaction and Productivity* (Cleveland: Department of Organizational Behavior, Case Western Reserve University, 1975), p. 52.

17. H. H. Carpenter, "Formal Organizational Structural Factors and Perceived Job Satisfaction of Classroom Teachers," *Administrative Science Quarterly*, 16 (1971): pp. 460–65. L. W. Porter and E. E. Lawler, III, found, in a survey of managers, that flat organizations seemed better for self-actualization, while tall met security needs, in "The Effects of 'Tall' Versus 'Flat' Organization Structures on Managerial Satisfaction," *Personnel Psychology*, 17 (1964): pp. 135–48. A laboratory experiment using 15-person organizations with either two or four levels concluded that the tall

organization was superior in decision-making performance, but the simulated organizations lacked many features common to real bureaucracies, such as status and reward differences and restriction of certain information to top levels, which could make tall organizations less efficient. See Rocco Carzo, Jr., and John N. Yanouzas, "Effects of Flat and Tall Organization Structure," *Administrative Science Quarterly*, 14 (1969): pp. 178–91.

18. Gene W. Dalton, Louis B. Barnes, and Abraham Zaleznik, *The Distribution of Authority in Formal Organizations* (Boston: Harvard Business School Division of Research, 1968); Walton, "Innovative Restructuring of Work."

19. Tannenbaum, et al., *Hierarchy in Organizations*.

20. Louis Davis and Eric Trist, important figures in the socio-technical school, argued that when supervisors are given more technical and professional responsibility, they won't supervise as closely. See "Improving the Quality of Work Life."

21. Jerald G. Bachman, Clagett G. Smith, and Jonathon A. Slesinger, "Control, Performance, and Satisfaction: An Analysis of Structural and Individual Effects," *Journal of Personality and Social Psychology*, 4 (1966): pp. 127–36.

22. Recent research has shown that number of subordinates is not necessarily related to closeness of supervision, a style I take as a sign of powerlessness. See Gerald D. Bell, "Determinants of Span of Control," *American Journal of Sociology*, 73 (July 1967): pp. 100–109.

23. Carl D. Jacobs, "Job Enrichment of Field Technical Representatives—Xerox Corporation," in *The Quality of Working Life: Cases and Commentary*, L. E. Davis and A. B. Cherns, eds. (New York: Free Press, 1975), pp. 285–99.

24. Derek W. E. Burden, "Participative Management as a Basis for Improved Quality of Jobs: The Case of Microwax Department, Shell U.K., Ltd.," in *The Quality of Working Life: Cases and Commentary*, L. E. Davis and A. B. Cherns, eds. (New York: Free Press, 1975), pp. 201–15.

25. Evidence about the need for employee sharing of management information is in Walton, "Innovative Restructuring of Work"; and Paul Bernstein, "Necessary Elements for Effective Worker Participation in Decision Making," *Journal of Economic Issues*, 10 (June 1976): pp. 490–522. The issue of valid information appears throughout Chris Argyris' work; for an application to the question of individual efficacy, see "The Incompleteness of Social Psychological Theory," *American Psychologist*, 24 (October 1969): pp. 893–918. The Selznick reference is to Philip Selznick, *Law, Society, and Industrial Justice* (New York: Russell Sage Foundation, 1969).

26. One top manager from General Electric, reflecting on his early days as a trainee, recalled the camaraderie of his training group and the lasting friendships made. It also turned out (not surprisingly) that that "fine bunch of people" all became high executives, and the esprit de corps was translated into advantageous peer alliances. See George W. Downing's report of his experiences in "The Changing Structure of a Great Corporation," in W. Lloyd Warner and Darab B. Unwalla, eds., *The Emergent American Society: Large Scale Organizations* (New Haven: Yale University Press, 1967), pp. 158–240.

27. Even progressive companies may become conservative in times of financial pressure. See William O. Lytle, Jr., " 'A Smart Camel May Refuse that Last Straw': A Case Study of Obstacles to Job and Organization Design in a New Manufacturing Operation," in *The Quality of Working Life: Cases and Commentary*, L. E. Davis and A. B. Cherns, eds. (New York: Free Press, 1975), pp. 110–37. The case is about Polaroid, well known for its advanced and humanistic personnel policies.

28. Raymond A. Katzell and Daniel Yankelovich, *Work, Productivity, and Job Satisfaction: An Evaluation of Policy-Related Research* (New York: The Psychological Corporation, 1975).

29. A vast amount of economic and sociological literature on the effects of organizational size is summarized in Barry A. Stein, *Size, Efficiency, and Community Enterprise* (Cambridge, Mass.: Center for Community Economic Development, 1974). See also E. F. Schumacher, *Small Is Beautiful* (New York: Harper Torchbooks, 1973); Bernard P. Indik, "Some Effects of Organization Size on Member Attitudes and Behavior," *Human Relations*, 16 (November 1963): pp. 369–84.

30. Stein, *Size, Efficiency, and Community Enterprise*.

Appendix I

1. Michel Crozier, *The Bureaucratic Phenomenon* (Chicago: University of Chicago Press, 1964), p. 150.

2. Rosabeth Moss Kanter, *Commitment and Community* (Cambridge, Mass.: Harvard University Press, 1972).

3. Melville Dalton, *Men Who Manage* (New York: Wiley, 1959), p. 280.

4. Crozier, *Bureaucratic Phenomenon*, p. 112.

5. C. Wright Mills, *The Sociological Imagination* (New York: Oxford University Press, 1959). See especially his essay "On Intellectual Craftmanship."

Appendix II

1. Elizabeth Aries, *Interaction Patterns and Themes in Male, Female, and Mixed Groups*, Unpublished Doctoral Dissertation, Harvard University, 1973.

2. Rose Laub Coser, "Laughter among Colleagues: a Study of the Social Functions of Humor among the Staff of a Mental Hospital," *Psychiatry*, 23 (1960): pp. 81–95.

3. Nancy Henley, "The Politics of Touch," in *Radical Psychology*, P. Brown, ed. (New York: Harper & Row, 1973).

4. "Men, Enjoy It!, Says 28-Year-Old Woman President," *The MBA Executive*, 3 (May 1973): p. 5.

BIBLIOGRAPHY

Abrams, Richard M. "Brandeis and the Ascendancy of Corporate Capitalism." Introduction to Torchbook edition of *Other People's Money, and How the Bankers Use It*, by Louis D. Brandeis. New York: Harper & Row, 1967.

Acker, Joan, and Van Houten, Donald R. "Differential Recruitment and Control: The Sex Structuring of Organizations." *Administrative Science Quarterly* 19 (1974): 152–163.

Adams, Sexton, and Fyffe, Don. *The Corporate Promotables*. Houston: Gulf Publishing, 1969.

Ainsworth, Leonard H. "Rigidity, Insecurity, and Stress." *Journal of Abnormal and Social Psychology* 56 (1958): 67–74.

Alderfer, Clayton P. "Job Enlargement and the Organizational Context." *Personnel Psychology* 22 (1969): 418–426.

Alutto, J. A.; Hrebiniak, L. G.; and Alonso, R. C. "On Operationalizing the Concept of Commitment." *Social Forces* 51 (1973): 448–454.

Ames, Azel. *Sex in Industry: A Plea for the Working Girl*. Boston: James R. Osgood, 1875.

Annual Report of the Council of Economic Advisers. Washington, D.C.: Government Printing Office, 1973, p. 106.

Argyle, M.; Gardner G.; and Cioffi, I. "Supervisory Methods Related to Productivity, Absenteeism, and Labor Turnover." *Human Relations* 11 (1958): 23–40.

Argyris, Chris. "The Incompleteness of Social Psychological Theory." *American Psychologist* 24 (1969): 893–906.

———. *Integrating the Individual and the Organization*. New York: Wiley, 1964.

———. *Personality and Organization*. New York: Harper and Brothers, 1957.

———. "Some Limits of Rational Man Organization Theory." *Public Administration Review*, May–June 1973, pp. 253–269.

Aries, Elizabeth. "Interaction Patterns and Themes of Male, Female, and Mixed Groups." Ph.D. dissertation, Harvard University, 1973.

Armstrong, Thomas P. "Job Content and Context Factors Related to Satisfaction for Different Occupational Levels." *Journal of Applied Psychology* 55 (1971): 57–65.

Asch, Solomon E. "Effects of Group Pressure on the Modification and Distortion of Judgment." In *Group Dynamics*, 2d ed., edited by D. Cartwright and A. Zander, pp. 189–200. Evanston, Ill.: Row Peterson, 1960.

Associated Press. " 'It's Like Being a Prisoner,' Says Trudeau's Wife." *Boston Globe*, October 28, 1974.

Athanassiades, John C. "An Investigation of Some Communication Patterns of Female Subordinates in Hierarchical Organizations." *Human Relations* 27 (1974): 195–209.

Bachman, Jerald G.; Smith, Clagett G.; and Slesinger, Jonathan A. "Control, Performance, and Satisfaction: An Analysis of Structural and Individual Effects." *Journal of Personality and Social Psychology* 4 (1966): 127–136.

Balzar, Richard. *Clockwork*. Garden City, N.Y.: Doubleday, 1976.

Barnard, Chester I. *The Functions of the Executive*. Cambridge, Mass.: Harvard University Press, 1938.

Bartol, Kathryn M. "The Effect of Male Versus Female Leaders on Follower Satisfaction and Performance." *Journal of Business Research* 3 (1975): 33–42.

———. "Male Versus Female Leaders: The Effect of Leader Need for Dominance on Follower Satisfaction." *Academy of Management Journal* 17 (1974): 225–233.

———, and D. Anthony Butterfield. "Sex Effects in Evaluating Leaders." Working Paper No. 74-10, University of Massachusetts School of Business Administration, 1974.

Becker, Howard S., and Strauss, Anselm L. "Careers, Personality, and Adult Socialization." *American Journal of Sociology* 62 (1956): 253–263.

Bell, Daniel. "The Breakup of Family Capitalism." In Daniel Bell, *The End of Ideology.* Rev. ed. New York: Collier, 1961.

Bell, Gerald D. "Determinants of Span of Control." *American Journal of Sociology* 73 (1967): 100–109.

Bender, Marylin. "Women Managers and Marriage." *New York Times,* September 26, 1971.

Bendix, Reinhard. *Max Weber: An Intellectual Portrait.* Garden City, N.Y.: Doubleday Anchor, 1960.

————. *Work and Authority in Industry: Ideologies of Management in the Course of Industrialization.* New York: Wiley, 1956. Reprint. New York: Harper Torchbooks, 1963.

Benet, Mary Kathleen. *The Secretarial Ghetto.* New York: McGraw-Hill, 1973.

Bennis, Warren, and Slater, Philip. *The Temporary Society.* New York: Harper & Row, 1968.

Berg, Ivar. *Education and Jobs: The Great Training Robbery.* Boston: Beacon, 1971.

Berkley, George E. *The Administrative Revolution.* Englewood Cliffs, N.J.: Prentice-Hall, 1971, p. 86.

Bernard, Jessie. *Women and the Public Interest.* Chicago: Aldine, 1971.

Bernstein, Paul. "Necessary Elements for Effective Worker Participation in Decision Making." *Journal of Economic Issues* 10 (1976): 490–522.

Biggane, James F., and Stewart, Paul A. "Job Enlargement: A Case Study." In *Design of Jobs,* edited by L. E. Davis and J. C. Taylor, pp. 264–276. Baltimore, Md.: Penguin, 1972.

Birnbaum, Norman. *The Crisis of Industrial Society.* New York: Oxford University Press, 1969.

Blau, Peter M. *The Dynamics of Bureaucracy.* Chicago: University of Chicago Press, 1955.

————. "The Hierarchy of Authority in Organizations." *American Journal of Sociology* 73 (1968): 453–467.

————, and Schoenherr, Richard A. *The Structure of Organizations.* New York: Basic Books, 1971.

————, and Scott, W. Richard. *Formal Organizations.* San Francisco: Chandler, 1962.

Blauner, Robert. *Alienation and Freedom.* Chicago: University of Chicago Press, 1964.

Blaxall, Martha, and Reagan, Barbara, eds. *Women and the Workplace: The Implications of Occupational Segregation.* Chicago: University of Chicago Press, 1976.

Bonjean, Charles M.; Grady, Bruce D.; and Williams, J. Allen, Jr. "Social Mobility and Job Satisfaction: A Replication and Extension." *Social Forces* 46 (1967): 492–501.

Boothe, Viva B. "Women in the Modern World." *Annals of the American Academy of Political and Social Science* 143 (1929). Reprint. New York: Arno, 1974.

Borgatta, Edgar. "Analysis of Social Interaction and Socio-metric Perception." *Sociometry* 17 (1954): 7–32.

Bottomore, T. B. "The Administrative Elite." *The New Sociology: Essays in Social Science and Social Theory in Honor of C. Wright Mills,* edited by I. L. Horowitz, pp. 357–369. New York: Oxford University Press, 1965.

Bowles, Samuel, and Gintis, Herbert. *Schooling in Capitalist America.* New York: Basic Books, 1976.

Bowman, G. W.; Worthy, N. B.; and Greyser, S. A. "Are Women Executives People?" *Harvard Business Review* 43 (July–August 1965): 14–30.

Brannen, Peter; Batstone, Eric; Fatchett, Derek; and White, Philip. *The Worker Directors: A Sociology of Participation.* London: Hutchinson, 1976.

Braverman, Harry. *Labor and Monopoly Capital.* New York: Monthly Review Press, 1974.

Brown, J. A. C. *The Social Psychology of Industry.* Baltimore, Md.: Penguin, 1954.

Brown, Roger, and Lenneberg, Eric. "Studies in Linguistic Relativity." In *Basic Studies in Social Psychology,* edited by H. Proshansky and B. Seidenberg, pp. 244–252. New York: Holt, Rinehart, 1965.

Bruner, Dick. "Why White Collar Workers Can't Be Organized." In *Man, Work and Society,* edited by S. Nosow and W. H. Form, pp. 188–197. New York: Basic Books, 1962.

Burden, Derek W. E. "Participative Management as a Basis for Improved Quality of Jobs: The Case of Microwax Department, Shell U.K., Ltd." In *The Quality of Working Life*, L. E. Davis and A. B. Cherns, pp. 201–15. (New York: Free Press, 1975)

Burger, Chester. *Survival in the Executive Jungle.* New York: Macmillan, 1964.

Burnham, James. *The Managerial Revolution.* New York: John Day, 1941.

Burns, Tom. "The Direction of Activity and Communication in a Departmental Executive Group." *Human Relations* 8 (1954): 73–97.

———. "The Reference of Conduct in Small Groups: Cliques and Cabals in Occupational Milieu." *Human Relations* 8 (1955): 467–486.

———, and Stalker, G. M. *The Management of Innovation.* London: Pergamon, 1961.

Bryan, E. James. "Work Improvement and Job Enrichment: The Case of Cummins Engine Company." In *The Quality of Working Life*, L. E. Davis and A. B. Cherns, pp. 315–29. (New York: Free Press, 1975)

Caplow, Theodore. *The Sociology of Work.* Minneapolis: University of Minnesota Press, 1954.

Carpenter, H. H. "Formal Organizational Structural Factors and Perceived Job Satisfaction of Classroom Teachers." *Administrative Science Quarterly* 16 (1971): 460–465.

Carzo, Rocco, Jr., and Yanouzas, John N. "Effects of Flat and Tall Organization Structure." *Administrative Science Quarterly* 14 (1969): 178–191.

Chandler, Alfred D. *Strategy and Structure: Chapters in the History of American Business Enterprise.* Cambridge, Mass.: MIT Press, 1962.

Chinoy, Eli. *Automobile Workers and the American Dream.* Garden City, N.Y.: Doubleday, 1955.

Chow, Esther, and Grusky, Oscar. "Worker Compliance and Supervisory Style: An Experimental Study of Female Superior-Subordinate Relationships." Paper presented to the American Sociological Association, New York, August 1973.

Christensen, Jean. "Mr. and Mrs. Kleer Pak, A Smooth Team." *New York Times*, November 11, 1973.

Cochran, Thomas C. *The American Business System: A Historical Perspective, 1900–1955.* Cambridge, Mass.: Harvard University Press, 1957.

———. *Basic History of American Business.* Princeton, N.J.: D. Van Nostrand, 1959.

———, and Miller, William. *The Age of Enterprise: A Social History of Industrial America.* Rev. Ed. New York: Harper Torchbooks, 1961.

Cohen, Allan R.; Fink, Stephen L.; Gadon, Herman; and Willitts, Robin D. *Effective Behavior in Organizations.* Homewood, Ill.: Dorsey Press, 1976.

Cohen, Arthur R. "Upward Communication in Experimentally Created Hierarchies." *Human Relations* 11 (1958): 41–53.

Cole, Dollie Ann. "New Style of Corporate Wife." *New York Times*, December 2, 1973.

Collins, Orvis. "Ethnic Behavior in Industry: Sponsorship and Rejection in a New England Factory." *American Journal of Sociology* 51 (1946): 293–298.

Corwin, Ronald; Taves, Marvin J.; and Haas, J. Eugene. "Social Requirements for Occupational Success: Internalized Norms and Friendship." *Social Forces* 39 (1961): 135–140.

Coser, Lewis A. *Greedy Organizations.* New York: Free Press, 1974.

Coser, Rose Laub. "Laughter Among Colleagues: A Study of the Social Functions of Humor Among the Staff of a Mental Hospital." *Psychiatry* 23 (1960): 81–95.

Costantine, Edmond, and Craik, Kenneth H. "Women as Politicians: The Social Background, Personality, and Political Careers of Female Party Leaders." *Journal of Social Issues* 28 (1972): 217–236.

Cowan, Paul. "Connecticut's Governor Grasso Remembers How She Made It." *New York Times*, May 4, 1975.

Coyle, Grace D. "Women in the Clerical Occupations." *Annals of the American Academy of Political and Social Science* 143 (1929): 180–187.

Crowley, Joan E.; Levitan, Teresa E.; and Quinn, Robert P. "Seven Deadly Half-Truths About Women." *Psychology Today* 7 (1973): 94–96.

Crozier, Michel. *The Bureaucratic Phenomenon.* Chicago: University of Chicago Press, 1964.

———. *The World of the Office Worker*. Translated by David Landau. Chicago: University of Chicago Press, 1971.

Cuber, John, and Harroff, Peggy. *The Significant Americans*, New York: Appleton, 1965.

Culbert, Samuel A., and Renshaw, Jean R. "Coping with the Stresses of Travel as an Opportunity for Improving the Quality of Work and Family Life." *Family Process* 11 (1972).

Cussler, Margaret. *The Woman Executive*. New York: Harcourt Brace, 1958.

Dalton, Gene W.; Barnes, Louis B.; and Zaleznik, Abraham. *The Distribution of Authority in Formal Organizations*. Cambridge, Mass.: MIT Press, 1973.

Dalton, Melville. "Conflicts Between Staff and Line Managerial Officers." *American Sociological Review* 21 (1950): 342–351.

———. *Men Who Manage*. New York: Wiley, 1959.

Davis, Keith. *Human Relations at Work*. New York: McGraw-Hill, 1967.

Davis, Louis E., and Cherns, Albert B., eds. *The Quality of Working Life*. New York: Free Press, 1975.

———, and Taylor, James C., eds. *Design of Jobs*. Baltimore, Md.: Penguin, 1972.

———, and Trist, Eric L. "Improving the Quality of Work Life: Sociotechnical Case Studies." In *Work and the Quality of Life*, edited by James O'Toole, pp. 246–280. Cambridge, Mass.: MIT Press, 1974.

Davis, Margery. "Woman's Place is at the Typewriter: The Feminization of the Clerical Labor Force." *Radical America* 8 (1974): 1–28.

Day, D. R., and Stogdill, R. M. "Leader Behavior of Male and Female Supervisors: A Comparative Study." *Personal Psychology* 25 (1972): 353–360.

Deaux, Kay, and Emswiller, Tom. "Explanations of Successful Performance on Sex-Linked Tasks: What is Skill for the Male is Luck for the Female." *Journal of Personality and Social Psychology* 29 (1974): 80–85.

Dill, William R. "Business Organizatons." In *Handbook of Organizations*, edited by J. G. March, pp. 1071–1114. Chicago: Rand McNally, 1965.

Doeringer, Peter B., and Piore, Michael J. *Internal Labor Markets and Manpower Analysis*. Lexington, Mass.: D. C. Heath, 1971.

Dore, Ronald. *British Factory-Japanese Factory: The Origins of National Diversity in Industrial Relations*. Berkeley: University of California Press, 1973.

Downing, George D. "The Changing Structure of a Great Corporation." In *The Emergent American Society: Large-Scale Organizations*, edited by W. Lloyd Warner and Darab B. Unwalla, pp. 158–240. New Haven: Yale University Press, 1967.

Downs, Anthony. *Inside Bureaucracy*. Boston: Little, Brown, 1966.

Drucker, Peter F. *Management: Tasks, Responsibilities, Practices*. New York: Harper & Row, 1974.

Dubin, Robert. "Business Behavior Behaviorally Viewed." In Robert Dubin, *Social Science Approaches to Business Behavior*. Homewood, Ill.: Irwin-Dorsey, 1962.

———. "Industrial Workers' Worlds." *Social Problems* 3 (1956): 131–142.

Elbing, Alvar O.; Gadon, Herman; and Gordon, John R. "Flexible Working Hours: It's About Time." *Harvard Business Review* 52 (January–February 1974): 18–33ff.

Epstein, Cynthia. *Woman's Place*. Berkeley: University of California Press, 1970.

Etzioni, Amatai. *A Comparative Analysis of Complex Organizations*. New York: Free Press, 1961.

Fanon, Franz. *The Wretched of the Earth*. New York: Grove Press, 1965.

Fenchel, G. H.; Monderer, J. H.; and Hartley, E. L. "Subjective Status and the Equilibrium Hypothesis." *Journal of Abnormal and Social Psychology* 45 (1951): 476–479.

Ferber, Marianne Abeles, and Huber, Joan Althaus. "Sex of Student and Instructor: A Study of Student Bias." *American Journal of Sociology* 80 (1975): 949–963.

Fielder, Fred W. "Personality and Situational Determinants of Leadership Effectiveness." In *Group Dynamics*, edited by D. Cartwright and A Zander, pp. 362–380. New York: Harper & Row, 1968.

Fogarty, Michael; Allen, A. I.; Allen, Isobel; and Walters, Patricia. *Women in Top Jobs: Four Studies in Achievement.* London: George Allen and Unwin, 1971.

Follett, Mary Parker. *Dynamic Administration.* London: Pitman, 1941.

Ford, Robert N. "Job Enrichment Lessons from AT&T." *Harvard Business Review* 51 (January–February 1973): 96–106.

———. *Motivation Through the Work Itself.* New York: American Management Association, 1969.

Form, William H. "Auto Workers and Their Machines: A Study of Work, Factory, and Job Satisfaction in Four Countries." *Social Forces* 52 (1973): 1–16.

———, and Geschwender, James A. "Social Reference Basis of Job Satisfaction: The Case of Manual Workers." *American Sociological Review* 27 (1962): 228–237.

Frank, Linda L., and Hackman, J. Richard. "A Failure of Job Enrichment: The Case of the Change that Wasn't." *Technical Report No. 8.* Department of Administrative Sciences, Yale University, 1975.

French, David, and French, Elena. *Working Communally.* New York: Russell Sage Foundation, 1974.

French, John R. P., Jr., and Raven, Bertram H. "The Bases of Social Power." In *Studies in Social Power,* edited by D. Cartwright, pp. 150–167. Ann Arbor, Mich.: Institute for Social Research, 1959.

Frupp, Bill. "Transfers and the Executive Rebellion." *Boston Globe,* November 13, 1975.

Fuller, Ann L. "Liberating the Administrator's Wife." In *Women in Higher Education,* edited by W. T. Furniss and P. A. Graham, pp. 145–152. Washington, D.C.: American Council on Education, 1974.

Gamson, William A. *Power and Discontent.* Homewood, Ill.: Dorsey, 1968.

Gardner, Burleigh B. *Human Relations in Industry.* Chicago: Richard D. Irwin, 1945.

Garraty, John A. *The New Commonwealth, 1877–1890.* New York: Harper & Row, 1968.

Garson, Barbara. "Women's Work." *Working Papers for a New Society* 1 (1973): 5–14.

Gerth, Hans, and Mills, C. Wright, eds. *From Max Weber: Essays in Sociology.* New York: Oxford University Press, 1958.

Ginzberg, Eli, and Yohalem, Alice M., eds. *Corporate Lib: Women's Challenge to Management.* Baltimore, Md.: Johns Hopkins University Press, 1973.

Glazer, Nathan. *Affirmative Discrimination.* New York: Basic Books, 1976.

Goldman, Nancy. "The Changing Role of Women in the Armed Forces." *American Journal of Sociology* 78 (1973): 892–911.

Golembiewski, Robert T.; Hilles, Rick; and Kagno, Munro S. "A Longitudinal Study of Flexi-Time Effects: Some Consequences of an OD Structural Intervention." *Journal of Applied Behavioral Science* 10 (1974): 503–532.

Goodman, Ellen. "How Personal Can You Get?" *Boston Globe,* March 25, 1975.

Goodstadt, B., and Hjelle, L. "Power to the Powerless: Locus of Control and the Use of Power." *Journal of Personality and Social Psychology* 27 (1973): 190–196.

———, and Kipnis, D. "Situational Influences on the Use of Power." *Journal of Applied Psychology* 54 (1970): 201–207.

Gouldner, Alvin. "Organizational Analysis." In *Sociology Today: Problems and Prospects,* edited by R. K. Merton, L. Broom, and L. S. Cottrell, Jr., pp. 400–428. New York: Basic Books, 1959.

Graham, Ellen. "Many Seminars Are Held to Aid Women in Firms." *Wall Street Journal,* April 26, 1973.

Greenbaum, Marcia. "Adding 'Kenntnis' to 'Kirche, Kuche, and Kinder.' " *Issues in Industrial Society* 2 (1971): 61–68.

Grinker, William J.; Cooke, Donald D.; and Kirsch, Arthur W. *Climbing the Job Ladder: A Study of Employee Advancement in Eleven Industries.* New York: E. F. Shelley and Co., 1970.

Grusky, Oscar. "Career Mobility and Organizational Commitment." *Administrative Science Quarterly* 10 (1966): 489–502.

———. *The New Military*. New York: Russell Sage Foundation, 1964.

Guest, Robert. "Work Careers and Aspiration of Automobile Workers." *American Sociological Review* 19 (1954): 155–163.

Gumpert, David. "Women's Liberation Has All But Bypassed the Katy Gibbs Chain." *Wall Street Journal*, March 15, 1974.

Guttentag, Marcia. *Too Many Women*. New York: Basic Books. In press.

Hackman, J. Richard. "The Coming Demise of Job Enrichment." *Technical Report No. 9*. Department of Administrative Sciences, Yale University, 1974.

———, and Lawler, Edward E., III. "Employee Reactions to Job Characteristics." *Journal of Applied Psychology* 55 (1971): 259–286.

Halter, Marilyn; Schneider, Eric; and Weiner, Lynn. "Report from the 'Enormous File': A Case Study of Office Work." Xeroxed. Boston University Department of History, 1973.

Hamill, Katharine. "Women as Bosses." *Fortune*, June 1956, pp. 105–108.

Hampden-Turner, Charles. "The Factory as an Oppressive Environment." In *Workers' Control: A Reader on Labor and Social Change*, edited by G. Hunnius, G. D. Garson, and J. Case, pp. 30–44. New York: Vintage, 1973.

Hays, Samuel P. *The Response to Industrialism, 1855–1914*. Chicago: University of Chicago Press, 1957.

Hedges, Janice N. "Women Workers and Manpower Demands in the 1970's." *Monthly Labor Review* 93 (1970): 19–29.

Henderson, C. R. "Business Men and Social Theorists." *American Journal of Sociology* 1 (1896): 385–386.

Hendrick, Burton, J. *The Age of Big Business: A Chronicle of the Captains of Industry*. New Haven: Yale University Press, 1921.

Henley, Nancy. "The Politics of Touch." In *Radical Psychology*, edited by P. Brown. New York: Harper & Row, 1973.

Hennig, Margaret. "Career Development of Women Executives." Ph.D. dissertation, Harvard Business School, 1970.

Henry, William E. "Executive Personality." In *The Emergent American Society: Large-Scale Organizations*, edited by W. Lloyd Warner and Darab B. Unwalla, pp. 241–275. New Haven: Yale University Press, 1967.

Hetzler, Stanley A. "Variations in Role-Playing Patterns Among Different Echelons of Bureaucratic Leaders." *American Sociological Review* 20 (1955): 700–706.

Heydebrand, Wolfe V., ed. *Comparative Organizations: The Results of Empirical Research*. Englewood Cliffs, N.J.: Prentice-Hall, 1973.

Hickson, David J.; Hinings, C. R.; Lee, C. A.; Schneck, R. E.; and Pennings, J. M. "A Strategic Contingencies Theory of Intraorganizational Power." *Administrative Science Quarterly* 16 (1971): 216–229.

"The Hidden Proletariat." *Society* 11 (1975): 12–14.

Hill, Joseph A. *Women in Gainful Occupations 1870–1920*. Census Monographs IX. Washington, D. C.: Government Printing Office, 1929. Reprint. New York: Johnson Reprint Corp., 1972.

Hinings, C. R.; Hickson, D. J.; Pennings, J. M.; and Schneck, R. E. "Structural Conditions of Intraorganizational Power." *Administrative Science Quarterly* 19 (1974): 22–44.

Hinton, William. *Fanshen: A Documentary of Revolution in a Chinese Village*. New York: Monthly Review Press and Vintage Books, 1966.

Historical Statistics of the United States: Colonial Times to 1957. Washington, D.C.: Government Printing Office, 1960.

Homall, G. "The Motivation to be Promoted among Non-Exempt Employees: An Expectancy Theory Approach." Master's thesis, Cornell University, 1974.

Homans, George C. "The Western Electric Researches." In *Readings on Modern Organizations*, edited by Amitai Etzioni, pp. 99–114. Englewood Cliffs, N.J.: Prentice-Hall, 1969.

Hoos, Ida Rosakoff. "When the Computer Takes Over the Office." In *Man, Work and Society*, edited by S. Nosow and W. H. Form, pp. 72–82. New York: Basic Books, 1962.

Horney, Karen. *The Neurotic Personality of Our Time.* New York: Norton, 1937.

Hostetler, John. *Hutterite Society.* Baltimore, Md.: Johns Hopkins University Press, 1975.

House, James S. "The Effects of Occupational Stress on Physical Health." In *Work and the Quality of Life,* edited by James O'Toole, pp. 145–170. Cambridge, Mass.: MIT Press, 1974.

Hughes, Everett. "Dilemmas and Contradictions of Status." *American Journal of Sociology* 50 (1944): 353–359.

———. *Men and Their Work.* Glencoe, Ill.: Free Press, 1958.

———. "Race Relations in Industry." In *Industry and Society,* edited by W. F. Whyte, p. 115. New York: McGraw-Hill, 1946.

Hurwitz, Jacob I.; Zander, Alvin F.; and Hymovitch, Bernard. "Some Effects of Power on the Relations Among Group Members." In *Group Dynamics,* edited by D. Cartwright and A. Zander, pp. 291–297. New York: Harper & Row, 1968.

Iman, Stephen C. "The Development of Participation by Semiautonomous Women Teams: The Case of Donnelly Mirrors." In *The Quality of Working Life,* edited by L. E. Davis and A. B. Cherns, pp. 216–31. New York: Free Press, 1975.

Indik, Bernard P. "Some Effects of Organization Size on Member Attitudes and Behavior." *Human Relations* 16 (1963): 369–384.

Jackson, Elton F. "Status Consistency and Symptoms of Stress." *American Sociological Review* 27 (1962): 469–480.

Jacobs, Carl D. "Job Enrichment of Field Technical Representatives—Xerox Corporation." In *The Quality of Working Life,* edited by L. E. Davis and A. B. Cherns, pp. 285–99. New York: Free Press, 1975.

Janeway, Elizabeth. "The Weak are the Second Sex." *Atlantic Monthly,* December 1973. Reprinted in Elizabeth Janeway, *Between Myth and Morning.* New York: William Morrow, 1974.

Janowitz, Morris. "Changing Patterns of Organizational Authority: The Military Establishment." *Administrative Science Quarterly* 3 (1959): 473–493.

Jencks, Christopher, et al. *Inequality: A Reassessment of the Effects of Family and Schooling in America.* New York: Basic Books, 1972.

Johnston, Ruth. "Pay and Job Satisfaction: A Survey of Some Research Findings." *International Labour Review* 3 (1975): 441–449.

Jourard, Sidney M. *The Transparent Self: Self-Disclosure and Well-Being.* Princeton, N.J.: D. Van Nostrand, 1964.

Kahn, Robert L. "The Work Module: A Proposal for the Humanization of Work." In *Work and the Quality of Life,* edited by James O'Toole, pp. 199–226. Cambridge, Mass.: MIT Press, 1974.

———; Gurin, G. R.; Baar, E.; and Kraut, A. I. *Discrimination Without Prejudice: A Study of Promotion Practices in Industry.* Ann Arbor, Mich.: Institute for Social Research, 1964.

Kahne, Hilda, with Kohen, Andrew I. "Economic Perspectives on the Role of Women in the American Economy." *Journal of Economic Literature* 13 (1975): 1249–1292.

Kanter, Rosabeth Moss. *Commitment and Community.* Cambridge, Mass.: Harvard University Press, 1972.

———. "The Impact of Hierarchical Structures on the Work Behavior of Women and Men." *Social Problems* 23 (1976): 415–430.

———. "Interpreting the Results of a Social Experiment." *Science,* May 14, 1976, pp. 662–663.

———. "The Policy Issues: Comment VI." *Signs: Journal of Women in Culture and Society* 2 (1976): 282–291.

———. "Some Effects of Proportions in Group Life: Skewed Sex Ratios and Responses to Token Women." *American Journal of Sociology* 82 (1977): 965–990.

———. *Work and Family in the United States.* New York: Russell Sage Foundation, 1976.

Kasl, Stanislav V. "Work and Mental Health." In *Work and the Quality of Life,* edited by James O'Toole, pp. 171–196. Cambridge, Mass.: MIT Press, 1974.

Katz, Daniel, and Kahn, Robert L. *The Social Psychology of Organizations.* New York: Wiley, 1966.

Katzell, Raymond A., and Yankelovich, Daniel. *Work, Productivity, and Job Satisfaction.* New York: Psychological Corporation, 1975.

Kaufman, Carl B. *Man Incorporate: The Individual and His Work in an Organized Society.* Rev. ed. Garden City, N.Y.: Doubleday Anchor, 1969.

Kay, Emanuel. "Middle Management." In *Work and the Quality of Life,* edited by James O'Toole, pp. 106–130. Cambridge, Mass.: MIT Press, 1974.

Keene, Evelyn. "Cruising on a Collision Course: Policemen's Wives Vs. Policewomen." *Boston Globe,* November 2, 1974.

Keller, Morton. *The Life Insurance Enterprise, 1885–1910.* Cambridge, Mass.: Harvard University Press, 1963.

Kelley, Harold H. "The Warm-Cold Variable in First Impressions of Persons." *Journal of Personality* 18 (1950): 431–439.

Kennedy, J. E., and O'Neill, H. E. "Job Content and Workers' Opinions." *Journal of Applied Psychology* 48 (1962): 372–375.

Kerr, Clark; Dunlop, John T.; Harbison, Frederick H.; and Myers, Charles A. *Industrialism and Industrial Man.* Cambridge, Mass.: Harvard University Press, 1960.

Kirkpatrick, Jeane. *Political Woman.* New York: Basic Books, 1974.

Kohn, Melvin L. "Occupational Structure and Alienation." *American Journal of Sociology* 82 (1976): 111–130.

Korda, Michael. *Male Chauvinism! How It Works.* New York: Random House, 1973.

Laird, Donald A., with Laird, Eleanor C. *The Psychology of Supervising the Working Woman.* New York: McGraw-Hill, 1942.

Lake, Alice. "I Hate My Husband's Success." *McCall's,* July 1958.

Langer, Elinor. "Inside the New York Telephone Company." In *Women at Work,* edited by W. L. O'Neill, pp. 307–360. Chicago: Quadrangle, 1972.

Laws, Judith Long. "The Psychology of Tokenism: An Analysis." *Sex Roles* 1 (1975): 51–67.

———. "Work Aspirations in Women: False Leads and New Starts." *Signs: A Journal of Women in Culture and Society* 2 (1976): 33–50.

Lenski, Gerhard. "Social Participation and the Crystallization of Status." *American Sociological Review* 21 (1956): 458–464.

———. "Status Crystallization: A Non-Vertical Dimension of Status." *American Sociological Review* 19 (1954): 405–413.

Levenson, Bernard. "Bureaucratic Succession." In *Complex Organizations: A Sociological Reader,* edited by Amitai Etzioni, pp. 362–375. New York: Holt, Rinehart, 1961.

Levine, Adeline, and Crumrine, Janice. "Women and the Fear of Success: A Problem in Replication." *American Journal of Sociology* 80 (1975): 967–974.

Levinson, Harry. *Emotional Problems in the World of Work.* New York: Harper & Row, 1964.

———; Price, Charlton R.; Munden, Kenneth J.; Mandl, Harold J.; and Solley, Charles M. *Men, Management and Mental Health.* Cambridge, Mass.: Harvard University Press, 1962.

Lieberson, Stanley, and O'Connor, John F. "Leadership and Organizational Performance: A Study of Large Corporations." *American Sociological Review* 37 (1972): 117–130.

Lifton, Robert Jay. *The Life of the Self: Toward a New Psychology.* New York: Simon and Schuster, 1976.

Likert, Rensis. *New Patterns of Management.* New York: McGraw-Hill, 1961.

Lippit, R.; Polansky, N.; and Rosen, S. "The Dynamics of Power." *Human Relations* 5 (1952): 44–50.

Lipset, Seymour Martin, and Bendix, Reinhard. *Social Mobility in Industrial Society.* Berkeley: University of California Press, 1962.

Lirtzman, Sidney I., and Wahba, Mahmoud A. "Determinants of Coalition Behavior of Men and Women: Sex Role or Situational Requirements?" *Journal of Applied Psychology* 56 (1972): 406–411.

Litterer, Joseph A. "Systematic Management: Design for Organizational Recoupling in American Manufacturing Firms." *Business History Review* 37 (1963): 369–391.

Lockwood, David. *The Blackcoated Worker: A Study in Class Consciousness*. London: Unwin University Books, 1958.

Lopata, Helena Z. *Occupation: Housewife*. New York: Oxford University Press, 1971.

Lorber, Judith. "Trust, Loyalty, and the Place of Women in the Informal Organization of Work." Paper presented to the American Sociological Association, 1975.

Lynch, Edith, M. *Executive Suite: Feminine Style*. New York: AMACOM, 1973.

Lytle, William O., Jr. " 'A Smart Camel May Refuse that Last Straw': A Case Study of Obstacles to Job and Organization Design in a New Manufacturing Organization." In *The Quality of Working Life*, edited by L. E. Davis and A. B. Cherns, pp. 110–137. New York: Free Press, 1975.

Maccoby, Eleanor Emmons, and Jacklin, Carol Nagy. *The Psychology of Sex Differences*. Stanford, Calif.: Stanford University Press, 1974.

MacPherson, Myra. *The Power Lovers: An Intimate Look at Politicians and Their Families*. New York: Putnam, 1975.

Mann, Floyd C., and Williams Lawrence K. "Some Effects of the Changing Work Environment in the Office." *Journal of Social Issues* 18 (1962): 90–101.

Mann, Richard D. "A Review of the Relationships Between Personality and Performance in Small Groups." *Psychological Bulletin* 56 (1959): 241–270.

Manson, Grace E. "Occupational Interests and Personality Requirements of Women in Business and the Professions." *Michigan Business Studies* 3 (1931).

March, James G., ed. *Handbook of Organizations*. Chicago: Rand McNally, 1965.

———, and Simon, Herbert A. *Organizations*. New York: Wiley, 1958.

Marchak, Patricia. "Women Workers and White Collar Unions." *Canadian Review of Sociology and Anthropology* 10 (1973): 134–147.

Marcus, Philip M., and House, James S. "Exchange Between Superiors and Subordinates in Large Organizations." *Administrative Science Quarterly* 18 (1973): 209–222.

Marcuse, Herbert. *One-Dimensional Man*. Boston: Beacon Press, 1964.

Marglin, Stephen A. "What Do Bosses Do? The Origins and Functions of Hierarchy in Capitalist Production." *Review of Radical Political Economics* 6 (1974): 33–60.

Martin, Virginia H. *Hours of Work When Workers Can Choose: The Experience of 59 Organizations with Employee Chosen Staggered Hours and Flextime*. Washington, D.C.: Business and Professional Women's Foundation, 1975.

Marx, Karl. "Toward the Critique of Hegel's Philosophy of Right." In *Marx and Engels: Basic Writings on Politics and Philosophy*, edited by Lewis S. Feuer, pp. 262–267. Garden City, N.Y.: Doubleday Anchor, 1959.

May, Rollo. *Power and Innocence*. New York: Norton, 1972.

Mayer, Kurt B., and Goldstein, Sidney. "Manual Workers as Small Businessmen." In *Blue Collar World*, edited by A. Shostak and W. Gomberg, pp. 537–550. Englewood Cliffs, N.J.: Prentice-Hall, 1964.

Mayo, Elton. *The Human Problems of an Industrial Civilization*. New York: Macmillan, 1933.

Meadows, Paul. "Industrial Man: Another Look at a Familiar Figure." In *The New Sociology: Essays in Social Science and Social Theory in Honor of C. Wright Mills*, edited by I. L. Horowitz, pp. 444–463. New York: Oxford University Press, 1965.

Mechanic, David. "Sources of Power of Lower Participants in Complex Organizations." *Administrative Science Quarterly* 7 (1962): 349–364.

Megaree, Edwin I. "Influence of Sex Roles on the Manifestation of Leadership." *Journal of Applied Psychology* 53 (1969): 377–382.

"Men, Enjoy It! Says 28-Year-Old Woman President." *The MBA Executive* 3 (1973): 5.

Merton, Robert K. "Bureaucratic Structure and Personality." In *Complex Organizations: A Sociological Reader*, edited by A. Etzioni, pp. 47–59. New York: Holt, Rinehart, 1961.

———. *Social Theory and Social Structure*. New York: Free Press, 1968.

Miller, S. M., and Riessman, Frank. "The Working Class Subculture: A New View." *Social Problems* 9 (1961): 86–97.

Miller, William. *Men in Business*. New York: Harper & Row, 1962.

Mills, C. Wright. "The American Business Elite: A Collective Portrait." In *Power, Politics, and People*, edited by I. L. Horowitz, pp. 110–139. New York: Ballantine, 1963.

———. *The Sociological Imagination*. New York: Oxford University Press, 1959.

———. *White Collar*. New York: Oxford University Press, 1951.

Mintzberg, Henry. *The Nature of Managerial Work*. New York: Harper & Row, 1973.

Moore, Wilbert. *The Conduct of the Corporation*. New York: Random House Vintage, 1962.

Morse, Nancy. *Satisfaction in the White Collar Job*. Ann Arbor, Mich.: Survey Research Center, 1953.

———, and Weiss, Robert S. "The Function and Meaning of Work and the Job." *American Sociological Review* 20 (1955): 191–198.

Mulder, Mauk. "Power Equalization Through Participation?" *Administrative Science Quarterly* 16 (1971): 31–40.

National Manpower Council. *Womanpower*. New York: Columbia University Press, 1957.

Orth, Charles D., III, and Jacobs, Frederic. "Women in Management: Pattern for Change." *Harvard Business Review* 49 (July–August 1971): 139–147.

Orzack, Louis H. "Work as a 'Central Life Interest' of Professionals." *Social Problems* 7 (1959).

Packard, Vance. *The Pyramid Climbers*. New York: McGraw-Hill, 1962.

Palmer, A. W., and Beishon, R. J. "How the Day Goes." *Personnel Management* 2 (1970): 36–38.

Papanek, Hanna. "Men, Women, and Work: Reflections on the Two-Person Career." *American Journal of Sociology* 78 (1973): 852–872.

Parsons, H. M. "What Happened at Hawthorne?" *Science* 183 (1974): 922–932.

Patchen, Martin. *Participation, Achievement, and Involvement on the Job*. Englewood Cliffs, N.J.: Prentice-Hall, 1970.

Patz, Alan L. "Performance Appraisal: Useful but Still Resisted." *Harvard Business Review* 53 (May–June 1975): 74–80.

Pearlin, Leonard I. "Alienation from Work: A Study of Nursing Personnel." *American Sociological Review* 27 (1962): 314–326.

Pelz, Donald C. "Influence: A Key to Effective Leadership in the First-Line Supervisor." *Personnel* 29 (1952): 3–11.

Pennings, J. M. "Work-Value Systems of White Collar Workers." *Administrative Science Quarterly* 15 (1970): 397–405.

"Performance Appraisal Series." Reprints from *Harvard Business Review*, No. 21143.

Perrow, Charles. "The Analysis of Goals in Complex Organizations." *American Sociological Review* 26 (1961): 854–866.

———. "Hospitals: Technology, Structures, and Goals." In *Handbook of Organizations*, edited by J. G. March, pp. 910–971. Chicago: Rand McNally, 1965.

Phelps, E. S. "The Statistical Theory of Racism and Sexism." *American Economic Review* 62 (1972): 659–661.

Pheterson, Gail I.; Kiesler, Sara B.; and Goldberg, Philip A. "Evaluation of the Performance of Women as a Function of Their Sex, Achievement, and Personal History." *Journal of Personality and Social Psychology* 19 (1971): 114–118.

Piore, Michael J. "Upward Mobility, Job Monotony, and Labor Market Structure." In *Work and the Quality of Life*, edited by James O'Toole, pp. 73–86. Cambridge, Mass.: MIT Press, 1974.

Pollard, Sidney. *The Genesis of Modern Management: A Study of the Industrial Revolution in Great Britain*. Cambridge, Mass.: Harvard University Press, 1965.

Porter, L. W., and Lawler, E. E., III. "The Effects of 'Tall' Versus 'Flat' Organization Structures on Managerial Satisfaction." *Personnel Psychology* 17 (1964): 135–148.

Presthus, Robert. *The Organizational Society*, New York: Knopf, 1962.

Purcell, Theodore V. *Blue Collar Man: Patterns of Dual Allegiance in Industry*. Cambridge, Mass.: Harvard University Press, 1960.

Quinn, R. P.; Kahn, R. L.; Tabor, J. M.; and Gordon, L. K. *The Chosen Few: A Study of Discrimination in Executive Selection.* Ann Arbor, Mich.: Survey Research Center, 1968.

Reitan, Harold T., and Shaw, Marvin E. "Group Membership, Sex-Composition of the Group, and Conformity Behavior." *Journal of Social Psychology* 64 (1964): 45–51.

"The Relentless Ordeal of Political Wives." *Time,* October 7, 1974, pp. 15–22.

Reynolds, Sidney. "Women on the Line." *MBA* 9 (1975): 27–30.

Rieff, Philip, ed. *Freud: Sexuality and the Psychology of Love.* New York: Collier, 1963.

Roberts, W. R. "Executives, Wives, and Trouble." *Dun's Review,* January 1965.

Roe, Anne. "Womanpower: How is it Different?" In *Human Resources and Economic Welfare: Essays in Honor of Eli Ginzberg,* edited by Ivar Berg, pp. 198–228. New York: Columbia University Press, 1972.

Roetheisberger, F. J., and Dickson, William J. *Management and the Worker.* Cambridge, Mass.: Harvard University Press, 1939.

Rosen, Benson, and Jerdee, Thomas H. "The Influence of Sex-Role Stereotypes on Evaluations of Male and Female Supervisory Behavior." *Journal of Applied Psychology* 57 (1973): 44–48.

——. "Sex Stereotyping in the Executive Suite." *Harvard Business Review* 52 (March–April 1974): 45–58.

Rosenbaum, James. "The Stratification of Socialization Processes." *American Sociological Review* 40 (1975): 48–54.

Rosner, Menachem. "Direct Democracy in the Kibbutz." In *Communes: Creating and Managing the Collective Life,* edited by R. M. Kanter, pp. 178–191. New York: Harper & Row, 1973.

Rottenberg, Dan. "The Moneyweight Champion." *New York Times Magazine,* February 22, 1976.

Roussell, Cecile. "Relationship of Sex of Department Head to Department Climate." *Administrative Science Quarterly* 19 (1974): 211–220.

Roy, Donald. "Quota Restriction and Goldbricking in a Machine Shop." *American Journal of Sociology* 57 (1952): 427–442.

Ruml, Beardsley, "Corporate Management as a Locus of Power." *Social Meaning of Legal Concepts,* no. 3. New York University School of Law, 1950.

Rush, Harold M. F. *Organization Development: A Reconnaissance.* New York: Conference Board, 1973.

Ryan, William. *Blaming the Victim.* New York: Random House, 1971.

Sales, Stephen M. "Organizational Roles as a Risk Factor in Coronary Heart Disease." *Administrative Science Quarterly* 14 (1969): 235–336.

Sarason, Seymour. "Jewishness, Blackness, and the Nature-Nurture Controversy." *American Psychologist* 28 (1973): 962–971.

Sayles, Leonard R. *Managerial Behavior.* New York: McGraw-Hill, 1964.

Schmuck, Richard. *Strategies of Dominance and Social Power: Proccedings of a Symposium.* Ann Arbor: University of Michigan Department of Psychology, 1965.

Schoonover, Jean Way. "Why American Men Fear Women Executives." *Boston Globe,* March 27, 1974.

Schumacher, E. F. *Small Is Beautiful.* New York: Harper Torchbooks, 1973.

Segal, Bernard E. "Male Nurses: A Study in Status Contradiction and Prestige Loss." *Social Forces* 41 (1962): 31–38.

Seidenberg, Robert. *Corporate Wives—Corporate Casualties?* New York: AMACOM, 1973.

Seidman, Joel, et al. *The Worker Views His Union.* Chicago: University of Chicago Press, 1958.

Selznick, Philip. "Critical Decisions in Organization Development." In *Complex Organizations,* edited by A. Etzioni, pp. 355–362. New York: Holt, Rinehart, 1961.

——. *Law, Society, and Industrial Justice.* New York: Russell Sage Foundation, 1969.

——. *TVA and the Grass Roots: A Study in the Sociology of Formal Organization.* Berkeley: University of California Press, 1949.

Shepard, Jon. *Automation and Alienation: A Study of Office and Factory Workers.* Cambridge, Mass.: MIT Press, 1971.

Sikula, Andrew F. "The Uniqueness of Secretaries as Employees." *Journal of Business Education* 48 (1973): 203–205.

Smith, Judith. "The 'New Woman' Knows How to Type: Some Connections Between Sexual Ideology and Clerical Work, 1900–1930." Paper presented to Berkshire Conference of Women Historians, American Civilization Department, Brown University, 1974.

Smuts, Robert W. *Women and Work in America.* New York: Columbia University Press, 1951.

Sofer, Cyril. *Organizations in Theory and Practice.* New York: Basic Books, 1972.

Srivastva, Suresh, et al. *Job Satisfaction and Productivity.* Cleveland: Department of Organization Behavior, Case Western Reserve University, 1975.

Stein, Barry A. "Getting There: Patterns in Managerial Success." Working Paper, Center for Research on Women, Wellesley College, 1976. Xeroxed. Available through Center for Social and Evaluation Research, University of Massachusetts, Boston.

————. *Size, Efficiency, and Community Enterprise.* Cambridge, Mass.: Center for Community Economic Development, 1974.

————; Cohen, Allan; and Gadon, Herman. "Flextime: Work When You Want To." *Psychology Today* 10 (June 1976): 40–43, 80.

Stone, Katherine. "The Origins of Job Structures in the Steel Industry." *Review of Radical Political Economics* 6 (1974): 61–97.

Stone, R. C. "Mobility Factors as They Affect Workers' Attitudes and Conduct Toward Incentive Systems." *American Sociological Review* 7 (1952): 58–64.

————, and Mann, Richard D. "Sex Role Differentiation in Jury Deliberations." *Sociometry* 19 (1956): 3–11.

Strodtbeck, Fred L.; James, Rita M.; and Hawkins, Charles. "Social Status in Jury Deliberations." *American Sociological Review* 22 (1957): 713–719.

Strong, Bryan. "Toward a History of the Experiential Family: Sex and Incest in the Nineteenth Century Family." *Journal of Marriage and the Family* 35 (1973): 457–466.

Sutton, Francis X., et al. *The American Business Creed.* Cambridge, Mass.: Harvard University Press, 1956.

Swerdloff, Sol. *The Revised Workweek: Results of a Pilot Study of 16 Firms.* Bulletin 1846, Bureau of Labor Statistics. Washington, D.C.: Department of Labor, 1975.

Tannenbaum, Arnold S. *Social Psychology of the Work Organization.* Belmont, Calif.: Wadsworth, 1966.

————; Kavcic, Bogdan; Rosner, Menachem; Vianello, Miro; and Wieser, George. *Hierarchy in Organizations: An International Comparison.* San Francisco: Jossey-Bass, 1974.

Tausky, Curt. *Work Organizations: Major Theoretical Perspectives.* Itasca, Ill.: Peacock, 1970.

Taylor, Frederick W. *Scientific Management.* New York: Harper & Row, 1947.

Taylor, Shelley, and Fiske, Susan T. "The Token in a Small Group: Research Findings and Theoretical Implications." In *Psychology and Politics, Collected Papers,* edited by J. Sweeney. New Haven: Yale University Press, 1976.

Terkel, Studs. *Working.* New York: Pantheon, 1974.

Terry, George, R. *Office Organization and Motivation.* Homewood, Ill.: Dow Jones-Irwin, 1966.

Theodore, Athena, ed. *The Professional Woman.* Cambridge, Mass.: Schenkman, 1971.

Thibaut, John W., and Riecken, Henry W. "Authoritarianism, Status, and the Communication of Aggression." *Human Relations* 8 (1955): 95–120.

Thompson, James D. *Organizations in Action.* New York: McGraw-Hill, 1967.

Tichy, Noel. "An Analysis of Clique Formation and Structure in Organizations." *Administrative Science Quarterly* 18 (1973): 194–207.

Tiger, Lionel. *Men in Groups.* New York: Random House, 1969.

————, and Shepher, Joseph. *Women in the Kibbutz.* New York: Harcourt Brace Jovanovich, 1975.

Tillett, Anthony; Kempner, Thomas; and Wills, Gordon, eds. *Management Thinkers.* Baltimore, Md.: Penguin, 1970.

Townsend, Robert. *Up the Organization.* New York: Knopf, 1970.

Tracy, Lane. "Postscript to the Peter Principle." *Harvard Business Review* 50 (July–August 1972): 65–71.

Tresemer, David. "Assumptions Made About Gender Roles." In *Another Voice: Feminist Perspectives on Social Life and Social Science,* edited by Marcia Millman and Rosabeth Moss Kanter, pp. 308–339. Garden City, N.Y.: Doubleday Anchor, 1975.

Turner, Arthur N., and Lawrence, Paul R. *Industrial Jobs and the Worker.* Boston: Harvard University Graduate School of Business Administration, 1965.

Turner, Ralph, H. "Sponsored and Contest Mobility and the School System." *American Sociological Review* 25 (1960): 855–867.

Uesugi, Thomas K., and Vinake, W. Edgar. "Strategy in a Feminine Game." *Sociometry* 26 (1963): 35–38.

Ulrich, D. N.; Booz, D. R.; and Lawrence, P. R. *Maanagement Behavior and Foreman Attitude.* Boston: Harvard Business School, 1950.

U.S. Bureau of the Census. *1967 Enterprise Statistics.* Part I, General Report on Industrial Organization. Washington, D.C.: Government Printing Office, 1972.

———. *Occupational Characteristics.* Washington, D.C.: Government Printing Office, 1973.

———. *Occupations of Persons with Higher Earnings.* Washington, D.C.: Government Printing Office, 1973.

U.S. Bureau of Labor Statistics. *Handbook of Labor Statistics, 1971.* Washington, D.C.: Department of Labor, 1972.

———. *Handbook of Labor Statistics, 1975.* Washington, D.C.: Department of Labor, 1976.

Van Maanen, John; Gregg, Peter; and Katz, Ralph. *Work in the Public Service: An Economic Development Administration Technical Report.* Washington, D.C.: National Training and Development Service, 1974.

Vinacke, W. Edgar. "Sex Roles in a Three-Person Game." *Sociometry* 22 (1959): 343–360.

Walker, Nigel. *Morale in the Civil Service: A Study of the Desk Worker.* Edinburgh: Edinburgh University Press, 1961.

Wallace, Phyllis, A., ed. *Equal Employment Opportunity and the A.T.&T. Case.* Cambridge, Mass.: MIT Press, 1976.

Walton, Richard E. "Alienation and Innovation in the Workplace." In *Work and the Quality of Life,* edited by James O'Toole, pp. 227–245. Cambridge, Mass.: MIT Press, 1974.

———. "Innovative Restructuring of Work." In *The Worker and the Job,* edited by Jerome M. Rosow, pp. 145–176. Englewood Cliffs, N.J.: Prentice-Hall, 1974.

Warner, W. Lloyd, and Abegglen, James C. *Big Business Leaders in America.* New York: Harper and Brothers, 1955.

Warner, W. Lloyd, and Low, James O. *The Social System of a Modern Factory.* New Haven: Yale University Press, 1947.

Weissman, Myrna M., and Paykel, Eugene S. "Moving and Depression in Women." *Society* 9 (1972): 24–28.

Whyte, William F. *Street Corner Society.* Chicago: University of Chicago Press, 1943.

———, and Gardner, Burleigh. "The Man in the Middle." *Applied Anthropology* 4 (1945): 1–28.

Whyte, William H., Jr. "The Corporation and the Wife." *Fortune,* November 1951.

———. "How Hard Do Executives Work?" In *The Executive Life,* pp. 61–78. Garden City, N.Y.: Doubleday, 1956.

———. "The Wife Problem." *Life,* January 7, 1952, pp. 32–48. Reprinted in *The Other Half: Roads to Women's Equality,* edited by C. F. Epstein and W. J. Goode. Englewood Cliffs, N.J.: Prentice-Hall, 1971.

———. "The Wives of Management." *Fortune,* October 1951.

Wild, Ray. "Job Needs, Job Satisfaction, and Job Behavior of Women Manual Workers." *Journal of Applied Psychology* 54 (1969):157–162.

Wilensky, Harold L. "Varieties of Work Experience." In *Man in a World at Work,* edited by H. Borow, pp. 125–154. Boston: Houghton Mifflin, 1964.

Willett, Roslyn S. "Working in a 'Man's World': The Woman Executive." In *Woman in Sexist Soci-*

ety: Studies in Power and Powerlessness, edited by V. Gornick and B. K. Moran, pp. 511–532. New York: Basic Books, 1972.

Willmott, Peter. "Family, Work, and Leisure Conflicts Among Male Employees: Some Preliminary Findings." *Human Relations* 2 (1971): 575–584.

Winter, J. Alan. "Elective Affinities Between Religious Beliefs and Ideologies of Management in Two Eras." *American Journal of Sociology* 79 (1974): 1134–1150.

Wolff, Kurt H., ed. *The Sociology of Georg Simmel.* Glencoe, Ill.: Free Press, 1950.

Wolman, Carol, and Frank, Hal. "The Solo Woman in a Professional Peer Group." *American Journal of Orthopsychiatry* 45 (1975): 164–171.

Wood, Ann. "The Women at the Rim of Power." *Boston Globe,* November 28, 1973.

Worsley, Peter. "Bureaucracy and Decolonization: Democracy from the Top." In *The New Sociology: Essays in Social Science and Social Theory in Honor of C. Wright Mills,* edited by I. L. Horowitz, pp. 370–390. New York: Oxford University Press, 1965.

Worthy, James. "Organizational Structure and Employee Morale." *American Sociological Review* 15 (1950): 169–179.

Wray, Donald E. "Marginal Men of Industry—the Foremen." *American Journal of Sociology* 54 (1949): 298–301.

Yankelovich, Daniel. "The Meaning of Work." In *The Worker and the Job: Coping with Change,* edited by Jerome M. Rosow, pp. 19–47. Englewood Cliffs, N.J.: Prentice-Hall, 1974.

Yarmon, Betty. "Women Executives Gripe Too." *Boston Globe,* January 17, 1973.

Zagoria, Sam. "Policy Implications and Future Agenda." In *The Worker and the Job: Coping with Change,* edited by Jerome M. Rosow, pp. 177–201. Englewood Cliffs, N.J.: Prentice-Hall, 1974.

Zaleznik, Abraham; Christensen, Charles R.; and Roetheisberger, F. J. *The Motivation, Productivity, and Satisfaction of Workers: A Prediction Study.* Boston: Harvard Business School Division of Research, 1958.

Zeitlin, Maurice. "Corporate Ownership and Control: The Large Corporation and the Capitalist Class." *American Journal of Sociology* 79 (1974): 1073–1119.

INDEX